Letters from the
Light Brigade

Letters from the Light Brigade

The British Cavalry in the Crimean War

Anthony Dawson

Foreword by
Major-General Mungo Melvin

Pen & Sword
MILITARY

First published in Great Britain in 2014 by
PEN & SWORD MILITARY
An imprint of
Pen & Sword Books Ltd
47 Church Street
Barnsley
South Yorkshire
S70 2AS

Copyright © Anthony Dawson, 2014

ISBN 978-1-78303-027-9

Typeset by Concept, Huddersfield, West Yorkshire, HD4 5JL.
Printed and bound in England by CPI Group (UK) Ltd, Croydon CR0 4YY.

Pen & Sword Books Ltd incorporates the imprints of Pen & Sword Archaeology, Atlas, Aviation, Battleground, Discovery, Family History, History, Maritime, Military, Naval, Politics, Railways, Select, Social History, Transport, True Crime, and Claymore Press, Frontline Books, Leo Cooper, Praetorian Press, Remember When, Seaforth Publishing and Wharncliffe.

For a complete list of Pen & Sword titles please contact
PEN & SWORD BOOKS LIMITED
47 Church Street, Barnsley, South Yorkshire, S70 2AS, England
E-mail: enquiries@pen-and-sword.co.uk
Website: www.pen-and-sword.co.uk

Contents

List of Plates vi

List of Maps vii

Foreword viii

Preface ix

Acknowledgements x

Introduction: Letters Home 1

1. Going to War: 1 May–1 September 1854 5

2. Invasion of the Crimea: 14 September–1 October 1854 26

3. Prelude to Balaklava: 1–24 October 1854 59

4. Charge of the Heavy Brigade: 25 October 1854 72

5. Charge of the Light Brigade 123

6. Winter in the Crimea: 1 November 1854–1 March 1855 156

7. Remounts and Reinforcements: March–June 1855 193

8. Mopping Up: September–December 1855 206

Notes 217

Index 239

List of Plates

Trooper of the 8th Hussars at Balaklava by George Thomas.

Russian Cossacks by Henri Durand-Brager.

The Charge of the Heavy Brigade from the *Illustrated London News*.

The bloody repulse of the Light Brigade by Cossacks by John Gilbert.

The charge of the *Chasseurs d'Afrique* from the *Illustrated London News*.

The Cavalry Division transporting supplies, Winter 1854/5.

British troops' winter clothing from the *Illustrated London News*.

A French camp, January 1855.

British Army recruiting, Spring 1855.

British camp, Spring 1855, from the *Illustrated London News*.

Steeplechase in the Crimea, 1855, from *L'Illustration*.

The Charge of the 10th Hussars at Kertch, 21 September 1855.

A French depiction of the Battle of Kanghil, 29 September 1855.

The return of an Allied '*Razzia*' or 'Flying Column'.

Survivors of the Charge of the Light Brigade, 1900.

List of Maps

The Crimean Peninsula 4

General map of Kalamita Bay and its environs 27

Balaklava and its environs 73

Kertch and its environs 207

Eupatoria and its environs 208

Foreword

At a time when academic, media and public interest is focusing on the centenaries of the First World War, if not the bicentenary of the battle of Waterloo and the end of Napoleonic Wars, it is proper to remember also a major event – a seminal episode in European history – that bridged the two conflicts. The Crimean War, though not forgotten, remains a worthy object of study. While some authors examine primarily the grand and military strategies involved, dissecting the causes and consequences of the 'War with Russia', as it was once termed, others provide collections of personal accounts of those who took part, mostly set in a more tactical context. In order to understand that war fully, we need both these genres and perspectives.

Anthony Dawson's *Letters from the Light Brigade* offers us a rich source of authentic, very telling soldiers' experiences from the Crimean War. He presents this new collation with a concise, authoritative commentary on the deployment of the Light Brigade and its major actions in Crimea. Of course, that formation's famous charge at Balaklava is given due prominence, but not exclusively so. There are real gems of insight here, both historical and modern: much to fascinate and a great deal to learn. I for one, will never look at or describe the battles and battlefields of the Crimea again in quite the same way. Hence I am delighted to introduce and commend this work as a very valuable and compelling addition to the literature of the Crimean War.

Mungo Melvin, Major-General (retired),
President, British Commission for Military History

Preface

To quote Wilfred Owen, 'My study is the pity of war'. This book is not the study of battles or generals or weapons. It is the study, the story, of people – the extra-ordinary experiences of the ordinary men (and women) of the British cavalry brigades in the Crimean War.

One and a half centuries since the Charge of the Light Brigade, the events of 25 October 1854 continue to fascinate; in the last ten years alone upwards of ten books have been written on 'the Charge' – not only trying to identify those who took part but usually who was to blame – invariably to the detriment of the study of the Battle of Balaklava and indeed the Crimean War as a whole – and often using the same limited pool of contemporary accounts.

This project began with my Master of Art by Research at the University of Leeds – 'British Army perception of French support services during the Crimean War' – which entailed reading several hundreds (thousands?) of letters home from the front usually published in contemporary newspapers. Whilst collating these letters home it became obvious that here was an as yet untapped mine of first-hand accounts from the Crimean War, and yes, letters from survivors of the Charge of the Light Brigade. Thus *Letters from the Light Brigade* was born – an attempt to collect and present as many letters from the men of the British cavalry during the Crimean War – to put the human face and a personal voice on those calamitous events of so long ago. To let those who experienced the Crimean War tell their story, in their own words.

Acknowledgements

It is traditional at this point to thank all those who have helped the author in his or her arduous task of writing the manuscript. Firstly, I should like to thank my supervisor, Professor Edward Spiers of the University of Leeds, for his encouragement and enthusiasm for over two years during the writing of my thesis. Secondly I would also like to thank my partner Andrew Mason for the maps and also for his patience, cups of tea, a shoulder to cry on, and help on innumerable research trips. Thanks are also due to my brother, Paul Dawson, for his expert advice on all things equine.

I would also like to thank the staff at Huddersfield, Leeds, Manchester, Stockport and Wakefield libraries for access to microfilm copies of newspapers and answering innumerable questions; and also staff at Flintshire Record Office, Herefordshire Record Office, Lincolnshire Archives and the National Army Museum.

Introduction: Letters Home

The Crimean War was perhaps the first media war: it was not the first conflict to have war correspondents or the first time letters from the front were published in the press, but it was the first fought under the scrutiny of the domestic press.[1] Increased levels of literacy allowed private soldiers, rather than just officers, to write home 'from the front'. This meant that the ordinary soldier now had a 'voice' which could be heard, thus reconciling Britain to her army: the letters caused 'the heart of the nation to go out to its soldiers as it had never before'.[2] The period 1854–6 saw the readership of newspapers massively increase as well as the broadening of the scope and social diversity of their readers. Newspapers, via their readers, developed a degree of 'political clout' heretofore unknown.[3] For the first time the common soldier in Britain was commemorated in death and awarded medals, such as the newly-instituted Victoria Cross. No longer were the officer and the class they represented the war-hero, but now it was the everyday soldier who won Britain's wars in spite of the blunders of its generals: a narrative which would run through British military history to the Second World War and beyond but may have indeed held back serious reform.[4] The same was true in France, Britain's ally during the war; the common soldier was seen no longer as a drunk and miscreant but a national hero, and the army an instrument of that unique French quality, *La Gloire*.[5] The cult of the solider, in particular the veteran, became more focused through Napoleon III's introduction of the *Médaille de Saint-Hélène* (Saint Helena Medal) for veterans of the army of the First Empire in 1857.[6]

The period 1854–6 also saw the readership of newspapers, and their social diversity massively increase. Newspapers developed a degree of significance heretofore unknown.[7] This led to the newspapers becoming the biggest maker of opinion in mid-century Victorian Britain. The press saw its readership increase during the Crimean War due to demand for information on the war and also from the abolition of stamp duty. More jingoistic than its military counterpart, the domestic press could build itself up into hysterical 'war fever'.[8]

The Provincial Press
Whilst the impact of the reports from the Crimea by W.H. Russell of *The Times* (which had the largest circulation in Britain, 60,000 copies being sold per day), it was the provincial press which, through its publication of Russell's reports and letters home from local soldiers – that gave Russell's accounts both local colour and verification – turned the mood of the country against the Aberdeen government and towards the soldiers at the front. Many of the leading provincial towns and cities had their own newspaper, often several, usually one liberal and the other Tory. Indeed, the majority of the letters presented here were published in the provincial press, rather than the metropolitan titles, as they provided much needed 'copy' and were full of local (human) interest. Manchester, for example had three papers, of which the radical, Nonconformist *Manchester Guardian* was

the most widely read and influential (circulation of 23,000 per day in 1855) of the provincial dailies, both in the north and nationally. The liberal, tri-weekly *Leeds Mercury* was the next most influential (circulation of 10,000 per day) of the northern papers.[9]

The Ordinary Soldier

Letters from ordinary soldiers and the despatches of the various 'special correspondents' that were full with the human drama of the war contrasted greatly with the official, somewhat terse despatches of the British commander in the Crimea, Lord Raglan.[10] Furthermore, as the 'official' version of events often arrived after 'unofficial' accounts, suggested that Raglan was writing to contradict the press. In most of his correspondence with the Duke of Newcastle (Secretary of State for War and the Colonies, 1852–4; Secretary at War 1854–5) or Sidney Herbert (Secretary at War 1852–5), Raglan was writing a stream of rebuttals to complaints about him and the army in the press.[11] Lord Panmure (Secretary of State for War 1855–8) noted that Parliament relied on the 'vast number' of letters home written by officers in the Crimea, 'which we hear daily quoted and hear daily read'. Lord Raglan did not 'deny' what was written in the letters home, but simply 'despised' that they had been written at all.[12]

Letters like those published here are both useful documents for revealing not only how the ordinary soldier lived and spent his time in the Crimean War, but also his response to and feelings towards the war. These letters became all the more important because of the 'human interest' they generated in the plight of the common soldier in those 'on the home front' and also political ramifications they had, in bringing about a change of government and also fuelling reform of the British army, reforms which would see the day-to-day living conditions of the British 'Tommy' and his family vastly improve.

Critical Analysis

Newspaper editors were keen to publish letters, especially provincial papers, those from local soldiers. Some papers, such as the *Nottinghamshire Guardian*, unable to afford a 'Special Correspondent' paid soldiers for their letters and indeed commissioned local soldiers from regiments stationed in and around Nottingham to send a monthly letter reporting on the events in the Crimea. It will be noted that, despite the title of this book being *Letters from the Light Brigade*, the majority of the correspondence was generated by the Heavy Brigade; and this pattern is not just due to the relative proportion of casualties resulting from the Battle of Balaklava as the trend is observable in the months preceding that battle. This trend may be due to different literacy rates between the Heavy and Light Brigade or that the men of the Heavy Brigade regiments had greater opportunities to write home. Furthermore, the Heavy Brigade correspondence is further biased toward the Scots Greys – perhaps because as a Nottingham regiment some of their rankers, such as Sergeant-Major Sturtevant were commissioned by the *Nottinghamshire Guardian* to send letters home. Similarly, because Corporal Thomas Morley was a Nottinghamshire man, letters from the 17th Lancers dominate the Light Brigade material. Correspondence from the Scots Greys is also more frequent in the metropolitan titles than other cavalry regiments, and naturally so in the Scottish press.

Most letters home contained three main topics: the health of the writer, the writer's travelogue (many soldiers having never served outside the British Isles) and comments on their allies. Most writers were also self-censoring: these letters are not literal blow-by-blow accounts, but only include details that the *writer* deemed were important or felt were of interest to the reader at home. Most writers often reserved the more gruesome sights of the battlefield for a male reader to preserve the modesty and feelings of a female reader. Many writers commented that their readers would be universally surprised by the French soldiers and how well the allies got on, and reflected naïve belief that the war would be quick and over by Christmas. Letters provided an immediate, snapshot level of immediacy and intimacy that the official despatches or those of Russell *et al.* did not.[13] Whilst letter writers record events that they remember and deem of sufficient important or interest to write home about, these are not objective or literal records of the events the writer has been involved in. The writers are reporting events they *believe* they remember or perceive; the closer to the event the letters were written the more likely the reporting is to be uncontaminated from other sources and closer to the experience of the writer. The more detached in time from the event, the less reliable the recording, often contaminated by what has been absorbed from other sources (usually the media, books, contact with other soldiers), subsequent experiences or distorted by a sense of grievance or, usually, self-importance. As Paul Fussell notes, oral history and memoirs tend toward being a combination of historical fiction and autobiography, stressing the role or importance of the writer than any objective or literal form of history *per se*.[14] The further the written narrative shifts away in time from the events which took place, the closer the written narrative becomes to a figurative fiction. The recollection of crucial events will be re-evaluated and re-contextualised throughout the life of the author to the point of creating the written record – personal memoirs become influenced by the socio-political, socio-economic environment and experiences of the author will have an impact on how they recall and event. Furthermore, as critical or evaluative historians, we must also take into consideration that observers do not always understand what they saw or thought they saw.[15] Ultimately, however, these are personal narratives, written down by combatants: each of the writers of the letters included in this work, had a personal and unique experience of the Crimean War – what they experienced will be different from participant to participant, but it is useful to note the shared experiences between different accounts, too.

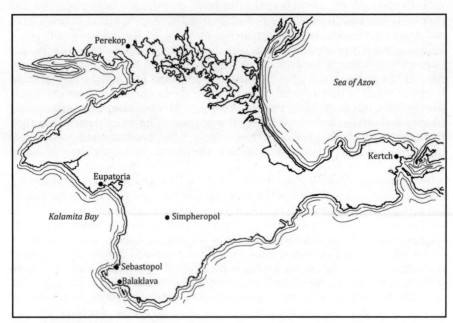

The Crimean Peninsula, showing the major towns.

CHAPTER 1

Going to War:
1 May–1 September 1854

Preparing the Cavalry for War

British cavalry regiments had seen little or no active service after 1815, being mostly employed in a policing role, such as at the 'Peterloo Massacre' or the Bristol Riots.[1] The Scots Greys, for example, hadn't seen active service since 1815 whilst the 8th Hussars had not served outside mainland Britain since 1823. Four regiments of light cavalry, however, served in India during the first and second Anglo-Sikh Wars: the 3rd and 14th Light Dragoons and the 9th and 12th Lancers. The 14th Light Dragoons fought at Ramnagar (22 November 1848) and famously charged at Chillianwallah (13 January 1849) where they were nearly destroyed; and the 14th together with the 16th Lancers fought at Aliwal (28 January 1846). Lack of service abroad made the cavalry highly attractive to rich *flâneurs*, who merely 'played' at soldiers and spent more time hunting and socialising than with their regiments, and when their regiments went on active service went on half pay or sold-out.[2] Officers who had seen active service or were promoted on merit were considered inferior to those officers 'born' to rank.[3] Because of this, many subaltern officers in the cavalry were totally ignorant of drill or their duties in garrison or in the field and worse, had no desire to learn.[4] Lieutenant-Colonel Hodge (4th Dragoon Guards) despaired that his subalterns and even his Adjutant displayed 'such ignorance' even with regards to equitation: 'not one of them knew by sight the lower part of the breastplate [part of the horse harness]' and they certainly did not how to pitch their tents or live in the field.[5] Lack of education and basic horsemanship was common amongst cavalry officers because they were accustomed to having grooms and servants do that work for them; they also had little interaction with the men they commanded which further widened the social gulf.[6] This lack of education was not just due to apathy, but due to a lack of any educational material.[7] General Sir Charles Napier considered that education for cavalry officers was vital. They had to be more educated than infantry officers because they were more often called to act independently. He thought that an uneducated officer could not lead his men or inspire confidence; badly led cavalry was not effective on the battlefield and could end in disaster. Bravery and chivalric conduct were no replacement for education.[8] The British cavalry officer came in for much criticism in the press during the 1840s because of the various scandals of the Earl of Cardigan;[9] cavalry officers were much ridiculed for their noble birth, fanciful uniforms and mannerisms (such as speaking with an affected lisp or pronouncing Rs as Ws[10]) most notably by *The Times* newspaper,[11] *Punch Magazine*[12] and the social reformer Charles Dickens in *Household Words*.[13]

In order to augment those regiments being sent to the East, men and horses had to be begged, borrowed or otherwise. Hodge records how his regiment received fifteen horses transferred from the 1st (King's) Dragoon Guards and a further five from the 3rd Dragoon Guards. The twenty Hodge gave them in return were 'young ones – a great set of brutes as ever I saw. I felt quite ashamed of the transaction'. In the following month he received an augmentation of 100 men and had an order to 'buy fifty more horses'.[14] Similarly, the Scots Greys purchased 3,000 tons of forage from merchants in Leeds in March 1854 and 150 'dark bay, brown and chestnut' horses at the York Horse fair for remount purposes.[15] The problem faced by most commanding officers, however, was the dramatic increase in the price of horseflesh following the declaration of war. At the Drogheda Horse Fair 'first class cavalry horses' sold for £80–£100, double their usual price,[16] and at Doncaster:

> two or three army agents, who it is said have a commission to purchase 1,000 horses for cavalry and artillery purposes [were present]. Only about 50 could be picked up, and those at very high prices. Good nags and roadsters were also scarce, and realized from 30L to 60L each ...[17]

Amongst the private soldiers of the cavalry division was a mix of recruits, experienced men and those who had joined up in the New Year of 1854 on the surge of patriotism generated by the 'Great Russian War'. Private Brookes (13th Light Dragoons) had served from 1842 and had fought during the Sikh Wars (1845–6 and 1848–9) whilst Trumpeter Smith (11th Hussars) had been in the ranks from 1836 and fought in Afghanistan (1839). Amongst those who had enlisted out of patriotic fervour was Private Thomas Tomsett, a former bricklayer, who enlisted in the 4th Light Dragoons 25 January 1854 or George Wootton, a baker, who enlisted two days later in the 11th Hussars.[18] Private William Henry Pennington (11th Hussars) had only been with his regiment for a few months by the time he was ordered to the East. His father, Albert, wrote on 23 December 1854:

> ... my son, a youth of 21 years of age, who last spring, in a military fit, enlisted in the 11th Hussars, and in the incredibly short time of six weeks has passed through all the rough riding and other drills in to his troop as a competent soldier, though the extent of his horsemanship before was a pony ride on Blackheath![19]

Mobilisation for war also led to desertion: two bandsmen from the 17th Lancers (the brothers Deakon) absconded from their regiment and joined the orchestra at the fashionable Argyle Rooms in London.[20]

The Voyage Out
Overall command of the cavalry was vested in the Earl of Lucan. The Earl of Cardigan was to command the Light Brigade and Sir James Yorke Scarlett the Heavy Brigade. Captain Lewis Nolan (15th Hussars) was to superintend all the 'cavalry arrangements' and left Manchester on Monday 13 March 1854 for that purpose. He also carried 'special instructions' to purchase 1,000 cavalry remounts in Constantinople.[21]

The 11th Hussars and 4th Dragoon Guards departed Dublin on 11 March 1854, accompanied by Captain Maude's troop of Royal Horse Artillery.[22] The 1st Royals were barracked in Manchester and sailed for Turkey from Liverpool, 'where nothing could exceed the hospitality and kindness' of the inhabitants.[23] According to Lieutenant-Colonel Yorke, they were to sail in five vessels: forty-eight horses and men on board *The Gertrude* (1,300 tons); fifty on board *The*

Coronetta (850 tons); sixty-eight on board *Rip Van Winkle* and a final forty-eight on board *The Pedestrian*. In addition there was a small 'luggage steamer' which accommodated a further thirty horses.[24] They sailed for Boulogne from 'London Dock' on 12 May 1854.[25] From Boulogne the regiment was to sail to Marseilles and thence 'for such a destination as deemed advisable. This route . . . is said to be determined for keeping the horses in condition ready for action.'[26]

Getting the horses on board the transports was no easy matter. Albert Mitchell (13th Light Dragoons) described how:

Each horse was led up the ship's side . . .; a sling was placed beneath the horse's belly, and fastened to the tackle on the main-yard. The order was given to 'hoist away', when about a hundred convicts manned a large rope, and running away with it, the poor Trooper was soon high in the air, quite helpless.[27]

Sergeant-Major Smith (11th Hussars) notes it took four hours to embark all forty-six horses of his troop on their transport because 'some of the horses resisted violently'.[28] The horses were next lowered into the hold – which had been well padded – where each one was 'provided with a separate stall. They were placed with their heads towards the ship's side, and heads towards each other, with a passage between them.' The animals had no means of laying down and had to stand throughout the voyage.[29] This method of transporting horses proved controversial, however. Retired cavalry officer W.J. Goodwin suggested that during the Napoleonic Wars (1800–15) horses had been transported 'with their heads to the side of the ship' and, crucially, had larger stalls, which allowed the horse to lie down to rest and also to lie down during storms at sea. Most importantly horses, which had 'stood for six weeks' were in much worse condition than those which had had room to move and lay down.[30]

The 17th Lancers embarked at Portsmouth between 18 and 25 April. Headquarters, under Lieutenant-Colonel Lawrenson were on board the *Eveline*, one troop under Major White onboard *Pride of the Ocean* with the remaining troops on board *Ganges*, *Blundell* and *Edmunsbury*. Captain Godfrey Morgan records that the *Edmunsbury* had on board forty horses, four of which belonged to him, and eighty men of his troop and their horses. Also on board was the paymaster and an Irish doctor and his wife. The ship was dirty, the food poor and Morgan reported that he soon tired of the company of the doctor. In the Bay of Biscay they sailed into a gale: 'My first real gale at sea truly awful sight, with 40 horses on board kicking and plunging and dashing themselves to pieces.'[31]

Morgan's troop lost one horse on 1 May from sea sickness and others quickly followed: Morgan's second charger, 'Atheist', died on 4 May; one troop horse died on 5 May and another on 9 May. By the time the 17th Lancers arrived at Constantinople at the end of May, they had lost twenty-six horses and, whilst camped at Varna, lost four more.[32]

Lieutenant-Colonel Hodge and the 4th Dragoon Guards embarked at Kingstown 25 May on board five transports; The 5th Dragoon Guards, quartered in Ballincollig under Sir James Yorke Scarlett, left for Dublin at the end of March and sailed from Kingstown in the *Himalaya*.[33] Hodge had forebodings about things to come: he insured his horses 'pretty largely, as I fear we cannot help losing some' and was very concerned about how the horses were to be fed and quartered once in Turkey, fearing that they would 'soon fall off' in condition.[34]

All was not plain sailing. On 14 May the transport *Harkaway* carrying fifty-six cavalry horses had a 'narrow escape' after getting in to a strong current and drifting toward rocks on the Portuguese coast. With the aid of 'two boats and thirty men' she was refloated.[35] But worse was to come. The Inniskillings sailed from Plymouth on Tuesday 30 May on board five transports: tragedy struck just one day later when the *Europa* carrying the HQ, 'portions of each of the four troops and 13 officer's chargers and 44 troop horses' caught fire 'about 200 miles from Plymouth'.[36]

The Scots Greys and the 4th Light Dragoons were the last cavalry regiments to sail for the East. The Greys were quartered in Nottingham Cavalry Barracks. The barracks had been built in 1819 due to fears of civil unrest from unemployed silk weavers. The regiment consisted of three squadrons, each squadron consisting of two troops. One squadron was quartered in Loughbrough Cavalry Barracks (built in 1839 as a conversion from the former workhouse); one troop was quartered in Mansfield and the remainder were in Nottingham.[37] The order to Prepare to Embark was received at Nottingham on Monday 3 July 1854: the Greys were to proceed to Manchester via Chesterfield, Matlock and Buxton prior to embarking at Liverpool for Turkey.

In Manchester they were quartered in Preston and in the Hulme Cavalry Barracks along with the 3rd Light Dragoons. Due to lack of stabling for the horses, 'wooden sheds' were erected 'on the gardens' at Hulme Barracks for the horses of the Light Dragoons as the horses of the Greys had priority for stabling. They left Manchester at 8 a.m. on Monday 23 July, 'played out of the yard' by the band of the 3rd Light Dragoons and they were accompanied out of Manchester by Colonel Unnett of the 3rd Light Dragoons along Regent Road. They rested on Monday evening in Prescot before resuming their march to Liverpool on the following morning.[38]

The Greys embarked 299 men, 14 officers and 294 horses on board the *Himalaya* in '12 minutes under the hour' on 26 July and got under way on the 27th.[39] By all accounts the Greys had an uneventful voyage to Turkey, often with the band playing to entertain officers and men alike on the quarterdeck, with dancing organized on the forecastle.[40] They passed Gibraltar on 30 July and arrived at Malta on 4 August to take on coal and water. Sadly, whilst at Malta one man fell overboard and drowned. So comfortable were the officers of the Greys that upon arrival at Scutari (7 August) they presented Captain Adam Kelloc and the Purser Daniel Lane with engraved silver plate and a handsome purse. They were barracked at the cavalry barracks at Kullalie, which were in a filthy condition. For a time the Greys had to share them with a battery of Royal Artillery, commanded by Major Townshend, and a squadron of Turkish lancers.

Letter from Lieutenant **Robert Scott Hunter**,[41] Scots Greys, to his sister Helen Carnegy Hunter.[42]

H M S Himalaya[43]

My dearest Holly   At Sea, July 27th 1854

We got away all right yesterday & are having beautiful weather. This is a most splendid ship, & the best idea I can give you of her size is that she is *80 feet longer* than the "Duke of Wellington".[44] We are now getting near the Bay of Biscay, & the ship as you may see by my writing is rolling *a few*, besides our screw makes such a thumping that it really is not easy to get the letter straight.

We shipped all our horses in *12 minutes under the hour*. They are all right as yet & none of them have been sea sick nor any of us but Miller the Adjutant.[45] We had a very rainy night and the decks this morning were very wet but now (11.40) the sun is coming out & the officers of the ship say that they think the afternoon will be fine. I don't suppose I shall get this finished today, as such there is no use in doing so as we do not *touch* anywhere till we get to Malta where we are to be 12 hours. Andrew came out as a far as the "Bell Buoy" with us whence the Pilot left us. I was very glad as it gave me two hours more of his company. He dined with me on board the ship the day before & will be able to tell you how well we *feed*. We get breakfast at 9, Lunch at 12. Dinner at 4. Tea at [blank] and *grog* at 9 & you know learn how we eat. I do so. I can tell, for besides the fact of my being hungry, if I happened to be sick. I should be more comfortably so, than if I had an empty bread basket. We have been allowed to take off uniform & go about the queerest figures imaginable, with all sorts of hats, wide awakes, caps, coats, boots &c. &c., & enjoying the good life in its highest sense. We expect to be by at Malta this day week – July 31st – Dearest Holly we have just passed Gibraltar. The morning is lovely & the view perfect. The rock is most curious & as we passed we cheered like anything, & our band played "Rule Britannia" which was answered by the garrison lining the walls & returning the compliment. There never was anything like the beautiful weather we have had. The Sea has been so smooth, & but for the heavy rolling of the ship with the enormous ground swell, you could have hardly told you were at Sea. We made land last night about 10 o'clock after looking [at] it all day from Cape St. Vincent. Just before getting to Gib. We got a splendid view of Tangiers on the African Coast & Tariffe on the Spanish side. Both sides are very rocky, especially the African, where the mountains are enormous & their summits are quite lost in, or appearing above the clouds. We expect to be at Malta about Wednesday, where we are to anchor for 12 hours.

Footnote: This ship is 364 feet long! Her engines 700 horse power & they work up to 1200!!! Imagine her size. Her mainyard is 84ft long!!!!

Letter from Sergeant **John Hill** (number 976), 1st Royal Dragoons, to relatives in Dublin.[46]

Karajusin Camp,
Dear Mary, -   July 31st, 1854.[47]
When I last wrote to Tom, we were about to disembark at Varna. We remained at Varna, encamped on the sea-coast about week, and then received orders to march for Devna. We remained on Devna plain, a fine open piece of ground close to the city – for a week, when we were removed in consequence of the cholera breaking out amongst the infantry regiments to Karajusin, where we remain encamped for the present. It is expected that a great portion of the army will move in the direction of Sebastopol very shortly, where it is intended to quarter for the winter. I had scarcely time, when I last wrote, to give you even a short sketch of Turkey, but I will endeavour now to do so. The country itself is certainly most beautiful, and abounds with the loveliest scenery you can imagine, and if cultivated by an industrious class of people would be one of the finest countries in the world: but the inhabitants are an idle, lazy race, and seem to have no thought of improvement or invention. They must be a thousand years behind the British in civilisation and art. Every article that you look at

it so primitive that it reminds one very much of the accounts given of the Easterns [*sic*] in Scripture History. The roads here are very bad, and you may ride 20 miles without seeing a human being or habitation, and when you happen to meet either they are the picture of poverty and filth. When they kills a beast for their use, the offal is allowed to decompose in front of their cabins; but this is in the country parts, and in the towns and cities it is only a shade better. They always sit on the ground cross-legged, like so many tailors, and eat their food with their fingers; but they adhere strictly to religious duties, as they never sit down to a meal without offering up thanks to their Prophet, and the same when rising. We find them, too, very honest in the dealings with us. Great numbers of French troops preceded us on our march. The poor Turks are not very partial to them for their excesses, and they say they are 'no bono;' but the English, they say, are 'bono.' Bread and meat are very cheap, but the bread is very coarse and black. We can buy a very nice sheep here for 1s. 6d. Soap, candles, cheese, salt, and many other necessaries are very dear. Soap, 1s. per 1lb; cheese, 2s.; small candles, 3d. each; a bottle of porter, 2s.; and salt difficult to be had at all. The cholera has cut off a great many of our troops lately at Varna, chiefly the infantry, but we have not had one case in our regiment as yet. The doctors attribute the sickness to the men eating green fruit and drinking inferior wine, which is sold here at the rate of 6d. a quart. I wish very much to get a line from you, and a newspaper; the latter would be a great treat here, as we get more information from a peep into an English newspaper, as so to how the war is proceeding, than we could here for a month. I never got better health than I am enjoying at present; and you may tell O'B[censored] that my horse Paddy is as brisk as a bee, and was never in better condition. Write soon, and direct according to the printed instructions.

Letter from Troop Sergeant-Major **Matthew Brown** (number 517), Scots Greys, to the editor of the *Nottinghamshire Guardian*.[48]

Malta.

Dear Sir, -   August 4, 1854.
From the extreme kindness shown to the Greys by the inhabitants of Nottingham, on leaving for the East, I have no doubt that they still feel a deep interest in our welfare. I have therefore presumed to send you, for the information of your readers, the following rough sketch of our voyage from Liverpool, should you deem it worthy a place in your valuable journal.

On the 24th July, at 7 a.m., we marched from Manchester amidst the cheers of the populace, and halted for the night at Prescot. We were next morning again on the road for Liverpool at 4 a.m., and arrived there about 6 a.m., where, notwithstanding the early hour, thousands followed us, some of them only half-clothed, to witness our embarkation at the Docks. By 10 a.m. were all on board, the horses in their stalls, and them as comfortably put up as circumstances would permit. The ship then slipped her moorings and steamed out to the middle of the river where we cast anchor. During the whole day steamers, crowded with dense masses of people, were continually putting off from the shore, and steaming around the Himalaya; bands playing lively and appropriate airs, and the people saluting us with cries of "God speed the Greys," and loud and protracted cheers that could only be surpassed by the good people of Nottingham. Next morning, at 8a.m., we weighed anchor, and steamed down the Mersey, in gallant style, our band playing the "Queen's Anthem." The quays being lined with immense crowds of people, saluted us as we passed with deafening cheers, which were returned by our men in a manner that evidently showed that the pain of leaving home, friends, and all that were dear to us, was buried, for the time, beneath the heart-stirring feelings of enthusiasm which animated every one on board. On getting clear out to sea we doffed our soldiers' clothing, and were quickly rigged out in duck trousers and smocks, which caused no small amount of merriment amongst us, as each man was inclined to laugh at his comrades grotesque and comical appearance: but we soon got reconciled to our garb, and we soon found the comfort of it, for on getting in to warmer latitudes our usually warm clothing would have been quite insufferable. We sighted Cape Finisterre on the 29th, at 4 a.m., and when day broke next morning we were steaming at full speed round Cape St. Vincent. At noon on the 30th we were abreast Gibraltar, close in shore; our band struck up "Rule Britannia," and in an instant the gallant 92nd Highlanders – now stationed on the Rock – came rushing down to the batteries, and cheered us so lustily that we could almost fancy they were heard by the Moors on the opposite shore! On the same evening we passed close to the opposite shore. On the same evening we passed close to the mail steamer Tagus, steaming towards Gibraltar. Our band struck up "Cheers, boys, cheer,"[49] and the usual cheering was prolonged on both sides as long as we could hear each other. Nothing further happened to us worth committing to paper, excepting seeing Algiers in the distance on the 2nd inst., until we arrived at Malta to-day, after a passage of nine days from Liverpool. We expect to stay a day or two here to take in coal and water; but whether any of us can get ashore to see the town of Valetta or not I cannot say, as I merely penning this as we have cast anchor, to be ready for the mail. We will next proceed to Constantinople, where we will get orders where to land. So you will perceive that it is impossible for me to say in the mean time where our actual destination is, or when it may be likely be that we may have the satisfaction or measuring our swords with the Russians. But this I *can* say, that we are all very anxious to meet the enemy; and should our success in fighting be commensurate with our anxiety to meet the Russians, I have no doubt that we will add fresh leaves to the laurel of the Greys. I am very happy to say that we have arrived here without any casualty whatever. The horses are all well, and the men in excellent health and spirits. Our passage, so far, has been remarkably fine, the sea all the way being so smooth that it put one forcibly in mind of some beautiful lake that he has seen described in the pages of some fairy tale. The only thing we could complain of was the oppressive heat that commenced with us at Cape St. Vincent, and has been increasing every day since, until it has reach a point that is truly oppressive. Still our spirits are not out of tune, for in the cool of the evenings, at the request of our worthy Colonel, the men assemble aft on the quarter deck, where the band plays some lively airs, and the song, the tale, the joke, and laugh go round as merrily as if we were gathered round the board of some good old host on the shores of merry England; while others, who prefer dancing, assembly forward, and with a good flute player mounted on the capstan head, they dance Tulloch Gorum [*sic*, Tullochgorum] and the Flowers of Edinburgh to perfection.[50]

I hope your goodness will forgive me for intruding thus far on your space; but I cannot close without conveying to the inhabitants of Nottingham, through the medium of your columns, the lively sense of gratitude that is entertained by every man in the Greys for then, for their extreme kindness and generous bearing towards us on leaving them, and our humble hope is that in the struggle before us we may prove ourselves not unworthy of the respect of such a kind and generous people. We should be very happy if you would be kind enough to send us a paper occasionally – it would be a great luxury to us.

Letter from an anonymous officer of the Scots Greys.[51]

Constantinople,
Aug. 12th, 1854.

Her Majesty's recently purchased Steamship Himalaya arrived at Scutari, after a rapid passage from Liverpool of 10 days and 22 hours, on the evening of the 7th instant, and having received orders from Admiral Boxer, proceeded the following morning to Koulalie, a cavalry barrack about three miles up the Bosphorus [*sic*], on the Asiatic side. A stage having been constructed by Captain Kellock, similar to the one used at Liverpool, on the following day, viz., the 9th, the whole of the Scots Greys and remounts, numbering 370 horses, were disembarked in nine hours without accident, and the horses in as good condition as they were when embarked at Liverpool. The loss on the voyage amount to one, a horse of some 18 years of age, whose lungs could not stand the change of climate or excessive heat which was experienced during the passage out.

On the evening of the 11th the Colonel had a parade in Full Dress, and so gay and lively were the horses, that if one of the officers, Captain Toosey,[52] had not been [a] pretty good 'cross country' man, he must have been kicked out of his saddle, for his mare sent her hind legs up for about 10 minutes, as though she meant to send her rider up to Beicos. It was really a very fine sight to see a whole regiment, and such a regiment! after a journey or voyage of 3,100 miles, just as fit to go into action and gallop over a squadron of Cossacks as they would have been the day after leaving Nottingham.

Colonel Griffith[53] and the officers were so gratified at the result of the voyage, and so pleased with the attention that had been paid to and care which had been taken of them, their horses and men, that they presented to Captain Kellock, and Mr. Lane, the Purser, a handsome piece of Plate, with a letter of thanks, and a suitable inscription, expressive of their feelings at the termination of the voyage.

Life in Turkey

Lieutenant-Colonel Hodge's forebodings about the resources available in Turkey to supply the cavalry appear to have been true. Lawrence Godkin, the 'special correspondent' of the *Daily News*, reported that:

Oats are not to be had. Here and there a bad quality, little better than chaff, is to be met with, but contains no nutrient whatever. All horses here are fed on barley ... about ten pounds per day. Hay is rarely to be had ... Barley ... very scarce.[54]

An anonymous cavalry officer writing home painted a similar picture:

The French are lost in admiration at the beauty, the symmetry, and the activity of the English cavalry horses ... There is, however, a drawback to them; it is thought by the Frenchmen, as well as some persons in the English army, they are perhaps *too* well bred. How are they to be fed? Will these pampered creatures stand rough work of a campaign on short and sometimes bad rations – moreover, as a change of diet, for oats and hay are not to be had?[55]

Living conditions for officers and men were little better; Lieutenant-Colonel Hodge thought he would never 'get accustomed to the bad living' with only 'bacon and eggs, nothing else, and very little of that; no bread. The water at the camp at Devna is, I heard, good, but it is two miles off . . .'.[56] In an attempt to prevent having their 'knowledge boxes . . . boiled' the Heavy Brigade were issued with white calico helmet covers, but General Sir George Brown took a personal dislike to them, thinking them 'unsoldierlike [sic]'. He refused to let the men under his command (the Light Division) wear their shako covers.[57] The situation took a serious turn for the worse when cholera broke out in the Allied camp on 22 July 1854. Cholera is an infection in the small intestine caused by the bacterium *Vibrio cholera*. Its main symptoms – which can start very suddenly – are watery diarrhoea and vomiting. It is caught from drinking dirty water that contains faecal matter, but the bacterium that causes cholera can live in any environment. The severity of the diarrhoea and vomiting can lead to rapid dehydration and death.[58]

Hodge notes that the first victim in the 4th Dragoon Guards was 'Lupton of 'F' [Troop]' on 24 July. The cavalry was to change camp the following day, finally moving two days later. By 30 July the Inniskillings had forty-six men sick in hospital and the 4th Dragoon Guards had twelve: by 19 August Hodge had buried twenty-three men from his regiment.[59] W.H. Russell of *The Times* estimated that the Guards had lost 100 men to the disease and had 'around 600 sick;' the Light Division 112 and the Cavalry a similar number.[60] Of the cavalry regiments, the 5th Dragoon Guards had the highest number of casualties from cholera: three officers and forty other ranks. To make matters worse, the Lieutenant-Colonel of the 5th – Scarlett – was absent in command of the Heavy Cavalry Brigade so command devolved onto the Major who was absent sick. The senior Captain, Duckworth, assumed command but he died from cholera on 24 August, so 'a young officer', Captain Adolphus Burton, then took the reins.[61] Thus having no effective command, 'what remained of the officers and men were incorporated into the 4th Dragoon Guards' leaving only two effective Heavy Cavalry regiments – the Scots Greys and the 4th Dragoon Guards (the 1st Royals and Inniskillings having lost half their horses).[62] Sergeant-Major Henry Franks suggests that Scarlett 'took up his quarters with the 5th Dragoon Guards', and wanted the regiment placed under the supervision of Lieutenant-Colonel Hodge (4th Dragoon Guards) but Hodge 'could not be in two places at the same time' leaving Burton in command.[63] Worst affected by far was the French army, which lost 4,500 out of a total force of 13,000.[64]

Lucan and Cardigan

The petty bickering between the Earls of Cardigan and Lucan appears to have intensified under the strain of active service. *The Times* believed the 'private relations between the two men, they become responsible for disaster'.[65] In May Cardigan left for Varna to command the leading elements of the Light Brigade, without receiving permission from his superior, Lucan, to do so. Lord Raglan, the Commander-in-Chief, compounded this error, by not consulting Lucan.

This led to Cardigan believing he had an independent command and that he was responsible to the Commander-in-Chief alone. Lucan only got to hear of Cardigan's departure via a staff officer who wanted to know what instructions he was to give the latter![66] Lucan wrote several indignant letters to Lord Raglan and to General James Estcourt (Adjutant General), none of which appear to have brought his insubordinate brother-in-law in check.

Cardigan and Lucan both succeeded in 'annoying everyone': 'he [Cardigan] does all he can to knock up both horses and men before the work beings in earnest.' Captain Shakespeare RHA thought Cardigan 'the most impractical and most inefficient cavalry officer in the service ... We are all greatly disgusted with him ... We wish we were with Scarlett and his Heavy Cavalry.'[67] Fanny Duberly, wife of the paymaster of the 8th Hussars, was of a similar opinion, relating in a letter how 'Poor Col. Shewell who has been weeping nearly ever day over the way Cardigan overworks his men is now nearly frantic.'[68] Meanwhile, Lucan was making an embarrassment of himself because, according to Major Forrest of the 4th Dragoon Guards

> ... he has been so long on the shelf that he has no idea of moving cavalry, does not even know the words of command and is very self-willed about it ... If he is shewn by the drill book he is wrong, he says 'Oh, I should like to know who wrote that book, some farrier I suppose.'[69]

Many officers expressed a lack of confidence in both Lucan and Cardigan: Major Forrest felt that a 'row with Cardigan was imminent',[70] whilst Captain Robert Portal (4th Light Dragoons) thought that Cardigan was 'one of the greatest old women in the army' and

> He has as much brains as my boot. He is only equalled in want of intellect by his relation the Earl of Lucan. Without mincing matters two such fools could not be picked out of the British Army to take command.'[71]

Lord Paget suggests that Lucan insisted on using the old drill which he remembered: 'Instead of bending to the new order of things, he sought to unteach his troops the drill which they had been taught ...'[72] Lucan held a meeting with his commanding officers where Lord Paget managed to make his superior back down with regards to drill.[73]

On 25 June Cardigan was ordered to take a squadron each from the 8th Hussars and 13th Light Dragoons to lead a reconnaissance toward the Danube to ascertain the position of the Russians following the lifting of the siege of Silistria. This would go down in history as the 'sore-back reconnaissance'. For seventeen days Cardigan pushed his men and horses to the limit, covering a total of 300 miles. Day by day the condition of the horses and men deteriorated from the intense heat, lack of water and heavy loading and that Cardigan insisted on a 'cracking pace'. Food and forage were short and in total some 100 horses were lost. Fanny Duberly saw them return:

> A piteous sight it was – men on foot driving and goading the wretched, wretched horses, three or four of which could hardly stir. There seems to have been much unnecessary suffering, a cruel parade of death.[74]

Finally, with morale at an all-time low and drunkenness at an all-time high, the order was received to prepare to embark for the Crimea.

Letter from Corporal **Thomas Morley** (number 1004),[75] 17th Lancers, to his
father, William Morley, Inspector of Licences, of Hounds' Gate, Nottingham.[76]

Dear Parents, -

Camp at Aladdyn, near Varna,
June 25th, 1854.

I take the opportunity of writing these few lines to you, hoping to find you all
quite well, as it leaves me at present, thank God. We arrived quite safe at
Turkey. We had one or two very rough nights at sea. One night we lost six
horses; we lost eight horses in the ship I came in, and all the ships lost some;
some lost five and six. It took five ships to bring us over. I was 33 days on water.
We sailed from Spithead on the 19th of April, and landed at Constantinople
on the 23rd of May. The ship I came in was called the "Ganges". The first
place we stopped at was Malta, where we stayed four or five hours, just to get
fresh water, and then went on to Gallipoli. We stayed there about an hour, and
we were towed by steamer to Constantinople, and stayed there about a fortnight; and then we embarked again for Varna, about 160 miles further up the
country. We stayed in Varna two days, and then came on to Yeni; we have left
Yeni, and are going on to Shumla, where the head quarters of the Turks are.
We are not in any town, but are all in camp betwixt great mountains, something like the Peak of Derbyshire, only worse. If we should get to a town as
we call them I cannot describe them to you as bad enough. If you get a few mud
cabins or old broken-down barns, and a lot of wooden stables, with the thatch
chucked on the roof, an old mud cart, some sheds, and take and chuck them
into a field any how – that would be some-thing like a Town in Turkey. There
is no such thing as streets or roads in the town where we are now. When I was
at Constantinople we were in the Turks' barracks, and a very dirty barracks it
was; we were eaten up with fleas, and they *were* fleas – the largest ever I saw.
We had no beds; it was worse than being in camp, and that is needless to
explain. I took the pains of going a little through Constantinople. When on the
water I thought it was a beautiful place; but when I got into the town I could
not believe myself. To hear people in England talk about Constantinople, you
would think it was something like London; but a dirtier town you never saw.
I never thought there was such in the world. The streets you can hardly walk,
they are so badly paved; there are no footpaths, and the streets themselves only
about three yards wide. I thought Constantinople was bad enough, but as I
came further on I found it was a city of a place compared to the towns I have
seen since I left it. The Turks are a dirty, lazy lot of people; they think about
nothing but smoking. They never cultivate the ground – only sow a bit of
barley; and I think they never turn the ground over, or dig it, or anything. I
have never seen any one at work in the fields since I have been in the country.
There are no potatoes, or peas, or cabbage, or anything like that in the country;
I have not seen anything of the sort yet. We get a pound of beef or mutton, and
a pound and a half of bread, but it is black, or nearly so; the bread is made from
barley, and the tea and sugar comes from England – they are very bad rations.
Neither the beef nor mutton is fit to kill – there is not a bit of fat on them; but
there are plenty of eggs, and geese and fowls are very cheap. You can buy four
eggs for a penny; and we can buy a fowl for 4d., and a goose for 8d.: everything
is cheap in this country that they have got excepting salt and ink. Salt is very
scarce, and ink is too; but what produce they have in the country, such as it is,

is cheap. There is no butter or cheese in the country. I could tell you more, but that I will do should I come back again.

We have not been in any engagements yet, and I have not seen any of the enemy. The Turks are fighting about 20 or 30 miles from where I am stationed now. There are the 8th Hussars, the 13th Light Dragoons, and the 5th Dragoon Guards all together; and we expect 20,000 English to march on to where we are, and form the English division, and them march into the field; but I think Nicholas will be glad to give in before long. You can get more news in England than I do out here. Sometimes there is one report, and sometimes another, so that we do not know what to believe. The Turks look very curious as soldiers, and they are very badly mounted; their dragoons are all mounted on ponies! If they can keep the Russians back and keep gaining victories, which I believe they do, I do not know what will remain for the English and French to do; I think the Russians will not stand long. It will be a regular slaughtering match with poor Russia; they will get well licked if ever they should go into the field. I should like to go into the field before I come back, as I have come so far not to. They say the Turks have been fighting four and six to one, and I am sure one Englishman is worth six Turks. The English cavalry could ride over the Turks without any arms. You would not believe what cattle they have. The little pony which you had would make a Turk a good horse. They have little bits of swords; their firelocks all go off with flint, and they alarm the Russians with them, and they can take an aim with them at half a mile's distance. There is a fine army out in Turkey, the finest ever England sent any where [*sic*], with the finest cannon ever sent from England. There are about 30,000 English landed, I believe, and about 70,000 French; and I believe there are plenty more on the road; but the English will not take the field till all the army is together. They seem to say we are going to Sebastopol for winter quarters, and to Odessa. I believe our fleet and the French fleet are playing the devil with their fortifications by water. When I landed at Constantinople the only person I saw that I knew was young Neep; he is full farrier and doing well. We had a good spree together in Constantinople; he was there about five days, and then went on to Varna; and when I got to Varna I saw him again in a day or two. He told me to mention to you that he was along with me, so that you could tell his uncle. I must conclude. Give my best love to all, and accept the same yourself.

PS I was made full Corporal the day I landed. I do not know when I shall be able to write to you again. I have sent two letters to Derby, and told Betsy to write and let you know I had written, and that I was quite well. I hope I shall be in England again before long. When you write send me the [Nottinghamshire] "Guardian" newspaper; the latter will come for a penny; just put a stamp on, and it will come free. I do not know what my letter will cost you coming, but I think 2d.; and if they go through France they will cost you 3d.

The ground in Turkey is full of vermin, such as lizards, snakes, and black ants; particularly black ants and lizards. There is also a kind of rat that lives in the ground running about the tents; and they say there are many wolves about, but I have not seen any of them. If, however, a horse dies, there are hundreds of vultures come off the mountains and eat him up in a few hours. I have seen 500 round a horse at once.

When you write do not forget to send me a newspaper. Direct for the future, Corporal Thomas Morley, 17th Lancers, British Army, Turkey, *via* Marseilles, and put three postage stamps on the letter, than I shall have it in 12 or 14 days. Send me all the new you can.

The Russians and Turks are hard at it ding dong, and some of the 8th Hussars and 13th Light Dragoons have gone in great haste this 25th of June (Sunday); I cannot tell you whether they will be engaged or not. We are expecting to go every hour now. I shall be able to tell you more in my next letter.

Letter from Corporal **George Senior** (number 1386), 13th Light Dragoons, to his brother in Lockwood, near Huddersfield.[77]

Encampment, Devna,
29th June 1854.

Dear Brother, -

This is the first opportunity of writing I have had since I landed in Turkey. We arrived at Varna on Wednesday evening, the 21st inst., and disembarked on the following day. We had a great deal of trouble in disembarking the horses. We anchored off shore about half a mile, and had boats for taking horses and ourselves on shore. All belonging to our vessel ("Calliope") were fortunate in getting the horses safe on shore; but other had not been so fortunate, for, on lowering them into the boats, several in plunging had not only got themselves into the sea, but taken men and other horses with them, which had been let down before them; some of the horses were drowned, but the men were saved. We staid [*sic*, stayed] all night at the place where we landed, and on the following day marched about three miles, to the encampment of English, French, and Turks. There were about 40,000 French, and, I should think, from 15,000 to 20,000 English. You would be surprised to see the good feeling existing between the English and French soldiers; the latter you might often see kissing our men and pulling them about, particularly our Guardsmen, whom they appear to be very partial to. 'Tis quite laughable to see a tall Guardsman with two or three French soldiers leading him home to his tent, with about as much wine on board as he could carry in a most easy humour, and they pulling and jumping on his back, kissing and fondling him about as if he was some pet animal, and the French chattering away as fast as they can, and he responding to them with a nod of the head or "Yes," "No," or "Oui;" in fact, to see them at a distance you would imagine them understanding each other to the greatest nicety, when at the same time neither party understood what the other was saying.

The night after our arrival at the general encampment another corporal and myself went up to the French lines: we were soon surrounded with ten or a dozen, for the corporal who was with me was born in France, consequently, could speak French better than the generality of the Frenchmen he was speaking to, at least they told him so; however, they were delighted to find some one of the English to converse with; they would not allow us to go until watch-setting, at which time we had to be at our lines; they treated us to several bottles of wine, which we returned, and showed us round their tents, in fact, appeared to be delighted that we had come to see them, although we were not the only party who was there, for I think there must have been two or three hundred of the Guards, whom they were pulling about in all directions. Now, you must have a little patience in reading this letter, for I am at the present writing this laying on my back, and shall be most likely be in a different positions before I have done, for it is so excessively hot, and the innumerable flies and insects tormenting me, that it requires the greatest resolution to continue writing.

On Sunday evening, after our arrival, we received orders to march further into the country, where two troops of ours had already gone, also the 8th Hussars and 17th Lancers. The orders were for reveille to sound at one o'clock in the morning, and march at three. The reveille sounded at the time ordered, when we all commenced to saddle our horses. Such confusion I never saw in my life (for this is new to most of us, and we have so many things to look after that you are sure to lose something); one man you might hear – "Can you tell me where my horse is?" – which might have been loose during the night and got to some other place than where he left it the night previous; another, "Can you tell me where my saddle is?" "Who has got my bridle?" and a hundred other things; however, I managed to get my horse saddled, with two days' provisions of barley. We also had two days' food given out for us to carry, but I was unfortunate in not getting any – going for it too late. I started without breaking fast, or tasting a drop of any-thing to drink. We commenced our march along with a troop of artillery, at about five o'clock, the sun at the time excessively hot, in fact, if you were only able to see us, or most of us, particularly myself, you would think I was a Turk, as far as colour goes, for I am nearly black. The road which we came was something like a cart-road, through a wood, just sufficient width for the guns to pass, and horses up to their fetlocks in dust. We rode for miles in a continual cloud of dust; I many times had to gasp for breath; and during my stay in Varna I one morning went to bathe, and thinking it a good opportunity to wash my shirt, did so and went without one until it was dry; the consequence was, the sun burned my shoulders and neck so much that if I had a blister plaster on I could not have been more blistered than I was with the sun. Well, what with the dust and the irritation of my neck and shoulders, I was nearly mad (I was not the only one who was blistered with the sun, hundreds of us are suffering from it). On arriving here I was obliged to come to a hospital, where I am now, writing this letter, for I could not bear my jacket on, much more my pouch, & belt, and some other articles which we have to carry. We arrived here about five o'clock in the evening, having been twelve hours in marching about nineteen miles, not having tasted food, only about a biscuit and a half with a pint of milk, the horses not having had a mouthful of anything but water, which we gave them on the road. We found out that all the Russians had been seen by the party here previous to our coming up (two days previous), and a part of cavalry had gone, the day we arrived, further into the interior to ascertain the whereabouts of the enemy. The news here is that all the Russians are re-crossing the Danube, and that they will not fight the English and French. They have raised the siege of Silistria; the Turks took six guns from them, which I saw on the road between Varna and Devno, an escort of Turks were taking them on to the former place. The party which I mentioned above having marched further into the interior (which consisted of one squadron of the 8th Hussars and one of the 13th Light Dragoons),[78] took three days' provisions with them; they have not yet returned, but two of our men returned with some horses which were knocked up this morning. They give a sad account of the country, which has been in possession of the Russians; nothing whatever in the shape of provisions can be found. Lord Cardigan has command of this reconnoitring party, and, I understand, five more days' provisions have been sent to them this day to continue their march in search of the Russians. I am certain, we can only come up with them, we will annihilate them altogether; both French and English are burning to be at them; I wish it was over, for you have no idea of the fatigueing [*sic*, fatiguing] duty we have to put up with. The second day we were in Devno [*sic*, Devna] we had nothing to eat but a mouthful of biscuit, the salt meat given out to us for two days was all eat the night we marched in here; the consequence was, I might say, we had nothing to eat; and, what was worse, we could get no money, for the Turks in this place would not give more than 18s. for our sovereign. Speaking of the Turks, I never in my life saw such a degraded, dirty, idle, lot, and they rob us whenever they can, particularly in changing money; they are sure to give you wrong change. The French detest the sight of them, and say, "Turks, no good;" "English good." It surprises me that they will not give us the value for any silver pieces, but that being scarce, we are not obliged to lose a penny in each shilling, which I did this morning: 4d. in 4s. This, of course, causes a good deal of grumbling amongst the soldiers, for our pay is small, and it is hard to lose it here, when I am sure it is worth its value in any country; and this, too, with the people we are come out to fight for, makes it worse. I think there is not distinction of people, for in the country here all are dressed alike – in the most miserable, dirty plight. We expected to see some Turkish gentlemen, but no such distinction, I think, exists. I must now close, for it is getting dark, and I believe the mail goes to-morrow morning, so must send this to our office, otherwise shall have to keep it until the next one goes. I duly received your kind letter in Constantinople, which gave me much pleasure, and I trust you will write me regularly, and, for my own part, I cannot say when I shall have an opportunity of writing again, but should I. you may rely on my doing so. I trust all are in good health at home; give my love to all and believe me to be your ever-affectionate brother.

Letter from Corporal **Thomas Morley** (number 1004), 17th Lancers, to his father.[79]

Dear Parents, -

Camp, Varna,
July 24, 1854.

I am at Varna in charge of a Letter Party that is to take despatches to the troops up the country. I have been here for three weeks. It is a great deal better than being with my regiment knocking about the country. All the troops are going up the country to attack Sebastopol, which is the greatest fortified place in Russia. The Czar has got a strong army there, but we are going to tackle it by land and sea. Eighty thousand French have landed at Varna and about thirty thousand English. I did think the Czar had come to terms, but it appears not. I think he will soon be glad to do so. It is said here that there is some other place to attack before we get to Sebastopol. There are many reports about on that subject. My regiment moved this morning higher up the country. I do not know where they have gone to yet, but I shall know to-morrow, as I have an orderly in from the regiment nearly every day. Eight days ago there were reports that we should all be embarked by this time for Sebastopol. I hope they will soon do something, as I am tired of this life. It is frightful to see the men die in this country. They are dying by hundreds of the cholera and fever. There is a general hospital about a mile from where I am staying. I have occasion to there with letters every day, and so I know how many die – about a dozen die every night, and sometimes more. If anyone goes into the hospital at Varna, it is 100 to 1 if he ever comes out again alive. I have been very lucky myself. I have not been sick yet, but many are taken off in a few hours. They sell wine and drink of all sorts here very cheap, but it is very bad, and so I never drink any of it. I can get a good bottle of brandy for 2s 8d. or 2s. 6d. – the best Cognac brandy I ever drank; but the other descriptions they sell for 10d. and 11d. a bottle, and wine at 6d. a quart. It is, however, shocking stuff, and I think many of the deaths are attributable to it. I have not drank a quart of wine this month. I did drink a little of it before, but since there has been so much sickness I cannot bear the sight of it. As soon as the men die they are sewn up in a blanket and sent off in a wagon [*sic*] to be buried. There are no such things as coffins in this country.

Letters from Lieutenant-Colonel **John Yorke**, 1st Royal Dragoons, to his sister, Etheldred.[80]

My Dear Ethel, -

Kara-Hussein,
August 7th 1854.

...

Since I last wrote I am sorry to say that we lost a man from Cholera and another now remains without hope of recovering. Fever is likewise prevalent, and poor young [John Glas] Sandeman[81] still remains in a precarious state. Poor Ferringe [?] of the Horse Artillery (the vacant Jacket expected at Lt. Church) is dead having taken too large a dose of laudanum to cure neuralgia. Poor fellow we were at a Field Day very recently & he had been looking well, in a good spirit, and now he is [illegible]. Colonel [Lauderdale] Maule (79th Regt.) died of Cholera, in the next camp to me. I had received a letter from him only 2 days before his death having written to him to assist us in forwarding our letters to England.

Other officers have likewise died recently these not acquaintances of mine. We buried our poor man at an early hour on the 4th [August] & I read the Funeral Service over his grave. He was one of the oldest soldiers in the Regt. and belonged to my old Troop. His name was Wheatley which I mention in case you are writing to [illegible] as I [illegible] would well know him. He was at a Field Day the morning of his death. I fear we shall lose others as there are some bad cases in the Hospital.

I moved however to new ground immediately after the death of this poor fellow. You likewise have been witnessing a sad funeral close the windows of Holywell. I do hope and trust that your [illegible] will be from London. Another mail has however arrived but no letter for me but newspapers dated 23rd and 24th. I have not time to read them and the post is leaving a day sooner than we expected and I am in some haste. Poor Fred. Fancy. I hope he is not dangerously ill. I have felt the heat very much these last few days, but I am still better than my neighbours. Peter Godby is well. The Major's brother is in the 19th Regt. and frequently comes over here, and we have a joke about my reporting Peter Godby. Well it seems he is a very idle fellow but wants to come over to call on me (this he can never make up his mind to move [)]. We have not a hint of news. I begin to think the Cavalry will do nothing this year, indeed if we can keep tolerably well it is all we can hope for. I have established a table made of old deal boxes which would be a great advantage but the tent is too hot ● to write in, and remaining outside is worse as a breeze occasionally blows the paper about. I am therefore quite in a fix and much wound up in despair this time as it is quite impossible to get on. God bless you all.

PS 22 Troop Horses of the unfortunate 'Coronetta' have been shot, and 2 officers' horses. So much for [illegible]. Stacks, he is still at Varna with the remainder. My horses are quite well.

Kara-Hussein,

Dear Ethel   August 12th 1854[82]

Since writing my last, sad calamites have befallen us, but thanks to God I now think the terrific plague has passed, but I can much describe our distress & depression on the 8th, & 9th. We lost one man on the 8th of Cholera, whose illness I mentioned in my last. He was the Majors second servant. At 2 the following morning I heard the Major bringing up his other servant to the Doctors Tent on account of symptoms which I at once set down as Cholera. In a few hours after another man appeared with the same terrible symptoms at about 8[am] two more officers servants and a Woman who cooked for the officers were reported in the same condition, another man Choleric in hospital was reported worse, and at noon the whole were dead.

At this time I had moved the Regt. to fresh grounds, about a mile distant, which is considered the only hope of checking the Plague. The day was intensely hot, the occasional puff of wind feeling like the fumes from an oven. I say upon my horse, and just balanced myself, at a walk, being perfectly incapable of any further exertion. Depressed in body and mind, my pulse beating about 45. I never passed such a day of trouble indeed. I may say my dear Ethel, after you and me have witnessed calamites, and prolonged sufferings of those we loved most in this word, still we had time for reflection and resignation and were in a measure prepared & felt relief when the sad hour came. It was just so on the sad 9th I felt extremely ill, at a great distance from relatives in a climate unwholesome [?] Cast down with sorrow, and feeling that just one of our lifes were with one hours [illegible]. It was an immense exertion to set up our new camp, and as soon as this labour was ended for the men they had to return to the old ground to dig graves for their comrades. In doing this sad office our only remaining spades ... Night came on the funeral took place by the light of one miserable lantern. The poor woman was a Catholic but her husband wished her to be buried with the others [.] We gave her a separate grave and placed 3 Officers servants in one. This ended the sad 9th of August. The Majors excellent servant who was thus suddenly carried off was our perfect factotum, and, his loving wife most respectable and uncommonly handsome, was our cook, and we really were most comfortable, but my ... We were thus deprived of both their services, without the means of replacing them, and with all my depression and foreboding of further misfortunes I had to cook over a kindling fire, but most fortunately a small dose of laudanum and Peppermint which I took at night afforded me the greatest relief for at an home in the morning I was ordered over to the 5th Dragoon Guards to preside over a Board of Inquiry over Intrenching Tools. I had likewise on my return a ... edition of the same tedious affair over my own Regt. In my arriving, however at the 5th, about 5 miles distant I witnessed a second sad scene and saw men taken to hospital with hope of recovery. On the following morning we heard 9 men had been buried. The same fearful plague having visited here, and death even more ... than with us. Fortunately on arriving at this new ground I received a supply of Cholera Belts from Varna which I had sent for, I was also after to space two of them for the 5th Dgn. Guards ... and since the issue of these most useful preventatives we have had no case of Cholera, and trust no repetition of our recent distress will visit us. I think there was something in the air which affected everyone, for I was myself very unwell and as dear Mr A's Powder did me no good I took the Laudanum & Peppermint and intend to keep a small quantity on me always. Yesterday a fresh calamity reached us in the distruction [*sic*, destruction] of the Town of Varna by fire, and the whole of the English & French stores, this bringing the Commissariat Arrangement to a complete stand still, our Poor Horses have not even seen barley for 24 hours, and I am making preparations to fall back on the standing crops of the neighbourhood and pay a fair price whether the ... But to tell the truth I had always thought it an unfortunate ... to make the little Town of Varna the Depot for stores & ammunition. It has always been understood the Greeks ... our enemies, and even Russian stragglers have been seen in the Town. Who can ... at its destruction by incendiaries, Ld. Raglan will I should think be K ... for this for would it not have been more prudent to have use store ships in a fine harbour than a filthy rotten Town.

I have just heard General Scarlett is unwell with some Cholera symptoms but I trust not serious. The Surgeon of the 5th D.G. is likewise in a similar state. Two of our Doctors are sick. Doctor Banner will be invalided to England, Colonel Elliott of the 79th Highlanders is dead, likewise an officer of the 93rd in fact our poor Army is in a sad state, and in comparison with other Regts. we may still consider ourselves fortunate, but what our movements are now to be nobody can form an idea. I heard yesterday the Duke of Cambridge was unwell, having had a recent attack of gout which has been followed by Encephalitis, at the present state we shall have a scarcity of Generals and other officers, we ... it is most difficult to ... great in this climate, and there is no escape from ... when it comes. I hope however that my next will return to the news, and the your next will give better accounts of the dear girls, but Pollie appears to have got over the tetastation of the Will better than Ethan, Carlo & Tuttie seem to flourish. Your dear letter of the 21st contained this good news, it was sent to the 4th Light Dragoons by mistake but reach me on the 10th and afforded me the greatest comfort after my sad day of troubles.

August 13th. I am happy to hear General Scarlett's illness was untrue, but the Doctor of the Regt. & Capn. Duckworth had the Cholera. Thank God we have no fresh cases, and yesterday & today have been many degrees cooler, and it is stated by the natives that after the middle of this month the Eastern heat ceases and we have reason to hope it will not be followed by any more unwholesome weather. I was amazed at old Wesly Binck's surprise at my being in command of the Royals but as you his ... sawmills occupy his mind too much to think some which will account for it. I do hope you will get away from

Holywell shortly. London will be so nice for the dear girls. It is wonderful how we respect England now we are in this banishment for it is truly the ... country to live in.

Letter from Lieutenant **Robert Scott Hunter**, Scots Greys, to his sister.[83]

Kullali Barracks

My dearest Holly,   August 22nd 1854
Here we are still you see, & from all accounts here we are likely to remain as we can get no information about any movements. We were landed here at first on accounts of the dreadful state of Varna which is really as bad as it is represented. Men & officers are dying off like rotten sheep, & the Duke of Cambridge[84] is very ill indeed & it is expected will be obliged to return to England. People may say what they like but this country is anything but a pleasant place of residence, at least for arriving men. It is all very well for persons who have good houses & can live in Turkey in the midst of English comforts & cleanliness, but for us poor officers to have to rough it rather under Canvas or in a dirty barrack, & live on common soldiers rations, it is anything but pleasant. However, it is a change, & we have no grumbles. We would all prefer life at once under canvas, as our present quarters are thoroughly *Turkish* in dirt & all. Everything else abominable. The people themselves are dirty & smell very high. Their dress however is in most easy, very clean & pretty, mostly composed of muslin with jaunty scarfs and calico shirts printed in large patterns of birds & flowers. However it is only the outside. I'm afraid that does to look at for you have only to go into a room to tell whether a Turk is there or not. A great proportion of the natives is black. The old thorough bred Turk is now almost a rarity but you meet them about the street of Pera, Jalala and Stamboul. Still sticking to the long furred robes & usual Turban & as you pass they scowl & mutter Gairun & sometimes spit on the ground, & look as if they would very much like to make cold meat of some of us. I have just heard that the Duke of Cambridge has today arrived in Constantinople unable to bear the climate any longer, at least for some time. Some go so far even as to say that his health is very much undermined.

More French troops have been heading up the Bosphorous today, & the 41st Foot (English) went past this morning in the Simla from Gallipoli. They however are only going as far as Beicos Bay where we have now a large Encampment. It is only 6 miles from this, & some of us are constantly going over to see them. I can tell you soldiers on service are very sociable fellows. I cannot imagine how it is that I have received no letters from anybody. Surely some of you could send a few lines just to jolly one up a bit. We get no news, & no papers, & when we get no letter we fell quite inclined to stop writing on our part, *till we do*. I have been advised by all the accidents here not to prepay my letters. The people take more of letters when they are only expecting the money, but on the other, *letters from home should be prepaid* as otherwise *they do not come to our British army post office*, but are sent to the *French one*, & there they may sit to all eternity, & *no one* the wiser. I bought a large sketch book the other day & have been commencing today with a large sketch of our Barracks (which are really splendid *to look at*!!) with the Bosphorus & the "City of the Sultan" in the distance. If I can only shake off my laziness I shall fill it & send it *home*, but you have no idea of the oppressive feeling in the air during *the day*. We are obliged to lie down, & then you are sure to fall asleep. The Sunday night we had a fire in the Barracks, but the Turks and our men got two small engines & and a lot of immense poles with hooks at the end and luckily out it out in about ½ an hour, with a loss only of the ceiling of one room, a fireplace & flue & divers tiles & rafters out of the roof. We have now got a company, battery I mean, of artillery with us, under the command of Major Townsend.[85] They came by the "Jason". I daresay you will see about them in the paper. They are very small fellows (*half a dozen* officers) & we get on capitally together. They have 230 horses & we 248, so we are well off for nags. You would laugh to see the Turkish regiments of cavalry. You *never* saw such louts – we have the 2nd Lancers here, you never saw such *devils* in your life, & their horses are little bits of ponies, but well bred, & some of those belonging to the officers, who by the way are hardly to be distinguished from privates, are very handsome. We had very heavy rain yesterday, & thunderstorm. The consequence of which is that today it is very cool & comfortable. You should first see the grapes here, (the only first I ever touch). You can get two immense bunches in ½ a peastre [*sic*, piastra],[86] sometimes less than a halfpenny & most delicious they are & so cool. I have a bunch every morning. Another delightful thing here is the bathing. The water is as clear as [illegible] but *very* deep & rapid. It is the greatest luxury we have now …

Letter from Troop Sergeant-Major **Richard Lawrence Sturtevant** (number 868),[87] Scots Greys, to the editor of the *Nottinghamshire Guardian*.[88]

Kululie Barracks,
Turkey in Asia
25th August, 1854.

My Dear Sir, -

I trust ere this that you will have received my former letters. Since I wrote to you last the Jason arrived here with a battery of artillery, and with ours completely fill the barracks, more particularly the stables. We have them packed very nearly as close as at Chobham last year. I hear that the artillery will soon move up country. But as for us, we hear nothing, and actually do not know so much about the movements against Russia as you do … The Duke of Cambridge arrived here the day before yesterday, or rather at Constantinople. He has come for a few days only for the benefit of his health, he is suffering from gout. Whether it is that we are getting used to the weather, or that it is actually getting a little cooler here I cannot say, but the most of us do not feel so uncomfortably warm as at first, and we get nice and cool with bathing in the Bosphorous in the mornings. I do not think this place is mentioned in the maps, if it is not I will try and explain it to you. One the left shore previous to entering the Bosphorous is the city of Constantinople, which runs along the shore and is joined to Galetta, which again joins Pera, this latter place is where the English residences are; well, on the right shore opposite to Constantinople is Scutari, and five miles, or about, from that is *Coolalie* (that is the way it is pronounced), which is nearly opposite Pera. It is a beautiful country about here and fit for cultivation; there are lots of vineyards, and the grapes are excellent eating; will get as many here for one half-penny as you will get in England for a shilling. Over the hills at the end of the barracks is a very good piece of level ground for drilling, and yesterday morning at half-past four a.m., we had a good field day; all the drills are ordered to be over by eight a.m. because of the heat. Everything you see looks delightfully pleasant some distance off, but when you go close you see everything going to decay, or most of it. The Sultan is getting a new palace built between Galetta and Pera, and a very handsome place it is; almost all the dwellings are built close upon the water's edge. The place originally meant for the Russian embassy is a very extensive building. I went over to Constantinople the other day, and a filthy, dirty place it is; I went through the Grand Bazaar, and most of the articles sold are trash, the only things I saw really good were some embroidered shawls worked by the men; tobacco pipes and mouth-pieces are certainly good, but very dear, and they have some good caps worked with gold, and the slippers are good; I asked the price of a pair nicely worked, and they asked me 30 piastres or 5s. The dollar is much used; each dollar is worth 4s. 2d., and for an English pound (gold) you can get 23s. 6d. in Turkish money, but there is such a quantity of different coins it would puzzle the Devil to make them all out; for instance, there is the French franc worth 10d., and half ones; there are all sorts of English coins, and lots of Florins, Russian money; there are 8d, and 1s. pieces; small change seems very scarce in English, French, Turkish and Russian coin; they deal also in paper money here, 3s. 4d. and 1s. 8d. notes. I send this note to you without paying for it, that is unless I can get the officer who takes the letters to pay for it for me; the post-office is at Pera, but they charge you 2s. for a boat, for it is nearly two miles broad and a very strong current running, and a circular that the post-office authorities have issued says that it is optional to pay, and that if not paid in advance only 3d. will be charged to the party receiving the letter; there is a post from here five times a month, via Marseilles. I should be very glad if you could now and again send me a newspaper, for we get nothing to read here at all, and we have not made enough progress in Turkish to be proficient in reading. There are no tables in barracks, and only two or three chairs, so of necessity we squat on the ground with our mess tins on our laps. Our coffee issued is in the bean and green, so we have to roast it, or rather burn it, and then pound it (a very troublesome job), the bread is very black, and the meat lanky and lean and plenty of it, so we make pretty good soup with rice. The horses get barley and no hay, a little chaff or what remains after the bullocks have trod out the corn we mix with the barley, but the horses eat very little of it. They have no beds. The Turkish cavalry here dry the horses' dung in the sun and use it for litter. We have no bedsteads, but lie on the ground with one blanket and cloak, and are nearly carried about the room by the detestable fleas; if you pull a board down you can take them up in shovels full; however, they are getting better for we kill some 50 to 100 in our blankets every morning when we rise, a slight occupation for an appetite for breakfast. We make our-selves as comfortable as all this will permit. It gets dark soon after seven and watch sitting [*sic*, setting] is at half-past eight. Todd[89] is sent to Scutari in charge of our heavy baggage, and we have only a slight kit with us, and fit for the field at a very short notice. We have no casualties, although the Rifles and 68th encamped about seven miles from here, have had some cases of the cholera; and altogether our men are healthy. I think I have given you a pretty correct description at present, and will continue to write until you should let me know to the contrary.

CHAPTER 2

Invasion of the Crimea:
14 September–1 October 1854

The Landings

The Allies landed at the aptly named Kalamita Bay on 14 September 1854. The French disembarked first, at 7 a.m., using the same plan of campaign as used in their 1830 invasion of Algeria. By 10 a.m. they had 6,000 men ashore and the *Tricoleur* was flying from the French beachhead. The British, meanwhile, took two frustrating days to disembark. Unlike the French who used their *tentes d'abris* (shelter tents carried on the knapsack or saddle) the British had no shelter from the incessant rain for their first night in the Crimea; the large bell tents, reputedly left over from the Peninsula War, were still on board ship. Trooper Albert Mitchell of the 13th Light Dragoons was on board the *Jason* on that first night: 'the rain poured down the hatchways with such force it soon flooded the floor on which we lay. When we arose in the morning we found our blankets soaking wet.' He further notes that those men who had disembarked with their horses had spent a worse night than he, as they were 'obliged to hold their horses all night, they could not lay down for a short time ...'.[1]

The horses were landed by being lowered onto flat-bottomed rafts that were towed by rowing boats, which proved to be a traumatic moment for man and horse alike; Trooper Mitchell had to re-assure his animal by letting him nuzzle him and feed him some hard-tack biscuit. As soon as each raft reached the shore 'Each man then had to watch for a retiring wave, and then take a leap with bridoon rein in hand' and 'in nine cases out of ten the horse would follow him'. Ashore, the 13th Light Dragoons went in search of forage for their horses and clean water, the horses tethered to their piquet pegs.[2] The 4th Light Dragoons were the last to land, and one troop remained at Kalamita Bay with part of the 4th Infantry Division after the bulk of the armies had marched south.[3]

Cavalry Patrols

Almost as soon as they had landed, the cavalry were sent out on patrols; around 4 p.m. on the afternoon of 14 September, Captain Louis Nolan and a company from 2nd Battalion the Rifle Brigade (commanded by Colonel Lawrence) headed toward the village of Kentugan in pursuit of 'large Russian Convoy'. Nolan witnessed 'Col. Airey ... ride at the head of the column, & stop the Carts which was done' and in the process captured '80 waggons laden with flouer [*sic*] and drawn by excellent teams of oxen ...'[4] Nolan spent the night 'at the country house in Kentugan' where he had a 'suite of apartments with polished floors ... a bottle of red wine like good French claret' and a piano to play.[5]

The following day, Nolan accompanied a patrol of the 13th Light Dragoons, commanded by Captain Goad and led by Captain Wetherall (Deputy Assistant Quartermaster General) 'to the front'. Whilst on patrol, the party was attacked and, according to Nolan, 'surrounded by Cossacks who however did not attack.

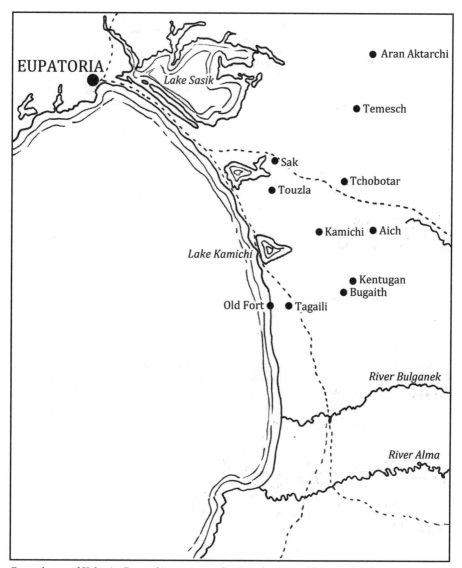

General map of Kalamita Bay and its environs, showing the major villages and settlements.

We captured some Cossacks and I caught my friend Schneider [a wealthy German living in the Crimea taken prisoner by the British], who attempted to escape.'[6] The Light Brigade spent 15 and 16 September patrolling the surrounding country to procure 'carriages of all sorts' to transport the tents and wounded, but only 'sufficient ... for the sick & for some of the [tents of] Officers of higher ranks'.

Nolan led a reconnaissance by the 4th Light Dragoons on 17 September ostensibly to find supplies to feed the army. The 4th were commanded by Lieutenant Harry Adlington, riding out through the village of Sak toward Tchobotar. They spent the night at 'Biouk Aktash' where they 'collected some carts and horses' and returned to camp the following day.[7]

Skirmish on the Bulganek

The advance on Sebastopol began on 19 September – the French had been ready to move from dawn, whilst the British were still not ready at 9 a.m. The advance guard consisted of the 11th Hussars and 13th Light Dragoons, commanded by the Earl of Cardigan; the 8th Hussars and 17th Lancers marched as the flank guard whilst the 4th Light Dragoons under Lord Paget – minus one troop – were the rearguard. During the march the British troops suffered greatly from thirst and hunger. Lord Paget noted that it had been 'a fearfully hot day without a drop of water'. Advancing as he was in the rearguard, Paget came across 'stragglers ... lying thick on the ground ... Men and accoutrements of all sorts lying in such numbers, that it was difficult for the regiments to threat their way through them.' He thought the entire scene 'resembled a battle-field'.[8] Albert Mitchell relates how the advance guard begged, borrowed or purloined carts from the local villagers to transport the 'young men (mere boys) of the Rifles, many of whom had never marched a days' march before ... many of them, laid down by the wayside ... some would not move, or attempt it'.[9]

Around midday, the French advance guard made contact with the Russians at the River Bulganek. A French naval officer attached to the Staff wrote:

> At midday, our advance guard crowned the hills of Zembrouck ... separated by a vast plain two kilometres wide which extended from Zembrouck to the [River] Alma ... the *Maréhcal* [Saint Arnaud] was halted for a time at Zembrouck, but he went to the heads of the column to attack a party of the Russians in the plain, on the right bank of the Alma. [*Général*] Canrobert descended to the east ... and in a moment fell on the right [flank] of the Russians engaged in the plain. Until two o'clock in the afternoon, Menschikoff remained immobile, entrenched behind the village of the Alma, on their inaccessible plateau on the left bank.
>
> At two o'clock, or thereabouts, during our immobility ... for a hesitation to allow us to consult the formidable position, there debouched into the plain a strong column of cavalry (Dragoons of the Guard), supported by a column of infantry marching in close column.
>
> The Russian cavalry then deployed, and executed a beautiful manoeuvre, [and] we admired their speed and precision. They attacked our advance posts and we fired several volleys of artillery, and they replied, the infantry forming square and marching resolutely forward. Our line remained immobile ...[10]

During this 'hesitation', Saint-Arnaud remarked to an ADC that he did not wish to

> jeopardize my benefits by too much precipitation, we must not be forced to the attack, we must battle with the troops rested and with the advantages of time. It is too late tonight I'll wait until morning. I will prepare my plan, and bring together all generals.[11]

Obviously, Saint-Arnaud thought it too late in the day to bring the Russians to battle and he was feeling too ill. As a result, the *Maréchal*'s tent was set up to allow him to rest – he had been in the saddle since 5am and was terminally ill from congenital heart disease. Canrobert's Division was deployed in line, supported by artillery. Dr Cabrol, Saint-Arnaud's personal physician, remembered 'A regiment of Russian cavalry was seen to approach our *grand gardes*,[12] [and] several shells were fired [at them].' At the first cannon shot, Saint-Arnaud 'sprang up' and left his tent crying '*À Cheval!*' His favourite horse, Isabelle, was made ready and in several moments he and his staff were galloping off, sabre in hand, toward the scene of action.

Down in the plain, *Capitaine* Marie Octave Cullet (*20e Légère*) thought contact with the Russians was more by accident than by design; an advanced piquet from the *20e* found 'some parties of Cossacks' 'hiding' around a burned out farm in the middle of a valley, and on the opposite facing slope, much to their surprise, 'there was a body of cavalry'.[13] Colonel J.J.G. Cler (*2e Zouaves*) described the Russian force arrayed before the Allies as 'a few squadrons of cavalry, with a battery or two of horse artillery' which had been sent to reconnoitre the Allied armies, who 'even exchanged a few cannon-shot with the English'.[14] *Caporal* Édouard Minart (*1e Zouaves*, part of Canrobert's 1st Division) wrote to his mother that:

> On the 19th, after a long and very fatiguing march in grass and scrub that was waist-high, we saw Russian sharpshooters. Immediately we dropped our knap-sacks [*sacs à terre*] and went forward in cover ahead of the main guard ... the enemy Cavalry wanted to attack, but the cannon began to shoot and they were dispersed.[15]

The French columns had been led by a native Tatar guide, and around 12-noon the advanced pickets of the 1st Division (Canrobert) reported to French HQ that the way ahead was blocked by the Russians. Saint Arnaud and his staff arrived on the 'summit of the hill' at the gallop and ascended a rise from where he saw a major Russian force 'batteries established half a score, troops reached the top of the heights and taking defensive positions; before the [River] Alma, in the plain, the enemy cavalry was advancing'.[16]

By all accounts, the British did not arrive until 4 p.m.; Saint Arnaud had been impatiently waiting for their arrival but then deemed it too late in the day to bring on a general action.[17] One observer suggests that the British had rather stumbled upon the Russians: 'the men, in spite of their fatigue, were chasing the hares in the long grass, amid shouts of laughter: when suddenly the cavalry pickets came down' informing them that the Russians were 'in force in the vale beyond the hills'. The officers of the 88th Foot (Connaught Rangers) had been having 'an al-fresco lunch ... when suddenly the deep boom of a gun struck upon my ear ... and in an instant it was followed by another and another'. The Light Division under Sir George Brown was ordered forward along with the cavalry under Lord Lucan.[18] Cresting the heights the British saw:

> ... an immense deep valley, the south side of which was formed by the mountain range which encloses Sebastopol, and four squadrons of our cavalry were down in the centre of the valley, and facing them, and distant about 600 yards, were 18 or 20 squadrons of Cossacks.[19]

Captain Nolan remarked in his journal 'Some Cossacks appearing on the heights the Earl of Cardigan was ordered to advance with the 11th and

13th Drg[ns].'[20] Regimental Sergeant-Major George Smith (11th Hussars) remembered that the leading skirmishers were found by the 13th Light Dragoons, and that when 'half way across a valley, we halted; the Cossack skirmishers were twice as many as ours'.[21] Nolan states that

> One Troop was pushed forward and in crossing the heights a strong body of Horse was seen on the Plain in Front whilst another body concealed by the undulations of the ground was discovered by the QMG [Quarter Master General, i.e. General Airey] in person in the Valley on our Right.[22]

Private Mitchell confirms Nolan's observation. He notes that on cresting a hill 'we came in sight of a line of the enemy's skirmishers ... They allowed us to get within two hundred yards of them, when they retired.' According to Nolan, the Russian cavalry was drawn up in three lines and retired slowly across the plain, trying to induce the British cavalry to follow, '& disappeared over the next ridge about 2 miles from the Boulganek'. The four squadrons of British cavalry advanced slowly, cautiously, 'at a walk,' toward the Russians. Lord Raglan then ordered forward the 4th Light Dragoons, 17th Lancers and Maude's troop of Horse Artillery: 'Skirmishers were thrown forward & presently the Enemys [*sic*] light horsemen came down to meet them.'[23] Half of Private Mitchell's troop were sent out as skirmishers, and it was on the higher ground that the Russians 'made a stand': the 13th Light Dragoons advanced to 'within about a hundred yards' of the Russian skirmishers and a fire-fight commenced, which lasted for around half an hour. None of the 13th were wounded. At this point the Russians brought up a battery of horse artillery and 'let fly a couple of round shot', one shell 'struck a troop horse ... It struck him in the side, bursting inside the horse, cleaned him out as though a butcher had done it.'[24] Captain William Richards (Royal Artillery) wrote to his aunt that

> On the morning of the 18th [*sic*, 19th] we arrived at the river Belbec where we first saw the enemy consisting of about three or four thousand Cossacks, with some guns. The Cavalry and Horse Artillery had a skirmish with them, some few horses were killed, and a few legs taken off by round shot, but no prisoners.[25]

Corporal William Hargrave of the 7th Royal Fusiliers watched as

> Our artillery and cavalry went up to reconnoitre. They sent three shots at us before they were returned, when ours gave them one, which dismounted their gun. We then gave them six more, when they scampered off.[26]

Bombardier George Spence (Royal Artillery) related to his uncle that 'they [the Russian artillery] opened fire on us; upon which two of our batteries and one troop of horse artillery, along with our light cavalry, charged them, and three of our division were wounded'.[27] Colour Sergeant Spence remembered seeing 'the Light Division formed in line, and our Artillery got their guns into play, and soon made them side off'.[28] Meanwhile the French were getting the worst of it. Watching from the fleet, 'Travelling Gent' Sir Edward Colebrooke recorded that:

> After an hour of two of inaction, heavy masses of cavalry advanced from the Russian right over the broad plain. They came on slowly and cautiously, and as

they approached the French position, our Allies, who at first were gazing idly at this demonstration of the enemy suddenly ran to arms and form up on the crest, while some guns were advanced and opened fire . . .[29]

Capitaine Cullet wrote that 'Hardly had the officer returned [to] our camp than a regiment of *Uhlans* [Lancers] descended into the valley . . . and made straight for our outpost . . . our . . . men prepared their arms to defend themselves, one against twenty.'[30] This was about 4.15 p.m. The Russian cavalry attacked *Général* Canrobert's 1st Division which:

> formed three squares, flanked by their supporting artillery. My God! How the heart in me beat! They would be destroyed by that mass of 3,000 horsemen launched at the gallop. But no! A terrible cannonade of musketry and artillery fire; the horses fell to the ground, a great number running around without riders in all directions, and the mass of cavalry fell into disorder and quickly reformed behind their infantry. Bravo! Bravo![31]

Watching from the Fleet, Admiral Brouat and his staff were 'in fits of delight' at the 'first triumph of [their] countrymen'.[32] Despite the initial French success, the Russian cavalry reformed out of artillery range and prepared for a second charge, which was similarly met with a 'furious' fire of artillery and musketry. Once again the Russians were stopped in their tracks, and forced to 'turn their backs'.[33]

It was at this point that the Earl of Cardigan and his superior, the Earl of Lucan, 'had an animated controversy': Cardigan wished to charge the Russian cavalry whilst Lucan wished the cavalry to retire. The debate was cut short by Lord Raglan ordering the cavalry to retire, a movement covered by the fire of the Horse Artillery and done in 'beautiful order & as steadily as at a Field Day' by alternate squadrons. This was much to the chagrin of the Light Brigade who had to forgo the 'yells & hootings' of the Russian cavalry as well as of the British infantry. W.H. Russell of *The Times* saw 'Our Lancers and Light Dragoons were preparing to charge' when the Russian cavalry 'practiced a *ruse*, of which our Generals should have been aware': 'They very coolly opened their ranks, and disclosed a battery of ten or twelve field pieces, which instantly opened a heavy fire on our cavalry.'[34] Despite most of the Russian shots passing 'over the heads of our men', 'one of our dragoons lost his leg, and another his foot, one horse was killed, and another wounded'.[35] Nolan who was 'with the skirmishers' 'spoke to the Men to prevent their returning fire of the Cossacks'. The retrograde movement of the British cavalry was covered by fire from the British artillery, which 'soon induced them [the Russians] to shear off'.[36]

Whilst carrying a message from Lord Raglan to Prince Napoléon, ordering the latter to take ground to his left, so as to reduce the gap between the French and British armies, *Lieutenant-Colonel* Lagondie of the *État Major*[37] was taken prisoner. Lagondie and *Chef d'Escadron* Jean-Pierre Vico were both attached as French liaison to the British HQ. Nigel Kingscote, one of Lord Raglan's ADCs (and also his nephew) thought Lagondie 'like a great fat cook' whilst Vico was 'not a bad fellow'. His fellow ADC, Somerset Calthorpe (also Raglan's nephew) agreed with Kingscote's estimation of the pair.[38] *Capitaine* Cullet and Dr Cabrol both relate how Lagondie had poor eyesight, and rode straight into the middle of the Russian cavalry whom he had mistaken for British![39]

Chef d'Escadron Vico's rather terse report of 21 September to *Maréchal* de Castellane summed up the 'Affair of the 19 September' as

... a demonstration made by a numerous Russian cavalry who were accompnied by horse artillery and the distant masses of infantry. The Russians tried to dispute our passage to the Alma, but was shown the resolution of the English cavalry and horse artillery, and battalions of the French army, whose artillery was able to take a few shots. This decided the retirement of the Russians. The English had, that day, three or four men wounded and few horses killed by the Russian artillery fire.[40]

With the action over, Saint-Arnaud and his staff rode amongst the gunners, infantry and Zouaves of the 1st Division to congratulate them and their commander, Général Canrobert. Édouard Minart relates how

Le Maréchal Saint-Arnaud came to see the artillery, then my battalion that supported. We started to shout '*Vive le Maréchal*' but the brave man told us: 'Go and rest my children, because tomorrow we will have to fight a grand battle, and shout "*Vive les Zouaves*", instead of "*Vive le Maréchal!*"'[41]

Saint-Arnaud also offered the following advice to his men:

Well! my children, I promised that you would see the enemy; I have kept my word: the Russians are ahead of you, they will experience you tomorrow ... If, if, my children, you are willing to wait, they will fight well, but we do not fear them. I recommend especially do not shoot much or waste your powder, aim carefully, slowly, coldly, and do not pull your blows; remember that [in the] battle, there are not French and English, but there are only braves![42]

Letter from '**G.C.**', a 'private in the 8th Hussars' who 'Enlisted, much to the annoyance of his parents, who are *very respectable tradespeople* [in Bristol]' to the Right Hon. Francis Henry FitzHardinge Berkeley, MP for Bristol.

　　　　　　　　　　　　　　　　　　　　　Encampment, near Varna
Honourable Sir –　　　　　　　　　　　　　31st August, 1854.[43]
This letter may very probably be the last I shall have the honour of writing to you.

　　　　　　　　　　　　　　　　　　　Transport Steamer, "Himalaya"
　　　　　　　　　　　　　　　　　　　3rd Sept., 1854.
I had just commenced to write to you, when we got the order to prepare for immediate embarkation. When I wrote last we were near Shumla, but a week yesterday we got orders to march back to Varna, and there to embark for the Crimea. Sebastopol is to be taken next week.

　　It was a great surprise to a good many who had fancied all along that there would be no war, to find themselves near to it. The 11th Hussars marched first; the next day the 8th Hussars, the 13th and 17th followed them. We had three days' march, and then halted near Varna, and on the next day marched down to the Quay, and there embarked on board the "Himalaya." I have often read of this vessel, but had no idea of her immense size and splendid accommodation. When I went on board, after my horse had been taken from the slings, I went down a staircase, and the polished railings, gilded mouldings, and splendidly-lit Saloon put me more in mind of a palace than a troop-ship. It made me wonder where they could put 400 horses, for in the transport ship I came out in, which was 1020 tons, we could only find accommodation for 54 horses. This vessel ("Himalaya") is able to carry two regiments of horse and [or?] one of infantry. We have now 300 horses on board, and 32 more are to be shipped this afternoon; the whole of one regiment (8th Hussars) is on board and one squadron of the 17th Lancers. Lord Cardigan and the whole of the staff are coming on board to go up to Sebastopol. We expect to leave Varna on Monday, one day's steaming will bring us in sight enemy. We all feel it is now coming to an end. It is said that Wednesday is the day fixed for the landing of the troops. This is now Sunday, and therefore two days before the fight. Many wear a very downcast look, that never did before; men that were regular bullies and brutes, because they were big and strong, are now talking seriously, and are as easily managed as lambs; this is the time to find out what a man is, when he knows not that he will be alive in three day's time. I was talking to an old boatswain on board that had come with a party from the "Leander" to assist in getting the horses on board; he tells me that "it will require every ship and every gun that the allied forces can muster to take it [Sebastopol]." He says, "It is the strongest fortified place in the world, and, admitting you land, as some of you may, under the fire of the whole of your guns, you will have an army of 80,000 to walk over before you will come to the garrison, and that has 60,000 more inside it. If they land, as they dare not, every soldier, marine, and sailor there is, and fight well when they are there, it will take them a week to master it, and then it will be with a tremendous loss of life to you." My reply was, "Well a man that is born to be shot will never be drowned." So as the song says – Cheer up, Sam, and don't let your spirits be down.[44]

I intend to look to myself as much as is consistent with my duty, keep up my spirits, and leave the rest to fate. We cannot all fall; every man says, why should not I survive as well as any one else? I am sorry to say Captain Longmore of my troop died this morning from cholera; he came on board two days ago as well as I did; he is just buried.[45] About a fortnight ago there was an order from Lord Lucan that 10 men out of every troop of 70 men were to be cooks, and relieve one another weekly. I was one of those sent to cook, and when we marched from Yuah Bazaar, the cooking was no easy task, for after marching with the rest all day under a burning sun, and having cared for and watered my horse, I, with a subordinate, had to cook and scour the country for wood wherewith to light and keep up a fire – many and many were the adventures I encountered inn this strange place in search of fuel.

I generally used to make for some village, and always took my haversack over my shoulder, in case I met with any bread or eggs or cheese; and my calabash as well, in case I met with that great luxury milk, and whether I could get that or not, it was an excellent weapon in the hands of an active man, for it has a strong leather thong attaches to the wooden barrel, bound round with iron hoops, capable of containing three pints. Any man, therefore, that got a blow from it must go down if he got it on the head. I went to one village, and after looking about for the most comfortable home or cabin, went to one that had recently been white-washed, and found a venerable Turk outside, smoking, of course. I asked him for some *echmeck* (bread) at the same time showing him three piastres; he told me to go to the door, and called to his wives to serve me.

I saluted them very politely, and as one of his wives had about four or five words of English, and I had about a dozen of Turkish, we got on very well. I bought some bread, and filled my calabash with milk for two piastres; as for eggs they were, according to our money, four a penny. I was coming away congratulating myself upon my good fortune, when, in passing the old Turk, and giving him a nod with the usual salute, "Bono Turco," I was stopped by him, saluted by a slap on the shoulder and "Bono Johnny," and signs were made to me to go back into the house.

I went, the Turk motioned me to sit down, which I did cross legged like himself; he them spoke to his wives, who brought out a leg of lamb, with some vegetable marrows, cheese, cucumbers, and vinegar; I fell to with no little gusto, for we had had a long march with nothing before it but cold coffee (without sugar) and biscuit; after I had done he gave me a chibouque,and as the tobacco was mild I smoked with the Turk. But what surprised me most of all, was his bringing out a bottle of English porter. I began to question him as to where he got it from, as well as I could, but there was no difficulty, the word Varna settled the matter. The Turk's kindness did not end here, for telling him that I wanted some wood, he put 4 or 5 logs upon his araba or bullock waggon [*sic*], and sent a boy with me to bring it back. I must here mention a circum-cstance that occurred while I was dining and smoking – a girl, of about 18 or 19 years of age, came into the room for some domestic purpose, and stared very hard at me; no wonder, she had probably seldom seen an English soldier in full uniform, with the exception of the shako, sitting dining and smoking on the best terms with her grave father. Well, when they all went out to put the wood upon the araba, I went for my havresack [*sic*, haversack] &c., and found her intently and curiously gazing upon the number and name inscribed upon it. She was so absorbed in this task that she did not at first notice me, no, indeed, till I was close upon her. She started up, for she was kneeling, and vuest into tears, perhaps, as a Turkish girl, thinking herself guilty of some forwardness or impropriety, they have h ad odd notions on such points. At this moment, her father entered, and seeing his daughter in tears, no doubt imagining that I had in some way offended, perhaps insulted her, he directly drew his knife. I started at him, seized his arm, while his daughter spoke to him and I imagine assured him I was not to blame. He, however, ordered her out of the room; but it was all right, and I was "bono Johnny" and he was "Bono Turco" as before. I thank him for his kindness as well as I could, and went back to the camp, thinking over the fortunes of war. At the next place we went to I was still in office as cook, and had to cook the men's rations.

In a very dark night I had to go forth about midnight to look for wood. I stumbled upon an old farm-house, with a dry wooden stake fence round it, and as there was a scarcity of fuel, I was pulling up three or four of the stakes, when a whole legion of dogs were let loose upon me; it was a good job for me that they were not English dogs, or my campaign would have ended on that spot, but the Turkish dogs are the greatest cowards of their species that I have ever met with. As they advanced I put my back against the fence, and as they came at me I knocked the leaders down, seven in number, and the remainder then barked at a distance or went howling about the village. I must admit that I was very considerably frightened; in the dead of the night, no aid near, and full 20 hungry dogs with their infernal wolf-like heads about you; but, after all,

I got the wood, and the rations were cooked about two in the morning. At six we marched for Varna. I do not know, sir, that there is anything else to interest you; you will hear of our doings at Sebastopol, and, if I survive, I shall not forget your injunctions, and write you a full account of that which I see or take a part in.

Letter from Lieutenant **John Chadwick**[46] 17th Lancers to his brother Captain James Chadwick.[47]

Bivouac, Alma,

Dear James, -   22nd September, 1854.

I write this note from our Bivouac, upon the heights of Alma, taken by our army, on the 20th, in the most gallant style, after a fearfully dreadful struggle of about three hours, it is naturally the strongest position you can imagine, allowed by judges to be more than Torresbedras [*sic*, Torres Vedras[48]]. We disembarked on the 17th, marched on the 18th, and were turned out about 12 that night by an outlying picquet, who were fired on by Cossacks, but made nothing of it. The next day, the whole army formed and advanced in order of battle along the sea coast; we formed the rear guard, and protected the rear on the land side; on reaching the small river, on which it was decided to encamp, the cavalry, at least the 8th [Hussars], 13th [Light Dragoons], and ourselves, were ordered up over a ridge where we found about 5,000 Cossacks, formed up with skirmishers thrown out, after driving them back their artillery came up and opened nine-pounders upon us, killed two or three horses of the 13th, wounded three or four men, causing the necessity of amputation, one since dead. We were on the left, and taking ground, threatening an attack, and so escaping any damage. They ultimately retired upon some high ground, and we both kept position until dusk; the next day, the 20th, we marched in the same order, but without any rear guard, and when the sight of their lines with their army posted in them, composed of about 55,000 burst upon us, the greatest novice living could see that it was a fearful thing to undertake. However there was scarcely a pause made, the leading division, the Light (Sir George Brown's) deployed and advanced after the rifle skirmishers, and mounted the heights under a most murderous fire, and carried them in less than three hours from the time we sighed them. I cannot attempt to describe the action at present, we were ordered up to pursue, and our leading troops went on and took several prisoners, but a strong column of Cossacks suddenly showed and deployed on our men and we were recalled. About 90 of our officers were killed and wounded, and about 1,400 men, it is supposed, chiefly the Guards, 19th [Green Howards], 23rd [Royal Welch Fusiliers] and 7th [Royal] Fusileers [*sic*, Fusiliers]. The Russians, it is supposed, lost about 5,000; we took three guns, but they had 100, and it is said that had we been stronger in Cavalry we should have taken nearly all their guns and men.

They have another strong position between this and Sebastopol, but it has been telegraphed to the fleet that the whole [Russian] army entered Sebastopol that night. We march to-morrow [*sic*] morning for there, I suppose, and have drawn three days' rations, so that we expect fully to go right on. It has must been reported that two of their ships of war have escaped, and gone to Odessa for reinforcements. I saw about 900 Russians buried this morning, that had fallen within the compass of 300 or 400 yards, and plenty moved alive, this morning, that had been unavoidably lying since the day of the bloody struggle. God grant I may never again see such sights as I have seen the last two mornings!

Letter from Sergeant **James Shaw** (number 596), 13th Light Dragoons, to his brother Joseph Shaw of Lower Head-Row, Leeds.[49]

Dear Brother, -
Scutari Hospital,
Sept. 25, 1854.

I wrote to you when we sailed from Varna. We were near a fortnight ere we reached the vicinity of Sebastopol. We had part difficulty in landing, but met with no opposition from the enemy.

I like the inhabitants here much better than I did the Turkish people; the former are more kind and more willing to oblige us, and don't appear to look upon us as enemies.

The cavalry have been very severely harassed, reconnoitring night and day, and sometimes no grub, and when we could lay down, no tents, and the nights fearfully damp and cold.

On the 18th we came in sight of the enemy at a small river, where we deliberately watered our horses and filled our bottles, but we had soon to look sharp, for the enemy began to fire, and the bullets came about us like hailstones. Lord Cardigan sent our right troop against them; we act on the defensive for a short time, then ordered to five to fire, which we did for near half an hour, and they stood like stones.

We were then ordered to form up with the 11th Hussars to charge. Counter orders were immediately sent for us to retire, which we had no sooner done than the enemy showed about 1,000 cavalry and artillery, the latter took the ground to the right and brought their guns on us. Our guns then rushed to our aid, but not before they had killed eight serjeants, and wounded three more: I happened to be one, a ball struck my sword scabbard, doubled it up, passed through my horse, broke my spur, and wounded my right ankle, hit the man next to me, and wounded him worse than me. My horse never stirred again. We were carried to the rear, and our guns soon silenced theirs, and they retired for the night.

A general engagement took place the next day, particulars of which you will have seen 'ere this. A Russian general and his son or nephew were brought prisoners on board the 'Olden' where I was. He said they only expected to meet *men* in the fight but they found them devils (that's the way he talks.) They expected to keep their position for three weeks, and our men took it in as many hours.

Were you here, amongst 1,000 sick and wounded, you could indeed see the horrors of war. We are very much short of attendance on the sick and wounded: the sufferings of some from that causes are dreadful. I have not time – or rather I am not able – to sit up and tell you more, but with me I hope the worst is past, and that I shall soon be right again.

Give me kindest love to my dear children, and tell them that my grey horse, on which they have so often rode, is dead. Where we shall go once Sebastopol is taken I don't know. I for one shall be glad when it is over, so that I can again visit dear Old England, and be united to my wife and children.

Letter from an anonymous NCO in the Light Cavalry Brigade.[50]

English Camp, in front of Sebastopol.
Mr Dear, [censored], -   Oct. 1st, 1854.

I scarcely know what you will infer from the heading of this letter, for I believe we are not within four miles of Sebastopol, nor are we in sight of it, although I have seen it twice at a long distance. It appeared to me a square town, walled all round, with a very strong fort at one corner, at which I cannot say, for I was out of sight almost as soon as in; but let me begin from our disembarkation, which was completed on the morning of the 19th ult. about 25 miles from Sebastopol. However, I cannot speak certainly as to the distance. The Cavalry, having moved forward the day before (18th) about three miles, saw some villages on fire, and were disturbed once during the night by a party of Cossacks. The whole of the army moved forward about five o'clock on the morning of the 19th. The French on the right close to the shore, the Turks in the centre, and the English on the left, covered by the Cavalry. They advanced about 12 or 14 miles, when we came in sight of the enemy. He was quickly driven back by our skirmishers, and seemed to be strong in cavalry and artillery. The 8th and 11th Hussars, 13th Light Dragoons, 17th Lancers, and two troops of Horse Artillery were then ordered to the front. The latter silenced the fire of the enemy's artillery after firing four or five rounds, and he then paid attention to his cavalry, and disappeared in about an hour. Our artillery then drew off; but the cavalry remained until dark, when they were relieved by the infantry outlying picquet, and all was quiet for the night.

At six o'clock on the morning of the 20th we moved toward the stream (or river as it is called) Alma, with immense heights in rear, on which the Russian army was posted in entrenchments. The allied army was in the same order as yesterday, viz., French on the right, Turks centre, and English on the left, with their flank covered by the four regiments of cavalry abovenamed. The English division under General Brown, on the right; the Guards, under the Duke of Cambridge, on the left and the other division in the rear. This was the order in which we advanced, and such was the ardour of our men that not a single regiment was relieved during the whole of the fight, although two or three regiments of the Light Division, which was in the hottest part of it, and before a village which was set on fire to retard their progress, caused some little confusion; but this was soon put to right. Notwithstanding they were under a tremendous fire of shell and shot, they soon after gained the first height, and then a second, almost as formidable, when a troop of Lancers skirmished a little way down the hill, and took a few prisoners. This completed the battle of Alma. The French lost about 1,400, ourselves about 1,600. I have not heard what was the loss to the Turks, but the enemy lost 6,000 or 7,000. The cavalry lost none, this being an affair almost entirely of scaling heights. But there was about 5,000 of the Russian cavalry waiting for something to do, which, however, they could not get, on account of our (cavalry) position, and I do not think they much admired us.

We encamped the night on the field, and the two following days were employed in attending to the sick, conveying them aboard ship, and burying the dead. We (the cavalry) then took two short marches to the front, and the next day were ordered out, the Greys having joined us on the 23d, and made a ramble for about three hours in the wood, dismounting and loitering about, until we were all in single files, and grazing our horses. All at once we heard the sound of our own artillery wheels, upon a hard road close by, and got the order to mount. Off we were like a shot. The artillery unlimbered and fired four or five shots, and then off they were again, and away went the Lancers in hot pursuit. The Greys dismounted, took to the woods with carbines in hand, and commenced firing away 'like one o'clock.' There is said to have been 25,000 of the enemy before us, but this quite uncertain. However, I saw dead and dying of several regiments of infantry; three regiments of Hussars, viz., 2d, 12th, and 15th, and a lot of artillery. We captured about nine tons of powder, with lots of shot and ammunition, a carriage belonging to some person of note, with a great quantity of baggage of all descriptions, stars, medals, and orders.

We then came towards our own position, and the next day took up the one we now have.

The moon is going down a little, and I have nothing more to say, save that about 20 siege guns are up, and they will most likely commence to-morrow on Sebastopol. I have to go down with a patrol and Mr. [blank] to Lord Lucan by daybreak; so good night.

P.S. – We have no tents, but have to bivouack in the open air. The cavalry lost *five horses killed* and four or five men wounded in the first skirmish of the 19th with the artillery.

Letter from Gunner **John Horn**, Captain Maude's Troop, Royal Horse Artillery, to his parents in Lancaster.[51]

Within gun-shot of Sebastopol,
Dear Father and Mother, -   Oct. 6th, 1854.
I have just received your kind and welcome letter, and was glad to hear that you were all well, as this leave me at present, both fat, strong, and hearty, my clothes are getting too small for me. We live a great deal better in Russia than in Turkey. I have a great deal of news to tell you. A few hours after I despatched my last letter our troop was sent on board, and off we went to the Crimea. We landed about forty miles from Sebastopol, without a shot being fired at us; but a number of Cossacks gave us some trouble. Lord Cardigan took out two of our Guns with two troops of Light Cavalry to give chase to the enemy; I was one of them. We pursued them up the country for about eighteen miles, but they kept out of gun reach; night came on and we were obliged to return to our army, with empty stomachs. Slept very well on the sea sand, with my saddle for my pillow and my cloak for a covering. So much for our first day's work in the Crimea.

The French and English were all landed in three days. We then marched up the country, and on the 18th came in sight of the enemy; they, however, kept their distance that day. The following morning we proceeded on our route, and came in sight of the enemy about ten o'clock, on the top of a hill. Lord Cardigan with two troops of Light Cavalry and our Troop of Horse Artillery, received orders to reconnoitre. We started up the hill at full gallop; they were on the other side of the hill ready to receive us, so a few of our Light Cavalry were sent out as Skirmishers. The enemy also sent out a party of skirmishers, and they fired at each other for about fifteen minutes, when the enemy brought ten guns to bear on our Cavalry. Our troop then galloped up, the bullets whistling past our ears, which had a strange effect upon me till we were brought into action, then I had something else to think about and something to do. The very first shot I fired sent one of the enemy's gun barrels out of its bed. By this time the C Troop came to our assistance with a few of the battery's guns, and in a short time we sent them all flying; but it was a very severe skirmish. Our side lost four horses killed and four men wounded. The enemy's loss was much greater, about twelve horses killed and forty-five men killed. So much for the first touch of war. I thought if they called that a skirmish, what would a battle be, but I very soon afterwards saw the difference; for on the morning of the 20th we marched up to a large range of hills right in front of the enemy. As soon as we were within gun shot – bang-bang-bang went one great gun after another; shells and balls came whistling past us like lightning. The enemy set a village on fire to make a great smoke to blind our army. Our (the Artillery) guns were too light, being 6-pounders, so there was no way of taking it but by the gun and bayonet. Our gallant Infantry marched forward to the charge, and a splendid sight it was to see the Riflemen, the 23rd, 55th, 95th, 88th, 33rd and the Foot Guards march up to the enemy's batteries and bayonet the bears from their guns. You should have seen our little troop flying along with the Cavalry up the hill, under the fire of a heavy battery on the hill, it would have made you proud having a son in the Royal Artillery. The enemy flew before us like chaff before the win. We came into Action upon the hill, fired into the valley upon the enemy, and sent hundreds to their long home. We had the shipping on the right of us and they played beautifully upon the enemy. The enemy had a Grand Stand upon the hill for the great people of Russia to see the destruction of our army; but they were finely taken in, for the shipping sent a shell or two upon it (the grand stand) and sent them flying. The Russians had a great quantity of guns. They expected the battle to last for five weeks, but we won the day and set them off in four hours. So closed the great Battle of the Alma. It was an awful sight to go through the battle field, where thousands were lying dead, many of their bodies being frightfully mutilated. I had to go out at night for water through the thickest of the dead; I stumbled over dead bodies until I felt quite sick. Our army buried all the dead both of the English and Russians. This work kept us two or three days, and then we marched through a romantic country, but were not engaged again until the 25th.

While on the march our troop, with the Scotch [*sic*, Scots] Greys and other light companies were sent forward to reconnoitre. Our road lay through a level wooded country, where we could not see five yards on either side of us for thick bushes and underwood. For miles we went along expecting every minutes a volley of musketry fired into us. We proceeded until we arrived at a small opening in the wood, when we saw a large party of Russian soldiers and a train of ammunition, goods, and a great many carriages drawn by pretty ponies. We fired upon the soldiers and they took to their heels. We chased them, and they turned and fired into us, but no one was any worse. We took fifteen prisoners, and a great quantity of ammunition and carriages.

We have landed besides Sebastopol, and are getting the siege trains up to their stations. A constant interchange of shots is taking place, but the great siege will commence in a day or two.

Oct. 7th, Eight o'clock a.m.

We have just arrived from another skirmish. The enemy attacked our posts at five o'clock this morning. Captain G.A. Maude's troop was called out as usual to the front, likewise the heavy and light cavalry. We defeated the advancing party with great slaughter; they retired before our shell and round shot as fast as their horses could carry them. One of our heavy Dragoons was wounded; that was all the harm we sustained. We may have many such skirmishes before the siege commences, as our people have a great deal of work to do yet. We are lying about five miles from Sebastopol, on the east side of a small harbour, to keep the enemy in the rear, so that you see we are of some use.

Now I think I'll have my breakfast, for this morning's work has given me an appetite, but I do not want much to give me that, for I am as healthy and as fat as a pig. This country is much more healthy than Turkey. I forgot to say anything about the French. They fought on our right flank in the battle of the Alma. They are a gallant sent of men, and fought bravely; they pay great respect to our army. I could write all day, but I must have something to tell you by word of mouth when I come home. So good bye at present, and may God bless you all is the sincere prayer of your son.

Letter from Corporal **George Senior** (number 1386), 13th Light Dragoons, to his brother in Lockwood, near Huddersfield.[52]

Scutari Barracks,
Dearest Brother,-   6th October 1854.
... We continued our march about two miles further when we came in sight of the enemy, in great force, in a most formidable position, immediately on the opposite side of the River Alma. The position they were in was the hills, which by nature, was one vast fortification, and which extended for nine or ten miles from the sea shore into the interior of the land. Just opposite to where the English were advancing, the enemy appeared in great force, and one hill rising directly above another gave the Russians an opportunity of placing one fortification of guns above another until one hill overlooked the whole, and could observe all the movements of the allied army. We halted just without range of their guns, for Lord Raglan to make some observations. We had halted about an hour when the order was given for the Infantry to load with ball cartridge. The army again advanced. We soon came within range, when they opened fire with shot and shell from 130 pieces of artillery. The Infantry and our brigade continued to advance in the greatest order. By this time the shot and shell were bursting around us in all directions, but not doing much damage. The Infantry was now ordered to form line to the front, which they did, and kept advancing steadily. Just as we came near to a small village, which run along the banks of the river on our side, the enemy set fire to it, and the smoke and flames completely hid the Russians from us, although they knew our exact position, and continued to pour out shot and shell. The French were on the right, and reached to the beach, advanced up the heights, under the cover of ours guns from the navy. The "Terrible," which the Russians call "The Black Cat," kept sending forth her heavy shot and shell, which gave the French an opportunity of gaining the heights to the left of the enemy, and which they attacked on their left flank, driving them towards where the English were

attacking the forts on the right. The English infantry had great difficulties to encounter in crossing the River Alma. It was pretty deep in some places. I saw where the 23rd Regiment crossed; it was very deep: so much so that their pieces and ammunition got wet, they having to draw their charges under a very heavy fire of musketry from the Russians, who were behind barricades, also from shell, which killed a great many; – they suffered very much. Also the 33rd and 7th Regiments, 55th, the Guards, and 88th. The colours of these regiments were completely riddled with canister, grape, and musket shot. We lost a great number of officers. I am not acquainted with the details of casualties of each regiment. Just as the Infantry captured the last fortification and drove the Russians back in great disorder, we (the Cavalry brigade) were ordered to advance. We had to come down a very narrow lane, and could only ride in single file. We were obliged to halt, on account of some guns being in the way, something like a quarter of an hour. Had we or could we have charged up the heights when ordered to do so, we might have had an opportunity of charging the retreating Russians; but this delay gave them an opportunity of retreating. We came up to the top of the heights just in time to see them gain another of the heights, something in appearance to those we had then taken. When we came in sight they opened fire with some heavy guns, and several shells burst but a few yards away from where I was mounted. Our artillery opened fire at them, which must have done great execution, for their shells dropped right amongst them. I had a slight accident, when charging up the heights, by coming in contact with a large bush of underwood. I had no other alternative but to leap my horse at it, when, I suppose, the horse was not strong enough to clear it, caught it with his fore legs, which pitched him on his head. I also came on my head or shako (head dress), and the horse rolled on the top of me, but, thank God, did me no injury, any further than shaking me a little. When I got again on my horse I found it had shook the saddle nearly off, and knocked the bit out of its mouth, which hurt it very much, but that was all. I put things right again, and proceeded up the remainder of the hill, and joined my troop again. On gaining the top the Infantry were cheering in a most excited way, throwing up their caps and head-dress, and each successive regiment, as they gained the heights, which had cost so many lives and much blood in taking, was echoing from a thousand voices, which must have spread terror amongst the retreating Russians. Night was now coming on. We rode over a good deal of the ground where the battle had been the most severe. There the Russians were laying [*sic*, lying] in heaps, some dead and some living, and others had laid down and nothing the matter, but shamming. In one or two instances they got up, when some of the Infantry were going past, and shot them. The English behaved in the kindest manner to them. Two days were employed in burying the dead and carrying the wounded off the field to the hospitals. I went down to one hospital the second day after the engagement, and the most horrible sight met my view – men laying dead who had died under some operation, and others, in all directions, were undergoing amputation of either arm or leg, and heaps of legs and arms of all lengths were scattered in confusion over the place.

On the third day after the engagement a general march took place again. This was a sad day for me. I was taken with diarrhoea and vomiting. When we had got about six miles on the march I fainted and fell from my horse. When

I came round the doctor was standing over me; he asked me what was the matter; I told him, and he said I must mount again and go on to some led horses (a party leading spare horses). I mounted again, but was so bad that two men were obliged to go on with me and hold me on. In this way I was mounted until twelve o'clock, that I was nearly dead when lifted off my horse and laid down in the open air with my cloak and blanket round me, with not so much as a drop of water to quench my thirst. In this way I lay until morning when I was put into an araba (a kind of waggon [*sic*]), and in this I rode, or rather was jolted, until dark that night, having had nothing but water during that day. I have no recollection which way we marched. I was so ill the day appears a blank to me. That night I was also left as before, out in the open air, with some water to help myself to, which is rather a very bad thing for any one caught with my complaint. It was on this night that the cramps caught me in my legs and arms, and I was obliged to keep rubbing them most of the night. On the following morning a comrade corporal of ours made me a drop of tea, about a pint, which did me a great deal of good. I had then to walk about a mile-and-a-half to some arabas, which were for taking the sick on board ship. I got into one and travelled all that day with scarcely a drop of water. I was nearly exhausted when we got down to the beach. I was lifted into the boat and carried to the ship "Timandrew" of Liverpool. 130 men were taken on board that night, and not one man able to look after himself; had it not been for the kindness and human exertions of Doctors Pierce and Smith of the Navy, and the sailors on board ship, I think all of us would have died. The first night 25 were taken from amongst the living on the deck and thrown over board; next day four or five more died, and the second night either seven or eight. I saw these lying on deck. I for the first time had managed to crawl on deck for a little fresh air. Amongst this number was our Adjutant, Mr Irwin, who had died that night of cholera – indeed it was this complaint that all was affected with. During our passage to this place (11 days) 53 were thrown over board, and one who was dead that we brought on shore made 54, and many who were taken on shore could not survive the night. Myself, thank God, I got quite well on board by the kind attention of the doctors above-mentioned, and to whom, previous to leaving the vessel, I returned my sincere thanks for the untiring exertions they had used during the time we were on board, and kindness they had used to all under their charge; all was most thankful, and many thank them previous to disembarking. The first night I was on shore in this place I was taken ill again, and have since been very weak and can scarcely get about; but I trust in Providence that He will yet allow me to return to my native land and give me back my health. I have now been here a week. There has no particular news come down from Sebastopol, only that they have completely surrounded the place, and have landed the siege train and all the heavy guns from the shipping – in all from 900 to 1,000 guns. We heard yesterday they had commenced firing on the place, so you may soon expect to hear of its being in our hands, for it must fall. I intend to return by the next draft if I get a little stronger, for I was sorry to leave my regiment when in sight of the place we have heard of so much, and which, I trust, by taking, will put an end to the war. Give my kind love to all at home.

Letter from an anonymous Private in the Light Cavalry Brigade to his mother in Nottingham.[53]

Camp near Sebastopol,
My ever dear Mother, -   13th October, 1854.

Being on guard and having half-an-hour to myself I think I cannot spent it with more satisfaction to myself than in dropping you a line to let you know I am well and still among the land of the living. When I wrote last I had not a moment's time. Oh! my dear mother the horrors, the indescribable miseries, the most woeful sights of a campaign are beyond the power of my pen to express. On the 18th of last month we were attacked by the enemy, the Cavalry alone, we being some miles in front of the infantry) (only three regts.) the enemy some forty thousand strong. We kept them in check until the horse artillery came up, and when the bull dogs (our cannon balls) began to play they retired like infernal cowards as are. On the 19th we had a very sharp skirmish, only two or three of the English were wounded, an one of the 11th Hussar's leg blown off.

On the 20th we came to the River Alma, in front of which was a large village which the enemy had set on fire, so that the smoke would prevent us seeing their position; but the English spies were not to be done that way. They were about treble our number, and occupied a large hill – we were in a valley. The fighting began, and such slaughter I never saw nor could imagine. It lasted four hours, when our good brave army advanced up the hill, cheering, under a heavy cannonade of some hundred of the enemy's artillery. They charged and stopped their guns. We had great loss, but the heights were taken in three hours and forty minutes. Our generals expected it would take at least ten days to take. The enemy retired and we (the cavalry) pursued them about three miles. Oh God! The field after the action was horrifying, the ground for miles covered with wounded, their groans being dreadful – some laying without heads, some blown all to atoms, some without legs or arms. It took three days to take the wounded off the field and bury the dead. Oh my dear mother many a hardened wretch, who never knew what prayer was before, called on his God that day. The cowardly brutes of Russians never even sent in a flag of truce to bury the dead, and the English buried all of them, and the wounded enemy were all taken care of and sent to Constantinople. I will give you an instance of their treachery. An officer passing a wounded Russian gave him some brandy, biscuit &c., and as he was leaving him the Russian raised himself on his elbow and shot him dead with his gun which was laying beside him. He, the prisoner, was run through with a dozen bayonets by out soldiers who were passing. The treacherous brutes!

We were not attacked again until the last day's march here, when we were passing through a wood. We had some good fighting with little loss to us and a good deal to the enemy. We took 600 prisoners, and baggage, property, &c., to the amount of thirty thousand pounds (a lot of which the fighting private soldier will get). We are now lying in front of Sebastopol, and the siege train making every preparation for an attack, about two miles off, from Sebastopol, making entrenchments, the enemy continually firing but doing little damage. We have got 600 guns – 90 pounders – and mortars to play on it. I think it will soon be taken when commenced. The cavalry is about a mile and a half in the rear, to protect the rear of the army. We are nearly always saddled, booted, and belted. There are forty thousand Russians encamped over the hill four miles away, and they are nearly always out, but will not stand for a fight. They fire on our videts [*sic*, videttes] and picquets and retire. The weather is getting cold. We have to lay under the Canopy of Heaven all weathers – our blankets and cloaks are all. No tents; they were left behind. I leave you to guess what pleasures we enjoy. We are all lousy from the highest to the lowest and cannot help it. You would laugh to see the men lousing themselves every spare minute they have. Always our clothes on, and seldom clean linen. The people of England who sit by the fire and say – "We beat them again" little think of what WE undergo to bear them. If spared after this place is taken I will write again.

Letter from '**G.C.**', 8th Hussars, to the Right Hon. Francis Henry FitzHardinge Berkeley, MP.[54]

Honourable Sir, -

Camp, Balaklava, near Sebastopol. Oct. 14, 1854.

It is now some time since my last letter to you, and the scenes that have passed in the interval will, I think, be of more interest to you than the preceding ones. We landed about 30 miles from Sebastopol, on a flat sandy beach, and with nothing to oppose us. The first day the infantry landed, and then the next day the artillery and the cavalry; immediately after landing we saddled, and Lord Cardigan took us and the 17th Lancers about 15 miles up the country. Such a mad-brained trick I should was never played before. We started at ten o'clock in the morning, at length we stopped at a Russian village about 15 miles from the place we started from; here we fed our horses and remained an hour – in fact, it was getting quite dark before we thought of going back. We came over gigantic mountains, and as we were to go back the same way it struck us all how easily we could be attacked and the whole of us cut to pieces by men who knew the country; and, to mend the matter, his Lordship forgot the road. When we came up in the afternoon we had an immense sheet of salt water to ford, but it was only a foot and a half deep; on returning, when we came to the water, we found that instead of a foot and a half deep it was about five feet deep. We made a detour to the right, and found that the tide had, in our absence, come in, and the place we had forded in the morning was four feet deep. We were obliged them to make another detour to our extreme left, and at length got to a place where the water was only three feet deep, but it was nearly a quarter of a mile across. I thought how easily we could have been cut off when we were wandering about in search of a ford. When we got back to the beach it was twelve o'clock and the night very dark; our horses were picketed, and for the first time, I slept without a covering over me, but I slept as soundly as if I was in a decent bed, and the dashing of the waters on the beach served to make me sleep sounder. We had to get up at three in the morning, after about two hours' sleep; we saddled in the dark, and then learnt that we should not march until eight o'clock, which was afterwards changed to twelve. We took the road to Sebastopol, and stopped at a deserted village which had recently undergone pillage by the French, encamped near it (that is the 8th and 11th Hussars, the 4th and 13th Light Dragoons, the 17th Lancers and two Troops of the Horse Artillery), under the command of the Earl of Cardigan, but, to the satisfaction of all of us, the Earl of Lucan came up the same evening and assumed the command. We had on that evening an outlying picket of 60 men, who were stationed about a mile from the camp, and they threw forward some videttes. About one in the morning some of the videttes were driven in by a body of Cossacks, the officer of the picket reported the same to Lord Lucan, and the trumpet then sounded "Turn Out." I was comfortably asleep in my cloak by the side of a small wood fire, when I was awoke by the firing, and then roused by the trumpet. I ran to my horse – saddled and bridled her up, returned to where I left my horse, and found her gone – I looked around the stable, or out-house, where she had stood, asked my comrades about her, but she was clean gone. Seeing a horse lying down I made it get up, saddled it and mounted, and had the pleasure of finding the animal dead lame. In spite of myself I could not help laughing to think, if a Cossack should attack me, how I was to contrive a circle around him according to our rules, and beat him. Luckily they retired when they had got us all out of our beds, and we turned in and got two hours' sleep. The next morning we marched on the road to Sebastopol again, and I on my dear old mare, the chance of whose loss made me more sensible of her value. The whole of this day we fasted for want of food, and all we had the day before was a small bit of salt pork and a handful of small biscuit. I assure you, sir, the day's march was long and fatiguing. It chanced that I, with a party of 20 men, was in front of the whole body, with loaded carbines, and we expected an affair every minute. About five in the evening we came up to where all the infantry and artillery had halted, with Lord Raglan. At this point there was a company of Rifles thrown forward, who were advancing in skirmishing order, when all of a sudden the enemy opened fire on them. They retired behind us, and then we got the exciting words "8th Hussars, 17th Lancers, and Captain Maud's [*sic*, Maude's] Troop Royal Horse Artillery, draw swords! Gallop." Upon our advance we found the enemy with his artillery drawn up on a commanding height, so we halted, our artillery formed for action; the enemy commenced first by sending the shots of two well-directed 9-pounder guns among our men, one very narrowly missed hitting the colonel, but killed two horses; then our artillery opened upon the Russians, and Lord Lucan, who was close to us, said their firing was beautiful. The very first shot dismounted one of the Russian guns, and then the Russians, who were pretty strong, both with cavalry and artillery, thought to outflank us. As soon as this was seen, another division of our artillery was sent to meet these would-be outflankers, and send round, grape, canister, and shells among them so hotly that they judged it expedient to retire. In the meantime the main body of the enemy on the heights, thinking to come on our right flank, got within range of our fleet, about two miles off, and the Fury and Terrible terrified them so much with their heavy calibre [guns] that they were glad to regain their former strong position. Both sides then stopped firing, and the Russians sent a party to collect their wounded and dead. We then retired, and after this day's work all we received was a handful of biscuit and half a quartern of rum, and, to crown the whole, I was on guard all night.

The next morning was the 20th, and long before you received this, sir, you will have heard of the battle of the Alma. We, of the cavalry, were not engaged until near the close, as we had to watch the enemy's cavalry, who were waiting for an opportunity to charge our infantry on the flank. I had a splendid view of the whole – nothing could be stronger than their position: a complete range of mountains, with guns covering the whole. It was a good, Lord Raglan said, as twenty to one. On the glories and losses of that day it is not my province to speak in this letter, they were not the doings of my branch of the service, but surely never did men, as *the* Frenchman [i.e. Napoleon] would say, "Cover themselves with Glory." One little anecdote, perhaps, you will pardon. The 33rd lost their colours for about five minutes, and they were being borne into a square of Russian infantry, when the colonel said, "We can't retire, boys, without them," and, cut to pieces as they were, they charged, and in that glorious effort they lost their colonel, three captains, and more than a hundred fine fellows, but they got their colours. Well, sir, we picketed our horses after the battle, and in those very lines there were thirty wounded and dead Russians. I slept side by side with two dead Russians, who were killed by a cannon. I was not aware of their close proximity until the next morning. We stopped here for two days to bury the dead, dress the wounded, and send the captured guns and prisoners to be shipped. On the day of the battle, which was thought one of the bloodiest ever known, all the troops fought on was the usual pound of biscuit a man; their rum was not served out until it was over. The two days we stopped here we got plenty of fresh meat, as there was a great quantity of captured cattle, to us quite a God-send. I saw numbers eat it raw.

After we quitted this miserable spot, we marched through a dense wood, that is the 8th, 17th, and a battalion of Rifles, to see that the enemy were not in ambush; the main body took the High Road. We were divided into two parties, our regiment, and the 17th, each having half the Rifles attached to us. The Rifles were in advance, and we were dismounted, and what with being up all night the three last days, we were no sooner on the ground than we fell asleep, we were in this state when the alert the Rifles heard the sound of wheels and cavalry, "Mount and Gallop" was the word, and through the wood we went. I forgot to say that Captain Maud's troop of Artillery was with us. On we came into a narrow lane, through a thick wood, and there we found a quantity of baggage, with a strong cavalry escort and three guns, which proved to be a general and his staff thus accompanied, making his was to Sebastopol.

They drew up their guns and let fly at us, we returned with some round, grape, and shell, and canister to finish up with, and then our regiment was ordered to "Charge." We had moved off for that purpose, when a smart fire of musketry was opened on us from behind and on either side, but we could not see a man; then the artillery sprinkled the wood with a few shells, and in we rode to cut them down. We had some pretty smart cutting and slashing here; I had hardly got in, when two Russians came forward and one fired at me, I suspect the other had not time to load, and had he fired two inches more to my left my fighting would have ended. They both separated and made off; but I kept my eye on the gentleman that fired, and was up with him in a minute, and I had my sword raised to cut him down, when he threw his musket down, and went on his knees with his hands clasped as if in prayer; he was an old man, and I could not strike him, but made him a prisoner, and brought him in. We took an immense quantity of valuable baggage, gold lace, watches, and jewellery. My paper cannot contain much more, so I must come to a conclusion. We have now been a fortnight before Sebastopol, and this fortnight has been the hardest part of my soldiering for me; that is, the light Cavalry were posted in the rear to keep in check a division under General Luders. Hardly a day passes but we have a skirmish with those cowardly Cossacks. The attack on Sebastopol commences to-morrow at one in the morning, and it is said will only take three days to reduce. May I request you to send this to my father and mother, for I have not materials nor time for writing more, and I beg to subscribe myself, honourable sir, yours, respectfully and obediently.

Landing of the Heavy Brigade; Pursuit of the Russians

The Heavy Cavalry Brigade did not sail for the Crimea until 7.30 a.m. on 22 September. Lieutenant-Colonel Hodge (4th Dragoon Guards) on the same days as the landings took place (14 September) described how:

> Rain continuing in torrents. My tent luckily has stood it as yet … Looked thro' the lines of horses. The poor brutes … were standing in canals of muddy water, their coats staring, themselves shivering, and looking only fit for dogs. The saddlery lying saturated with wet.[55]

In a portent of worse things to come, the officers and men – who were 'soaked to the skin … suffering much' – had 'no warm clothing, not a winter waistcoat … and but thin worsted socks'.[56] The Greys sailed for the Crimea aboard the *Himalaya* on 22 September and landed at the River Katcha two days later. On the 26th they bivouacked on the plain outside Balaklava. Sadly, during September there were 120 cases of diarrhoea in the regiment (nearly half the effective strength), and three men and one officer (Captain Freeman) died from cholera.

En route to the Crimea, the transports carrying the Heavy Brigade headed in to a storm, so graphically described by Private George Hunt and John Yorke below, whose regiment (1st Royals) lost 150 horses and was reduced to a 'single squadron in strength'. This was the second disaster to strike the Inniskillings: they lost seventy out of the seventy-eight horses aboard the *War Cloud* whilst the 1st Royals lost 100 horses aboard the *Wilson Kennedy*.[57]

Following the Battle of the Alma (20 September 1854) the Allied armies rested for two days, ostensibly to collect the sick and wounded and to bury the dead. The Light Brigade had 'no share in the glorious victory', which many officers found 'most galling'.[58] Nolan raged in his diary that the cavalry should have been used to pursue the defeated Russians and prevent them from withdrawing their artillery from the field. The Allies commenced their march on Sebastopol on 23 September, the Cavalry forming the Advance Guard commanded by the Earl of Lucan, camping at the Belbec river for the night. The Scots Greys joined the army on 24 September 'and were heartily cheered as they passed to their encamping ground. Their horses looked in fine condition & the men in high spirits.'[59]

At 9 a.m. on Monday 25 September the Scots Greys, 8th and 11th Hussars, 13th Light Dragoons and 17th Lancers were ordered out on a 'strong reconnaissance' under the Earl of Lucan to 'examine the roads leading towards the Tschernaya [*sic*, Tchernaya] to ascertain they were not occupied by the Enemy'. The 4th Light Dragoons again brought up the rear and one troop of the 8th Hussars under Captain Chetwood formed Lord Raglan's escort. Around 11.30 a.m., Captain Nolan, together with the single troop of the 8th Hussars, was 'ordered to push ahead' as a report from the cavalry reconaissance had come in saying that the roads ahead were clear. Twenty minutes later, Captain Nolan found this report to be in error:

> About 10 mins before twelve I came to the clearing at Mackenzia and … saw the Enemy in some force[.] They had one Regt. of Cav[a]l[r]y[,] one batt[alio]n inf[antr]y[,] some Guns and a large convoy of carriages and carts.[60]

Nolan then 'requested permission' to order Captain Maude's troop RHA 'and at once attack them before they recovered from their surprise'. This, however, was not agreed to 'for fear of exposing our artillery without sufficient support'. The delay gave the Russians valuable time to make ready; Captain Chetwood led his troop of 8th Hussars into the open, accompanied by two guns of Captain Maude's battery which unlimbered and prepared to open fire. Seeing an easy target, the Russian cavalry 'advanced upon them at the Trot' but luckily for the gunners, the Earl of Lucan led the main British cavalry force 'out into the open' whilst 'Maudes Troop with the foremost at once galloped forw[ar]d [,] unlimbered & fired'.[61] The 8th Hussars now advanced toward the limbered Russian guns and baggage carts, but stumbled upon a Russian infantry battalion in square. 'The Hussars, sword in hand were galloping at them,' when the Earl of Lucan ordered them to break off their attack and 'shouted for Guns to come to the front', Maude's troop 'rode up, unlimbered & with a volley from the guns scattered the battalion who threw themselves into the wood both sides & then fired upon their pursuers'. In order to clear the woods of the Russian infantry, the Scots Greys were pushed forward and one troop of the Greys dismounted to skirmish on foot with their carbines.[62] The Russians were pursued for about a mile by 'Two Reg[imen]ts of our Cavalry [Greys and 17th Lancers]' during which time they captured, by Nolan's estimation, twemty-two wagons and horses as well as Prince Menschikoff's fine carriage and all his baggage![63] One officer of the Guards remembered seeing

> … the Scots Greys and some of our artillery in advance … where they intercepted a Russian army of some 15,000 men and a large convoy of provisions and ammunition. The party of Greys was only twenty strong, but so cowd were the Russians and taken by surprise, that half their army cut off … Every waggon [*sic*] was destroyed, the flour given up to our men, powder scattered, cartridges destroyed, camp equipments thrown over the precipices …[64]

The British camped on the banks of the River Tchernaya for the night and on the morning of 26 September two regiments from the Light Brigade were detached under the Earl of Cardigan to 'intercept a convoy making its way to Sebastopol'. Cardigan, however, was unable to intercept the Russians because of the 'totally unfit state [of] the English Troop Horse'. They were so weak that 'they can hardly raise a Canter' despite having done any actual real work; The horses 'soon dropped down' from exhaustion and the pursuit of the convoy was called off.[65]

Letters from Lieutenant-Colonel **John Yorke** (1st Royal Dragoons), to his sister Etheldred.

                                            Camp, Adrianople Roads, Varna,
My Dear Ethel,   Sept. 3rd 1854.[66]
Since my last, all has been well and the embarkation for the Crimea progresses splendidly but there is rather a deficiency of Transport for so large an expedition, and the Heavy Brigade has to remain here until some ships return to

convey us. This delay has caused all sorts of murmurings that the Heavies will not be engaged if the present force can accomplish all without them, but I do not for the moment think an attempt will be made without us, indeed it would be an unfair proceeding and I find the idea of such a thing with the following sets off in our favour – but that we shall have a quick embarkation and an easy disembarkation that we shall have the chance of being late for any service and in ample time for Victory and further reap the benefit of a short period of exposure after landing prior to this great struggle which appears, incidentally, I have returned some very good Trophies from England in lieu of those destroyed for plunderers, in fact the mortality of the men has been so much greater than we expected, and consequently these remount horses near useless to the other Regts. and Ld. Lucan was quite pleased to hand them over to me, he has likewise come upon the Royal to find his orderlies for the Field, which is considered a compliment, and I am considered the most effective Regt. in the Heavy Cavalry Brigade, and I think am in favour with the great people for last night I received a most king letter from the Ld. Raglan beginning 'My Dear Col. Yorke' and introducing an officer late of the Greys to me in the hopes he might be useful to me in place of the Adjutant, as lately the said officer had been disappointed in a good marriage and wanted to enter the service again which had induced him to take the benefit of introducing him to me. So kind a letter from so great a man ... and I immediately sent my answer, and expressed my gratitude with the hope he would recommend Mr. Westen [?] to be transferred to another Regt., and replace him with a fellow now, as I can have no fear of getting a [illegible], I have received no orders as yet and Ld. Raglan & Lucan are embarking for the Crimea, but all is well, and it is great good fortune for me to be thus employed at such an eventful time. The little delay will likewise be of service in restoring the health of the men who are gradually gaining their spirits, even my servant plucks up; indeed I told him fairly I would hope no more crawling about the place, he must work for me, or in the ranks, in the sick marquee but not crawling about the place which was getting quite an arteficial [*sic*] malady, and was most depressing to look at, as well as infectious to others & a bad example ... we lost one more by fever since I last wrote, making our deaths 13 in this country but this number is far beneath most other Regts. My health is really wonderful my dear Ethel tho' my constitution has itself changed Viz. not the slightest tendency of heat in the flesh ... and I think I before said my *wart fell off*, as it could not stand the climate, this is had remained on my finger and increase in size for at least 10 years. – I am a good sleeper likewise, which was a thing unknown to me, I even gestured to take effect at night and it did not disturb me altogether. I am doing well – and I have discovered a dodge with the ration beef, which has improved our condition. I scrape the meat with an old razor, and cook it with a spirit lamp with Horse Raddish sauce, set, and obtain *wonderful* countenances, and make it quite tender.

Sept. 4th. I have been waiting in hope of a mail which has been expected every hour for the last 2 days. I have no doubt I shall receive a letter from you this evening my dear Ethel, but unfortunately I must close this without as the mail leave early. Poor Captain Longmore of the 8th Hussars and Mr Saltmarsh [*sic*, Saltmarshe] of the 11th [Hussars] died yesterday. It is quite terrific how the officers and men die off, but we hope for better times still. You may depend on my writing again before I take ship, which must make up for this most stupid letter. God Bless you all and as much love.

PS I believe no man living can forsee the result of our invasion of the Crimean. Sir John Bourgoyne may be supposed to have the most [training?] as he is an Engineer Officer. *Captain Wrottlesley married his daughter* & has gone home sick, but I look upon the opinion of any man such as worthless, and time must prove the result.

Camp, Adrianople Road[67]
September 16th, 1854.

My dear Ethel, -
Since the embarkation of the troops for the Crimea all communication has ceased between us & then and likewise the packets have ceased to deliver in secure mails at Varna, in fact they go direct from Constantinople to the Crimea and return direct to the former leaving us in utter ignorance of all matters and without means of communicating with England. I have therefore receive no letter from you since I last wrote and now fear this delay in my writing will cause you anxiety but I have no [illegible] and now hope no news whatever to communicate.
...

Last week we had a very serious change in the weather commencing with a deluge of wind which continued for 18 hours, and followed by extreme cold, indeed winter appear to have set in for earnest and unfortunately the Commissariat supplies again failed in the way of forage and for 3 days in this miserable weather the horses were nearly starving; in fact I feared all my efforts to re-establish their constitutions would fail, but fortunately a second summer has followed, supplies have come in from the distance, and all is again prosperous but we hope to be removed shortly from this for fear of a repetition of difficulties & bad weather. We conclude the landing in the Crimea has been affected without opposition but it is not at all improbably that the real state of things will reach England before this, which appears almost [illegible] but we are so completely isolated and know nothing here.

I received a second most kind letter from Ld. Raglan thanking me for mine and stating he had communicated my wishes to the Horse Guards and the arrangements should be carried out. This letter was written the day of his embarkation. We like Genl. Scarlett very much indeed, and what is better he likes us, and we are a very united Brigade of Heavies, and it would never do for us to be left behind, but not with standing this delay I still think we shall arrive in good time but it would be unsafe to send the Transports back for until all was made secure for defence on shore in the Crimea. The French have likewise at least 15,000 Troops to send who are likewise awaiting Transports.

Pour young Currie[68] of the Inniskillings has been extremely ill & is now I understand but in a state of convalescence. I have not seen him but the Colonel reports to me about him and hopes he will be able to remain out with the Regiment. They have several sick officers in the Inniskillings and wonderful horses we have none, but a great number of men continue very sickly. Whenever I feal ill I take immediate steps to right myself, and have so far succeeded wonderfully. And I have twice taken good Mrs. Ewings [?] remedies with good effect. Indeed it is a terrible climate and care must be taken with the stomach other wise the [illegible] results may follow ...

Rip Van Winkle, Bay of Varna,
My dear Ethel,   Sept. 25,1854.

Thank Heavens I am once more safely embarked on board an English Transport, and altho there was a great scarcity of men & water men to tow off the Horse Boats, we effected an excellent days' work yesterday (Sunday) and embarked the whole Regt. without any accident. We have collected every vessel for a move to the Crimea for another week here would have been very difficult to accomplish as we had ... exhausted the country and it was very [good] news to hear our Transport have arrived. We marched down to the beach on Friday and the 4th & 5th Dragoon Guards embarked but did not complete all before Saturday evening, and then the Inniskillings & ourselves began but we were much more fortunate in the portion of our ships and the Inniskillings are still busy putting Men and Horses on Board the French steamer which will likely tow the ships to Euphatoria. I dined on Board the French steamer ... The Illustrated [London] News has a reporter and you will instantly see a drawing of his in the Paper. My horses are perfectly well. I am happy, busy ...

Rip Van Winkle[69]
Sept. 30th [1854]

I send you my dear Ethel the commencement of this letter, tho' how changed are circumstances, and it is very sad what 24 short hours at Sea may cause to poor horses – all mine are dead – pony likewise.

We sailed from Varna at Sunset on the 26th in tow of the Trent each under convoy of the Spiteful (Steamer), The Simla, Jason, Emperor, steamers, towed the Pride of the Ocean, Wilson Kennedy, War Cloud (transports), containing the whole of the Heavy Brigade. The wind freshened towards night, but I felt so secure in the two of a steamer that I went to bed, but did not sleep as the storm increased, I was however [illegible] in my cabin until 4.15 [a.m.] when I was suddenly informed all the officer's horses were dead. It was a sad shock to me, as you may suppose and I rushed on deck to ascertain the worst. I then saw the whole of the deck fittings which contained the officer's horses had been swept to the lee side, and under about 24 Tons of spars and long boats. I concluded (in the darkness) my poor horses dead, at this time, however a fearful scene occurred. The gale had increased to a hurricane, we parted one warp from the Trent and about the same time the fittings between decks gave way, and the poor Troop Horses actually poured down the holds. It was totally impossible to render or devize any measures under such fearful circumstances and great effort would probably have lead to great sacrifice of life. The Captain and crew were as helpless as myself and the Soldiers. They had never witnessed so terrific a gale. There was nothing to be done, but do hold on to save ourselves, which we continued to do for 30 more hours. We suffered much from sea sickness, & exhaustion, and myself from extreme anxiety of mind. At 6 [a.m.] daylight appeared and we were either cut adrift by the Trent, or our other warp parted of its own accord. She appeared in great distress. We saw the War Cloud had also parted from her steamer. We were now at the full mercy of the wind, and worse, the ship rolled in the most fearful manner, and [illegible]. I saw my poor Chestnut horse's white face appearing from amongst [illegible] of pack saddles, it was 24 more hours, however, before I could approach him. He was there poor fellow, still alive, but much exhausted.

I tied his legs together, and cut pack saddle panels out and made a couch around and under him, and lay upon his head to keep him steady, until my servant could come to my assistance, but all to no purpose for he died about noon on the 28th. It appeared he had broke his collar rein, and breast [illegible] and released himself, when alarmed, at an immense cask containing 250 gallons of water rolling down the hold he had been brought up by the Pack Saddles, & fallen, and whenever he got up the sea threw him down again. The grey pony fell down the main hatchway, and was nearly divided in two & on the 29th, we were able to extricate the dead horses and I think from Pollies & the Brown, must have died instantaneously by the whole weight of all rested upon them, & [illegible] scored the deck of the ship. Particularly old Pollie, every bone in her body appeared broken. I suppose such a cold night has never before fallen to 4 officers, Captain [George] Campbell lost his 3 Horses. Mr Wrey Hartopp his 2, and Mr Philips of the 8th Hussars, who had been left behind sick, and was about to rejoin his Regt. his 2 likewise. The poor Troopers[70] still continue to die from the effects, and out of the 62 Royals 31 are dead, 5 of 14 of other Regts. attached are dead, and others are not likely to recover & in the meantime we know nothing of the remainder of the Brigade who may have suffered equally, or may have escaped, and landed at Sebastopol, and it would be a sad affair if I were to arrive to late to Command the Regt. in any great affair. This is my present anxiety my dear Ethel, and is perhaps the cause of my fealing my loss better than I should otherwise have done. I think there can be no doubt that Government will allow me £120 for my losses, as we were actually sailing under convoy, and have been [illegible] when making for an enemy's shore. It is therefore perhaps better that I should just at such a time be encumbered with mutilated horses – and have selected a good Trooper which shall be my charger for the present. Including all things, I am not disheartened my dear Ethel and hope better times await one, but God only knows when we shall land, we lost all reckoning during the gale. We lay towards Sinope, now we have sighted the Sulina mouth of the Danube, but the sun has never shone since we left Varna, and the weather is [illegible], but God grant all may yet be well again, and I will not in the least despair, and I only hope, this sad account will not rest heavily on you, for we may be thus thankful no life has been lost in this ill-fated ship – But what I most fear is, the affair may prove a National Calamity, for if the other Regts. have at all suffered in proportion, the Brigade would be rendered ineffective, but I positively trust this is not the case; as Pride of the Ocean & Wilson Kennedy had each more men of the Regt. on board. I put the servants on these 2 ships, and am without one myself. I have a fearful deal of sickness I am sorry to say, but Good Mrs Emery's Powders come to my aid, & I hope I shall not lose a man. During the rest of the gale I was unable to reach my patients, but it would have been impossible to give even a powder at that time, and it is in a measure the *want of proper nourishment* at that time, which is causing sickness but some recover rapidly now that I offer them Medical Comforts. The [illegible] powder has done wonders restoring the lining of the stomach. There may be a great enquiry into this sad affair, but though I have failed in saving these poor horses, I am convinced others would have posed as incompetent to myself, and that no human power could have saved them for the men were physically unequal even to water the horses during the gale, or to get him on his legs if he fell – the new fittings of the ship, which estimated to carry 119 animals, including ponies, were out [illegible] for *fine weather* and thus consequentially horses injured. I dreaded the affair very much, as the winter advanced; and one day said to the Major, if all my horses were lost, I should ride that mare [illegible] those I have now taken from my second servant (who I have recently taken), and who was knocked down, & rather hurt, when my Chestnut escaped. I therefore had a set of [illegible] about the fate of my horses, which have caused me much watchful care and grief ever since I left Liverpool. I now do not possess a horse in the world and after all my efforts to show a Good Regt., which I nearly succeeded in the opinion of all who had seen the Regt. and compred it with others, it is a great misfortune to have met with such a calamity by being a victim through the bad management in others, which, was quite beyond my control, but we hope for brighter days my dear Ethel, and I will still share to anybody what is needed of me. The hold of the Ship which had safely conveyed the same Troop from England, was completely choked with gabions (used for entrenchments) over which our horses clambered over after falling through the hold, seathing these baskets around, and completely cutting off communication below. This in equal manner, no doubt, added to our losses in the hold.

Oct. 4th. Several more horses have since died we have been detained by full winds & calms, but are now in sight of the Crimea. My detachment of the sick has recovered, and they are all convalescent. We know nothing of the army on shore as yet ...

Euphatoria.
4pm. Oct. 4th

Arrived here, and received orders to proceed at once to the Katcha River. Heard likewise the terrific tidings that the Wilson Kennedy Transport has lost the whole of the horses with the exception of 11, and put into Constantinople in distress. The poor Royals are annihilated, without a shot being fired – so great a calamity, mortally never occurred to any Regt. before.

Hear the Siege of Sebastopol commenced yesterday and hope not to be quite cut out, and have hopes of procuring horses from other Regts. Here the Pride of the Sea [*sic*, Ocean] arrived safe, have only 26 riding horses on board the ship, but much better fortune may yet favour the poor Regt.

Off Katcha River,
Oct. 5th

We are to be towed again by the Trent to Balaclava. The Trent lost no horses in the gale. The Captain gives a great succesful account of the English, but the 23rd suffered fearfully. Wynn is killed, poor Mrs Cresswell 11th Hussars is a widow, he died of cholera ...

Letter from Private **George Hunt** (number 754), 1st Royal Dragoons.[71]

Scutari,
Dec. 8.[72]

When I wrote to you before, we were lying at Kalycene. We left that a few days after, and marched down to Varna where we lay encamped for five weeks, expecting almost every day the order to embark for Sebastopol. At length the order came, and we marched down to the beach and embarked. We got the horses and everything on board all right, and set sail about four o'clock in the afternoon. The regiment went in three vessels, one steamer and two sailing vessels. One troop, and part of another, went in a sailing vessel, and was taken in tow by the steamer. When we left Varna the weather was quite fine, but as night came on the wind began to rise, and at ten o'clock it blew a complete hurricane. The steamer was obliged to cut us away, and leave us to get on how we could. The sea was running mountains high, and the vessel was pitching and tossing about so that neither men nor horses could stand on their feet. We had one hundred and eleven horses on board, twenty of whom were standing on the upper deck, and the remainder on the middle deck, and about twelve o'clock a great wave came and took over-board the horses and everything that was on the upper deck, with the exception of the masts and rigging. Some of the horses that were on the middle deck fell down, and could not rise again; others broke loose, and were dashed from one side of the vessel to the other; some were trampling over others, and others kicking (it was an awful time), and we could not assist them in any way, as we could not stand on our feet, and even if we could we should have been in danger of our lives to have been amongst them. The storm lasted all night, and then it was began to abate, and on the morning of the second day we were able to move about, and w hen we looked over the horses we found that ninety-nine out of one hundred and eleven were dead or dying; two others died the next day, and the remainder were so knocked about that they will never be fit for anything. We then had a very disagreeable job to get all those dead horses overboard. The stench from some that died first was dreadful. When we left Varna we expected to reach Sebastopol in about thirty-six hours, in place of which we were knocking about in the Black Sea nine days, and at last got drove down into the Bosphorus [sic], where we anchored in Beautry Bay, a few miles from Constantinople, and about three hundred and eighty from Sebastopol. The vessel was so knocked about that we could not proceed any further in her, so they sent a steamer from Constantinople to take us to Sebastopol, and we started off again and reached Balaklava, about eight miles from Sebastopol, in two days. We there landed, and having no horses we were obliged to walk about three miles up towards Sebastopol, where we were joined by the remainder of the cavalry, and found that the part of the regiment that came in the steamer had arrived all right about a week before; the remainder that was in the other vessel came in three days after, and had lost between forty and fifty horses, but, fortunately, like us, no men. We were there without horses for about a fortnight, and then we got some from one regiment, and some from another, and so got them made up in that way. We had several skirmishes with the Russians whilst we were there but out regiment was very fortunate as regards the loss of men. We only lost two, and several others wounded, amongst which was the Colonel, who had his leg shattered by a cannon ball. We then shifted our camp up to within two miles of Sebastopol.

When we first arrived in the Crimea the weather was very hot, but after we had been there about a month it came on wet, and through that I got a cold which brought on the diarrhoea, and I got that weak I was obliged to go into the hospital. I was there about a week, and I was sent along with about 200 others – some of our regiment and others belonging to different regiments – down to Scutari to get round a bit. I have been here about three weeks, and I am happy to say that I am got quite well again. I am as well now as ever I was in my life, but how long I shall remain here I cannot say; it might be only a few days, or it might be a month. There is a great number of sick and wounded here. As soon as a sufficient number gets round they are sent back again to make room for others. Scutari is opposite to Constantinople, on the other side of the Boshporus [*sic*]; it is a most splendid view across the water, one of the finest I should think, in the world. Constantinople, with her gilded domes and mosques looks quite grand at a distance, but when you are close to it, it is a dirty looking place.

I don't know how they are getting on at Sebastopol. I have not heard any news about it since I came here; you hear the news in England a deal sooner than we do here, indeed we get the most of our news from England, but when I left Sebastopol they had been bombarding it for about a fortnight. We have a much longer and harder job there than we expected to find. War is a dreadful thing in a country where it happens, it spread desolation and destruction all around. When we arrived in the Crimea orders were issued that we were not to destroy any property, but we had not been there many days before the town of Balaklava and its neighbourhood were in ruins – houses were torn down, furniture of all descriptions was broken up to cook our victuals with, fruit trees were cut down, and even then we began to get short of fuel, but then it appears such a wanton destruction of property, I hope it will never happen in our own country.

The weather here has been very fine, more like the month of September, and there has not been any appearance of winter yet; it has been raining very fast all day to-day [*sic*], but it is very mild.

Letter from Troop Sergeant-Major **Robert Lawrence Sturtevant** (number 868), Scots Greys, to the editor of the *Nottinghamshire Guardian*.[73]

Sir,-

Camp Crimea, Near Sebastopol,
28th Sept., 1854.

Knowing as I do the great interest you and the inhabitants of Nottingham feel towards to the welfare of the Greys induces me to send you the following brief sketch of our movements. The long expected order at last arrived for us to proceed from Kullullie by the Himalaya. She passed down the Bosphorus on the 19th instant, having a board on her bows on which was written "Get ready the Greys," which could be seen with a glass from the barracks; but it being early in the morning no one saw it, and indeed it was a question with most of us whether or not it was the Himalaya. It was soon, however, explained by her coming back in a few hours from Constantinople, where she had to proceed to get orders. We were all very glad to see her, and joy appeared on every face.

On the 20th she took in coal and water, and the following day we embarked. She got up steam during the night, and in the morning we were steaming towards the Black Sea.

On the 23rd we arrived on the coast of the Crimea, a few miles from Sebastopol and disembarked some of the horses that night. The following day all were disembarked and we joined the army with any tents of camp equipage.

On the 25th we were saddled at day-break and off through brush-wood, going through at single-file and making our own track. After about four hours thus marching in a broiling sun we got the words "Greys to the front." We were still in the bush, and hard to charge in single file. We soon came on the road, and after a charge of about two miles caught the enemy's rear guard, and sent them flying into the bush, and we also dismounted a troop, and sent them out skirmishing, and did great execution, while on the other hand not a man or horse was hurt. We killed a good many of the enemy and took many prisoners. By being thus surprised we captured the whole of the baggage of a division of the Russian army, and although we had only the 17th Lancers, two or three guns, and a few Rifles, they were too cowardly to face us, although there were thousands of them. The post is going; we are in front of Sebastopol and have a day's rest. The siege guns are being landed, and the town will be attacked in a day or two.

Letter from Lieutenant **Robert Scott Hunter**, Scots Greys, to his sister.[74]

Camp, Balaklava, Crimea
September 30th 1854

The place we landed was the mouth of the Katchcar River but where we first went to was the scene of the Battle of Alma[,] which you will have had news of. We were all so disappointed at being done *out* of the scrimmage, we were only three days late. On the 24th we finished the disembarkation and marched to join the army, which we took up at about 3pm on the afternoon and about dark for to our bivouack [*sic*] at Balaklava in a beautiful valley. I write to Andrew the other day, so you will get a description of the scenery in that epistle. On the 25th we were off again at 7½ am, a most wearisome march and awful sun; about 11 got our first signs of being close to the Enemy by a shot being fired from the bush at an A.D.C. We rushed straight on through an awful country for cavalry & at 12 the guns opened in our front. We had come plump on their rear & baggage. The "Greys" now went off at a Gallop to the front & while one squadron cut off a lot of their baggage. I was sent out to the underwood with about 30 men to skirmish, so I pulled out my revolver & (tho' I did not like it much) went at them[.] We shot some who would not come out of the bush & made a lot of prisoners & there was great plunder at the baggage. Our fellows got a whole lot of wine & things & in my skirmish I captured a cross of the order of St. Catharine, a very handsome trophy, I can tell you. I also got a capital horse[.] On the 26th we march and came to the plain [,] below which we are now & the forts at the mouth of the harbour were taken by the Light Division & some guns, in cooperation with the fleet. The Enemy fired two shells at us & then bolted or rather surrendered & we got 16 guns and 600 prisoners I hear[.] Next day (27th) we came to this ground, to a most lovely position commanding a glorious view. The scenery is exactly like Scotland, but such devastation you never saw & vineyards destroyed & houses half pulled down, & completely *gutted*; hay, furniture cooking utensils & all sorts of rubbish lying pell mell amongst the bivouack fires & *all* the inhabitants had bolted. In fact all you read of as "horrors of war" in books. *We* have landed most of the siege train & have already got some of *Lancasters'* guns in position, & yesterday *Lord Raglan* went up with 9 of *them* & tried one or two, which threw *their shells* slap into the middle of the town at 4 miles distance!!! They are potting at each other all day, but I believe the siege does not commence till Monday.

The Russians never expected any Enemy on this side, & they (I mean our people) say they must surrender immediately as they *cannot* hold out against our force by land & sea. There is still I'm sorry to say a great deal of sickness in the army. Cholera. We have only as yet lost 3, 2 men & 1 officer, my Captain, poor Freeman.[75] He died at 3½ am yesterday. The best fellow we had & and *unfillable* gap (to make a word) in the Regiment has been made by his loss. Today *we* have 4 bad cases. The Infantry have all marched on but the Guards & the Highlanders & the French have been going past all morning, a Turkish regiment has also just passed now. I should close this so good bye. I shall write again as soon as I have time.

Letter from Troop Sergeant-Major **John Norris** (number 803), 1st Royal Dragoons, to the editor of the Nottinghamshire Guardian.[76]

Dear Sir, -

Camp two miles in rear of Sebastopol
Oct. 17, 1854.

It was with great pleasure I received your note this morning, also two 'papers, for which I return you my sincere thanks. I do assure you it gave me great pleasure to hear from you. Forster[77] is in the same tent with me, and has been all through the campaign. I am glad to inform you that we are both enjoying good health at present; we have both been very ill. Forster, I was much afraid, would never recover, but he took a turn for the best, and is as well as ever. There is not a man out here but that has been ill more or less; we have lost about fourteen men since we left England, with the disease of this country; but, thank God, we have not been so unfortunate as other regiments. Since our arrival here, our men have had excellent health, a few have died; but they were all ill previously to coming to this country. You have seen by the papers the great loss the heavy brigade had in crossing the Black Sea: our regiment lost about 130 horses, killed and wash overboard.[78] My troop lost 29 horses, but we are getting horses from the Light Dragoons to re-mount us;[79] they have a great many men sick in Scutari. We mount two good squadrons still. There are 10 cavalry regiments encamped opposite Balaklava, which is our place of unshipment [*sic*]. I cannot say one word about the entrenchments, as we are not allowed to move a foot from our horses, for there is a large army of Cossacks and Russians in our rear, waiting and trying to get into Sebastopol, but it is of no use. They annoy us very much by skirmishing with our pickets and outposts; but they will not stand and fight us. We made an advance on them one morning with the whole of our cavalry, ten regiments, and Captain Maude's troop of horse artillery, but they escaped and fled into the mountains. The artillery fired twelve shots at them, but they were rather out of range; but we saw many horses without riders. They next day our pickets went out in search of them, but they had returned. The ground was all covered over with every sort of regimentals, and camp equipage of every description, saddle-bags, helmets, carbines, swords, lances, pistols, and some very richly embroidered gold belts. Everything is good except their arms, &c. Many silk shirts, belonging to officers, our men got, and not before they were wanted, as most of the cavalry had left their kits on board ship, to lighten their horses, except one coat and a pair of overalls; some of them have not been undressed during the last six weeks. I have not been undressed for a fortnight. We turn out of our tents at half past four every morning, and the whole army is drawn up in their places at a quarter to five o'clock; it is pitch dark and we remain until daylight; and we then look round the country well, and see that all is right, after which we go to breakfast on hard biscuit and hot tea, but hunger is sharp thorn, so we manage to make shift. We remain saddled all day until night, then, it all is quiet, we make down our nice beds and go to sleep, without rocking for about three or four hours. It would make you laugh when we turn out at night, when the d—d Cossacks drive in our outposts, to see, if you could, the soldiers bustle in reality – eighteen men in a small tent, and only four minutes allowed to turn out, – pitch dark is no joke, and every person singing, "Look sharp! Look sharp!" – fellows half asleep, I suppose, rubbing their eyes until they find out what is the real cause of our sudden turn-out; but as we are out they run away. The battle of Alma gave them a belly full of the "Devils dressed in red" as they call our troops.

Exactly at half-past six this morning our guns, at least part of them from land, and some steamers opened fire on Sebastopol, and have continued firing on their batteries all day; they knocked down one fort in twenty minutes that has been annoying the French very much while making their entrenchments. I have been told there never was such an engagement made as our army has made – twelve thousand men working day and night, under a heavy fire for three weeks, day and night, kept up without ceasing, and we did not fire a single shot in return until to-day [*sic*]. On the hill this fort had a large swivel gun, that got nearly into our range, so they were obliged to open fire on it this morning, and the second shot we fired knocked the gun clean off the fort. They have blown up two of their powder magazines; and I was told the Russians have blown up one of the French magazines, but I do not think that is true, for we only heard two explosions, and the sound seemed to come from Sebastopol. But I think they are going to open all guns on them to-morrow morning for a quarter of an hour, and then cease, to see what they intend doing; if they do not give in then, they will soon have the place about their ears. You wish to know what I think of the French cavalry; they made do for skirmishing very well, but in the field, against such as ours, they would be nowhere to be seen. I have seen the whole of them, – good little horses, but too small, and too slight.

The morning I left Manchester I could not get time to reach my much-respected friend, Mr. Smith. I do assure you I was very sorry indeed, for I promised to call the night before. I have not one minute to spare I do assure you. I am never done; everything to do as in barracks, and no place to do it in. I am now sitting, dressed, ready to mount in a moment, for we do not know the moment the enemy may make an attack to annoy us. I am sure they will not stand to fight us, but just to break our rest. Give my kind respects to all my old acquaintances at –'s; I am exceedingly glad to hear that he has recovered from his illness. I will write to Mr. Smith the first opportunity after this place is taken, if I live, and let you know all the particulars. I must conclude: I am tired of sitting on the cold ground, for it makes my neck and back ache writing on my knees for a table. Forster, Tripp,[80] and Cruse[81] desire to be kindly remembered; they are all in good health. The guns have ceased firing on both sides at present; they only killed twelve men in our entrenchments in three weeks; some thousands of their shells never burst, we put in fresh fuses and sent them back to-day [*sic*]. Excuse this scrawl, for I am half asleep ...

CHAPTER 3

Prelude to Balaklava:
1–24 October 1854

As the Allied armies settled down to the formal siege of Sebastopol, the cavalry was engaged in patrols and advanced pickets, probing the Russian positions and preventing the Russians from doing the same. The cavalry 'stood to' from 3 a.m. every morning (an hour before daybreak) and remained in the saddle until an hour after sunrise, because the Allies were 'constantly expecting an attack from the Russians, who have been largely reinforced'.[1]

On campaign pickets (in-lying and out-lying) were to be posted one hour before daybreak. An outlying picket, or *vidette*, consisted of half-a-dozen mounted troopers under the command of an NCO to observe the movement of the enemy and also mask their own unit. The in-lying picket was larger, commanded by an officer, and as the name suggests, placed closer to the camp. Captain William Douglas (10th Hussars) wrote that 'An Outlying Picket ought to be concealed entirely from observation, either by natural or artificial obstacles' but in many cases in the Crimea the pickets were badly placed due to unfamiliarity with the routine of a campaign: those watching the entrance to Balaklava were either too close to the camp to be of any use, or in fact readily observable by the Russians, in one instance on the slope of a hill, which, whilst giving the picket a good view left them 'entirely exposed'. The Russians, conversely, had their picket on Canrobert's Hill and were thus able to look down on the British positions.[2] If the enemy made a serious approach, the outlying picket would fire their carbines, more as a means of raising the alarm rather than having any effect. They would then circle their horses to the left if infantry were approaching and to the right for cavalry; the speed of the circling gave some indication of the size of the force – the faster the circling the greater the numbers. After the picket had returned to camp, a trooper's first priority was to ensure his horse was fed, and watered. Each trooper than had to clean all his tack, groom his horse before getting his breakfast.[3]

The daily routine of the cavalry thus took on the familiar monotony of barrack life. The horses were to be fed and watered four times a day – even on campaign. *Standing Orders* of the Scots Greys states that 'Morning Stables' was at 5.30 a.m.; 'Noon Stables' was at 12 p.m., 'Afternoon Feed' was at 4 p.m. and 'Evening Stables' at 6 p.m. The veterinary surgeon and the farrier-major inspected each horse at 'Morning Stables'.[4] In addition was the business of providing the out-lying and in-lying pickets. This was hard, tiring work with officers and men in a constant state of alert, ready to 'turn out at any notice'. Captain Nolan's journal reveals just how tiring – and frequent – these duties were:

> 3d October Tuesday. A Patrole [sic] of the Scots Greys report the advance of a Russian Army into the Valley of the Tshnaya [sic, Tchernaya][.] No notice whatever taken of them or their movements[.]

4th Wednesday
Rode out to the extreme right on a Reconnaissance with Genl. Airey & Sir De Lacy Evans ...[5]

Général Canrobert reported on 6 October that 'At the point of day, an enemy reconnaissance, of around 3,000 men and 1,600 or 1,800 cavalry, supported by two batteries of horse artillery' approached the British positions; the British artillery 'fired several shells' into the Russians, which caused them to retire.[6] The 4th Dragoon Guards and the Scots Greys were surprised by a Russian reconnaissance in force early in the morning of 7 October. Two regiments of Hussars, a regiment of infantry and 'an untold number of Cossacks' crossed the Tracktir bridge and attacked the British pickets, taking three members of the 4th Dragoon Guards prisoner. The alarm was raised and 'large detachments of ... Greys and Dragoons were sent out, accompanied by two troops of Horse Artillery. Among them was Captain Maude's Troop of horse artillery ...' who opened fire on the Russian Hussars, forcing them to make a 'sudden retreat.' For 'some unknown reason' the British cavalry did not pursue. A second 'light skirmish' took place in the evening when Cossacks again probed the pickets of the Greys and 4th Dragoon Guards.[7] Nolan records:

Saturday the 7th Octr
I was awoke at 6 o'clock AM by a report by Mr Woomwell [*sic*, Wombwell] 17th Lancers that the Russian Army had forced our Picquets in the [Tchernaya] Valley & were marching in great force on Balaklava.[8]

This was a Reconnaissance in Force; they had surprised a patrol of the 4th Dragoon Guards under Cornet Edward Fisher Rowe and drove them in, killing two men and taking a third prisoner. They were thus able to cross the Tchernaya and advance toward Balaklava. Captain Nolan received orders that 'should the attack be pushed home' for the 93rd Highlanders under Sir Colin Campbell to retire from the village of Kadikoi to 'the conical hill in the gorge' [Canrobert's Hill]. The Cavalry Division was ordered to 'oppose the Advance of the Enemy but if driven back by superior force to retire[,] throwing back its right so as to fall back towards our own position.'[9]

The Russians could be clearly 'seen with the Telescope on the further side of the River' from the Balaklava Heights where the Earl of Lucan had drawn up the Cavalry Division. According to Nolan, Lucan was content to simply observe the Russians rather than deploy in the valley to check the Russian advance. Lucan allowed Nolan to detach one squadron from the 17th Lancers to 'go forward to see what they [the Russians] were doing' and in so doing counted '8 Batt[alio]ns Inf[antr]y and five Reg[i]m[e]nts of Cavalry'.[10] *Général* Canrobert also records that later on the same day, there was a second Russian reconnaissance in force, but this time directed towards the French: 'At 11 o'clock at night, a column of the enemy, of two battalions of infantry, two pieces of artillery, and a squad [*peloton*] of cavalry ...' probed the French left near the 'burned house' [*Maison brulée*]. They were repulsed with much loss; the French suffered just two men wounded.[11]

On 13–14 October 3,000 Turkish troops from Constantinople landed at Balaklava to reinforce the garrison. They were immediately set to work building five redoubts on the causeway heights, which were armed with twelve iron 12-pounder guns. At the same time, the French built a redoubt on a conical hill

christened 'Canrobert's Hill' after the French Commander-in-Chief. One officer
estimated the garrison of Balaklava to be 500 Royal Marines with six field guns;
the 93rd Highlanders; Maude's Troop RHA and, of course, the cavalry. The
usefulness of the cavalry in the plain before Balaklava was open to question,
however, due to the rocky broken ground. The cavalry was also thought to be of
even less use during a night attack.[12] Opinion was divided as to whether the
Russians would attack or not: one officer believed the Russians would – and in
force[13] – whilst a second believed that the Russians would be foolish to attack
because of the presence of HMS *Agamemnon* in Balaklava Harbour whose guns
'will sweep them [the Russians] away by fifties ...' and also the division of *Général*
Bosquet on the heights.[14]

The first bombardment of the Siege of Sebastopol commenced at 6.30 a.m. on
17 October; there were major Russian incursions into the plain before Balaklava
on 18 and 20 October. One anonymous officer reported seeing 'about 12,000
Russians – half of whom are Cossacks' advance into the Balaclava plain and came
under fire from the Turks in the redoubts on the Causeway Heights.[15] An officer
of the Royal Marines continues the narrative:

> ... I had scarcely ... taken my *al fresco* ablution, and was preparing for breakfast
> ... when our drums beat to arms – the Highland pipes brayed – and all was
> accoutre and arm. The Russians, in force, were on the plain below – artillery,
> cavalry, and infantry – in all about 10,000. Their cavalry appeared to be their
> largest arm. Our cavalry and horse-artillery, with some Turkish battalions ...
> advanced ... the Russians retired without coming to an action. Our field-guns
> opened on them; but they retired, out of range.[16]

It was thought that this had been a reconnaissance in force, rather than a 'strong
attack'. It was considered that the Russians would not attack the redoubts
protecting Balaclava due to the presence of 'The Devils in Red' and 'had we [the
Royal Marines] not been here they might have seriously inconvenienced the army
before Sebastopol, by taking them in the rear'.[17]

The Russians had first been spotted by the French about midday; an officer
reported to *Général* Canrobert that the Russians were 'making a general attack
on ... Balaklava'. *Général* Bosquet was advised to 'make dispositions for battle'
and Canrobert set off for Balaklava whilst French staff officers sought in vain to
find Lord Raglan – Canrobert met him on the way. On the left, on the heights,
was the brigade of *Général* Vinoy, and in the plain the 93rd Highlanders and
the cavalry under Lucan. Canrobert remembered how it was 'the Turks alone
engaged; the Russians did not want to seem to push the matter. They were content just to observe.' Unlike British observers, Canrobert (realistically) estimated
the Russians to have been 'only about two or three thousand men.' The fire soon
ceased and the Russians retired toward Tchorgoun.[18] The garrison remained on
the alert for the remainder of the day; 'many officers returning retired to their
tents, and slept uncommonly well after being under arms all day.'[19] That evening
Canrobert and Raglan held a meeting to discuss the defences of Balaklava.[20]
Following this meeting, Canrobert wrote to Lord Raglan:

My Dear General,
. The cavalry of the enemy, who are very numerous, and are growing in strength
every day is composed of Dragoons that pass for being good troops; their

infantry is also numerous: these considerations have caused me to examine this evening your defensive position and I have suggested the following disposition:

I would create at the Pass of Balaklava a barrier, which would be sufficient obstacle to the cavalry. It is the matter of a few pickaxes to make. If, at some point, the totality of the Russian infantry marched against the left and against the English right, this would certainly give serious problems ... and if at the same time the enemy launched on the pass of Balaklava with six thousand cavalry that might go galloping on, three squadrons wide, it be more than a few guns or gunshots that would stop this avalanche. Your right would be turned and the besieged at your back.

Always lend the force to the enemy, and in this order of ideas, we must predict as I indicate. Make therefore tomorrow your ditch. It must be a sufficient obstacle to stop the momentum of a large body of cavalry.[21]

The Russians made another feint two days later. The 'Special Correspondent' from the *Illustrated London News* reported on 20 October:

The Russians attempted a diversion, by marching several battalions of infantry, and a quantity of cavalry and guns to the front of Balaclava. The Turks fired several rounds at them from their new redoubts [on the Causeway Heights], and Sir Colin Campbell thought it necessary to send for reinforcements. General Goldie's brigade moved out at three in the morning to the front of Balaclava. Lord Lucan's brigade of Cavalry struck tents, but the Russians retired without having molested us ...[22]

According to one officer of Royal Marines the Russians appeared in the afternoon 'in great force, and Sir Colin Campbell ordered the whole of the division to be on the alert'. Two companies of the Marines were sent down into the plain where they remained until evening but not before being startled with two false alarms. The first caused by the 'Turkish advanced sentries firing at – perhaps Russians' the second 'by our own people firing with rockets and great guns on – I think, brushwood (it was a very dark night)'.[23] Five days later the Russians would attack in earnest.

Letter from an assistant-surgeon, 8th Hussars.[24]

Cavalry Camp, near Sebastopol,
October 4th, 1854.[25]

My Dear Major, -
Here I am in the thick of it; within shot hearing at least, if not within shot of the notorious Sebastopol. After leaving Scutari I went to Varna, and from thence to Eupatoria, encountering a gale by the way, and in amazing fear of finding ourselves prisoners to the Russians. From Eupatoria we sailed to Sebastopol, and from then to Baliklava [*sic*, Balaklava], where we finally disembarked, and joined the army. On passing in front of Sebastopol, we saw part of the fleet engaging Fort Constantine. The village of Baluklava [*sic*] is the queerest place in the world. Fancy a creak quite invisible from the sea, in which we found several line-of-battle ships, lying within ten yards of the land, one of the great "Agamemnon". There were besides dozens of transports, all busy disembarking the siege train, and the heavy cavalry. I landed with what clothes I stood in (a hussar jacket and trousers, and Busby, full dress in fact), my horse was got ashore, and off I started for my regiment, but as night was nearly on I

was lucky to find a troop of my regiment, being Lord Raglan's escort; and with them I put up. The officers had a room in a deserted cottage, and it was funny to see an honourable subaltern and his captain, eating with gusto a piece of ration pork, and washing it done [*sic*, down] with some coffee water out of a broken pannikin, cautioning me at the same time that I was not to fancy that the fellows in camp lived nearly half so well, which I afterwards found to be true enough. Next day I joined the head-quarters of the 8th, encamped with all the cavalry except two regiments, on a plain in rear of the heights above Sebastopol. We bivouac in the open air, and as for eating, I have plenty of biscuit, and occasionally am lucky enough to get a piece of meat, but, for the charity of my neighbours, however, I must eat it raw, as I have no cooking utensils, no drinking cup, no plate. I generally eat off a piece of deal, or the lid of a tin, if lucky; in fact I am pretty near starving. One thing we have in plenty, grapes; there are hundreds of vineyards, and we gorge all day long, in spite of cholera, which carried off some forty or fifty daily – in fact it is decimating us. My regiment is a prefect skeleton. They days are very hot; the nights are very, very cold, with the heaviest dews I ever saw. We lie down in boots and spurts, and dress jackets, covered with a cloak, not to sleep for it is too cold for that, but to rest. We (the cavalry) are watching the Russian army which is assembled for the relief of Sebastopol; its outposts are about four miles off, and every now and then the Cossacks gallop up, and after turning out our whole line, coolly trot back again. This took place yesterday, and indeed they bother us a good deal. The regiment is so weak that all our servants are put in the ranks; a lucky thing for me, as this morning my servant brought back a hen, which he had plundered when on patrol. By the way, we have plundered the country awfully, and the French have in addition destroyed everything they could not carry off. Our patrols sweep the valleys and bring in everything eatable, but they are now quite bare. I went up two days ago to the infantry camp, and saw my old friends the 55th, who, poor fellows, suffered sadly in the action [at the Alma]. I went as far as the outlying picket, within a few hundred yards of the Russian outlying posts, and saw into the streets and harbour of Sebastopol – it seems a very fine town, and is full of ships, though they have sunk a number at the mouth of the harbour. The Russians have erected large field works to cover the unprotected parts, but these are already crumbling under their own fire, for as yet we have not fired a shot. The French are encamped on our right, and they broke ground last evening with little loss. We are ready to begin this evening: our siege train is all up, and is the most formidable ever before used. It is said that we might with a little sacrifice take the place by assault, but the generals prefer a siege, which will not last many days, and in a week from this I expect to be inside Sebastopol, or else in pursuit of the relieving army. The Russians sent in a large reinforcement yesterday, but we are so certain of taking the place that the generals do not care how many men are in it, at least so gossip goes. The Russians pitch both shot and shell into our camp (infantry), and occasionally knock over some poor fellow; we (cavalry) take no notice of such compliments.

October 5 – Another day without fighting, but the report of a strong Russian force in our rear, coming on, is the talk, and the cavalry is going to move nearer them to-day [*sic*]. The pickets yesterday had a little affair with the Cossacks.

The batteries open to-morrow [*sic*], and it is expect that forty hours will be enough to bring them to their senses – but you know camp gossip cannot be relied on. I suppose you saw in the 'papers full accounts of the late fight. There is *no doubt* that the Coldstreams and 23rd Fusiliers *wavered* and *retired a little*, but came on again, and it is said that the fire from the Russian batteries on the heights was so severe, that the Duke of Cambridge ordered his division to retire, but old Sir John Campbell [*sic*, Sir Colin Campbell] said, "The Heelanders [*sic*, Highlanders] niver [*sic*, never] retire with an enemy in front, your Royal Highness," and on went the Highlanders with the bayonet; they made mincemeat of the Russian. That is the story, and I believe a true one. Brigadier [Richard] Airey is said to be the man of resource in our army; in fact, its real head-piece; [Sir George] Brown is not half so bad as the newspaper make out; [Sir George] Cathcart is very popular, from his dash and form, his genuine good heartiness.

October 7 – This morning, at sunrise, the trumpets sounded "boots and saddles," and in a short time eight regiments of cavalry, and a troop of horse artillery were trotting away to the assistance of our pickets. The writer, with the rest, after going a mile or so, came on a very large body of Russian regular cavalry, the artillery unlimbered and sent 8 or 9 shells among them. They evidently had a body of infantry near, so we did nothing else but observe for a couple of hours, and then returned to our camp, where we are not with horses saddled, ready to turn out. I expect that we are not far off a battle with the relieving army, as their pickets and ours come into collision daily. General Luders, and a large convoy, got into Sebastopol the evening of the 5th. Something wrong, I fear. Our Lancaster Guns are now in position, and it is said that we open this evening on the "Twelve Apostles", the Russian admiral's flag-ship, which throws shells at us all day. The cholera is still raging, the last account I heard was that forty-five had died that day, but really the wonder is that any are left alive. We (that is the men and regimental officers) are either starved, or eat food against which our stomachs turn, and in order to live we are obliged to eat loads of grapes from the vineyards close at hand. The days are very hot, the nights are very cold, and our clothing consists of one suit on our backs, the dew wets us through every night, just like rain. When taken ill we have no medicines, no place to be nursed in, no one to care a straw about us, no place to mense mortality has made and invariably so, everyone more or less callous. In fact, people taken ill may recover, but by a sort of miracle. One officer of the 77th, Crofton, a man I knew, died in a ditch by the road-side, with as little ceremony as a dog.[26] When the officers are so badly off, I leave you to guess how the men are. I am myself so weak from diarrhoea that I can hardly sit on horse-back, indeed, I am quite prepared to see it turn to cholera, as I cannot stop it. I feel low spirited about my sister, and I am in bad condition to resist disease. I went to the General Hospital yesterday, and the horrible sight of so many dying of cholera, and all suffering horribly, quite stunned me. The surgeons have all along done their duty well, and have died in heaps. If I were not pressed for time I could write pages, but one has plenty to do here, and can only write at intervals. I would give the world if I were quietly settled down in the country in England, as surgeon to some workhouse, as I positively loathe [*sic*, loath] and drug doctors dishes. Give me a letter if you have time, as I know you have. I see by the last newspaper you sent me the Berwick post mark, and conclude you are at [censored], so I send this letter there on chance. With kind remembrance to [censored], and my uncle.

Letter from Lieutenant-Colonel **John Yorke**, 1st Royal Dragoons, to his sister Etheldred.

Camp between Balaklava and
Sebastopol
October 1854.[27]

My dear Ethel,

After this sad misfortune I am again rising like a Phoenix [from] its Ashes, & instead of hearing complaints against me for the calamity (which usually follow back luck) all console with me at the fearful destruction of the Regiment, and I take my place in the Brigade as a single squadron instead of two, and the same share of outpost duty &c. and what is better still I have purchased a horse for £30 which I [illegible] worth £100. It is really wonderful how matters have mended for me since that fearful night on which the Regt. lost more horses than at Waterloo. The 'Wilson Kennedy' lost 99 and the only 12 surviving ones are still at Scutari. The Major and his men & horses landed here most discomfited. My ship lost 43 of the Reg. and landed 4 out of 26 remaining in a mutilated condition. The 'Pride of the Sea' lost 8: *total 150*, 24 of them were officers chargers and expected loss cost is 200, and the sums approaching that high figure. Such a loss of horses at Sea has never occurred in the annals of the Army. The only Sailing Ship ('War Cloud') the Eniskillens [*sic*] lost 71. There is no doubt the officer will [receive] the Regimental allowances, Viz. £45 for a 1st Charger and £35 for a 2nd. This will be but a mite to everybody but me, but having already [illegible] myself and actually pocketed £15 from [illegible], I am in a fair way for mounting another at the [illegible] of the Chestnut & Brown. It is very singular and sad that poor old 'India' (quite understandable at his great age) should have thus died a melancholy death, and left me a legacy after carrying me thousands of miles, and never offending me, poor old thing he certainly owed me nothing. My new horse joined the Regt. at Brighton having cost £130. He is a Chestnut and likewise high spirited and the Young Cornet could not manage him and consequently sold him to the Quarter-master[28] for £120. He then got neglected, and was never properly ridden, but I hope, and indeed feal [*sic*] certain I can manage him as his temper is good, and having only one [horse] he will be well looked after.

Yesterday was a fearfully cold day and we feared winter was upon us. Some Woodcocks appeared [?] over the camp, and there was an appearance of Snow, but this day fortunately is *two greatcoats* at least warmer, and if it will last this climate will be perfection.

The Russians have been keeping up a constant fire on our entrenchments but the shells have not done much damage as yet, and our encampment is beyond the rang, still we have a most important post to defend and we are all mounted at 4-30 in the morning turning out in total darkness. Some of our Piquets [*sic*] had skirmishes with Russ. Yesterday but not mischief beyond a couple of horses killed. The Russians must have been greatly alarmed at the appearance (in the distance) of our cavalry one Thursday last for they quit off [and] fled in the disorder and threw away their arms and appointments, one of the Patrols saw Chacoes [*sic*, shakos], broken carbines, cartridges and as well jackets strewed on the ground, which was straight in and I gave then men 5 shillings for it [all], and had a great unpacking in my tent with General Scarlett, and the head of the Bashi Bazouks. The contents were wonderful ... There was a full dress Hussar Pelisse of the celebrated 12th Regt., a full dress jacket, quite new, a smock frock, 2 shirts, 2 towels and a quantity of excellent Russia leather for aprons bearing on each piece the Imperial Stamp. I have kept the clothing, leather and Valisse, and given the other articles to the finder, and sent the [rest?] on board the Gertrude ...

Without the Gertrude on hand I could not find any security for any articles, as it is difficult to calculate what one moment bring, relative to a move now that we are in advance, and so near the enemy, but we feel perfectly secure by day and endeavour to fancy ourselves so by night – though it is an open plain the greater part of the distance, but we think the Cossacks are afraid of us. How strange just as I am writing this I am interrupted by the tidings that the Patrol of 4th D.G. are engaged with the enemy. 40 men of the Regt. and 60 of theirs have just left the camp to reconnoitre. The remainder of my small force are foraging 3 miles distant and I am calling them in, but believe it is only Cossacks who are annoying the Patrols, and it will come to nothing, but how difficult to wait when every moment may cause an alteration in my opinion. 6 men of the 42nd were killed by a shell in their tent last night. There is now a great deal of firing from the Town upon us, and we cannot ascertain the cause. The whole management of this mighty siege are a mystery but it is clear Ld. Raglan never intends to provoke an action otherwise Ld. Lucan would be said to have missed two good opportunities. He is a very strange man & generally abuses everybody and everything, but yesterday his unexpected civility to me was as extraordinary as it was unexpected. He strode up to me in the camp, offering me his hand, and said he never could think of me and my fine horses without the deepest sorrow, the more so as it was through the *bad management of others* that it occurred. He said he had carefully read my report, and repeatedly said it was a remarkably good & clear report detailing every circumstance, and that he should send it on to Ld. Raglan. He was greatly pleased likewise that I had, as well as several other officers, purchased horses I needed. He was more than surprised at our effort and when I asked if I might hope to mount the spare horses of other Regts. and thus form a 2nd Squadron, he said he would do whatever he could for me. So it may happen in a measure to fall on my legs again. I think this move will certainly come to pass and that the fine Royals will once more be effective in the field & trust my dear Ethel I may not have the misfortune to send any more bad news to distress you.

The Piquet has returned stating that Patrol had been engaged with Cossacks and think they have killed 2 horses of the latter. The firing from the Town has not again commenced, but our people a vat time in completing the positions of the heavy guns. Last night it was ascertained the Village of Balaklava. ... Would ... not, but great preparations were taken and nothing,

The [illegible] now is anchored [illegible] of the valley and it is wonderful to see so large a ship in such a pond. The whole arrangements are indeed wonderful and nobody can form a true opinion how the winter is to be prepared for, few constitutions amongst the men and horses would stand such exposure through a winter even if it were not colder than yesterday. This has ... work ... but unfortunately the Vineyards around the Camp caused increased sickness which it would be impossible to keep down if the men are so impudent as to eat unripe grapes ...

Ld. Cardigan looked *extremely ill* at the Parade about 4 days since, and returned on board ship, he accepted a packet of powders and assured me he would give them a [illegible], but I have not seen him since. General Scarlett has been and many others, and the 1st packet is getting low, still I do not know whether it would be prudent to spend Uncle Wynne's kind present as yet, as the winter is so near at hand and climates alter.

Oct. 12th – Heavy firing on our Entrenchments during the night and day and constant alarums of Cossacks, they are again reported in the plain but always fly & when pursued. My suspicion now is that we can hold the most important Post and that no great attack will be made upon us in the rear, but that the whole of the Russian force will Sally out of Sebastopol and attack our entrenchments, which are so near the Town. It is quite wonderful to me that they have not done so sooner and we are most anxious for the guns to be planted and the affair to commence. The French guns are of a much greater distance and rather more to the east. I am now receiving 11 or 12 Troopers for my men to ride from the 5th D.G., and in a few days expect 40 horses more ...

Letter from an anonymous officer of the Scots Greys.[29]

Heights of Balaklava,
Saturday, Oct. 21

The pounding of Sebastopol has now been going on for five days, and amid the thunder of artillery in the front I snatch a few moments to write to you. Our position here is the same, and we are in constant expectation of having something warm upon our hands.

On the 18th, early in the morning, a vidette was seen "circling left" most energetically – and here, in a parenthesis, I must explain that when than when a vidette "circles left" the proceeding signifies that the enemy's infantry are approaching, while to "circle right" is indicative of the approach of cavalry. On this signal was immediately heard the roll-call to "Boot and Saddle;" we, the Scots Greys, and a troop of Horse Artillery assembled with the remaining cavalry on the plain; the 93rd got under arms, and pickets were seen to advance, and a dragoon dashed over the plain with the intelligence that the enemy was advancing quickly. Then cavalry and infantry moved upon the plain, remaining in rear of the eminences from which the movements of the videttes had been observed. This, position in front, the Turks opened fired from their advanced intrenchments [sic] on their summits from 21-pounder howitzers, firing several rounds from two batteries. At this moment we were informed that the enemy "meant advancing," and that they numbered several thousands, and that we should have a hard day. We were thorough prepared for them, and remained in status-quo. The Moskows, however, halted in their onward course, and in the evening lighted their watch-fires about 2,000 yards in front of our videttes, the blaze showing bright and high in the darkness. The Russians had made reconnaissance three weeks ago in this directions, when there were not works here, so had not bargained for a first reception at this point. Of course, we were on the alert all night, and before the day broke were particularly attentive to our front. If the Russians had intended to attack us at that time, they could not have had a more favourable morning, a low dense white fog covering the whole of the plain. The sun rose, and the mists disappeared, when it was found the Russians had vanished also. The next day (19th) we naturally expected would be a quiet one, and that we should not be annoyed by remaining at our arms for our final work. Not a bit of it; we had just laden ourselves with haversacks to forage among the merchant shipping in the harbour, when a vedette [*sic*, vidette] was seen to "circle right" most industriously. "Boot and Saddle" again resounded through the cavalry camps, and Sir Colin Campbell again ordered all to be under arms, and another was passed like its predecessor, the enemy finally once more retiring, this time without advancing near enough to a short from the Turks. The next day [20th] I had a foraging expedition, and returned with a goose, butter, preserved milk &c. – a very successful foray, and a full haversack. Of the price of provision you will have some idea when I tell you that a small ham is sold for £3; tins of preserved meat fetch £1 16s; and for sauces, curry-powders, and marmalade the prices sound fabulous. I have known a pot of marmalade fetch one guinea, and frequently 10s is given for this luxury. We were just beginning our meal of commissariat beef and pork, tempered with the contents of the aforesaid haversack, when away when the vedette [*sic*] again, first circling right and then reversing as suddenly to the left. Again sounded trumpet, bugle, and drum through the plain, and masses again moved into position upon it. So we remained till dark, a night attack on the Turkish position to our front being anticipated, and the batteries received orders to fire upon any troops perceived in certain eventualities, and so we again stand all ready for some hours, during which the only amusement is in the hands of the Turks, who fire a round or two; darkness finds us similarly occupied. About nine o'clock a smart fire of musketry is heard from the Turkish heights, and its light sparkles over the hills; we now feel that our vis-à-vis means something; then again all is unaccountably quiet, until some batteries open a pealing fire, and then the bursting shells illuminate the sides of the hills. We strain our eyes in the darkness, and wonder what the deuce it means; afterwards all is still, and the men lie down in their cloaks to rest, though ready for momentary action. No camp fires were allowed to burn during the night; the men were dismissed at eight o'clock for two or three hours, and the vedettes [*sic*] have at present allowed us tranquillity.

Noon. – We learn that the Turkish musketry was directed upon some Cossacks, and that the batteries had mistaken the preparations for chibouque lighting[30] of a striking Turkish advanced picket for the flashes of musketry, and blazed away – fortunately, in thick darkness of the night, having given their guns sufficient elevation for the shells to pass harmlessly over the heads of our astonished allies, and burst far beyond. Our Russian friends of yesterday are said to have entered Sebastopol by the north side. I imagine their object was to annoy and harass us, so as to compel a large force to remain here, and weaken as far as possible, the number of assailants in the Front.

Sir Colin Campbell is a fine old fellow, and frequently pays us a visit. I hear that in the attack of the fleets on the 17th the "Albion" was so much injured than she will have to return to England immediately. The "Agamemnon" led in (she was within 500 yards of Fort Constantine, and had only two feet of water under her bottom), and the "Albion" made the signal "Where you go

I will follow." One of her lieutenants (Chasey) was killed, and 70 men killed and wounded; Greathed (lieutenant in batteries of Naval Brigade was killed yesterday, and Ruthven (lieutenant) very badly wounded. The Colonel of the Grenadier Guards was killed two days ago. Captain Peel ("Diamond") has much distinguished himself, and threw a Russian 8-inch shell over the parapet of his battery, which burst on the other side. The "Arethusa" suffered much, and will have to return home. It would have been a great thing had some of the heavy lumber of the ships of the Baltic had been sent here, where they are wanted, instead of encumbering the Baltic fleet, where circumstances prove they were not wanted.

Today [21st] is the fifth day of our cannonading Sebastopol; the impression there was not felt much till to-day [*sic*], which appeared to be an excellent day for us. The town was on fire three times; the Round Tower was silenced on the first day; by the second morning, however, the Russians had again raised one gun upon it, which was soon knocked over. Sebastopol is the Woolwich of Russia – at least, this part of it, and with their appliances, spare guns, carriages, &c., the Russians have been quickly able to effect their each night. Sir Edmund Lyons was at such close quarters with Fort Constantine that the upper tier of the guns of the fort could not be brought to bear on the "Agamemnon."

Evening. – Sir Colin Campbell's Aide-de-Camp has just been in to say that the enemy are again menacing us, and again cavalry and infantry are waiting in expectation in the plain for some hours; we have just, however, returned again; this constant turning-out is very wearying. When we stood to our arms the whole of the other night, I was amused by the remark of one of the men, "Them Rooshans is too ugly to show their faces by day; I wish the brutes would come on and take their licking without so much bother."

Sunday Evening [22nd]. – Undisturbed day here, but firing in front. The last three days have been very satisfactory, the Russian fire having greatly diminished. There is some talk at assaulting at day-break to-morrow. There is a report that yesterday evening the Russian made a sortie upon the French, who repelled them, and entering one of their own batteries with them, took it and twenty-three guns. There is a large bright reflection upon the clouds as I write, which speaks of fires in Sebastopol. We have been most fortunate in the weather, which is lovely. A very few days now would settle Sebastopol. What a pity it is that false reports of its fall should have appeared in the English papers! My bed upon the clean straw looks so very inviting that I cannot resist its appearance any longer.

Monday Morning [23rd], 7 o'clock. – Just returned to my tent, having been under arms (as is customary in an enemy's country, since an hour before day-light – four o'clock. All quiet here this morning, but the firing is going on as usual. The Moskows in our front sent out feelers yesterday afternoon to the French line of batteries and fired upon them. We shall look carefully for our friends here on the day of the assault in the front, where no doubt they will imagine the greatest number possible of our troops to be engaged. On the day of our first alarm here (four days ago) the Brigade of Guards and the Highlanders marched up to reinforce us after the enemy had retired. Three regiments marched to reinforce us. An officer of the Guards was taken prisoner yesterday in the Trenches.

Letter from Lieutenant-Colonel **John Yorke**, 1st Royal Dragoons, to his sister Etheldred.

Balaklava,
My dear Ethel,   Oct. 22nd 1854[31]
I have only time for a gay few lines just to say all is well with me and indeed I consider myself most fit.

...

On the 18th we were during the entire day in expectation of an engagement, and when in the field all our tents were removed to the rear to another ground to unite with the rest of the army. It was a hard day for me as I had only just been returned from 24 hours duty and had been riding considerable distances during the day & night, and in the darkness searching for the Piquet ... The Videttes of the Russians were clearly visible, and by night almost upon ours, with the view, no doubt, of ascertaining our exact position in front. To-day [they] advanced but the fire of our artillery & that of the Turks who have redoubts on the heights turned their movements and we believe they entered Sebastopol. On the 20th we had a similar attempt but much later in the day, we halted their advance in like manner but this army ns the coolest manner Bivouaced beyond the range of the Guns with their Bands playing. We were just at the time out commencing our dinner upon one sent back to keep warm, but instead of returning we remained out from 3pm until 9am, and during the entire night we were in a dense fog, without Cloaks. Most unfortunately for me I had turned out without an under waistcoat which I always wear on the early morning duties, and I was in a state of things ... I never passed so miserable a night but I am thankful to say I have escaped illness.

Our next misfortune is Lord Lucan. When there is the least appearance of alarm he being excited to madness, and abuses everybody, and in the most uncourteous [*sic*] manner. The last night he sent round an A.D.C. to say we were to remain stationary during the night, and, as if the doubted our obedience to his orders his message added that (in the presence of the men) that he would send any officer home under arrest who left his post as well as the Commanding Officer who permitted it. Poor General Scarlett can do nothing with his Brigade – Lord L. by nature opposes everything he does not think of himself and we are consequently fearing his *want of temper and judgement* should anything serious occur. He is known to do something and then throw the blame on others. He is very unfit man to Command such a Brigade; a hot-headed, nit-wit, Irish man. I believe he shines on the Bench at Castlebar as he can put down the Almighty.

We fired shot and shell into the enemy that night in the fog, and in the morning they had fled, and we suppose damaged the town much. The Brigade followed this night affair, without blankets or cloaks, mornings cold and un-commonly dark, but such a change after hot days in fine weather, as now nearly as warm by day as night. I find myself in command of a Brigade, viz. the 5th Dragoon [Guards], Royals & Enniskillens which made one rather hoarse after my previous days' duty but I slept 'till booted and saddled the following night and shook off all ill effects. To-day Major White of the 17th Lancers died leaving his Regt. in command of a Captain. Col. Lawrence has gone away sick;

Poor Col. Hood Gren. Guards was killed by a Cannon Shot & E.B.R. [illegible] senior officer of the 3rd Battn. he came down yesterday to see me but left word Col. Hoods articles would be sold tomorrow. I was out on duty when he called but conclude he is quite well. Ld. Dunkellin[32] is taken prisoner being very short sighted – he could not see the Russians coming ... Sebastopol ... is all fire and smoke and we see nothing ...

CHAPTER 4

Charge of the Heavy Brigade: 25 October 1854

Attack on the Redoubts

On the morning of 25 October 1854 the men of the cavalry would have been cold and wet. One anonymous Royal Artillery Captain recoded the weather conditions in his journal:

> October 23, – A cloudy night, followed by rain. A hazy morning. Wind still from the south, and mild.
>
> . . .
>
> Oct. 24, – A dark, cloudy night; followed towards daybreak by some smart showers. Rain continues at intervals all day, and falls heavily towards night.
>
> . . .
>
> Oct. 25, – Rain continued at intervals during the night, but towards morning the clouds broke, and it became starlight.[1]

A Russian cavalry officer recounts how he had to huddle underneath his schabraque from the rain as they had no tents or any form of shelter.[2] After the prolonged heavy rain the conditions under foot and hoof would have been soft and muddy. On that particular morning, everything had seemed 'normal' to the men of the cavalry.[3] Sergeant McGrigor of the Greys related:

> The whole of the cavalry parade every morning at five o'clock, and on that morning, as usual, we were in front of our lines, when the enemy opened fire upon one of the batteries which was manned by Turks.[4]

The Heavy Brigade was alerted to the presence of the enemy 'by hearing firing from the outlying picquets'.[5] The picket of the Scots Greys was commanded by Lieutenant Robert Hunter, who noted that all was quiet until 5.30 a.m. when 'an immense Column of the Enemy' suddenly appeared and attacked the British outworks on Canrobert's Hill (No. 1 Redoubt); the advanced picket of the 5th Dragoon Guards was commanded by Captain William Inglis who 'fell back on our support' when the Russians appeared. Adjutant Moodie of the Greys thought the Russian attack started 'at daybreak', as did Corporal Gough (5th Dragoon Guards) whilst Trumpet-Major Forster (1st Royal Dragoons) 'around' 6 a.m. 'W.B' (5th Dragoon Guards) thought the attack 'commenced at half-past six o'clock a.m.' whilst Private James Prince of the same regiment thought the attack was as late as 7 a.m.[6]

The outlying picket of the 4th Light Dragoons had also observed the Russians: at around 5.30 a.m. Captain Alexander Low on his way toward the vidette at the village of Kamara spotted 'a party of Cossacks trying to steal up on the village' which his own men had not seen.[7] Private Farquharson of the same regiment reported

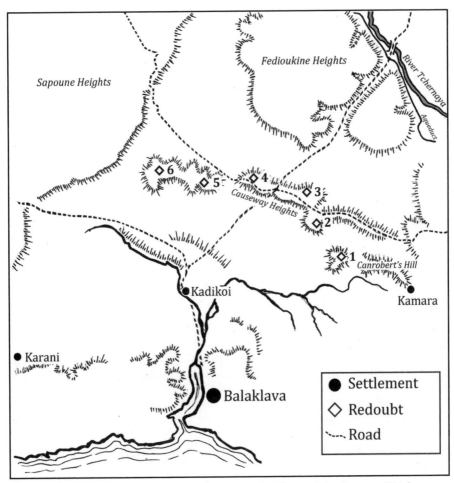

Balaklava and its environs, including the North and South Valleys and the Causeway Heights.

The videttes were circling to right, and also to left, some of them being at a trot. These combined movements signalled to us that the enemy were showing both infantry and cavalry.[8]

Sergeant-Major Loy Smith (11th Hussars) had observed the videttes of his regiment circling 'rapidly' as this meant that the enemy force must have been significant: the speed of the circling signified the size of the enemy force present.[9]

The Earl of Lucan, commanding the Cavalry Division, had ridden forward just as the pickets had been posted to inspect the redoubts on the Causeway Heights. With him were Lord George Paget (4th Light Dragoons), Lord William Paulet and Major Thomas McMahon. From their position they were unable to see the cavalry videttes circling, but they were able to see the signal flags in the redoubt on Canrobert's Hill. The two red signal flags, one above the other, indicated that the enemy was approaching. Because the flagstaffs had only been erected the previous day, Paget suggests no one in the party knew what they meant until the guns in the redoubts started firing![10] This may not be strictly true, given the number of Russian sorties into the Balaklava plain during the preceding twenty days. Paget and his companions then 'scampered' to the Earl of Lucan, who had been riding about fifty yards in front of Paget *et al.*, whilst Paget rode over to command the Light Brigade in the absence of the Earl of Cardigan who was still aboard his yacht.[11] Lucan is then reported to have sought out Sir Colin Campbell, who was in command of the defences at Balaklava: conversely, Kinglake suggests Campbell was riding with Lucan inspecting the redoubts. Lucan sent back Captain Charteris, one of his Aides de Camp, to Lord Raglan to inform him of the unfolding events.

'Eight Squadrons of Heavy Dragoons ... to support the Turks ...'

Lord Raglan arrived on the Heights sometime between 7.30 a.m. and 8 a.m.; the French Chief of Staff, *Général* Martimprey's official report to the French Minister of War records that *Général* Canrobert arrived on the heights overlooking Balaklava at 7.30 a.m., whilst Canrobert himself recalled meeting Raglan around 8 a.m.: 'at the time the two Generals met, the sun had risen, a greyish autumn sun and not very warning ...'[12] At approximately 8 a.m., Raglan ordered both cavalry brigades 'to take ground to the left of the second line of redoubts occupied by the Turks'.[13] This is a very ambiguously-worded order. There was only one line of redoubts, those on the Causeway Heights, unless Raglan interpreted the redoubt on Canrobert's Hill and the Highlanders as the *first* line. Secondly, 'to the left' whilst making sense to Raglan from his position and orientation make little sense to officers on the ground. Lucan correctly interpreted this order as meaning the cavalry should take post to the west of the Causeway Heights.

Whilst the struggle for the redoubts raged, Lord Raglan ordered 'Eight squadrons of heavy dragoons to be detached towards Balaklava to support the Turks who are wavering.'[14] In other words, the Heavy Brigade was ordered to advance down the south valley towards the beleaguered Turks. The Turks are traditionally believed to have fled before the Russian attack, but the 'Special Correspondent' for the French state newspaper, *La Moniteur*, writing on 30 October believed the 'Turks defended themselves with much courage, but, succumbing to the numbers, they were forced to yield'.[15] Another French observer wrote that '425 Turks with two cannons resisted for an hour against considerable forces' and:

> At 7 o'clock they [the Turks] were seen on the march, retiring in good order, but this movement encouraged the other garrisons [to do likewise], and around 8 o'clock the Russians were masters of the heights. The situation is very grave. The enemy continued his march, proceeded by 2,500 Cossacks of the 11th Regiment of the Duke of Weimar and number 12 of the Prince of Lichtenstein [*sic*, Leuchtenberg], and they deployed down in the plain with every intention to attack the camp of the Turks.[16]

Another French observer, writing on 30 October, thought the attack commenced at 6 a.m. and that the Turks had also '... defended themselves valiantly first; but overwhelmed by the growing number of enemies, they had to withdraw, leaving all their redoubts to the Russians'.[17]

Withdrawal of the Cavalry

The weight of artillery fire caused the Heavy Brigade to withdraw back towards their camp; Captain Inglis estimated a distance of two miles and done 'very unwillingly' although an NCO from the 1st Royals suggests double that distance, the Heavy Brigade taking post to the rear of their former camp, 'having ridden over all our tents and their contents'.[18] General Scarlett's Orderly Trumpeter, Thomas Monks, suggests that the Heavy Brigade retired 'by alternate Squadrons', 'Left [Squadron] in front,' towards its old camping ground.[19] This formation is confirmed by Private Auchinloss of the 4th.[20] Major William Forrest of the 4th Dragoon Guards notes that 'we had very bad ground to advance over', initially through the vineyard and then 'over two fences, bank & ditch, then thro' the camp of the 17th Lancers'.[21]

One NCO of the Greys indicates that the Heavy Brigade may have retired in two phases: firstly out of range of the Russian guns, and secondly out of the range of the captured guns in the redoubts, 'to get away from our own guns, which were opened upon us by the Russians as soon as they took them'.[22] Paget suggests that this movement took around an hour to complete, during which time 'we had the mortification of seeing all the redoubts occupied by the Turks ... abandoned one by one'.[23] Trumpet-Major Forster interpreted this retrograde movement as 'to let them come from the hills and have a fair fight', a challenge which was duly accepted.[24] Not only had the Heavy Brigade to withdraw, but so too had the artillery: according to Corporal Gough due to running out of ammunition and casualities (men and horses) sustained. Furthermore, Gough suggests the withdrawal of the British artillery precipitated the flight of the Turks from the redoubts.

There are two key controversies surrounding the Charge of the Heavy Brigade: the orders given to the Brigade immediately before the charge, and its formation and direction of travel. Kinglake suggests the Brigade was advancing back into the south valley from the position it had withdrawn to, at the head of the valley, on or near its old camping ground, whilst Trumpeter Monks and Private Auchinloss both suggest the Brigade was retiring immediately before the charge. However, given that Auchinloss suggests that the Brigade was making an oblique movement to his right and then changed front to the left would suggest that the Brigade was advancing in an approximately easterly direction into the south valley; the vineyard which caused the oblique movement being at the north western end of the south valley, almost at the foot of No. 6 redoubt.[25]

The 'Thin Red Streak'

Following the protracted capture of the redoubts, Russian cavalry appeared on the heights, of which two regiments veered off to attack the 93rd Highlanders, Royal Marines, artillery and those Turks which had rallied with them. One Sergeant of the 93rd believed that the Russians had mistaken their long grey greatcoats for Turkish uniforms. Colour-Sergeant J. Joiner (93rd) watched as 'the cowardly Turks ran away, Sir Colin was looking-on, and turning round, said, in a calm determined way "Men, here we must all die."' The Russian cavalry was 'still advancing' and the Highlanders fired first at 800 yards and finally at 20 'they found it too hot to come any further' so

> Wheeling round they fondly thought of turning our right flank, but we brought our left shoulder round, presenting a new front, caught *them* on the

flank, when volley after volley was fired into them so fast, that they could not advance, as their own dead and dying choked their way.[26]

Private Donald Cameron (93rd) saw:

The Russians coming again toward us, we opened fire on them for a second time and turned them. They seemed to be going away. We ceased firing and cheered. They wheeled about and made a dash at us again. We opened fire on them the third time. They came to a stand, wheeled about and rode off at a canter. We ceased firing and cheered. Our heavy guns fired after them.

The Russian Cavalry

Russian cavalry present at the Battle of Balaklava was the 4th Light Cavalry Division attached to the 6th Infantry Corps. It was two brigades strong: 1st Brigade (Hussars) of two regiments; 2nd Brigade (Reserve Lancers) also two regiments. In addition was one regiment of Cossacks (Ural Regiment) and a battery of horse artillery (Battery Number 12). It was the Hussar Brigade, consisting of the Duke of Leuchtenburg's Kiev Hussar Regiment and the Duke of Saxe-Weimar's Ingermanland Hussars, commanded by Major-General Jabrokritsky, which were engaged by the Heavy Brigade, although Russian sources indicate only a single regiment may have actually been engaged – the Leuchtenburg Regiment. The Ingermanland Hussars were dressed entirely in sky-blue (shakos, dolmans, and pelisses) with yellow lace, whilst the Kievski wore red shakos with a dark green dolman and pelisse, both with yellow lace. The Reserve Lancer regiments were the Orenburg and Siberia Regiments.[27]

Both Allied and Russian sources have exaggerated the number of cavalry present: General Scarlett and General Todleben argue that the Russian cavalry was 1,400 strong, whilst Kinglake argues the number of Russians could be no less than 3,000,[28] and *The United Service Magazine* calculated that both Russian Hussar regiments had a combined strength of 1,800.[29] Lieutenant-General Liprandi suggests there were 2,000 British cavalry[30] whilst General Rhyzov believed the British Heavy Brigade outnumbered his Hussars.[31]

A Russian Hussar regiment had an authorised strength of seven squadrons, each 170 men strong at full strength. Each regiment was divided into three divisions, each two of squadrons. According to the regimental history, only five squadrons (therefore 850 sabres) of the Saxe-Weimar Hussar regiment were engaged compared to all seven (1,190 sabres) of the Leuchtenburg.[32] This would suggest that the cavalry force which the Heavy Brigade attacked had a strength of approximately 2,000 men, considerably less than the majority of British estimates. This estimate is close to those of Scarlett, *The United Service Magazine* and General Todleben of between 1,400 and 1,800, and therefore probably close to the likely number of Russian cavalry engaged. The eight squadrons of the Heavy Brigade, contrary to the belief of General Liprandi, numbered no more than 650. There was some confusion amongst the Allies as to the identity of the Russians: British observers generally describing them as 'belonging to the Imperial Guard,[33] whilst *Général* Canrobert incorrectly identified the blue-clad horsemen as the Leuchtenburg Hussars.

Lieutenant-General Liprandi in his report on the battle says that two brigades of cavalry were engaged, commanded by Major-General Jabrokritsky two squadrons [*division*] of the regiment of hussars of the Grand Duke of Saxe-Weimar, and two detachments [*sotnias*] of the regiment No. 60 of Cossacks (of Popoff [Popov]), advanced upon the heights to the left of our cavalry, and occupied them. Our cavalry hardly had time to form in order of battle beyond the right flank of our infantry, when, from the other side of the mountain, where the redoubt No. 4 was raised [located], the English cavalry appeared, more than 2,000 strong. Its impetuous attack induced Lieutenant-general Ryjoff [Rhyzov] to turn back upon the route to Tchourgoum.[34]

General Rhyzov, who commanded the Russian cavalry at Balaklava, says that under his command were two regiments of Hussars (Leuchtenburg and Saxe-Weimar), one regiment of Ural Cossacks, one *sotnia* of Guards Crimean Tatars and Horse Artillery Battery No. 12.[35] The Russian cavalry officer Lieutenant Koribut-Kubitovich confirms this and also identifies the Hussars as the Leuchtenburg and Saxe-Weimar regiments. He also says it was the Cossacks who attacked the 93rd Highlanders and were 'bowled over' by the 'cool' fire of the Scots. He suggests the two Hussar regiments

> ... moved forward in fine order and started to deploy, heedless of the artillery fire. The [Saxe-]Weimar Regiment deployed in the first line, extending six squadrons with four guns on each flank, these being covered by a squadron in column on each flank, too. In the second line were the Leuchtenberg men in attack columns.[36]

Conversely, General Todleben suggests that six squadrons from the Saxe-Weimar Hussars and the Don Cossacks charged the 93rd Highlanders and it was the Leuchtenburg Hussars and Ural Cossacks who charged the Heavy Brigade.[37] Rhyzov in his account of the Charge suggests that the British cavalry were superior in number to him and he was 'amazed' that the Heavy Brigade did not attack sooner, as they allowed him time to deploy and manoeuvre 'with freedom'. Contrary to Koribut-Kubitovich, Rhyzov recounts:

> First to ascend was a division of the Leuchtenberg Regiment under the command of the truly brave Colonel Voinilovich, whom I ordered to bear to the left as much as required to be face to face with the red English dragoon guards. As the rest of the divisions each came up the slope, I directed them to parts of the enemy formation, since to conform to the extended English front *I was forced to also stretch out both my regiments in a single line, and was left without a reserve.*[38]

In other words, the Russian cavalry was deployed in a single long line, the regulation two ranks deep and with no reserve to counter-charge the British attackers. It is therefore no wonder that the charge of the British cavalry into the centre of the Russian line broke it, with the Russian cavalry being thrown around the flanks of its assailants in an attempt to encircle them and to cut off their reserves. Lieutenant Arbuzov of the Saxe-Weimar Hussars couldn't understand why

> ... the dragoon guards, the flower of the whole English cavalry, received us standing in place, not moving forward a single step. This considerate favour on their part gave us greatly improved chances in the attack. Had they struck us a full speed with the weight of their big horses, in all likelihood our own horses would not have had the strength to withstand them. All the more so since before our attack made contact with the English, we had to overcome two

obstacles – tables and horse lines which could not help but prevent us from maintaining a tight formation. Besides this, we were already weakened by significant casualties from being shot at and had to attack the enemy uphill. When two masses of cavalry attack each other, it often happens that one of them gives way even before the actual impact. Here, however, and as explained above, the actual clash occurred under conditions which were completely unfavourable for our hussars, and then there began a furious slashing away while standing in place.[39]

The Leuchtenburg Hussars, 'with God's help', 'slashed away at a standstill for about seven minutes' and, contrary to British accounts, 'forced the enemy to show his rear'.[40] Rhyzov estimates that the Leuchtenburg regiment lost 18 officers and 122 men killed or wounded and the Saxe-Weimar 12 officers and 105 other ranks and despite these losses he believed he had overcome a superior enemy force and it was difficult to stop his Hussars chasing after the Heavy Brigade. Instead, he withdrew in good order out of the range of the British artillery and took up a position occupying the whole width of the valley with artillery on each flank.[41] Arbuzov also states that the British cavalry were forced to retire and that Rhyzov had difficulty in restraining his men from pursuing what they believed was a broken enemy.[42]

The Charge
The Greys were the first regiment to charge, but thereafter there is controversy whether it was the 6th Inniskillings or 4th Royal Irish Dragoon Guards which charged alongside the Greys or charged next in sequence. Lucan's aide de camp, Captain Walker, believed from what he had been told that the Russian cavalry were received by 'the Greys, 6th Dragoons, and 4th Dragoon Guards, assisted slightly by the 5th Dragoon Guards, and not at all by the Royal Dragoons, so that actually only eight squadrons were engaged'. He further suggests that the Greys and only one squadron of the Inniskillings charged first, the second squadron of the Inniskillings and the 4th Dragoon Guards charging together on the flank.[43] Sir John Yorke denies that a flank charge occurred.[44] *Général* Canrobert thought that 'the general advanced his wings to a form a half-circle; then, when the Russians were at five hundred metres, he put all his line at the trot ... When he was two hundred metres, he ordered the gallop.'[45] In other words, Canrobert believed Scarlett extended his brigade as wide as possible prevent them being out-flanked. Paul de Molènes, who commanded Canrobert's 'Duty Squadron' of *Spahis*, only identified two regiments of British dragoons, the Greys and Inniskillings, because he could only see two uniforms: bearskins and helmets. At a distance it would be hard to see the different facing colours of the helmeted regiments. De Molènes remembered seeing:

> ... two regiments of dragoons; one of the regiments wore helmets; the other, if it was not for the scarlet colour of their coats, recalled in all points, the *Grenadiers à Cheval* of our Old Guard. They are the Scottish Regiment of Grey Dragoons. They derive their name from the colour of their horses.[46]

Général Canrobert also admired the uniform of the Greys with their 'enormous white leather gauntlets and their black bearskins, mounted on grey horses ... looked like giants at a distance'.[47]

Lieutenant Hunter (Greys) suggests the Greys and one squadron of the Inniskillings (the first line) charged first, followed by the 1st Royals and the 5th Dragoon Guards (second line).[48] This is confirmed by Captain Walker,[49] John Yorke,[50] and Major Forrest.[51] That the Greys and Inniskillings charged first is also confirmed by an officer of the Greys writing to friends in Manchester,[52] and by Troop Sergeant-Major Sturtevant.[53] Trumpeter Thomas Monks of the Inniskillings was at pains to point out it was his regiment that charged simultaneously with the Greys,[54] a point contended by Isaac Stephenson (4th Dragoon Guards) who believed it was the regiment, the 5th Dragoon Guards that had done so.[55] Monks implies that one squadron of the Inniskillings charged at the same time as the Greys and the second squadron 'said one to the other, "do you see that?" "Come on", says the Greys to us, and at that moment we went right and left at them.'[56]

An NCO of the 1st Royals also supports this: 'The Greys and part of the Inniskillings were the first to meet them,'[57] whilst Trumpet-Major Forster suggests it was the Greys alone who charged the Russians,[58] a view also shared by *The United Service Magazine*.[59] Colonel Yorke wrote that 'the Greys and Inniskillings did all' and because the 1st, 4th and 5th were held in reserve did very little because the Russian cavalry had already been 'turned' by the Greys and Inniskillings. The 1st Royals, therefore, did 'not deserve much glory in this charge'. He also states that there was no flank charge as described by Lucan in his report.[60] Colonel Hodge argues that the Greys and Inniskillings charged first. His regiment (4th Dragoon Guards) were held in the reserve line, and seeing 'The Greys in a little confusion and retiring' charged on the flank of the Russians 'and settled the business'.[61] Private Auchinloss of the 4th Dragoon Guards argues that his regiment was the second to charge,[62] as does Private James Morrison.[63]

Scarlett's 300

Kinglake suggests that the Greys and Inniskillings attacked the centre of the Russian cavalry; 'W.B.' however suggests that the Greys attacked the Russian right flank,[64] whilst Private Auchinloss argues that the Inniskillings attacked the Russian left flank,[65] and Captain Walker notes that the Greys and one squadron of the Inniskillings attacked the front of the Russians whilst the 4th Dragoon Guards and the remainder of the Inniskillings attacked the flank.[66]

Lieutenant Hunter notes that his (the left) squadron of the Greys was faced by an entire regiment ('their right regiment') and one squadron from the second.[67] An anonymous officer of the Greys wrote that

> They regularly surrounded us. I belonged to the left squadron (likewise the left of the line), and had two squadrons, each double our strength, who tried to turn our flank, opposed to us.[68]

Captain Inlgis confirms that 'a whole troop or squadron overlapped them [the Greys] and took them in flank'.[69] Major Forrest saw how 'the Russians met them, well out-flanking them, wrapped around both flanks and took them in front, flank and rear'.[70] This flanking attack by the Russian cavalry, according to the testimony of Lieutenant Arbuzov of the Saxe-Weimar Hussars, may not have been deliberate:

> Our regiment's 2nd Squadron, being pressed from the left side, veered to the right at full gallop, pushed on the 1st Squadron and forced it to unwittingly do

the same. As a result, the Leib-Squadron's 1st Platoon, which I commanded, did not have any enemy facing it at the moment we collided with the English, since the foe's left flank ended opposite the right flank of our squadron's 2nd Platoon.[71]

Taking advantage of this, Arbuzov ordered his platoon to charge the left flank of the Scots Greys, and 'hewed into it', which, in his opinion, 'seriously disorganized' it. From his position in the rear, however, Sir John Yorke denies that there was 'no appearance of an encircled affair'.[72] It was at this point, with the Greys in difficulty, that Colonel Hodge states that the reserve line, including the 4th Dragoon Guards, attacked;[73] other members of the 4th Dragoon Guards (Privates Auchinloss and Morrison) state that they were the second to charge.[74] Thomas Monks states that the second squadron of the Inniskillings attacked at the same point, in support of the Greys.[75] Sir John Yorke implies that the second line (1st Royals, 4th and 5th Dragoon Guards) charged simultaneously, the 1st Royals passing to the left of the Greys,[76] and this makes sense of the conflicting claims from survivors as to which regiment charged in support of the Greys and Inniskillings.

Major Forrest suggests that after the Greys and Inniskillings had been surrounded: 'our first line retreated' and 'we saw the greatest part of the men come back, upon which the 4th [Dragoon Guards] charged the Russians'.[77] This is confirmed by the surgeon of the Greys, Dr Ramsey Brush, who although writing in 1868 states that the 4th and 5th Dragoon Guards charged simultaneously. He further states that there were two, not one, charges of heavy cavalry: the first made by the Greys and Inniskillings, the second by the 1st Royals, 4th and 5th Dragoon Guards. Dr Brush further states 'In the interval between these two charges, the Russians retired a short distance up the hill and re-formed, the Greys and Inniskillings [*sic*] following suit.'[78] In other words, the Greys and Inniskillings had been forced to retire due to being outnumbered and surrounded and the reserve line – 1st Royals, 4th and 5th Dragoon Guards – charged in support.

Letter from 'a Non-Commissioned Officer in the 1st Royals',[79]

Camp, Balaklava,
October 26.

Through God's mercy I have been saved from one of the most horrible engagements that ever British soldiers were engaged in. But, before I proceed further, let met acknowledge the receipt of your kind letter of the 7th instant, which I received this morning. I have not as yet received the newspaper, but I dare say that I shall get it to-morrow, as it takes along time to sort them. Well, to proceed. I informed you in my last that we were mounted and under arms every morning a little after three, as we were constantly expecting an attack from the Russians, who have been largely reinforced; so yesterday morning we were, as usual, drawn up opposite our encampment, while the General[80] went to reconnoitre. About half-past six the guns (which had been placed by us at the commanding points at the end of the plain which extends about three miles at the end from Balaklava, and near the village of Camara [*sic*, Kamara]), began to open fire upon the enemy, who were advancing in great numbers. These guns were held by Turks. We advanced to the end of the plain and within range of the Russian guns, which began to play upon us in a very rapid manner. A large 32-pound shot passed through our squadrons, breaking the legs of two horses, and we soon began to think it was time to move off, as in another a minute a ball struck a man right in the head, and of course, killed him instantly. Several other casualties took place in the Right Squadron, but I was too busily engaged with my own lot to take notice of all that passed. I am sorry to say that the Turks gave way very soon, and the Russians sent up vast columns, took the heights, drove the Turks away; and, of course, captured all the guns which had been placed there in the earthworks. Our light field guns were no match for the immense artillery which the enemy brought against us: besides, our artillery began to suffer severely in men and horses. As we were not supported by British infantry, of course we were obliged to retire, which we did for about four miles, or about one mile in the rear of our camp, having ridden over all our tents and their contents. There was half a regiment of Highlanders stationed near our camp on the left of several thousand Turks, commanding the road into the village of Balaklava. As we expected, the Russians advanced in great force, the Cossacks skirmishing, and after them about 2,000 regular cavalry. They drove in the whole of the Turks, but, seeing a body of infantry standing firm in line, advanced in capital order to charge. They advanced to within 300 yards of them, when the Highlanders poured such a fire upon them that some dozens of saddles were soon empty. It was now our turn; the Russians increased in great numbers, when we advanced. The Greys and part of the Inniskillings were the first to meet them, and, to do the enemy justice, they advanced in much better order than we did; but they could not stand a moment the charge of British Cavalry, for one squadron of Grays [*sic*] upset a whole regiment of them. We were soon at the support, and the enemy retired, but not in confusion. I fully expected we should follow and charge them again, as I am confident we could have taken the whole of them prisoners, but, marvellous to say, the order was given to Retire, and a more confused rabble was never seen. However, the Russians retired beyond the heights which they had won, and very soon after our infantry began to arrive, as the news had reached Lord Raglan of our perilous state, and he sent the First and Fourth Divisions to our aid, and I felt quite comfortable as the Guards and High-landers came in. I was never was so vexed in my life to think that 3,000 Russian cavalry were within the grasp of our small force, and our commander allowing them to retire unmolested!

October 27.
I could not write any more yesterday, as we were constantly on the look out, expecting the enemy to attack us. I will now go on with my horrible narrative of the doing of the eventful 25th of October. As our infantry began to arrive at noon we again advanced to the heights which the Russians had won, and which the Turks had so shamefully abandoned. We could see them bringing up immense reinforcements, and their artillery quite outmatched our light pieces. We advanced to the heights, and got on the edge of a plain (or I may call it a gorge) on the other side of the heights, and there we rested, waiting for orders, or for an opportunity to get at them again, but the chance was lost. About two o'clock Captain Nolan, who was one of Lord Raglan's aides-de-camp, came galloping down from Sebastopol, his horse quite blown, and, as he rode past,

he inquired for Lord Lucan, who was close by. He said "It is Lord Raglan's Order that you force the enemy to retire, there they are – charge them." Lord Cardigan was immediately ordered to charge with the Light Brigade, who took them up in gallant style, in two lines. They had to gallop, I should say, upwards of a mile and a half. We were the next support, the Grays [*sic*] on the right of us, and the other heavy regiments in our rear. The Light Brigade went so rapidly that we almost lost sight of them, for a more horrible fire was never heard than what was opened upon us. We were actually under a cross fire of thirty guns in our front and ten on each flank from the heights. Just as we got under the cross fire I could see the remains of the Light Brigade returning, scarcely a mounted man, and dozens of poor fellows crawling along on foot to the rear. Lord Lucan saw that a great error had been committed, as we were now under the fire of fifty heavy guns and just within the Russian Riflemen, who poured in their shot like hailstones. We were, I should say, steady under this horrible fire for upwards of half a minute, and how a single man of us escaped is quite a mystery. I cannot tell you all the casualties, but just as we were about to return, Colonel Y[orke] got his leg shattered by a shell; Captain E [lmsall], Captain C[ampbell], and Mr. H[artopp] got severed musket wounds. I have every reason to by thankful to God Almighty for my safe deliverance from such a horrible scene. R—'s horse was shot dead just on my right, little Trumpeter S[tacey][81] was severely shot on my left, and a young lad named A— had his arm blown off by a cannon shot just in front of my face.[82] In fact the shot and shell from fifty pieces of cannon, and supported by some tens of thousands of infantry and several thousand cavalry, was too much for about 1,200 cavalry. So we were obliged to retire, which we did without the least confusion, till we just got out of range of their guns. But I should here observe, a regiment of French Cavalry had opportunely arrived and charged the batteries on the left heights, and forced the Russians to retire their guns from that point, so that the poor Royals were saved the loss of many other poor fellows. I cannot tell you the number of men killed or wounded either in our own or any other regiment, but no doubt a complete list will be published in due time; but this I can say, that after the fatal charge, the Light Brigade did not bring 190 men out of action, who went upwards of 800 into action. They behaved most gallantly; they charged through the immense battery of thirty guns in front, cut down every gunner, and took nearly the whole of the guns, but they were then exposed to the fire of several immense squares of infantry, and were, I may say, almost totally destroyed. I never saw poor Lord Cardigan in such a way in my life; he only obeyed orders and how he escaped God alone knows. Poor Captain Nolan, who brought the fatal order to Advance, was immediately afterwards killed by a large shell striking him in the breast. Our loss has been immense, and I could not attempt, nor would I wish, to describe the horrible sights which I saw on the field that day; but, if it should please God to spare me to return to you, many a long tale of horror I shall be able to describe.

We retired just out of range of their guns, and we then dismounted, as some of our infantry had advanced, with the Rifles in front, and a reinforcement of the French at the same time arrived on our left. It was not getting towards nightfall, and neither men nor horses had tasted food or water the whole day. Little W— just at this time came up from our camp with a load of corn for the horses and some biscuit and rum for the men, which refreshed them very much; and as it was now getting dark, L— and I made a fire and boiled a drop of water in a mess tin and made some tea, which much refreshed us. T— and L— escaped. N— had his horse shot from under him, and he has gone to Scutari, as his health has been very bad for some time past.[83] About 9 o'clock we made immense fires to deceive the enemy, and, after posting a strong picket, we retired to our lines, but not to rest, as we had to get up our picket poles, pack up our baggage, and retire about another mile nearer to Sebastopol, and it was 12 o'clock before we could lie down that night, having been under arms and mounted nearly 21 hours.

Yesterday, the 26th, we again shifted camp another mile nearer to Sebastopol, and it was in the afternoon after we had got to our new ground that I commenced this scribble. I must now bring it to a close as soon as possible, as the mail leaves to-morrow morning, and I am afraid the letters will not get posted unless sent off in good time to-night [*sic*]. We heard this morning that the Russians made a sortie out of Sebastopol yesterday to try and take our batteries, as they thought the force was very much weakened by the infantry coming to our support. I am glad to inform you that the loss the Russians sustained yesterday made up in a measure for our loss the day before. I have not heard particulars, but the Russians lost about 2,000 men, and an immense number of prisoners have just passed Balaklava to go onboard ship. I believe our loss was little of nothing; part of the 49th Regiment kept several thousands of the enemy at bay a long while, till they were reinforced. We hear various reports of how they are getting on at Sebastopol, but I believe the Russian fire is getting very slack. I do not know when it will be stormed; this makes the eleventh day of cannonading. Our position here is very critical. I believe we shall have to abandon Balaklava, as the enemy are bringing up some large guns and reinforcements. We scarcely have the bridles out of the horses' mouth, and our belts are scarcely off our backs. I heard some old staff-officers say that no cavalry in the annals of war were ever exposed to such a fire as we were on the 25th.

I could relate lots of anecdotes about it, and I hope it will please God that I shall be able to do so at some future time. You would be surprised at the skeleton appearance or our small regiment now, and, of course, it is too late in the season for reinforcements. How my portmanteau and baggage have escaped is a mystery to me. Should they be lost I do not know what I shall do for firing materials.

Letter from 'A soldier of the First Royal Dragoons who was present at Balaklava', to his relatives in Manchester.[84]

Cavalry Camp,
27 October

... In about one hour's time after they [the Turks] retreated, Lord Lucan collected all the two brigades of cavalry which consisted of five regiments of the light dragoons and five of heavy dragoons, with two troops of horse artillery. We were ordered to advance, which we did, and showed fight a second time, which I am sorry to say played the very deuce with us, as we were in a very dangerous position, a triangular one; we were exposed to the Russian batteries on our right and left, and in front to the whole of their cavalry, artillery and infantry. They peppered into us nicely, as our artillery could not act. Presently,

Capt. Nolan (who you will remember reading about, and who came out to purchase horses for the army before we started), galloped up to Lord Lucan with an order from Lord Raglan to charge the light brigade against the Russian artillery, which he did, and led them himself. They charged right through 21 pieces of artillery, driving the enemy from their guns, cutting away the traces, and spiking the guns. We pursued them about half a mile, when two or three infantry regiments came out of ambush. Of course our cavalry were obliged to retire. It was then the damage was done, for the Cossacks met them retiring and slaughtered them in all directions. The light brigade charged 850 strong, and came back 190 of all ranks. The heavy cavalry were advancing all the time, under the hottest and most destructive fire that ever was witnessed by Lord Lucan or any other man on the field. The long shot, with grape and musketry, came amongst us like hail, whistling through the air like a gale of wind through the rigging of a ship. I saw one huge shot drop on the left of our front, which I expect would sweep the whole line from right to left. Had it not been for the French cavalry, who stormed the battery on our left, and obliged them to cut and leave it, we should all have been mown down like grass. But, fortunately, we retired with few casualties of broken limbs. I am sorry to say, my poor brother George got a shot through the thigh, which passed right through. If you remember, some person wished the Colonel [Yorke] to be the first man shot. This person verily got his wish, for, I believe, after the first man of our regiment was killed, he was the next that had his leg shattered. Capt. Campbell, I am sorry to say, got shot through the shoulder, Captain Elmsall and Mr Hartoph [*sic*, Hartopp] are also wounded. We had several privates wounded. Two of them had their arms blown away. I got too close to one of the big shot myself, for had I not reared my horse up just at the moment I did, I must have had it, for the officer riding alongside of me caught it in the chest of his horse, which dropped in a moment ...

Letter from Lieutenant **Robert Scott Hunter**, Scots Greys, to his sister.[85]

Balaklava,
My Dearest Holly,　　　　　　　　　　　　　　　　　October 27th 1854

I don't know whether I have written to you since the siege commenced. At any rate I'll give you a secret now. We began on the 17th & are still at it, with no further effects that I can see, then having knocked the parapets about, & by all accounts from deserters, killed a good number inside. But now for my news. We have at last had a *fight* & I have "fleshed by maiden sword". I was on picquet on the morning of the 24th, & all was quiet at 3 AM & afterwards, till day break (about 5½ am) when an immense Column of the Enemy, & our fire opened from our field works, which unfortunately as you will see were entirely manned with Turks. The Russians stormed, & *took* them the Turks only making a stand at one work, but bolting as soon as the bayonets crossed. The consequence of this, was, that the Russians soon got up a number of guns & turned our own captured ones upon us, & commenced at 6 o'clock to pepper us, with shot, shell & rifle balls. We had *no* infantry, & stood their fire for some time, losing a few, but were obliged to retire as the fire got hot. The Turks absolutely ran away from the other batteries, before the Enemy got there, & we lost our position, & 9 guns, & retreated slowly towards our Encampment.

About 12½ their Cavalry came suddenly over the Hill, with a Cloud of Cossacks, who speared the unfortunate Turks, who were running away, & begging for mercy, in all directions. We came trotting up, wheeled into line & our little Regiment & one squadron of the Inniskillings charged, & broke 4 Regiments of Regular Cavalry & about 100 Cossacks, they were 5 to 1. There were 2 regiments of Blue Hussars, & 2 of Light Dragoons. The latter were big fellows, & my Squadron, the left (I commanded the left Troop) was opposed to their right Regiment & one squadron of the second. The scene was awful, we were so outnumbered & there was nothing but to fight out way through them, cut & slash. I made a hack at one, & my sword bounced off his thick coat, so I gave him the point, & knocked him off his horse. Another fellow just after made a slash as me, & just touched my bearskin, so I made a rush at him, & took him just on the back of his helmet, and I didn't wait to see what became of him, as a lot of fellow were riding at me, but I only know that he fell forward on his horse, & if his head tumbled like *my* wish, he must had have it *hard* and as I was riding out, another fellow came past me, whom I caught slap in the face, I was bound his own mother wouldn't have known him. They all by this time were broken, & running, our fellows gave some awful cuts & the 5th Dragoons & Royals had now come up & finished what we began. Lord Raglan saw it from the heights & sent an A.D.C. to say "he was delighted with the Greys". The Light Brigade, viz. 8 & 11 Hussars, 17th Lancers, 4 & 13 Light Dragoons went to the front, the Royals & Greys following, & pursued. The Lights went ahead, & answered for a great many more, but were led too far by Captain Nolan (15th Hussars), an A.D.C. who suffered for his rashness with his life & I am sorry to say, were cut to pieces! Their loss is about 600!! We were following, & got into the cross fire, which cut them up. Three batteries (two of them captured ones) turned on the Royals & us, & such a shower of round shot, shells, grape, canister & rifles played on us that we were obliged to retire. Every officer of the 17th but *3* were killed or wounded, & the only brought out about 45, out of action. The 4th about the same, the 13th have only about 35. In short they are quite *annihilated*. Our loss was 4 officers wounded, but only one obliged to go to the ships, & 44 men wounded, 2 killed, our escape was miraculous. The round shot bounced around us, Shells bursting before, behind and about us, & anything like the balls from canister & rifles you cant imagine, but by the awful results. A grape shot struck my cloak, & bounded off, it was just 2 inches above my knee. I have much cause to be and am thankful for my escape. It was an awful time & the men were falling, & horses on all sides. The din deafening, & the poor fellows who were struck screamed awfully. A man riding beside me had his leg shattered just below the knee by grape shot, a fellow of the one no doubt that hit my cloak. The Russians we allowed to hold the positions, as it is now useless to us, & we have had fallen back upon the heights.

There was a desperate sally made yesterday afternoon from the Town but the 3rd Division received them, & beat them back I am told with immense loss. Their artillery is superb & they fire magnificently as we (Cavalry) can tell, but I don't think so much of their other troops. The Turks are useless cowards, & will need to do much to work off the stain they have put on their name here. There is a report that we are to leave Balaklava, as our force not sufficient to hold these and extended positions. This looks, it strikes me, very much as if we were getting the worst it. From our lines & the door of my tent, we can see the Russians working like bees all over the place. They are intrenching themselves, but General Bosquet with a division of French went away I believe, last night, at it is supposed is going to take them in the rear, but his instructions were not made known – at any rate he has gone away over the hills in front of our position, & that looks like it. But its very little use telling you all this, for you will get all the news in the papers. Do send me any that may have anything in about us … If you get a good Punch send them, …

… I hope soon to be able to tell you that we have taken the town, & licked the Russ again, but I have not much time now to write, as most days we are out all day, & very often at night too. It is disagreeable work & we have all a good many hardships to go through, but altogether we are *jolly*, & look forward hopefully to go home some fine day.

… Our red coats are crimson, and black stains all over them: epaulettes no one wears, they are done away with; & we have to carry telescopes and haversacks & pistols so that with our brown faces & patched clothes, we look queer figures I assure you …

Letter from Cornet and Adjutant **Daniel Moodie**,[86] Scots Greys, to the editor of the *Nottinghamshire Guardian*.[87]

Camp, Balaklava,
Sir,-   27th October, 1854.
Since the date of my last letter we have never been out of the roar of the enemy's cannon. I told you how we expected to take Sebastopol, but it was a very different job from what was expected. We were employed until the 17th instant in getting up the cannon from Balaklava, and then opened on the forts with 200 pieces, and we are also assailed by an army in our rear which the cavalry alone has to contend with. We are never done day or night, but the worst job we have had was on the 25th, which commenced at daylight by the Russians attacking our outworks and driving back the Turks at the point of the bayonet and capturing three forts. We were under shot and shell from daylight till four p.m. The slaughter was dreadful, we were attacked by a numerous body of Russian cavalry who thought to drive everything before them, but our cavalry charged, and our regiment leading, went in in fine style. Such a "mill" you could not imagine. We fought hand to hand, but we proved our superiority as swordsmen by beating them off the field. You must excuse me going into details now, as I have not time. The charge made by the regiment was admired by everyone, and proved that the Young Greys were equal to the Old ones.

Lord Raglan complimented Colonel Griffiths on the gallant conduct of the Regiment, and, in doing so, asked him if he had any favour to ask. The Colonel told him he had recommended me a month ago for a commission on the death of Captain Freeman by cholera, and he hoped he would give me a commission. His Lordship told him that, by all means, I should have it.

You little know how I am situated. For ten days after we arrived in the Crimea we had no tents or covering of any kind, and had to bivouack on the cold ground. Our duty obliged us to stand at our horses heads all night. We have got our tents now, but we might almost as well be without them, as there is not rest to be had, night or day. At this moment (10 p.m.) I see the Russian watch-fires two miles from us.

I suppose the engagement of the 25th will be called the "Battle of Bala-klava." Our losses have been severe, Colonel Griffiths, Major Clarke,[88] and Mr Prendergast[89] have been wounded: and Henry Campbell,[90] of D. Troop killed. Thomas Traill[91] was severely wounded and has since died. Altogether, fifty-two men have been wounded,[92] some of them severely, amongst whom I may mention Galbraith,[93] Serjeant Kneith [*sic*, Kneath],[94] William Seggie[95] (a ball through his head), Douglas Gardner [*sic*, Gardiner],[96] A. Thomas Donaldson,[97] S. Land,[98] and Morris.[99] I do not think they can live long. The only thing I am glad of is that the regiment acted with the greatest courage; in fact, they were spoken of through the whole army. French, English and Turks all expressed the greatest admiration of our gallant charges. We have a strong garrison to contend with, a strong army in our rear to keep back, and the cholera raging in our centre. This is a strange life to lead. I have not washed my face for five days, and cannot get an opportunity to do it. Although we get good victuals, we cannot get them cooked, but chiefly live on biscuit and water.

PS I may mention I got off well. I never got a scratch although in the thickest of the battle the whole day. The non-commissioned officers got in for it a good deal. Serg. Majors Brown[100], Dearden,[101] Davidson,[102] Serjeants Wilson,[103] Gibson[104] & Kneith, wounded. We could not get poor Clifford's[105] body yesterday as we were burying the dead; but I went with two men this afternoon and we buried him in the corner of a nice yard. The field presented an awful spectacle. Horses dead, and dying, laying in all directions, and the bodies of many Russians. The place was stinking so much that I was glad to get out of it.

Letter from an anonymous officer of the Scots Greys, to his relatives in Manchester.[106]

Camp, Balaklava,
Friday, 27th October 1854.

I little dreamed that when I began this letter that I should, perhaps, never finish it, and also to finish it with bad news. An extract from my log of the 25th would be too long (but you shall see it, please God, some day); but on that day the Russians attacked the advanced forts and entrenchments of Balaklava, defended by Turks, who, great brutes! Ran away. They took possession of the forts, and they had the audacity to send thousands of cavalry to attack our poor handful. The Old Greys and Inniskillens [*sic*] had the honour of meeting the first charge of three times our number. They regularly surrounded us. I belonged to the left squadron (likewise the left of the line), and had two squadrons, each double our strength, who tried to turn our flank, opposed to us. We went clean through them, and back again, and you never saw such a fight. They say you could not see a red coat, we were so surrounded, and for *ten minutes* it was dreadful suspense; but they couldn't stand it, and were soon cutting away like anything, or re-forming. The realities of war were very apparent; excited cheering and congratulations from men covered with blood and cut about dreadfully. I mercifully escaped without a scratch, and only tried my maiden sword on one fellow's head, which must have given him a headache, thought it didn't draw blood. He was soon unhorsed, and I saved his life by making him a prisoner. Lord Raglan sent us a message of 'Well done, Grays [*sic*]' and the cheering was frightful. They say it was a magnificent charge; but it did not come up to my idea at all; it was more like a row at a fair. We immediately advanced over the field of our scrimmage, among dead and dying, and, would you believe it, I wasn't the least horrified. After an hour, the Light Brigade passed us on our left, and charged, ourselves and the Royals being their supporting line. This was the dreadful calamity and fatal mistake of the whole day. They had to charge some guns, supported by two lines of cavalry, ten times their number, and between a cross fire of innumerable guns and battalions of infantry. As if by magic, the whole brigade seemed to be either dismounted or annihilated. We were under the same fire, and it was something dreadful – shot, shell, and Minié balls, just like a hailstorm; and our men and horses falling right and left. The order to retire was never so thankfully obeyed, and for several hundred yards we retired under this fire, and at a walk, men falling every minute. Being under fire is the most frightful thing imaginable; I shall never forget it. I expect every minute would be my last. Our loss is 2 men killed, and 14 horses; 4 officers, 3 serjeants, 39 men wounded, and 21 horses. Captain Clarke has several cuts, and three wonderful escapes in the charge. Prendergast had a ball pass through his foot, but it broke no bones. A Cornet had two slight lance wounds; and our Colonel[107] retired after the charge from a bullet that passed through his bearskin, and came out on the same side. He joined us in the evening, after our great loss. A greater and more useless sacrifice of life never was made. You will learn, I have no doubt, from the papers the origin. Poor Nolan was killed. We buried him at the fort where we dismounted. The Light Brigade went in over 800, and 120 returned. Next morning it was pitiable to see them. The 13th Light Dragoons mustered 4 officers and 15 file out of 200. Poor Oldham[108] was killed; Goad, they are afraid, the same; and Montgomery is missing. The 17th Lancers has as great a loss; they have 3 officers and 23 file present. I got poor Webb,[109] a captain in them, whose leg was shattered just above the ankle, and put a tourniquet on him, and gave him some rum. You never saw a fellow so thankful; I rejoiced at carrying a tourniquet, as it may have saved his life; they say he is doing well. Altogether it was a sad day's work, and shows the necessity of *good generals*. Out of 39 wounded men, very few will join the ranks of the Grays [sic] again. In the evening, Lord Raglan came and complimented us in person; and I can assure you that it was quite a mercy that any of us are left to tell the story. We are now sadly out of spirits at our great loss; besides, the Russians are so numerous it is impossible to hold the extended line we have, so we have retired about half-a-mile, and they talk of giving up Balaklava.

Our attack on Sebastopol is still going on, and to our advantage. They attack our right flank yesterday, and found they had not Turks to tackle, so got frightfully licked, losing a general and 300 prisoners. It's tedious this work, so the sooner they take Sebastopol the better.

Fancy, all this for those brutes of Turks, who run before the Russians are within a mile!

As it is late, and I may not have time to-morrow morning to finish this, I will conclude *pro tem*.

28th October, half-past 6 a.m.
I had just shut my eyes last night when a frightful report and cannonade made me jump up like a shot, and in ten minutes we were in front of our lines, ready to received the 'wily Russe,' who attempted a night attack. The shell and

rockets light up the night beautifully. They never came near us, though we expected them down on us every second. After some time we were allowed to lie down again, but read to turn out at a moment's notice. At 4 a.m. we were out again, and about 100 loose Russian horses galloped into our lines. We took about a dozen ourselves; other regiments got about 20 or 30, and very odd all grays [*sic*]; and by the men's coats and buttons it seems that the Russian 'Grays' are the 2nd Dragoons like us. I got a medal off one of them, and mean to preserve it; it has got 1849 on it, so must have been for the Hungarian war. The fellows we tackled on Wednesday were the Hussars of the Imperial Guard, great swells in sky blue jackets with orange braid. The wounded Russians say it was the men with the tall bearskin caps on white horses that cut them up so frightfully. It is wonderful the good health and spirits I am blessed with, while others suffer so from illness. We have 8 officers out of 18 hors de combat, form sickness and most of them onboard ship.

Letter from Corporal **Joseph Gough** (number 1020), 5th Dragoon Guards, to his father in Lichfield.

Balaklava.
Dear Father and Mother –   October 27th.
I am glad to tell you that we had an engagement with the Russians on the 25th of this month. We turn out in marching order every morning at four o'clock; it is quite dark then, so we stand to our horses till about one hour after daylight, because we expected an attack before this, as they have been gathering their army about three miles from our camp, this last fortnight. They had before the action 34,000 men. Well, on the morning of the 25th, just as day-light was breaking, the cannon commenced firing from our batteries on the hills, and about seven o'clock we advanced just opposite our batteries under the hill. We could not see our enemies; but they kept firing at our artillery, and shell was flying over our heads and dropping all around us. Our artillery had to retire, as they had no more ammunition; so after a while the Turks started, left the batteries, and ran down the hill as hard as ever they could. Well, the enemy got possession of our batteries, and we could see them bringing their guns up the hill, and in a few minutes the shot and shell were coming pretty fast; they were firing 6-pounders at us, and we could see the balls coming, we shouted 'look out boys;' they came with such force against the ground, that they would rise and go for half a mile before they would touch the ground again. Us and the Greys lost some horses there. We had no infantry up at the time except the Highlanders, for the Turks had all run away, so their cavalry came galloping over the hills. Some of them went to attack the Highlanders, who formed squares, and popped them off nicely, so they retired from them. In the mean-time, another lot of cavalry came to attack us; I suppose they thought we should run. At first we thought they were our Light Brigade, till they got about twenty yards from us, then we saw the difference. We wheeled into Line; they stood still, and did not know what to do. The Charge sounded, and away we went into the midst of them. Such cutting and slashing for about a minute, it was dreadful to see; the Rally sounded, but it was no use, none of us would come away until the enemy retreated; then our fellows cheered as loud as ever they could.

When we were in the midst of them my horse was shot; he fell, and got up again, and I was entangled in the saddle, my head and one leg were on the ground. He tried to gallop on with the rest, but fell again, and I managed to get loose. While I was in that predicament, a Russian Lancer was going to run me through, and I could not help myself. Macnamara[110] came up at the time, and nearly severed his head from his body; so thank God I did not get a scratch! I got up, and ran to where I saw a lot of loose horses; I got one belonging to one of the Inniskillings, and soon was along with the Regiment again. When I have mounted again, I saw a Russian who had strayed from the rest; he rode up to try and stop me from joining the Regiment again. As it happened, I had observed a pistol in the holster pipe, so I took it out, and shot him in the arm; he dropped his sword, then I immediately rode up to him and ran him through the body, and the poor fellow dropped to the ground. Lord Lucan said, when we charged, that we were into them, and the devil could not get us away from them. Lord Raglan sent his compliments to General Scarlett, and said that the Heavy Brigade behaved gallantly. We had two men killed. Corporal Taylor[111] was one, and Ealing[112] was the other, and fourteen wounded. In the evening they wanted to give the Light Division a chance, and sent them to retake the guns. The poor fellows went, and not half of them came back. The Donalys[113] are safe. We expected an attack this morning, but they did not advance. We expect to be engaged to-morrow, but we don't care a pin about them as long as we have plenty of our infantry. That day there was none there but cavalry and artillery. I have no more to say at this time.

Letter from '**W.I.**' 'an officer of the 5th Dragoon Guards' to a friend.[114]

Balaklava,
Dear H–,   Oct. 27, 1854.[115]
Just a few lines to tell you that the day before yesterday, in support of and immediately after the Greys, we charged a column of Russian cavalry and entirely routed them; the Inniskillings [*sic*, Inniskillings] were engaged, and, I believe, one squadron of the 4th Dragoon Guards. Perhaps I had better begin at the beginning.

I commanded the Advanced Picket. Large forces of infantry, cavalry, and artillery advanced on our positions. I fell back on our Support. The ridge of hills in our front was defended by four forts, or properly earthworks, thrown up by us, and garrisoned by Turks. The whole of our cavalry were formed up in rear of the ridge, and an express was sent for infantry, thinking, of course, that the Turks would hold the forts until assistance arrived; but no sooner did the Russians advance than the Turks poured out of the forts, and did not even spike the guns. We then retired about two miles across a plain, under a very heavy fire. This we did very unwillingly, at a walk; but of what use could we be against artillery planted on hills, behind earthworks? Emboldened by their success, they sent their cavalry pouring down into the plain, and their first attempt was against a long line of Turkish infantry, who, on the Russians getting pretty close, bolted outwards, and disclosed the 93rd, the only foot we had; these opened a fire, and the Minié bullets had the desired effect. The Russians fled, but soon rallied; and, fancying from our retreating previously that we were afraid of them, they advanced in a column at a gallop, but as they came close this gallop degenerated into a walk. They were then about 150 yards from the Greys, who went in at them with a yell. The Russians were so much more numerous than the Greys that a whole troop or squadron overlapped them and took them in flank. Then we went in and gave them what they will not forget. They stood for some ten minutes; then fairly turned and ran. Corporal Tayler[116] and Bernard Callery[117] were killed in the charge. Cornet Mr Neville[118] was un-horsed, and has three wounds on his back and one on the head. Swinfen[119] was slightly wounded in the hand and breast. Brigadier-General Scarlett led the charge with Elliot[120] and Sergeant Shegog,[121] his aide-de-camp and orderly. The brigadier was slightly wounded. Abbot, of F. [Troop],[122] stood over Neville and defended him; certainly saved his life. Private McNamara[123] killed three men and had a very narrow escape; a lance went through his sleeve and caught on a button and dinged it in, not hurting him. Sergeant-Major Green[124] was cut down and ridden over, but not hurt. Sergeant-Major Stewart[125] had two horses shot under him, and Sergeant Russel[126] had one. A shell burst in the rear rank of my squadron, but killed no one.

In the afternoon the Light Brigade, by a mistake in the order received, got into a cross fire and were nearly cut to pieces; but came back past us in twos and three. 190 mustered out of the five regiments that went down the valley 800 strong. We got some of the cross fire, and were withdrawn. I have now told you as much as I have time to do.

Letter from an anonymous officer of the Heavy Brigade [Scots Greys?] on board the *Himalaya*.[127]

Balaklava Bay,
Oct. 27th.

Oct. 25th. – At daylight heard very sharp and heavy firing towards Sebastopol, and also near Balaklava, increasing towards nine o'clock, and from that time incessant. Could see occasionally shells bursting over the high hills by which the bay is surrounded; so as soon as possible I went on shore to my Regiment and found that a very heavy cavalry action, with artillery, was going on, the Russians having driven the Turks completely out of three batteries which had been erected and armed with our guns, and the Turks placed to man them. However, they got panic-stricken and fled and down came the Cossacks and the Russian cavalry (Imperial Guard) to attack ours, and a most bloody fight ensued, our Light Cavalry, viz., 4th [Light] Dragoons, 8th and 11th Hussars and 17th Lancers – being dreadfully cut up, having charged a battery of guns numbering thirty. They were supported by the Grays [*sic*], who have again distinguished themselves beyond praise, suffering, however, severely in the affair. They charged right through the Russian cavalry, who numbered about five to one; got surrounded by them, made another charge, and cut themselves out by sheer fighting. Colonel Griffith got shot in the head, Brevet-Major Clarke a sabre cut on the back of his neck, Cornet Prendergast[128] shot right through the foot, Cornet Handley[129] stabbed in the side and arm, being at one time surrounded by four Cossacks, three of whom he shot with his revolver, and the fourth was cut down by his cover-Sergeant. I saw this young gallant fellow a few hours after, and he was then getting ready to rejoin his regiment from the temporary hospital, not finding his two wounds of sufficient consequence to keep him from his post. The Colonel did the same after getting his head dressed. Major Clarke did not, I believe, leave the field. I also saw Lieutenant Elliot, 5th Dragoon Guards, riding into Balaklava, his face so covered with blood and his head bound up that we could not recognize him. The gallant Captain White, too, of the 17th Lancers, was laying on his back when we came up to him, with a round shot through his leg, with Sir W. Gordon, dreadfully cut about the head, both receiving, however, every attention and care from Surgeon Kendall, who was formerly at Southampton with Mr. Ward, surgeon of that town. In this garden and temporary hospital could be seen men with every description of wound, from the sabre cut to the grape and canister shot. One poor fellow's leg was taken off while we were there, nor can one easily forget the shocking scenes of such a day's fighting. The surgeons (Brush, and his assistant, Chappel, both of the Grays) were working away with the sleeves turned up, arms bloody, faces the same, looking more like butchers than surgeons, so hard they worked all day. During the afternoon, subsequently the Russians being repulsed with heavy loss, their object evidently being to take Balaclava, they retreated to the brow of a hill on the right, and formed themselves round the battery they had driven our allies, the Turks, out of; and our troops, with the Rifles in front were formed in line of battle, not more than three-quarters to one mile from them, occasionally trying the effect of the shells from the artillery guns, and the precision with which these missiles are directed is truly astonishing. I cannot conceive a more splendid sight than was witnessed during this afternoon, the two armies, the Russians being enormously strong, and our own, waiting for one or the other to advance, with an occasional shell by way of invitation or challenge. But for several hours they stood as if content with what had already taken place, and we so near the two, that with the aid of my glass (a good Dolland [*sic*, Dollond][130]), I could distinctly see the colour of their uniform (gray), and their standard, with an eagle on the top of it; I could plainly see the dead, both men and horses, on the scene of the late encounter. I observed one horse stand fully an hour by the side of his dead rider, while others were wildly galloping about, no knowing which way to turn their riderless course. One of the most wonderful things I think is to see the way in which our Rifle-men go about in small detached parties, crawling along on the ground up the side a hill until they appear to be within 300 yards of the enemy, and this they lie on their bellies till a chance offers, when crack! goes a Minié, and down falls a Russian. I was informed most credibly that one of these brave fellows a few days since thought he would go and do a little business on his own account, got away from his company, and crawled up close to a battery under the shelter of a hill, lay on his back and loaded, and turned over and fired, when, after killing eleven men, a party rushed out, and he took to his heels, but, sad to say, a volley fired after him by this party, levelled him with the earth, and he was subsequently picked up with thirty-two balls in his body. A party of Russian sharpshooters made a sort of attempt to come up to the battery by the Marines, but a few well-directed shot from that gallant little body sent them back again, having taken nothing by their motion.

Lieutenant Maxse, Aide-de-Camp to Lord Cardigan, was severely shot in the foot and ankle, and was carried onboard his Lordship's yacht, the Dryad.

He was close to the unfortunate Captain Nolan, of the 15th Hussars, who was shot in the breast while cheering and gallantly charging the enemy, and who, after getting off his horse, made two or three staggers forward, and fell dead.

Whenever during the day you saw any of the Turkish soldiers, you saw the people hooting them and calling them cowards and runaways. I witnessed two Irishwomen actually driving four of those chivalrous gentry before them, making them carry some things for them, probably to their own wounded husbands, and saying, "Eh! Ye cowardly devils, this is all you're fit for, to be our servants; sure you are afraid to fight," and on our return I saw a young Middy [Midshipman] drawn up before some fifty of them, abusing them most heartily for having run away. One of them made a sign as if he was going to draw his sword, when master Middy sang out, "Oh," said he "I'm not afraid of you, such a set of cowards as you are," set his legs a-kimbo and then stood, the picture of a young lion, and, I should say, about as brave. Lord Raglan, after the Gray's charge, sent a message down to be told to the men, that he had never seen anything more brilliantly, or gallantly executed. Had our Turkish friends only spiked the guns before deserting them, it would have been far less disastrous; but that our own guns should be made use of, with our own ammunition, against us, and that through the cowardly conduct of these men, for whom we are sacrificing England's best blood and treasure, is too provoking and discreditable to write about; and I am sorry to say that, not content with deserting their posts, they plundered every thing they could lay their hands on, even to the very breakfasts which some men of the Grays were preparing for their officers who were then out in face of the enemy. The universal feeling is, that a very severe example should be made of this flagrant act of cowardice, the probably results of which will be another hard-fought battle, with a possibility of evacuating Balaclava!

The charge of the Light Brigade of Cavalry on the batteries of the enemy, some thirty guns strong, though brilliantly and bravely done, was most disastrous in its consequences to that gallant and devoted band, for it seems that out of 700 who went into the fray only 130 answered their roll when it was over; and it appears to have been done under a misapprehension of an order from the Commander-in-Chief. Lord Cardigan pointed this out to his superior officer the immense difficulty of charging a battery, flanked by another, into a sort of *cul de sac*, with the hills lined with rifles and guns; but, receiving the *positive order to charge*, at it he and his splendid Brigade went, and as they approached within a few hundred yards of the big battery a shell burst close to him, and struck Nolan in the chest, which caused the poor fellow to scream awfully, and his horse turned and galloped to the rear, when his gallant but impetuous rider was found lying dead. The Light Brigade still kept sweeping on till they were right in front of then, when a 32-pounder went off within two feet of Lord Cardigan's horse, quite lifting him off the ground, but he got in among then, and was, where he always will be when it comes to the point, in the first rank. It seems they rode right through the guns and turned, after killing the men that was serving them. Lord Cardigan was attacked by two Cossacks, who with their lances, gave him several pricks, and rather staggered him in his saddle; but his Lordship being well-mounted, and a good cross country rider, parried their thrusts, and escaped with lance-pricks in his legs.

Oct. 26 – To-day numbers of the wounded were sent onboard different ships in Balaclava harbour, and a most mournful sight it was to see the poor fellows carried down on stretcher, some minus a leg, others an arm; one with his face battered to pieces, another with a sabre cut in the back of his head.

Letter from an anonymous bandsman in the 5th Dragoon Guards 'who was formerly in the employ of Messrs. Brooke & Sons' of Huddersfield to friends in Huddersfield and 'read by John Brooke, Esq., at the Patriotic Meeting'.[131]

> Before Sebastopol,
> October 1854.

I wrote to George up to the 6th day of the siege, and its proceedings, which I suppose you have seen. We have been firing away as hard as possible, apparently with little effect. To make a long story short, we lost but a few men each day until the 25th instant, when the enemy attacked us in rear. They came in great numbers early in the morning, while we were cooking our breakfast. Most of them were Cossacks – they then attacked the Turks, caused them to give way, and took seven cannon from them. We, of course, were close up to Sebastopol, and they down at Balaclava, about six miles behind. They ran and gave the alarm to us – then you would hear the bugles sound "Stand to your arms!" The sound was quickly obeyed, and every man appeared both willing and pleased to meet the enemy. Off we marched the six miles in search of the enemy. When we got there the Russians were in sight; but I shall never forget the sight of the morning. Our Light Cavalry had advanced an hour before we reached the scene of the action. They had already charged the enemy, and they being too few in number for these Cossacks, they also charging before our infantry and artillery had arrived to their assistance, they were cut up like mince-meat, for cavalry are no use whatever in the field without infantry for their support. It was a foolish charge, and dearly they paid for it with the loss of the great part of our fine light cavalry. Although they lost so many before we got there, they had managed to re-take the guns the Turks had lost. If half the British troops had been there, they would not have lost the guns so soft. Well, when we got there, the cavalry were retiring in great numbers – all of them wounded, little or more; some without arms, others cut and mutilated in a shocking manner; some without horses and horses without riders. You would have pitied the horses, and to hear the soldiers talk and pity, and some of them curse again; others would say, "Bill, did you see my poor mare shot? Ah, poor beast, I was so sorry. My poor horse had its belly shot right away by a cannon ball, but I saw Jack So-and-So shot dead, so I took his horse and I mounted him, when both its hind legs were taken away by another shot, and at the same time half-a-dozen of them d[amne]d Cossacks got around me (excuse me, in using his own words), but I managed to send two of them to pay their reckoning with the loss of their heads. At last one of the – made a slapping cut at me, and took away one of my trotters, so I must hop to Old England with a wooden leg. No matter Doctor, I shall soon be well." That was the sort of conversation these brave fellows were using in the front of death. Well, onwards we went, when bodies after bodies lay one against the other, English and Russian, only some dead and others dying. Oh! it was dreadful to look on. It was our turn next to attack them – there they stood and there we stood facing them – not a stir for a few moments. They might have done great damage to us, but their soft hearts failed them. At last we were formed in three long lines, one behind the other, with our artillery on the right. The sight was imposing to look on; just like three red walls, so firm and stout, and every countenance looking so anxious to get a slap at them. Behind every regiment was its respective band, but not so clean and flash as we were at home; but our white coatees besmeared with dirt and smoke, so dirty, that if you saw me now you would not speak to me; and instead of our instrument, to cheer them up, we carried those frightful-looking articles, the stretchers, and a doctor along with us, every man not knowing but he might be the first carried on them. At length silence was broke by the report of their large cannon. We, of course, quickly paid them back with the same coin, shot after shot; and there we stood, balls flying over our heads, as firm as if we feared no death. They did not hurt for a long while; at last a ball struck a man near me on the arm and knocked it clean off. We were too far off to fire small arms, so they then also stopped firing, looking how they should turn to get a better advantage of each other. We stood looking on the enemy till dark, then we retired under cover for the night to our camps; they, too, made off up the mountains. We managed to get home about o'clock at night, safe and sound, another day, thanks be to God. We lay all the day after pretty tranquil till night came on, when they again made a rush on the French camp. Our First Division fortunately was close up to their backs. The Russians thought, as before, as it happened with the Turks, that we were four or five miles from them, but they were mistaken, and well we let them know it, for our men marched stealthily and steady along, unperceived by the enemy, and when they got near enough they let fly a volley of British pills which struck them with alarm and astonishment; they could do nothing, for we had them in the briers for once, and the affray last only a short time; we lost a few men only that were in front on the look-out. The enemy lost a vast number, and a great number of prisoners. I cannot tell the exact number of killed, for we cannot tell what is lost only in our own regiment for a certainty, although in the same field there are so many different stories – every man has his own yarn. I am very sorry that I gave you the wrong number of killed in the battle of the Alma; it is impossible for a man in the field to tell, only the official writers.

We are lying in tents at present, and highly we value them, especially in wet weather; yet, it is only every third night that we can sleep in a whole night, and then perhaps the Alarm would sound "Stand to your arms," for at two o'clock in the morning we have to go down to the trenches to support the big guns that are on the batteries there. We lay down in the trenches till about four o'clock the following morning. We then are relieved by another party who takes up our places. These trenches are about one and a half miles in length before Sebastopol, and big guns are placed at intervals, so you can see that if the Russians came out to attack our cannon, we should have only the old proverb. "Up Guards, and at them," for the enemy could not see a man of us till they were on top of us. We lay quiet and still all night and day, not scarcely allowed to speak for fear the enemy would hear us. Everything that is carried on in the way of shifting ammunition or men is done in the night. Some nights we meet parties of mules which reach a mile in length, and Turks, Arabs, and Tatars driving: they say to us "Bono Johnny" twice over. Sometimes the 28 hours that we are in the trenches are not miserable enough, for it rains to pouring, and we have not the least shelter. There we are like half-drowned mice, and nothing to eat to warm us but out water that we take with us, and our biscuit, for we cannot cook our meat there; also, our clothes must remain on till dry, for we have not a change with us. Yet, I can say with truth, that I am satisfied; I am cheerful and merry, and my spirits quite lively in the midst of all dangers and privations, for I really believe it a good cause, to maintain for England her future safety, and if that is the case, the God of Israel will be with us. I will also tell you that it was always my wish to go into the field of battle to witness what I have often read of. My ambition is now satisfied, but I am not in the least sorry. You might think I am when I tell you that my clothes have not been off my back since I left Corfu. The cannon reports are quite familiar now to my ears. It is now the 2nd of November, and the mail goes for England to-morrow. I will finish now, for I have had to steal a few minutes every day to write this, for time is very precious, also paper; so I will conclude with my love to all. Good bye; good by[e] all. Mistakes forgive, and all may be well yet.

Letter from Trumpet-Major **William Forster** (number 581), 1st Royal Dragoons, to Mr. J. Hurst, Chapel Bar, Nottingham.

Camp, Near Sebastopol,
Dear Sir, -   Nov. 2nd., 1854.
I have no doubt that 'papers will have told you by this time of our cavalry action on the 25th October – one of the severest actions on record. We were in the saddle a little after three o'clock in the morning, as we are every morning, and we stood to our horses until about six, when we were ordered to mount and to move forward, as the enemy were advancing in force.

I must now explain our position to you. In the first place we were encamped on a large plain surrounded by hills. On the right of this plain lies the harbour of Balaklava. About three quarters of a mile to the right and left front of the harbour were place two English batteries, and in front of the battery to the right were placed the 93rd and 42nd Highlanders, and to the left of them, facing the village of Camara was a Turkish battery, and on another hill to the left of them, facing the Black water,[132] was another Turkish battery. We advanced and were halted under these batteries, and the first intimation we had of the enemy's approach was by their round shot being fired into these batteries, and by many of their shot coming over the hill and into our ranks, killing one man and breaking the legs of many of our horses. The Russians advanced their Infantry and drove the Turks out of these batteries, and we retired to the other side of the plain to let them come from the hills and have a fair fight, and they were not shy in embracing this opportunity. There were two more batteries to the left of the Balaklava plain, overlooking a plain on the other side called Black Water Valley. From these batteries the Turks retreated, without spiking their guns, before the Russians could come up to them, for which their commanding officer was shot the next day by sentence of Court Martial. As I said before we retired across the plain, and the Russians threw our their Cossacks, and they skewered the Turks as fast as they could handle their lances. Our Light Dragoons advanced and drove the Cossacks back. They then advanced 3,000 of their Regular cavalry. These were our opponents. The heavy cavalry were ordered to advance; the Greys were in front. The Russians came on boldly and were met as boldly by the Greys, and then the cutting and slashing commenced; but they were so numerous that they surrounded the Greys, and when the Royals saw that they could not be restrained they gave one loud shout and let us at them, and without waiting for the command of officer or any one else away we rushed as hard as they could gallop at the enemy, and it became a frightful scene of slaughter. The Russians had to turn tail and run for it, driven back by the Greys and the Royals, and as soon as the enemy began to the retire, the Greys and Royals turned round and greeted each other with a real British hurrah. Two Hussar regiments of the enemy then made a most desperate charge upon the 93rd and 42nd Highlanders, and, by Jove, the Highlanders brought them down in hundreds, and they were soon glad to retire from there, leaving the ground strewed with their killed and wounded. The Russians then retired to the Black Water valley; that was a plain also surrounded by hills. The enemy had a battery on both sides of the plain. They were the two batteries taken from the Turks, and they now had an opportunity of turning our own guns upon us, and at the end of the plain they had a masked battery of 21 guns. Before these guns they had a regiment of Hussars. These, the Light Brigade were ordered to charge, which they did beautifully, and when they got near the bottom of the plain the Russians moved on one side and opened their guns upon them, and out of 700 that advanced to that charge only 195 returned. It was the most tremendous fire I ever heard of. There were the batteries on both sides of the plain, and the 21 guns at the end of the plain, all throwing their shot and shell at the same time. The Heavy Cavalry were then ordered to advance which we did in the face of that fire and got half way across the plain, but the fire was terrific, and the men and horses kept dropping so fast, that they gave us the order to retire. The French Chasseurs d'Afrique charged the Russian battery on the left and silenced it, which relieved us considerably. The French then threw out their skirmishers, but the enemy would not advance, and this closed the action of the 25th.

Colonel Yorke, Captain Elmsal,[133] Captain Campbell,[134] and Lieutenant Hartop[135] were wounded.

Letter from Sergeant **Charles McGrigor** (number 993), Scots Greys, to his brother in Greenock.[136]

	Crimea, Camp at Balaklava,
Dear Brother, -	2d. November, 1854.

Agreeable to your request, I hasten to let you know that I am alive and well, which you consider the more important when I inform you that, on the 25th of last month we had an engagement with the Russians which lasted fully two hours.

The whole of the cavalry parade every morning at five o'clock, and on that morning, as usual, we were in front of our lines, when the enemy opened fire upon one of the batteries which was manned by Turks, who fled, leaving the enemy to possess himself of the same. Emboldened by their success, in the course of twenty minutes the Russians came cheering over the hills in thousands – both horse artillery, cavalry, infantry – driving the poor Turks all in front of them. Only the British cavalry were at hand, and we were a mere handful them, but we were not to be done; our light brigade formed into line and charged them with vigour, though, poor fellows, they suffered severely; so the heavy brigade made the second charge upon them, swords in hand, waving them over our heads, cheering as we went. When within two yards of our enemy, they fired upon us with pistols; but ere they could get them out of their hands, we [were] into them with our swords like very devils, laying them low at every blow. On both sides the fighting was severe and the slaughter dreadful; here and there might be seen one of our men surrounded by half a dozen Russians, and the next moment two or three of his comrades flying to his assistance, leaving them lying dead on their horses' necks or cruppers, for being strapped into the saddle, they could not fall from their horses; and after peppering each other for some time, they retired.

We were highly praised for our gallantry and brave fighting. The Greys had two men killed and forty-four wounded, and also our brave Colonel, though, I am happy to say, but slightly; opposed to this, it is affirmed to us here that we killed five hundred. In our troop we have one man killed, sixteen wounded, and one officer.

The weather is getting cold, and this, with a bad pen and having to lie on the ground, will account for this scrawl. We are all under canvas, and don't expect to get out of it before Christmas. The siege of Sebastopol has been going on for nearly a month now, and we expect it will be stormed soon, and during the operation we anticipate another go in with the enemy in the rear, which will finish it for the present.

The French and we are great friends, they are in our tents every day; but we do not like the Turks, they having run away at the last battle and allowed the enemy to get upon us before we were altogether prepared to meet them. We have been reinforced by four thousand French troops; and it is said that our army here from the three empires is a hundred thousand strong.

Letter from Troop Sergeant-Major **Richard Lawrence Sturtevant** (number 868), Scots Greys.[137]

Camp, Balaklava,
2nd November 1854.

On the 25th morning, the Camp, being alarmed by hearing firing from the outlying picquets, in a short time we were in the saddle, and advanced with artillery. On arriving at the hills immediately in front of the village of Balaklava, we found a large Russian force advancing. The artillery commenced, and fired with shot and shell, which was kept up for some hours, both from forts and the Horse Artillery. The Russians, however, still advanced up the hills. The Turks fled from the forts without even spiking their guns, which the Russians used immediately upon us. The Cossacks soon came down the hill at the charge nearly into our Camp. Our cavalry, the heavy brigade, were, however, ready to meet them, and in which encounter the Greys and Enniskillins [*sic*] had the first of the encounter, in which a great many Cossacks were killed and wounded. You will receive officer details respecting the battle with this letter, so I will now soon close. I have no doubt but you and the inhabitants of Nottingham will find that the Greys did their part, although with many casualties; for we have four officers wounded – viz., Lieut.-Col. H. Darby Griffith, Brevet Major Clarke, and Cornet Handley,[138] all very slightly, with Cornet Prendergast with a wound of foot. The three first were not so badly hurt as to hinder them from their duty the next day. We have killed, Corporal Clifford and Private Henry Campbell, and Private Thomas Traill since dead; and 52 wounded, about one-third very seriously. Twelve horses killed, nine missing, and 20 wounded.

The Light Cavalry Brigade, in an encounter against the enemy's guns suffered severely, as also ours. The casualties in the Light Brigade are – 10 officers killed and 10 wounded; 14 serjeants killed and 8 wounded; 4 trumpeters killed and 5 wounded; 125 killed and 109 wounded men; with the loss of 293 horses.

On the 26th and 27th an encounter took place at Sebastopol. The enemy advanced out of the town, but were driven back with great loss of killed, and many prisoners. From the 17th to now, day and night, Sebastopol has been bombarded.

As I write lights and fires are ordered out. I now finish this at daylight, 7a.m. The cause of alarm proved to be a number of Russian horses, having broken loose and galloped to our Camp. It, however, made us saddle and be up all night. Something decisive is to be done to-day I believe. I now start of the post, having to go six miles, and the box closes at nine, so I cannot write more.

3rd November, 7.a.m.[139]
As I have five minutes more, I may say that since the affair of the 25th, the Turks have been looked down upon by all, and every one when he meets one shouts "Turks, no bono." The French are a lively set; and, although it was thought that the eagle upon our dress would still promote enmity between us, such is not the case, for they come to our watch fires and tents with a salute of "Bon English," and familiarise with us and try to make us understand them as much as possible, that they are now our brothers, and fighting for the same cause.

Provision ships come to the harbour of Balaklava, but everything is too dear for the soldier. Only fancy, bottled porter 3s 6d. per bottle; sugar, 1s a lb.; salt and flour the same; a box of lucifers, 3d; potatoes, 21s per cwt.; and other things equally dear.

The Russian army this morning have struck tents – with what object I can't tell; some think to leave the place altogether, others to make a movement. The ground this morning looked like covered with snow; but the sun, which soon sheds it rays over this fine country, makes things look smiling again. While I write this the bombardment is being carried on very heavily.

Letter from an anonymous Captain of the Inniskilling Dragoons.[140]

Camp near Balaklava,
Dear Jack, -   Nov., 2, 1854.
... I am, you see, alive at this date, but God knows for how long after. You have, I presume, devoured all the accounts which have been sent home as to our glorious charge. Oh, such a charge! Never think of the gallop and trot which you have often witnessed in the Phoenix Park when you desire to form a notion of a genuine blood-hot, all-mad charge, such as that I have come out of- with a few lance prods, minus some gold lace, a helmet chain, and Brown Bill's [the charger's] right ear. From the moment we dashed at the enemy, whose position, and so forth, you doubtless know as much about as I can tell you, I knew nothing, but that I was impelled by some irresistible force onward, and

by some invisible and imperceptible influence to crush every obstacle which stumbled before my good sword and brave old charger. I never in my life experienced such a sublime sensation as in the moment of the charge. Some fellows talk of it being "demoniac." I know this, that it was such as made me a match for any two ordinary men, and gave me such an amount of glorious indifference as to life, as I thought it impossible to be a master of. It would do your Celtic heart good to hear the most magnificent cheer with which we dashed forward into what P— W— calls "the gully scrimmage." Forward – Dash – Bang – Clank, and there we were in the midst of such smoke, cheer and clatter, as never before stunned a mortal's ear. It was glorious! Down, one by one, aye, two by two fell the thick-skulled and over-numerous Cossacks and other lads of the tribe of old Nick. Down, too, alas, fell many a hero with a warm Celtic heart, and more than one fell screaming loud for victory. I could not pause. It was all push, wheel, phrensy [*sic*, frenzy], strike and down, down, down, they went. Twice I was unhorsed, and more than once I had to grip my sword tighter, the blood of foes streaming down over the hilt, and running up my very sleeve. Our old Waterloo Comrades, the Greys, and ourselves, were the only fellows who flung headlong *first* in the very heart of the Muscoves. Now we were lost in their ranks – now in little bands battling – now in good order together – now in and now out, until the whole "Heavies" on the spot plunged into a forming body of the enemy and helped us to end the fight by compelling the foe to fly. Never did men run so vehemently – but all this you have read in the papers ...

I cannot depict my feelings when we returned. I sat down completely exhausted and unable to eat, though deadly hungry, and wept. All my uniform, my hands, my very face were bespattered with blood. It was that of the enemy! Grand idea! But my feelings, – they were full of that exultation which it is impossible to describe. At least twelve Russians were sent wholly out of the "way of the war" by my good steel alone, and at least as many put on the passage to that peaceful exit by the same excellent weapon. So also can others say. What a thing to reflect on! I have almost grown a soldier philosopher, and most probably will one of these days, if the bullets which are flying about so abundantly give me time to brush up.

My Dear Fellow, our Countrymen have not tarnished their fame in the Crimea. Gallantry and glory will never abandon the march of Celtic bands – never! Oh that I could have the patience to write you of such deeds of individual heroism as have come within my notice! Fictionists are shabby judges of true bravery. No novel had a sham hero who comes up to the realities I have witnessed. One of my troop, for instance, had his horse shot under him in the mêlée. "Bloody Wars," he roared, "this won't do," and right at a Russian he ran, pulled him from his horse by the sword hand in the most extraordinary manner – then deliberately cutting off his head as he came down, vaulted into the saddle, and turning the Russian charger against its late friends, fought this way. This took less time to do than I to tell it. I saw another of our fellows unhorsed, and wounded, creep under a Russian charger, and ran the sword up his belly. The animal plunged and fell on its slayer, crushing him to pieces ... We must take this doomed place, even as O'Grady says, if we be doomed who take it. Any one of our fellows is a match for three Russians. ... The Light Cavalry charge was a desperate but grand affair. Lord Raglan is blamed. The general belief is that Nolan gave his orders *literally* that the cavalry were to *attack*. Lucan is a regular fire-ball, but not mad enough to have done that without strict commands ... we want reinforcements very badly; without them we cannot continue to contend against fearful odds.

Letter from Private **James Prince** (number 1133), 5th Dragoon Guards, to his parents.[141]

Balaklava,
Nov. 3.

Dear Father and Mother, -

You must excuse me for not writing oftener. The paper, pen and ink is very scarce to be got, and time I have very little. I have been striving every day for the opportunity. I am very busy. I am in an enemy's country, and in sight of the enemy; one in front, and one in the rear. We had several scrimmages with them on the 25th of October. We had a general engagement, from seven o'clock in the morning until nine o'clock in the evening, under a continual heavy firing, and as hot as ever was known for any soldiers to be among. The first thing in the morning the Russians came up. We had the Turks on our main batteries on the outposts. The Russians rushed upon them, and they ran away, and the Russians took the batteries. We had very few of English infantry there at the time, but two Highland Regiments and all the cavalry, both heavy and light. The Russians came rushing upon us, about ten to one, all cavalry. We met all, sword in hand, and we all met in the charge. There was a great slaughter. There was some being with their heads half off, and some with their bowels out, and some with their legs shot off, with cannon balls and bomb shells dropping and sweeping half a troop of horses down at a time: the horses saved us the most, because they was undermost [*sic*], and they was in the most danger. But I escaped with God's mercy. We lost two men, and nine wounded. One that was killed my brother David knows very well. He is Corporal James Taylor. David can tell his friends about his accidents. He fought well till he dropped from his horse. He got his arm cut in eight places, and shot in the left side. The Light Brigade lost a great number of men and horses, especially the 4th Light Dragoons. I have been in Russia one month. I landed on the 1st of October, and I have been under canvas since. The British Army is suffering very much with fatigue and cold weather. The weather is very cold.

I shall be very well trained to hardship if I ever had the luck to come home. When I was in Turkey my health was very bad. I never was well all the time I was there. We have been cannonading at Sebastopol eighteen days. To-day we expect to take it by storm, with the point of the bayonet. Sebastopol is one of the strongest fortified places in the world. The French and the English have been bombarding these eighteen days. The French are very good soldiers, and very kind and good-natured. They will do anything for the English. They fight to the last man for the English. The Russians came on us several times in the middle of the night, and we all had to turn out. But the French laid a plot for them, and they have never disturbed us since in the night. The French made it up with some of our riflemen and Highland regiments, and they moved from their camps about a mile nearer the Russians, and kindled a great many fires. So the Russians thought to have a fine grab when they saw the fires. They came up as usual. The French retreated a certain distance from the fires. Upon which the Russians came up, and saw nobody there. They then came on further from the fires: the French could see them quite plainly between them and the fires. The French now went to work, and fired into them, and shot a great many as they retreated. The rifles and Highland regiments then came up behind them, and gave them a great beating, and then the cannon fired upon them, and made a terrible slaughter among them. The Russians are great cowards, always striving to take a mean advantage.

I cannot give a proper account of Sebastopol. We have been firing at it these last nineteen days. We are very busy: I cannot have time to wash a shirt. I have washed all my clothes ever since I came out. We are all very dirty, and in front of the enemy. I have suffered a deal of hardship since I left my own country. We have lost a great many men. We have lost forty-seven men with sickness, and three officers; and two men got killed. In all, what died, both what was killed, and died of sickness, is fifty-two.

If you get another letter from me after this one I shall think myself safe. My letter will be delayed about six days on account of the post only going five times a month. Send me a few stamps and wafers. I received your letter and stamps, and your newspaper. It is a prize to see a newspaper out here. Write back as soon as you can. Send a good envelope on your letter, so that I can turn it to do another, and send it back to you again. Pen, ink and paper is bad to be got. You that are at home do not know what I suffer abroad, or any other British soldier; but I have made my bed, so I lie on it: but a bed is the strangest of anything to me. It is nearly six months since I was on one.

I will give you a proper account of the war in my next letter, if God spares. Till then, give my kind love to all my brothers, and inquiring friends. I am glad to hear that you are all very busy. Sickness I know too much of: I hope it will soon cease. Accept my kindest love, my dearest father and mother.

Letter from an anonymous 'sergeant of the Scots Greys, a native of Edinburgh, and who was slightly wounded at Balaklava', to his mother.[142]

Scutari Barracks, Constantinople,
4th Nov.

Dear Mother, -

On landing in the Crimea we were struck by the general resemblance of the country to some part of England. On the second especially we seemed to be back in Hampshire, and riding through the New Forest. We had been marching slowly through the wood all day, when in the afternoon we suddenly came upon an army of Russians, just sitting down to dinner. At the sight of us the whole of them decamped as fast as they were able, leaving behind them everything. We pursued them for about three miles, and killed and took prisoners a few who had gone into a thick part of the wood to escape observation; and so they might have done, but, seeing only horsemen, they thought themselves secure where they were, and commenced firing. A part of us immediately dismounted, went into the wood, shot five or six, and the rest gave themselves up prisoners. We had another day's marching, and halted in the neighbourhood or Balaklava, near which we have been ever since, shifting a mile or so occasionally, just to change the ground, which soon gets very dirty on accounts of the horses. During the time that we have been here we have had innumerable alarms and sham fights, with a large force of Russians collecting in our rear, and daily getting strong.

On the 25th of last month they attacked us in earnest, but before you could understand my story I must describe the country. Looking from Balaklava, you look upon an extensive valley that stretches right and left of you, rising with a gentle slope, in all directions, and looking like a sheet held up by the corners, and dropping in the centre. Over the hill to the left front lies Sebastopol, and beyond the heights to the right front are the Russians, while on the extreme right, at the head of the valley, is a village that we had taken everything out of, from a haystack to frying-pan. Along the heights to the right front we had three batteries at little distances from each other, and another at the village. Beyond these batteries, there is another narrow valley separating them from a low ridge of hills, on which we had several times seen the Russians. The purpose of our being in this valley was to secure the means of retreat to the shipping at Balaklava, and to prevent this army of Russians in our rear from annoying the besiegers of Sebastopol. To accomplish this, there was left in the valley the whole of the cavalry, and the 93d Highlanders, and a number of Turks to man the batteries.

Early in the morning of the 25th, we heard heavy firing up at the village, mounted immediately, and went to see what was up. The Turks made a brave resistance at this point, being nearly all killed before they gave in, and we could give them no assistance. Having had some men and horses killed and wounded by shells that were fired amongst us, we retired a little out of the range of the guns. No sooner had we done so than we could see all the other batteries deserted by the Turk, and them flying along the hills, pursued by Cossacks, who were sticking them with their long lances in all directions. We retired a little further then, to get away from our own guns, which were opened upon us by the Russians as soon as they took them. The Russian infantry were followed up by their regular cavalry, who came upon us about four times our number. Close to Balaklava is another fort manned by Turks also, and as the whole shipping would have been at the mercy of the enemy if that had been taken, we proceeded to support the Turks at this point, in case they would run away here too, when the Russians, thanking that we were also running away, came down the hills as bold as Hector, to clear everything before them. We got the word 'Wheel into Line;' and the trumpet sounded 'gallop.' We have a hurrah and dashed at them in a charge, without any command, and rode over them and through them and back again, cutting and hacking them. Completely frightened, they galloped away helter skelter, and never stopped till they were on the other side of the hill. Sir Colin Campbell came up and gave us great praise, as the Russians, besides having the advantage of the hill, were four times our number at least. When the Russian infantry saw their cavalry flying, with us at their heels, they got afraid too and retired, leaving us our own batteries except the one at the village. In order to cut off this detachment from the Russian main body, we very foolishly, without waiting for our infantry which had been sent for at this time, went down into this narrow valley that I have spoken of before, but by the time we got about the centre of it, the enemy had their guns posted on the opposite hills and opened a tremendous fire upon us from our left, our front and right – the balls and shells flying about us like hail, and whistling like steam-engines. Horse and men fell on all sides, swimming in blood. We went 'threes about' and retired, and, when just feeling thankful to have escaped, a spent cannon-ball [*sic*] struck me in the ribs, and knocked me off my horse. I scrambled on again, and wondered whether I was killed or not, for I could scarcely breathe. All the wounded were sent away at once that very night, but I am perfectly well again, and will very likely be back in time to see Sebastopol taken. For the present I am as happy as a king, but I am to be off to the Crimea next week.

Letter from 'a Worcester man in the Scots Greys' to relatives in Worcester.[143]

> The Heights before Sebastopol
> 8th November, 1854.

... A mail being about to leave for England to-day, I take the opportunity to inform you how we are progressing with the bombardment of Sebastopol. This is the 23rd day of the siege and the French and our firing is as brisk as when we first commended. It is astonishing how a place can stand such a battering. There is no mistake but out people greatly underrated the place. They were going to settle it in three or four hours, but I think they have caught a Tartar. The Russians must have great resources in the place, for it we knock down and silence a battery one day, the next morning by daylight it is replaced and peppering into us as if nothing had happened. The French have advanced now close under the walls of the town, and it was expected we should have stormed it a day or two back, but owing to an engagement having taken place between our forces and the Russians on Sunday last, November 5th, it has been, I think, postponed for a time. Lord Raglan has been very averse, I think, to storming throughout. In the actual bombardment of the place we have lost very few men, our batteries being so well constructed. The Russians have lost a great number, so many that twice they sent out a flag of truce to us to cease the bombardment that they may have time to bury their dead, and a few hours were granted them. If we have to storm the place I have not doubt it will be at a great sacrifice of life, for the Russians fight very resolutely. They have their streets barricaded at every turn, and so much time has been given them, that large reinforcements have come up in the rear, and so soon as we storm Sebastopol the force in the rear will attack us, and as they are equal to us in numbers, and have a very powerful artillery, it will, I have no doubt, be dreadful work.

On the 25th of last month the Russians attacked us in the rear. The Turks guarded our outermost field-works and batteries, and fought away pretty well at first, but the Russians still advancing, the Turks took to their heels like so many sheep, and never stopped till they were in a place of safety. Through this several pieces were left in possession of the enemy, and they thinking they had it all their own way, advanced three squadrons of cavalry towards Balaklava, to take possession of the place, which is the key to our position; but here the 93rd Highlanders were formed up in line ready to receive them, and well peppered then. The 93rd were ordered to form into a square, to receive the cavalry, but they exclaimed – "No, no; let us receive them in line as men," and instead of the cavalry dashing through their ranks, they wheeled to their left, and retreated, when within twenty yards of our men, evidently not liking the look of the petticoats, after Alma. It was a beautiful sight to see the Highlanders; they were as firm as if on a parade at home. On their retreat, the Russian cavalry were charged by our regiment (Scots Greys), the 1st Royals, and 6th Inniskillings. It was the first time they had been engaged, and they behaved well. Our regiment had one corporal and one private killed, and about forty wounded, a great many of them very severely; and some have died since. They were all immediately sent on board ship for Scutari, so we have no particulars. Immediately after this the enemy retreated to their former position, leaving our batteries again in our possession; and now a fatal mistake occurred. Captain Nolan, one of the Aide-de-Camps, brought an order from Lord Raglan for the Light Brigade of Cavalry to charge and recover some of the enemy's batteries. It was misconstrued by some means or other. Captain Nolan was told to reconnoitre, to see if other batteries were in the way; but instead of that he led them, with Lord Cardigan, up the valley to the mouths of the guns, when a tremendous cross-fire opened upon them, and cut officers and men down like grass. Captain Nolan was the first to fall. The Light Brigade was cut all to pieces – a tremendous slaughter! I shall never forget it; I was up at the front at the time. Balls and shells were falling in perfect showers around us, but, thank God, I escaped injury. Lord Lucan was wounded in the leg by the bursting of a shell; his horse was also wounded. His Lordship and his staff were riding on top of the hill overlooking the valley; a ball came and cut Lord William Paulett's cap right across the top, within an eighth of an inch of his head, and then entered the side of Captain Charteris, a fine young officer, aide-de-camp to Lord Lucan, and his nephew, who fell dead on the spot. I can assure you there were some narrow escapes.

It is very hard work for all, and more than any of us expected. I suppose we shall winter out here now; it will be tremendously cold, but no one knows positively what will be done till Sebastopol falls into our hands. It is no joke sleeping under canvas, with nothing but your cloak and blanket. The days are warm enough, but the nights very cold, with heavy dews; and before long the rainy season will set in, so if we do not do something soon, I don't know how we shall manage. I must conclude as the post is now closing. I hope this will find you all in good health. I am first-rate now.

Letter from an anonymous private in the Inniskilling Dragoons, to his brother in Bristol.[144]

Camp, Balaclava,
19th. November 1854

... If I can assure you that writing has been altogether out of the question, for I have never any time scarcely to pull my boots and spurs off, and our horses often saddled for three or four days and nights together, standing to our horses heads all the time, or lying down on the damp ground, which is anything but pleasant, and perhaps wet through. Still, dear brother, thank God, I am in good health and spirits; never was better; but I am sorry to say many of our men are sick and dying from diarrhoea, caused by the cold and inclemency of the weather, for the winter is beginning to set in, and under canvass is no joke. But please God I hope to return one day and spend some pleasant hours together, and I shall be able to tell you many a tale you would scarcely believe or credit.

Of course, you have seen in all the papers. We had a glorious go at the Russians on the 25th Oct.; a day I shall ever re-member [*sic*] while I live. We charged them, and such cutting and slashing you never saw. The swords were flying about our ears as if by magic, but we drove them back in queer style, and we only lost three men killed and about fourteen wounded, that is our regiment; for myself I escaped without a scratch, and I was in the centre, and many a rapid cut and thrust I parried, and you may be assured I returned them with good interest. There is something grand and exciting in a charge; you brace up with all your nerves and prepare yourself for a mortal combat with weapons that when wielded with skill form a noble and beautiful science, but it is not very pleasant to have showers of musket-balls whistling over your ears.

We are about four miles from Sebastopol, and our guns are constantly playing on them, and have the last month. I am afraid it will be a long siege, and God help us if we stop here the winter without going into quarters. I little thought when I was with your last winter, and we were joking together, I told you that I would send you some Russian heads, but God knows there are some thousands here. It is sickening to see them. God grant we may never see a way in our country, for I can tell you it is awful. When we can here first, near two months ago, it was a beautiful country with miles of vineyards, and splendid grapes in large clusters, nuts, apricots, and all kinds of fruit, and nice houses. Now it is all in ruines [*sic*].

Letter from '**W.P.**', 1st Royal Dragoons, to his family.[145]

Dear Brother and Sister,-

Crimea, Balaklava,
Nov. 22.

I received your letter yesterday, and I was very glad to hear from you, as it is almost my only communication with England. You must excuse me for not writing oftener; but, situated as I am, it is almost impossible to write so often as I should like. I have been waiting day after day for Sebastopol to be taken, in order to send you the grand news, but it has take us in at an alarming rate. We have no been throwing shot and shell into it for 37 days; and there is no appearance of our taking it very quickly; yet Lord Raglan will not storm it, although several regiments have volunteered to do so. There are two forts we cannot play upon from the land, that is Fort Nicholas and Fort Constantine, neither can we play upon their shipping. I am at present about two miles from it, and almost deaf with the thundering of cannon night and day. Across the Crimea, about four miles from Sebastopol, is a body of Russians, reckoned at 45,000, who were increased yesterday by 12,000 more; these latter are supposed to have come from Silistria; they are very badly off. Some of our Light Brigade were taken prisoners; and, after ten days, one of them made his escape. He told us they were living in the open air, and three men were living upon one man's rations. Disease is also amongst them; in that lot they are dying at the rate of 120 per day. The English and French are also dying very fast; diarrhoea is carrying them off almost as quick as cholera. The weather is getting very cold, with plenty of high winds, rain, and snow. We are on the top of a very high hills, with no shelter but canvas; last week it came on a very high wind, and every tent was blown down, whilst we had to squat on the ground all night amongst snow and rain, and up to the knees in sludge and mud. I think it was the most miserable night that I ever passed. You may guess what it was when we found 25 horses dead in the morning from the severity of the weather. Thank God I am still alive yet, and have got better of the diarrhoea. We are sometimes three and four days without rations; but take them in general, they are pretty regular. I think nothing now of subsisting for days upon a piece of raw salt pork. We have very little accommodation for cooking, as the nearest wood is five miles off, and the water is very muddy. I blame the raw pork and water for so much diarrhoea. The French can make a very good meal of the rump of a shot horse, but I don't like such steaks.

The saddles are never off the horses' backs, for almost every day we have a skirmish. They generally attack us by night, or early in the morning. It is a beautiful sight to see the shells and rockets flying by night. We took a mud battery of 50 guns last night, within range of Fort Constantine. If we can keep it, we shall know in a few days how it will act. I have been in two general engagements, where the shot and shell were flying around me as thick as hail, and my comrades falling off their horses on either side of me, but thank God I am here still, and without a scratch. My first engagement was upon the 25th of last month. In the morning the Russians took four batteries from us, which were principally manned by Turks; afterwards the cavalry came in two bodies of about four thousands each, all of them Cossacks. The Scotch [*sic*] Greys, and 6th Inniskillings charged them. It was the first time I ever crossed swords with the enemy, and it was very sharp work, we having great numbers to contend with, all cutting and stabbing at each other. I never enjoyed such sport in my life; it was far beyond my expectations; I actually felt overjoyed meeting them at a gallop. We only lost three men in the charge, and a great number wounded. Upwards of 140 of the Russians lay dead. We took several prisoners, and the remainder went over the hill again like a drove of scattered sheep; we followed them over the hill, but the worst of it was to come. The heavy brigade had done their work, and the Light Division [*sic*, Brigade] was the first for the next charge. We followed for nearly two miles, down into a hollow in their own possession. They drew up 21 guns in front of the Light Brigade, and they poured the grape shot and canister into them to a great extent. They still advanced, and charged the guns, cut down every gunner, chased the cavalry supporting them into the side of the hill, and cut them up to a man. Immediately, a large body of Cossacks came round the corner of the hill, charged them in return, took back the 21 guns, and forced them to retreat, and in doing so opened a fire upon them from the 21 guns, besides two other batteries in front of them. Lord Lucan would not let us charge, but kept us advancing at a trot, and sometimes at a walk, and even halted us for upwards of five minutes in the midst of the three fires. I did not feel at all comfortable standing doing nothing, and so many "Russian Pills" flying about; shells sometimes bursting not more than a yard over my head, and sending dust and powder down in my face, but no hard pieces. We all retired, leaving the Russians to take our wounded as prisoners. Colonel Yorke was wounded, and Captain Campbell, and all our officers but two; we lost in all about 100, and the Light Brigade lost 320. I have heard since, it was a mistake of orders between Lord Raglan and his aide-de-camp: he did not intend us to charge into the enemy's possessions. By the appearance of the field, when retiring, we could count eight Russians for every British dragoon dead.

Paper is very scarce with us here, but I think you have got enough this time. I am certainly obliged to you for your kind offer of clothing; but situated as I am at present, any more than what is on my back is of little use to me. Sometimes I have very bad shoes and dirty shirt; but the first chance I get of a Russian's kit, I'll serve myself with clean linen, and throw the dirty one away. We are all annoyed with vermin, and it is no use to try to wash them off in cold water, neither am I particular about slipping a good pair of boots off a dead one's feet, if I think they will suit me. I just received yesterday from a Minister a first-rate blue flannel shirt, because he saw me with a very dirty white one on, I having worn it ever since the last battle, upon the 5th, and I did not expect to have a change until the next, whenever that may be. I had almost forgot to mention the storm last week that blew the tents down, and wrecked five of our ships, between Sebastopol and Balaklava. The Rip Van Winkle went down, and all hands were lost but three; one of our men's wives went down with her, and £100 in her pocket. I must conclude this rather quick now, for I just hear a terrible cannonading commenced from our front batteries, and I should not wonder if it be a turn out.

Letter from '**W.B.**', 5th Dragoon Guards, to his brother in Leicester.[146]

Dear Brother, -

Camp Before Sebastopol, Nov. 22, 1854.

I now steal the few passing moments which it has pleased the Lord to grant me, in addressing these few lines to you; but I cannot speak as to the future. I have only received one letter since I came out, but have written three or four; but I cannot account for the delay upon the road, Dear brother, since writing to you last you will not be the least surprised when I tell you that I have been in an actual combat with the enemy, sword in hand. I can assure you that the annals of history never could tell, nor ever has been read of, such a battle. This took place upon the 25th of October, commencing at half-past six o'clock, a.m., and terminating at 6.30p.m. They took one battery from us, which was held by the Turks, who fought bravely, but were compelled to retire, they, the Russians, having no less than twenty men to one of theirs, the Turks. The Russians have splendid artillery, which told greatly upon the small handful of men we had that day. We had no infantry, excepting a part of the 93rd, who were stationed at the village of Balaklava. We retired back to our very camp-ground, on purpose to draw the enemy upon the plain below the Heights of Connemara [*sic*, Kamara]. They came down upon us in thousands. They had infantry, but were kept behind their batteries in reserve. The first play, after we retired from their guns, was to send about 3,000 cavalry to attack the infantry, which were at the village, which they though were Turkish infantry; but they were never taken in so much in all their lives. The 93rd formed square, and sent into them such a volley of musketry that they fell in sections, when they were glad to retire. The 93rd then opened out, and then went in the artillery, which did fearful havoc. This was the first movement.

The next was, to send about 6,000 Cavalry, what he, the Emperor, calls his Imperial Guards, with a regiment of Cossacks, who came down upon the retiring Turks. They killed a great many with the lance. Our regiment formed the centre of our line – the 6th Dragoons on the left; the 4th on our rear; and the Grey's upon the enemy's right flank. They kept advancing upon us until they were within a very few yards. Then came the tightening of the reins, and grasping of swords. The 4th Dragoons got the word "Charge!," the Greys being upon the right flank. The 6th Dragoons were immediately surrounded. Then came *our* turn. Our impetuosity was very great to assist our comrades, who in a few moments would have been cut up. The next moment there was a shout and a cheer, and the 5th "Green Horse", dashed into the enemy's ranks, who soon made their blades strike fire in the air. For fifteen minutes there was nothing to be heard but the clashing of steel. Then the next movement was the retiring of the enemy. Some you would see with heads falling off, and arms broken at the charge. I felled two at once, by leaping my mare upon two of the Russians, when they were upon the point of retiring. Both horses and men fell never to rise again. I had often read of battles being fought, but never could it compete with this! To think of 500 cavalry attacking three efficient regiments! I never expected anything but immediate death. To see the columns which were advancing upon us! We remained upon the field of battle until nine o'clock the next morning.

The Light Cavalry were ordered to advance in rear of the enemy they succeeded in reaching the enemy's rear, and taking possession of 21 of their guns; but they could not retain them. It was a sorrowful movement for them: they got between the enemy's guns, and they kept up a tremendous cross fire upon them, which cut them greatly up. You could see nothing but dismounted soldiers broken-legged horses. We were ordered to advance to the relief of them, but the cannonading was too hot. We lost a few horses going to their relief. Poor J. Hill lost his life. He was killed by a grapeshot [*sic*] and was an awful cut up. I can assure you that it wants a stout heart to meet such an enemy as cannonballs.

Dear Brother, we have had some very rough weather here. Sometimes we cannot get any food, for not being able to light a fire. Not tents to cover our heads; everything wet through. Dear Brother, I can assure you that we are very near eaten up with filth and vermin. I have never had a clean article upon by back this two months; and as to washing my face, I may do so once in about fourteen days. The water is a long way from our camp, and sometimes we have none; so this will give you a little insight of how we are situated in this country. I believe that we are going to be encamped all winter. Well, if so, God help us, I say; for I am confident that the cold weather will take a great many of us off, not having anything to nourish the body. Sometimes we get a drop of coffee, without sugar or anything in it, for nourishment. Then we will get some salt meat, as dry and as salty that you have hard work to force it down. This is not half to what I could say. We are still hammering away at Sebastopol. They intend storming this month, sometime; but they have been for doing it for so long a time now, that I am tired of hearing about it.

Dear Brother, I have not seen my cousin since we left – . Let me have a few lines from you, immediately; as I am very anxious to hear from some of you. Give my kindest love to all my relations and receive the kindest love that your brother can give to all; and may the Lord bless and protect every one of you from all danger, is the best wish from your affectionate brother.

Letter from Trumpeter **Thomas Monks** (number 832), Inniskilling Dragoons.[147]

Camp before Sebastopol,
Dec. 4.[148]

My dear Father,-
I know take the opportunity of writing to you, hoping to find you all well, as this leaves me quite well, thank God for it. I suppose you have been anxious

about me because I did not write to you before, but the reason was, because I could not get any paper to write on. I was very glad to think that the little present came in so good time for you. I hope mother is better than she was. I was very ill myself for about six weeks with the bowel complaint. I was in hospital till we came to this country, and after we landed I got better every day. I thought it was all over with me, it made me so very weak.

I suppose you have heard about the battle we had on the 25th of October. If you could see the "Times" of November the 12th, you will see a very good account of our regiment, and the old Scotch [*sic*] Greys, who made a grand charge against double their number. The heavy brigade got great credit for that day; but I am sorry to say the light brigade got cut up. They lost about 600 men out of 800. It made me feel very much when we went out to cover them, to see them fall. It bought us under a very heavy cross fire from the enemy, the balls and shells bursting beside us. A ball [*sic*, shell] would burst under a horse and blow it to pieces, and never hurt the man. You would see men running back with arms off, and others bleeding from all parts of their bodies.

I can tell you, Dear Father, when one thinks about home, it is enough to make one cry; but I hope we will have sunny days for these yet. It is now December, and we are in camp yet. We had a great storm about a week ago. I was on Trumpeter's Guard at the time the storm came across the plain, accompanied with hailstones and snow, and it blew all our tents down. The only way to keep still was to lie down. I had to do so for fear of being borne amongst the dirt. You may think in what sort of state our tents were, as after it was all over, we had to lay down that night on the wet ground without anything to eat, the cooks being unable to keep the fires in. We had our grog and a bit of biscuit at night. Ever since then it has been very wet and cold. Our poor horses are dying by sections every day, and Sebastopol is not taken yet, though we have about seven weeks' hard firing at it. The Russians often make a sally out, but are driven back again. The Russian shipping is all that they can fire from, but we can't get at it yet. I was on picket the other day; we have to stay out all night with our horses, and it was very wet and cold. I don't think we can stand this much longer, but still we all keep our spirits well. I only hope we may get one more charge at them and finish it. I must now conclude for the present time ...

PS. The guns are firing away now. We about two miles off them, but we can see the flash and smoke.

You may guess what sort of state we are in when I tell you I have not had a chance of washing my face these four weeks, let along having a clean shirt. We are, I am sorry to say, in a state of filth, but we do the best we can.

Letter from Lieutenant-Colonel **John Yorke** 1st (Royal Dragoons), to his sister Etheldred Yorke.[149]

On Board the Arabia, Constantinople,
Dec. 5th 1854.[150]

In answer to your enquiries relative to the Balaklava Affair, I will give you an outline. Very early in the morning we advanced across the plain to our front, where the Turks held the redoubts and we had the mortification to see them all fall into the hands of the Russians, with very little resistance we thought, on the part of the Turks, in looking on on this work, we were what is erroneously called supporting the Turkish Batteries, that means we were so placed closely in the line of fire, that all the very large shot (32 lbs) that overcrowned the heights naturally bowled like cricket balls into our ranks, we should have been equally useful if we had been formed a few paces clear of the line of fire, but it was not so, the large shot came down upon us. The officers could easily escape: we had only to move our horses a few yards, to let the shot pass, which movement we effected frequently, but when a shot came opposite the closely packed Squadrons it generally took a front and a rear rank horse, and sometimes a man, or a single horse. In *this foolish manner* we lost 2 men and seven horses, but when the evil had passed (we suppose to prevent a re-occurrence of the same), we were sent to the rear and packed in enclosed vineyards. We had no sooner done so than the Russians entered the plain. We then advanced at once thro' the vineyards and at last, the advanced Regts., the Greys and the Inniskillens [*sic*] were fortunate to get on clear ground and with Genl. Scarlett dashed into the Russian cavalry. The 4th, 5th, & Royals came up as 'The Times' says, like 'an arrow from a Bow', which gave no appearance of an encircled affair but in justice the Inniskillings & Greys turned the Enemy before any of us actually arrived on a level with them. We then came upon stragglers, wounded men, & loose horses which were captured or cut down, but there was *no* 'Flank Charge' as appears in Lord Lucan's report, for I came up on the *left* of the Greys, though I was in the rear of everything, a few moments before. The Royals therefore do not deserve much glory in this charge, for they had the misfortune to be in support but we replaced our lost horses of the morning with Russian ones & were satisfied as the affair was perfectly successful, but the Greys and Inniskillings did all; the 4th, 5th nothing more. It is wonderful however what a vast deal is said about this charge, & it is fortunate as it counter balances the misfortunes of the Light Brigade & afford satisfaction to the Public & brings Honor [*sic*, honour] to the Heavy Brigade, *but* there is in truth a deal of *humbug* even in Battle, & the Pen, a fine language, smoothes [*sic*, smooths] the events & makes men appear great afterwards tho' their brains are in confusion during the affair.

After this there was a good deal of movement & we thought we might get back to breakfast. I put a sticking plaster on the Gen. Scarlett's hand, as he had a slight sword cut, when to my surprise the Royals & Greys were ordered to advance under one of the redoubts which had been abandoned but not taken by the Russians, just as I passed under it the Magazine blew up, & covered me with sand, as soon as they cleared off. I found myself in the now famous 'Valley of Death' & the Light Brigade just in front advancing at a more rapid rate than ourselves. The rest of the Heavy Brigade tho' stated to be likewise here, on Lord Lucan's report, were safe in the rear, for it was only Royals & Greys this time, & in a few moments we were in the hottest fire that was probably every witnessed. The Regts. were beautifully steady, I never had a better time on a Field Day, the only swerving was to the thro' the ranks the wounded & dead men's horses of the Light Brigade, which were even then thickly scattered over the plain. It was a fearful sight, I assure you, & the appearance of all who retired, was as if they had passed through a heavy shower of blood, positively dripping & saturated: & shattered arms blowing back like empty sleeves, as the poor fellows ran to the rear, during all this time there was a constant squibbing noise[151] around me, proving even in these improved days of gunnery what numbers of shot do no take effect, however another moment & my horse was shot in the right flank, a few fatal paces further & my left leg was shattered in this fearful manner. You know the rest.

Letter from Sergeant **David Gibson** (number 947), Scots Greys, to his parents in Glasgow.[152]

Scutari,

Dear Parents, -   9th December, 1854.

I now write you a few lines letting you know that I am quite well again. I have no doubt you will have seen by the 'papers that I was wounded on the 25th Oct. at Balaklava. I received seven wounds on that morning; but thank God that I am as well as ever again; I received a lance wound from a Cossack; and two swords cuts on the left hand, right hand, left arm; and two cuts on the head, one across the brow, which I will shew [*sic*] you when I come home. I am going up to Sebastopol tomorrow again, in the hope of giving some Russian a drubbing for the way they served me that morning. On the night previous to the engagement I was on night duty, and a little before daylight we saw the Russians coming over the hills in thousands; we had no infantry near us whatever but a few Highlanders, but they did their duty like men. The Turkish infantry ran like fury, and the Russian cavalry came at full charge on the kilties; but they gave them the rout very quick. We were coming to their assistance, but when we looked to our left we saw about five thousand cavalry coming on our rear. We received the order ' Threes About,' faced them, and went off at a trot to meet them; the trumpet sounded 'Gallop', then 'Charge,' and we were cutting our way through them like Greys when we received the word to rally again. I was on the left of our regiment, and somehow, when we were coming back, about twenty Russians surrounded about four of us and an officer, but they all managed to cut their way though them but me. I was in the centre, cutting right and left, when a Russian came in rear, and gave me such a clip on the bearskin that it came off my head, then I got two cuts on the cranium before I was aware of it. I thought it was all up with me: I was getting faint with the loss of blood, and quite blind, and to complete their task one gave my sword a crack and sent is spinning out of my hand; but God brought me out from them in his own way. Some of the men saw me, and came to my assistance, and the Russians, cowards they were or they would not have pressed me so hard, fled. I was led to hospital, and that is all I know of the fight of Balaklava.

Letter from a 'Private in the 1st Royal Dragoons – a Native of Wrexham'.[153]

Balaklava,
Dec. 12th.

I have been in the Crimea since the latter end of September, and I am going to let you know what I have gone through since I left Turkey. The day we sailed out of Varna bay was very stormy, and it took us eight days going up, which we could have done in two days had it been fine, and we were that near wrecked that we gave ourselves up for lost. 180 horses belonging to the regiment were lost. After we landed near Sebastopol we were camped in the rear of our infantry, on purpose to cut off the Cossacks from advancing on our infantry. We used to have many a skirmish with them, but on the 25th of October I had the honour of witnessing a field of battle. We were ready for saddle night and day, so on the morning of the 5th [*sic*, 25th] we had three batteries a little in front of us, to give us warning if the enemy was advancing; so this morning, about six o'clock, a salute was fired, and we were all immediately in our saddles, advancing towards these batteries. Ours were manned by the Turks, who ran away. The Russians got into these batteries and fired into us; then we retired out of their range.

There were about 30,000 Russians, when there was only ten regiments of ours, cavalry, and three companies of the 93rd Highlanders. So when these Russians saw us retiring the though we were afraid, and two regiments of their cavalry went at a gallop towards the Highlanders. They thought they were Turks, but the gallant 93rd opened such a fire upon them that you could see them falling out of their saddles like old boots. They turned threes about, and away with them back, looking like fools at one another. When they were going back our batteries opened a fire of grape upon them, which cut them up like turnips. When they say that that would not do, a large body of their cavalry advanced upon us, enough in number to swallow us up. "Never mind, boys," said Lord Lucan, "we will meet them directly." So when they were about 100 yards off, we got the word to charge at a gallop. Mind you, when we were nearly at one another, I was rather timid, but, says I, here goes for death or glory. As soon as we charged, you should have seen how the cowardly scamps turn round – away they went and we after them. So when we came back we were at rest until about one o'clock, when Lord Raglan gave the order to advance and charge the guns. The Light Brigade then advanced; there was a twenty-gun battery and two flank batteries playing upon us. But oh! it was awful to see the cannon showering upon us, there were shells, grape, and canister shot flying about like hailstones – it was awful to see – I never thought to come out of the field alive. That day Colonel Yorke had his leg broken by a shell. We had four officers and seven men wounded, and two killed. The Light Brigade got cut up awful, with their cannon. We were brought up again into the field on the 5th of November, but we were not engaged. E.H. is all safe after the awful fire he was under. I saw C–, of the 55th – he is quite well.

Letter from an anonymous private in the Inniskilling Dragoons from Peebles-shire.[154]

My Dear Mother, -
Camp Before Sebastopol,
Dec. 17, 1854.

I received your letter the other day, and a treasure it was to me. I was happy and thankful to God for the health and spirits you all seem to be in. J – [censored]'s letter I never received; in fact, campaigning as we are, on night here and another night away, in an enemy's country, you cannot expect postal arrangements to be very efficient. For the last three or four months we have been campaigning around Sebastopol, – that is, we have been marching and countermarching, driving back a very superior enemy, and undergoing all the dangers and vicissitudes of actual warfare.

You must have heard of our engagement at Balaklava, a most brilliant affair in the language of the press, but a most horrible event to the mind of a sensible, thinking man. This Balaklava is a small seaport village, but fortified. At this village we effected a landing – first the infantry and artillery, and, lastly, the cavalry. There were a few shots fired, and Nicholas' old forts began to totter – a smothered yell of revenge from the Russians and the village is ours. To us it was, and is, a valuable position: a spacious harbour contains all our transport and provision ships, and the village is only a few miles distant from Sebastopol, so that provisions and ammunition can be landed and forwarded to the sieging [*sic*] parties at Sebastopol, provided the weather is anything tolerable. Of a British winter you have an idea, but of a Russian winter you have no conception; and here we are, lying on cloaks to cover us, and half protected from the weather by our canvas tents; thousands of our men, both infantry and cavalry, are already useless. What with salt provisions and dry biscuit every day, and a constant exposure to wet and cold, the scurvy broke out amongst them and is playing dreadful havoc. Thanks be to God I never enjoyed better health, and I ought to be doubly thankful for escaping the many skirmishes, and more particularly that engagement at Balaklava.

We had awoke from our sleep, fed and saddled our horses, when in came our videttes or out-lying mounted sentries, with the cry of "The Russians are coming!" and in no mistake they were coming over the heights, about three miles distant. Lying before us on some smaller heights are some thousands of Turks, manning three batteries. The Russians come direct towards them; "pop" goes a gun, and then the sound of many; on goes the cannonade for about ten minutes, and then all is silenced. The smoke clears away, and we see the cowardly Turks running towards us; on comes the Russian cavalry, about 10,000, riding and cutting them down in hundreds. Between Balaklava, the point they were making for, and us, direct to our left, is a long red line, steady and immovable. The Russian and Cossack ride direct towards them. Elated with their easy defeat of the Turks, they think the game is their own, but what a mistake! There is a movement in the line, and a thousand Minié rifles from the gallant Highlanders empty the saddles of the dismayed Russians; and now comes our turn. "Do your duty, Inniskillings!" and in we go, along with the Greys, right into their centre; for a moment or two we are bewildered, but we soon recover, and then commences the work. It was awful. Too horrible to relate – suffice it to say, that after 20 minutes hard work they gave way and fled. We form up, Lord Raglan addresses us, heaps upon us laurels, and thanks us for our conduct. We retire to our camps, such of us are left, and all is over!

Letter from Corporal **John Selkrig** (number 807), Scots Greys, to friends in Dublin.[155]

Dear Friend,-

Cavalry Camp, Kaidkoi, 22nd December, 1854.

I suspect that you, long before this, will have imputed to me a "breach of promise," but you must not set it down to neglect, nor yet to forgetfulness, but to want of time and opportunity. 'Tis true that I was inactive in Kulalie for nearly six weeks before coming to the Crimea, but had little then to write about. I now take a rare opportunity to let you know a little. I am (thanks to Almighty God) in good health, and escaped as yet without a "scar." I need not trouble you with particulars of any of the engagements, as I have no doubt you have read all the accounts in the papers. I will only state that I was in the action at Balaklava, and early in the morning got my horse shot under me. I had only time to take off my carbine, leaving my kit to the Russians, and retire with the regiment. I soon caught another horse belonging to the 1st Royals, whose rider had been killed, and though not a "grey" he bore me through the great and successful charge[,] which I see so much spoken of in the English press. I exchanged immediately after with an officer of the 1st, who had picked up one of our horses. That charge must have been a fine sight to a looker-on, but we, who were engaged, had no time either to look, or think, as it was only the work of a moment from the time we formed in front of them, till we were among them. We were taken completely at a disadvantage, and could scarcely get our horses into a canter – whereas they were in full charge and down-hill, but we could plainly see them waver as we came to close quarters. A great many of the papers give quite a wrong account of that affair, *as there were none engaged in it but the Greys and Inniskillens*; but had the Light Brigade or the other regiments of the Heavy [Brigade] come up and flanked them, as I see it is stated in some accounts that they did, we could have either killed or taken prisoners ten times as many as we did; had the Russians stuck to one another as they ought to have done, scarcely one of us could have returned, as we were completely surrounded. As it happened we escaped remarkably well. We had only *two* killed on that day, and between forty and fifty wounded – a few of which have died since. But it was not in the Charge that our men suffered most. It was when we went down the valley to the support of the Light Brigade. We had got down a good way when we were halted right in between three cross-fires, besides being within musket shot of their infantry. It was the most awful sight I ever witnessed. The shot and shell flying about us and bursting among us in a most fearful manner; had we been riding quick through we would not have noticed it so much, but to be halted in it was awful in the extreme. A shell burst on a man's horse's crop, close to me – tore all the flesh of its hind quarters, cutting through the back part of his saddle and through his valise, and tore off his leg below the thigh. He has since died. There were many hair-breadth escapes, and it is only wonderful to me how we escaped it all. It was truly providential.

When we first arrived in the Crimea we had beautiful weather – very hot during the day, but very cold fogs during the night. We had no tents, and had to sleep in the open air for about a month, when the weather began to break. We then got our tents, but even then, in spite of all our precautions, they have been frequently blown away. The weather has been very coarse and wet this long time, and our horses are dying very fast. We are burying three or four almost every morning, and our "Bonny Greys," which were at one time the admiration of all in the Crimea, are now reduced so much that a man has many a time to look at the number on his collar or foot before he can recognise his own horse, and we are waddling up to our knees in mud for them. We have commenced to build stables amongst them, but our time is so much employed with our other duties, and the weather will not allow of our working much, so that I am afraid that we will have very few horses to put in them when they are finished, if ever they are. Sebastopol is still in the hands of the Russians, and we are all sick of the stories we hear, and can place no credit in them. It has been to be stormed every day nearly since the siege commenced, and when it will be God only knows, but we expect to hear some news very shortly.

We are about five miles from Sebastopol, close upon Balaklava, and our principal duty now is carrying up provisions – biscuits, &c. – to the lines in front of Sebastopol, and our own forage from Balaklava. We are expecting to winter here, and I believe there is lots of warm clothing coming out to us. We want it very bad, and the sooner we get it the better for me. Whatever they may do I do not think the horses will stand it, as they are very far through already, and we have had very little frost or snow yet, so I suppose we will requite a complete remount in the spring. The men are in general pretty healthy – a good many have been troubled with swollen feet and legs, and rheumatic pains, but that I think was principally owing to wet feet; we have now got plenty of boots and shoes, and I think we will now do much better. For our rations we get daily one pound of biscuits, one pound of salt beef or pork, coffee and sugar, and half a gill of rum in the morning and another in the evening, with sometimes a few potatoes. We can, for money, purchase a few luxuries, as they may be called here, in Balaklava:- Tea, 4s. per lb., sugar 1s., cheese 2s., and 2s. 6d., butter 1s. 8d. and 2s., ham 1s. 6d., brandy 6s. per bottle, porter and ale 2s., and other things *cheap* in proportion. I must now draw to a close, as my paper is near done, and the post leaves this afternoon. Remember me kindly to all my friends in Dublin, and let them know that many a pleasing reminiscence of the happy hours I spent amongst them floats across my memory in the dull routine of guard or picquet. I will mention no names, but with kind love to you all, wishing you all the compliments of the season.

Letter from Trumpeter **Thomas Monks** (number 832), Inniskilling Dragoons.

My dear Cousin, -

Camp before Sebastopol,
Dec. 17th., 1854.[156]

I received your kind and welcome letter on the 14th, and I was very sorry to hear that poor old uncle Joe was dead, but I hope he has gone to where we all hope to go to when we are called away from this world, to our Father which is in Heaven. I know very well that you will both feel it very much for awhile [*sic*], but we must all go some day. I have seen many a fine fellow go, who was all health and spirits, and in less time than I am writing this, I can assure you, my dear cousin, that last year at this time I little thought that I should have been in the battle-field now. I thought I should have had my Christmas dinner with you again; but the way things are in at present I have little hopes of seeing Old England again. Here we are in camp, and up to our knees in mud if we go out of the tent, and the inside of the tent is not much better, after we have all been out to the horses, and come back all over mud and dirt. Dear Cousin, I am glad to tell you that I am in good health at present, and I hope you are all well at home.

I suppose you read about battle in the paper. The 'Lancaster Gazette' gave a true account of it all. I hope you read about it. I tell you there were 3,000 Russian cavalry against us, and we only numbered 900, so you may think what sort of a battle it was. When our regiment and the Greys charged them, they tried to get round us, but our second squadron and the Greys, said one to the other, "do you see that? Come on", says the Greys to us, and at that moment we went right and left at them. After we charged them, each man had his work set out, for we fought hand to hand. Our regiment lost only two men and ten wounded. After we routed them, our Heavy Brigade dismounted for a while under the hill, but we got orders to advance after the Light Brigade, and that was where the "babies heads", as I call them, came hissing past our heads. You would see every man making a genteel bow as one came past us. We were right under a cross fire [*sic*] for a while that was when the Light Brigade got cut up so, we were covering them; it was a shocking sight to see some of them coming back cut up to pieces very near. I am thankful to say I came out safe. I believe there never was such a fight known before. We are expecting every day to take Sebastopol. They are erecting a new battery to play on the shipping, It consists of 21 guns, they call them Lancaster Guns; the Heavy Brigade are engaged taking up provisions to the army near Sebastopol, it is a dreary job, but then we know the poor fellows that have to lay for days and nights in the entrenchments, must have food, and this is the only way they can get it up because the roads are so very heavy with the mud. The only thing I do not like is going on out-lying picket, that is to watch the enemy all day and night, if it is raining cats and dogs we have to go. It knocks a great many of us off the hook. We have come down from the heights to Balaklava. We are in a valley. Before we came down the horses were all dying. They nearly all eat one another's tails and manes off;[157] they were nearly all starved, but they are coming round. It has been raining and snowing this last two or three days; it makes us all miserable, no fire to warm or dry us. I can stand dry weather very well, because we can then warm ourselves by walking about, but now we have hard work to walk being up to our knees in mud.

I must now conclude for the present. I hope the next I write to you that we will have taken Sebastopol. I believe it is ours at any time, only we want to take it without losing much life. I think we will get it for a Christmas Box. The Russian shipping makes great firing at our men, but they never do much damage. This is Sunday, but it does not look like Sunday to any one of us, because every day is alike to us; sometimes we do not know what day of the week it is. I only wish I may once more have the pleasure of going to church or chapel with any of you again. We all keep up our spirits very well, thinking we will have sunny days for these yet. The French and English soldiers have all turned against the Turks for being cowardly at the battle we fought so hard at. To see them run away made our blood boil to get at them. It was well for them they had a brave regiment to run behind, – the 93rd. To see *them* stand was a grand sight; they let the Russians know it was not the Turks they had to deal with, for as soon as they came to charge them they all fired a volley which made them glad to run back again; then after that we had a go in at them which made them call out for their Cossacks. I think our shout frightened them a good deal. I am very glad to say we fare very well considering everything. We get two glasses of grog each day, and we have all got a new Jersey shirt, a pair of flannel drawers, a pair of socks, and a pair of Long Turkish boots; long boots is the thing for this place. I wish I had a pair that would come above the knee. I am glad to say the scarfe [*sic*] you gave me comes in well, it keeps me warm. Now I think I have told you as much as I have room to spare, but I wish you would send me a few stamps and a sheet of paper and envelope, because it is a hard job to get them here. I don't forget Uncle Joe sending me them stamps. I little thought he would be dead by this time, but this is the time of year that would try him very much. I was very glad to hear that Uncle from Kidderminster was over; he did not know me. I suppose a great many often ask you about me. I was glad to hear that you told my father you had heard from me. I wrote to him since I wrote to Elizabeth at Preston, but got no answer. Give my kind respects to all acquaintances and friends, and accept of my kind love, and I hope Tom is better by this time. I often think about you; in fact, always hoping you may prosper and be happy, and I hope I will have the pleasure of telling you all about the war before long. No more at present.

PS Mind you write soon, and I wish you all a merry Christmas, and a happy new year.

Letter from Private **James Auchinloss** (number 996), 4th Dragoon Guards, of Maxwelltown, to his relatives 'on the other side of the Nith' in Dumfries.[158]

Camp Before Sebastpool,
Dear Parents, -   Dec. 27th, 1854.[159]

I hope this will find you all in the enjoyment of that inestimable blessing, good health, which none know better how to value than those who have suffered the pans of disease on the sultry heights of Varna, and now bear – under canvass [*sic*] the rigours of a Crimean Winter, with a powerful enemy in front, who loses no opportunity of harassing and annoying our courageous, but greatly over-wrought soldiers. Now, as I have a 'fair sheet of paper,' and a spare hour, I will endeavour to answer you with an account of things that have occurred, and part that I omitted in my last hurried scribble, which I am afraid you would scarcely be able to decipher. Well, as I hardly know what to begin with, I will write down what ever comes into my head first; and if it affords you any amusement I will consider myself amply repaid. I will begin with Sailor Jack, who is a private in my (F.) troop, '4th Dragoon Guards,' and one of the most amusing lads that ever reefed a topsail on sea or drew a sword on land. He combines the most remarkable courage with inexhaustible good humour, and often (when we have been sitting in our tents drenched to the skin) have his drolleries made the place resound with glee, and our sides ache with laughter.

On the 25th of October, Jack was about four files away from me in the ranks, and just when we had wheeled into line, off Jack bolted, and the rest of us with him; but, in consequence of the crowds of Russians, we had very little space for the use of our long swords. Well, Jack – who has a salve for every sore – finding he could not use his sword for a time, makes up to a huge Russian Lancer, who very politely 'presented' Jack with a pistol bullet, which he as politely 'refused,' by bowing to the pommel of his saddle, and receiving the ball in the hilt of his sword. 'Fair play, mate,' shouts Jack, and putting spurs to his horse, closed with the Russian, who was making off as fast as he could; and Jack, afraid of losing his prey, clasped the Russian with his left arm round the neck – or as boxers say, put his head in Chancery – and battered his face to a jelly with his sword hilt; then throwing him down, Jack went into the midst of them again, and I saw no more of him, as I was carried away among the retiring Russians, and had enough to do to make my way out from amongst them.

I have seen in various newspapers some very thrilling accounts of various officers and men who have signalised themselves in this campaign; and I can relate one which, though it may differ in its details from what would at Horse Guards be enrolled on the lists of 'Distinguished Service,' it is one which deserves to be remembered, and proves (to me at least) that there are other heroes than those whose heroism is built on the numbers slain by their own

awn by George Thomas and issued as a pair of prints by *The Graphic* (30 October 1875) to
mmemorate the twenty-first anniversary of the Charge of the Light Brigade, depicting a trooper
m the 8th Hussars 'charging to glory' and upon his return quoting Lord Tennyson's famous
em: 'Came through the jaws of death. Back from the mouth of Hell.'

populist depiction of Russian
ssacks by the French
wspaper *L'Illustration Journal
niversel* (7 October 1854), by
eir war artist Henri Durand-
ager, which appeared on the
nt page of the edition which
scribed the folly of the '*charge
la brigade légère anglaise*'.

The Charge of the Heavy Brigade – attack of the Scots Greys, as depicted by the artist of the *Illustrated London News* in November 1854.

The site of the Charge of the Heavy Brigade as depicted by a correspondent of the *Illustrated London News* in June 1855, looking towards Balaklava. The almost sheer faces of the heights on either side the valley are most apparent.

The bloody repulse of the Light Brigade by Cossacks by John Gilbert, issued as a commemorative print in 1854/1855.

The *Illustrated London News'* take on the charge of the *Chasseurs d'Afrique* – depicted here having already silenced the Russian artillery, attacking the infantry squares.

During the winter of 1854/5 the Cavalry Division found itself relegated to the humiliating and debilitating task of carrying stores from Balaklava up to the camp, a duty which sapped the morale and health of both men and horses.

An optimistic image from the *Illustrated London News* intended to bring comfort to the families at home, showing the troops in the Crimea how they were meant to be clothed – with thick furs and long boots. The reality was quite the opposite!

French soldier's depiction of his camp, January 1855. French cavalry horses were rugged up (unlike their British counterparts) and were also kept saddled in an attempt to keep them warm.

How the French saw British army recruitment during Spring 1855. Following the chaos of Winter 1854–5, voluntary enlistment into the army was at an all-time low. This led to an increase in the bounty offered to each man who enlisted and also the relaxing of requirements such as height and weight.

Spring 1855 came as a pleasant respite for the Allies – giving them a chance to reorganise, rest and recuperate before the Summer campaigning season began, as this sketch from the *Illustrated London News* clearly depicts.

During late Spring and early Summer of 1855, British and French officers attempted to resume their usual social life. Part of this were Steeplechases – here we see one such race depicted by the French newspaper *L'Illustration* – which proved a highly popular entertainment for officers and men alike with often considerable sums being won or lost betting on the outcome!

e Charge of the 10th Hussars at Kertch, 21 September 1855. A relatively unknown cavalry action
the Crimean War and one which nearly ended in disaster: two small squadrons from the
th Hussars had been sent on reconnaissance and were attacked piecemeal by Cossacks and it was
ly through 'repeated charges' that they could make good their escape.

French depiction of the Battle of Kanghil, 29 September 1855, where the French *4e Hussards*,
pported by the *6e Dragons*, charged a Russian artillery battery (supported by cavalry) in front and
t only captured the guns but routed the cavalry. Little-known in Britain, the charge of the
Hussards at Kanghil is one of the most celebrated French cavalry actions. The French cavalry
oughout the Crimean War consistently out-performed their allies.

The return of a *'Razzia'* or 'Flying Column' designed to sweep the surrounding area, to destroy crops and loot farms. This particular Allied *'Razzia'* was obviously a success: this illustration by Durand-Brager shows a motley mix of *Zouaves*, *Chasseurs à Pied*, *Dragons*, Highlanders and Heavy Dragoons all with comestibles and live animals.

Nine survivors from the Charge were the subject of a Benefit Concert arranged by the leading lady of her day, Mrs. Brown-Potter, held at the Palace of Varieties Theatre, London, in December 1900.

hands. Colonel Hodge,[160] commanding my regiment, was so ill that his life was despaired of, and he was left on board the 'Sans-Pareil', and was on board of her during the whole of the 17th of October – the day on which the shipping attacked Sebastopol. Well knowing that, as the attack had not the effect expected, the Russians would soon be down on us, who were so liable to 'surprise,' the Colonel came ashore and resumed the command, although at the time he was so reduced by sickness that he could not with safety leave his bed; yet, as soon as the guns began to fire on the 25th, we were all surprised to see our gallant commander come galloping to the head of his regiment and take command. Had you appeared before me, I could not have been more astonished. I kept my eyes on him for some time, and though pale and worn with sickness, he was as firm as a rock, and led us bravely during the whole of that disastrous day, never for a moment showing signs of fatigue, although I could at times observe a nervous twitching of the lips and chin which are the sure signs of great internal pain. Now, what does all this prove? Simply this, that our gallant commander looked upon health and bodily suffering as nothing, or as not having any claim on his consideration, when his country's cause required his presence. It is a lesson which ought to be treasured in our memories; and often when I have been inclined to grumble, I have said it is necessary for the good or our cause that I should do so and so, and I have gone and done what was required, if not cheerfully, at least without complaining – that is the lesson I have learn from him on that day. Sometimes or other I will give you an account of another of my heroes. Our hospital sergeant will be my next.[161] Queer heroes mine, eh?

I was highly amused with an article I saw in an old "Times" the other day. It was from the 'Special Correspondent,' who said he was an 'eye' witness of the heavy cavalry charge; but I much doubt whether he has an 'eye' or not, for he says the Greys and Inniskillings Dragoons charged in *the first line*. Now what does he mean by the 'first line,' I would ask? If the 'Corrspondent' [sic] of the "Times" knew anything of military matters, he would never have made such gross errors – I will not say mis-statements [sic], for really it was a want of correct information that caused him to give the account of that affair in the manner in which he did. I will tell you how we charged, and how we were placed when the Russians came upon us. After retiring out of range of the Turkish redoubts, which were in possession of the Russians, and, immediately after the Russian cavalry came over the hill to charge the Highlanders, when we came to our Front we were in Column, or rather, moving "en echelon" of Squadrons, left in front; and after getting through a vineyard, in which we were nearly bogged, we Changed Front to our Left, which brought us into Column of Squadrons. Now, as you may not understand these phrases, I will endeavour to demonstrate them, so that you can comprehend them in detail. "En Echelon" means a succession of parallel lines moving in an oblique direction, to the right or left – on that occasion we were inclining to the right – and when we Changed Front we were in Column of Squadrons which means a succession of parallel lines. Each regiment had two squadrons up, and there being five regiments, we had 10 squadrons. Well, while moving "En Echelon," the Inniskillings and 5th took too much ground to their right, which caused then, when we changed to the left, to be some distance to the right of the parallel, and when we Wheeled into Line our regiment was next to the Greys; and the

Inniskillings finding no space to act in front, attack the left flank of the Russians, whilst we, not five-seconds after the Greys attacked the front, charged the Russians' right flank; and, as Lord Lucan said, we fought more like devils than men. I enclose a piece of paper on which I have marked our movements "En Echelon" and Column of Squadrons; the 5th and 1st Royals formed the second line, and I hope you may comprehend their meaning, but I am no draughtsman, and for a desk I have my knees, and a large stone for a seat.

Letter from Private **Isaac Stephenson** (number 1011), 4th Dragoon Guards, to a friend in Lancaster.[162]

Camp, Front Sebastopol,
Dear Friend, -   January 3rd, 1855.[163]

You will think me very unkind for not answering you last before this; but then, you must excuse, for you must know how we are situated here for having time for doing those things. The weather here is both wet and cold, and we are still under canvass [*sic*] yet, with nothing to cover us at night only our blanket and cloak; and, when we get up on a frosty morning, you would think that we had been sleeping in the open field; and, after all that has been done for us by the good people of England, we have received nothing but one flannel shirt, one pair of drawers, and one pair of socks: they are very slow in giving out those that are sent for us, but, never mind, I hope that I will be able to pull through all, with the help of God. I was in hospital for 10 days with the bowel complain, but, thank God, I'm better, and hope that I will continue so.

We have had no more fights with the Russian since the 5th of November, though nearly every night the Russians make sorties out of Sebastopol, but are always repulsed back with great loss. The British have raised another battery, which they expect to destroy the Russian shipping with; and I hope it will, for they cannot storm the town until the shipping is destroyed, for it commands the whole place; and I believe that this battery opens to-morrow, the 4th inst. It is to be manned with 400 of the sailors onboard the "Queen."

Dear William, you would not believe the state that both Cavalry Brigades are in; to tell you the truth, there is not a horse that is fit to face a Cossack; and what they make us do with them now is to carry biscuit up to the front for the infantry, so now you see that we are Araba Gues instead of fighting soldiers. And, William, there is one thing that I want to mention to you, and, that is, about the assertions that are wrong concerning the fight at Balaklava: it was not the 6th Dragoons that charged in with the Scotch Grays [*sic*], but it was the 5th Dragoon Guards; and the Russians never gave way at all until our Regiment went into them. I could not do much execution myself, for my horse got unruly, and ran with me into the midst of the enemy's ranks, though I only got one slight cut on the arm, from a 'Cut 6,' by a Russian Dragoon, but he fell directly after, for, before that I could got to him, there was no less than three sabres of our fellows going on him thicker and faster, and me and my comrade was engaged with one each; but they got in a very short time what all the Russians may expect from a British soldier. And after we had repulsed them on this point, we followed them down the other valley, under a most raking hot fire, for both shot and shell rattled about our heads in all directions. They say that cavalry was never known to be under such a fire in any other battle that was ever known.

And now, dear friend, I hope that this will find both you, my mother, and sisters in good health. I'm much obliged to you for the newspaper that you so kindly sent me. Remember me to all inquiring friends, and I remain your sincere friend and well-wisher.

Letter from Trumpeter **Thomas Monks** (number 832), Inniskilling Dragoons, to the editor of the *Lancaster Gazette*, in reply to the letter of **Isaac Stephenson** (number 1011), 4th Dragoon Guards.

To the Editor of the Lancaster Gazette.   Camp, Balaklava,
Sir, –   February 23, 1855.[164]

Being a Lancashire man, and always feeling a pleasure in the perusal of your valuable journal, and especially when it relates to information respecting home affairs, I cannot refrain from doing what I consider my only duty in correcting any misstatement which may appear therein. In your publication of the 27th January is a letter from "Isaac Stephenson" but of what corps I am at a loss to know. I am well aware you will feel a delicacy in doubting any account of an engagement when given by one who appears to have borne part in it; but, at the same time, your informant should be as particular in stating only facts, and when he finds the same done by other and as good as authorities as himself, feel content in his belief of them, although they should not award to his regiment the praise to which he *individually* may consider it due. Had it not been a fact almost undeniable I should have taken no notice of "Isaac Stephenson's" letter, and much less thought it worth of contradiction, only that a very intimate friend of mine residing in Preston called my attention to it, and requested that the exact facts of the case should be stated. "Isaac Stephenson" states – " It was not the 6th Dragoons charged in with the Scotch Grays [*sic*], but it was the *5th* Dragoon Guards; and the Russians never gave way at all until our regiment went into them, we being the third Regiment what charged them."

Now, sir, this is about as consummate a piece of assurance as ever I heard of; for it not only contradicts the *reports official* of the general officers in command that day, but at the same time is an assertion which, *if present*, he must know to be incorrect. I will, for the information of those of your readers who are at all interested in the affair, explain to you why our regiment was the *second* in the charge – I should say *supposed* to be the second, for we were actually the *first*.

On the morning of the Battle of Balaklava, we advanced as the Heavy Brigade, "left in front", and had the nature of the ground allowed of it, the 5th Dragoons would have been the leading regiment, but the enemy's fire coming upon us from the redoubts captured from the Turks, we had been obliged to retire by alternate squadrons, and on this account the regiment *nearest* the enemy at the time of their advanced after being repulsed by the gallant 93rd, was the first to enter the charge. The Scotch Grays [*sic*] were undoubtedly the first to present a front to the enemy, but appeared reluctant to enter upon their duty without the regiment who had been before associated with them in deeds of valour, and who were then next to them, and perfectly willing to go hand and hand with them to face a powerful but equally cowardly enemy. This regiment, Sir, WAS the 6th Dragoons, and whatever corps Isaac Stephenson may be a member of, it he was present on that day, knows that this is the truth. We take no particular merit to ourselves for being the *first in*, but thank God we were so fortunate to *come out* with the loss of two men! As to the Russians never giving way until Isaac's regiment charged them must account for their making so speedy an exit, the whole of the brigade having barely sufficient time to come to the attack before they were "over the hills and far away." I am sorry in one respect Stephenson does not mention his regiment in the epistle to which I allude, as I then could have saved myself the contradiction of his statement by the request that he would do so himself.

It would appear selfish to devote the whole of a letter to this one point; – I will, therefore, give you what information I am able respecting the state of affairs at present. Sebastopol stands at present; but it is now reported amongst us that all the errors which have existed have been corrected, and that its speedy fall is certain. We are now being pretty generally accommodated with wooden houses, which are far more comfortable (especially as the weather continues very inclement), than the canvas tents. Our supply of warm clothing also has been very good, but the other creature comforts, which we have been so long looking and wishing for, cannot be disembarked on account of the scarcity of labour.

On the 20th we had a most extraordinary duty to perform, the object of which, to a certain extent, remains a mystery with every soldier engaged in it. At twelve at night we turned out, it having then commenced to rain and snow, and before we had proceeded far a severe frost attended us. So fierce was the storm that men dare not open their eyes, and their faces were actually covered with ice. Several of our regiment are now suffering from the frost-bite then received either in the ears or other extremity, and appear to suffer much. The enemy offered no opposition to our advance, which extended over quite five miles of their ground; but from the unfavourable state of the weather, we were obliged to return at about nine in the following morning, without having the satisfaction of even routing a party of Cossacks. This is the only adventure I have worthy of recording, but should you consider my letters worthy of insertion in your columns, I will forward you the particulars of any new features which may present itself, and which you may rely upon not calling for contradiction by any man of another corps.

Our railway from Balaklava to Sebastopol is progressing favourably, and it is stated will be completed before the end of next month. Should this be the case it will afford a better opportunity for us to enjoy a few moments, and likewise free the infantry from a deal of labor [*sic*].

Hoping that all friends in Lancaster are well, and that trade may continue to prosper, and also that I may once again have an opportunity of meeting those to whom I am known.

CHAPTER 5

Charge of the Light Brigade

'Damn those Heavies'

The officers and men of the Light Brigade had sat motionless as two Russian cavalry attacks had been repulsed: the first by the 93rd Highlanders, the second by 'Scarlett's 300'. Albert Mitchell thought that if the Light Brigade had been allowed to pursue 'we should have cut many of them up'.[1] Captain William Morris, in command of the 17th Lancers, was even more frustrated by their inaction, pleading with the Earl of Cardigan to charge, who rebuffed Morris' entreaties three times. This was later denied by Cardigan:

> 'My Lord, are you not going to charge the flying enemy?' 'No,' replied Cardigan, 'we have orders to remain here.' 'But my Lord it is our positive duty to follow up this advantage.' 'No, we must remain here.'[2]

Lord Raglan had ordered Cardigan to remain where he was to defend the position; the Earl of Lucan confirmed this but also added: 'You are to attack anything and everything that shall come within your reach, but you will be careful of columns or squares of infantry.' Obviously, Cardigan wilfully ignored the instructions given to him by his immediate superior, sticking to the letter of the orders issued by Raglan. Indeed, his version of events differs from that of Lucan:

> I had been ordered into a position by Lieutenant General the Earl of Lucan, my superior officer, with orders on no account to leave it, and to defend it against any attack of the Russians; they did not, however approach the position.[3]

These two conflicting accounts were written after the event, with both of their writers trying to clear themselves from any blame for the disaster. Cardigan also denied ever having received a note from Lucan reminding him that:

> Lord Cardigan would always remember that when he [Lucan] was attacking in front, it was his duty to support him by a flank attack, and that Lord Cardigan might always depend upon receiving from him similar support.[4]

'Cavalry to advance and take ... any opportunity to recover the heights.'

At around 10 a.m. Lord Raglan sent his third order to the cavalry:

> Cavalry to advance and take advantage of any opportunity to recover the Heights. They will be supported by infantry which have been ordered. Advance on two fronts.

The first part of the order seemed clear enough: because the Causeway Heights, topped with the redoubts manned by the Turks, bisected the Balaklava plain into two valleys, Raglan obviously desired the cavalry to advance, one brigade along each of the valleys, parallel to the heights. The second half caused some confusion. Lucan moved the Light Brigade to the entrance to the north and held the Heavies at the entrance to the south valley, waiting for the infantry 'which had been ordered' to arrive. Given that Lord Raglan issued his now famous 'fourth' order, which ordered to the cavalry to advance 'immediately' and 'rapidly' 'to the front', Lucan had probably not fully understood the order: Raglan intended the cavalry to advance and use any opportunity to retake the heights and that infantry was on its way and would arrive later. Presumably Lucan believed that he was to wait until the infantry arrived. Read in conjunction the 'third' and 'fourth' orders, it becomes clear that Raglan intended the cavalry to advance 'on two fronts', down the north and south valleys, and to attempt to re-take the heights, although what use cavalry would be against earth redoubts it is difficult to say. General Airey thought that the order was perfectly clear:

> The Brigade of Guards was ordered by Lord Raglan to advance to the redoubts, and Lord Lucan ... was directed to hold the ground with the cavalry till they came up.[5]

Thus, Lucan not moving his cavalry until the infantry support arrived was perfectly understandable. *The United Service Magazine* thought, however by 'some unaccountable wilfulness' by Lucan 'the cavalry never moved' which necessitated Raglan to send his 'fourth' order.[6]

This moment of inaction allowed the men of the Light Brigade a chance to snatch a hurried breakfast and have a quick smoke, much to the chagrin of Lieutenant-Colonel Shewell, 8th Hussars:

> I saw that as he passed in front of us, that all at once his face expressed the greatest astonishment. 'What's this? What's this? One, two, four, six, seven men smoking! Sergeant! Sergeant Pickworth! ... Sergeant advance and take these men's names.'[7]

The men of the 8th Hussars had been 'warming our noses with a short black pipe' and thought there was 'no harm in the matter'. The Lieutenant-Colonel, however, took a very different view and ordered Sergeant Williams and others to 'fall back to the rear' and 'take off his belts' in punishment.[8] Lord Paget of the 4th Light Dragoons had just lit up a cigar, and watching this display from Lieutenant-Colonel Shewell and pondered whether he should 'set a bad example' or throw away his cigar: 'The cigar carried the day.'[9]

Lord Raglan, however, was watching from the Sapoune Heights, probably with growing impatience at the inaction of the cavalry. A staff officer, who was forever to remain anonymous, mistakenly shouted out that the Russians were dragging away the guns on the Causeway Heights, and this triggered the 'fourth' (and final) order from Raglan to the cavalry:

> Lord Raglan wishes the Cavalry to advance rapidly to the front – Follow the Enemy and try to prevent the Enemy carrying away the guns – Troop Horse Artillery may accompany – French cavalry is on your left.[10]

The United Service Magazine, citing General Airey, suggests Lord Raglan was 'amazed at the inaction of the British cavalry' as he watched 'the light squadrons of the enemy scouring over the ground', and artillery horses moving up to the redoubts to draw-off the captured guns.[11] Raglan therefore dispatched his fourth order to the cavalry, but by the time Lucan had 'received this order, the enemy had actually carried off the guns, and re-entered his lines' so that 'the time for action had gone by, the guns could not be recovered'.[12] To attack, as the Light

Brigade did was 'impossible' and 'only to expose it to destruction' especially as *The United Service Magazine* emphasized, the order contained the phrase 'to *try* and prevent the enemy carrying away the guns': Lucan was to use his discretion and had not been ordered to attack.[13]

Raglan's nephew and ADC, Somerset Calthorpe, had been next in line to carry his orders, but Raglan chose Captain Nolan instead. Calthorpe noted that his uncle and General Richard Airey both gave Nolan 'careful instruction' as to the meaning of the order, so that if questioned, Nolan would be able to provide any further clarification. As Nolan turned to find his horse, Raglan fatally shouted after him: 'Tell Lord Lucan the cavalry is to attack immediately.'

Captain Nolan

Around 11 a.m. Captain Nolan cantered up to the Earl of Lucan carrying the order from Raglan. Their conversation has caused controversy ever since. Letters from eyewitnesses from the Light and Heavy Brigades presented in this book cannot agree whether the two officers did have the heated exchanged as reported by Kinglake. Crucially it appears in *The Times* before it does in letters home, which might suggest letter writers were influenced by what they had read in the newspaper. Those who do mention it tend to agree that Lucan demanded from Nolan where the Russian guns were and Nolan showed him with an outstretched arm. One cavalry officer from the Light Brigade 'who knew the ground' in a letter to *The Morning Chronicle*, however, states that it was not possible from where Lucan and Nolan were to see the Russian battery at the end of the valley. This is confirmed by the Earl of Lucan who stated that 'neither enemy, nor guns were within sight'.[14] W.H. Russell of *The Times* also agreed that it would have been 'impossible' to see guns at the end of the valley or on the heights from Lucan's position.[15] Agreeing with the version of events as described by General Airey, that the situation on the ground was changing whilst Nolan was carrying the order to Lucan, Russell wrote that:

> As an eye-witness of the scene, I may here state that the Russians had succeeded in carrying off our guns out of the Turkish redoubts before Captain Nolan had well left the plateau and got down to the plain where the cavalry were stationed. ... I had been looking through my glass at the Russians drawing our guns away from the back of the redoubts, and retiring with them toward the rear of their lines.[16]

One anonymous private from the 1st Royal Dragoons believed that Nolan had been sent to reconnoitre, whilst a second observer believed Nolan had reconnoitred the Russian position before giving his order to Lucan whilst a third suggests that Nolan and a few men from the 11th Hussars went to reconnoitre during the exchange between Nolan and Lucan, so ascertain where the 'guns' referred to in Raglan's order were.[17] Lucan, writing to exonerate himself during spring 1855 wrote that 'After carefully reading this order I hesitated, and urged the uselessness of such an attack' but Nolan informed him they were Lord Raglan's 'positive orders' and he was to 'attack' immediately. Lucan believed Nolan had behaved disrespectfully and impertinently toward him, but 'so positive and urgent were the orders delivered by the Aide de Camp, that I felt it was imperative on me to obey'. Subsequently, Lucan denied having had any 'altercation' with or grudge against Nolan.[18]

One 'Travelling Gent' who was watching from the heights thundered in a despatch to the *Daily News*:

> Those in High Places assert that Captain Nolan who had to convey the orders, mistook an order to charge in the flank for one to charge in face of the batteries. Capt. Nolan may or may not have made a mistake, but one thing is clear ... is that if the order was as insane, as it is acknowledged to have been, why did Lord Lucan or those in command execute it?[19]

The same writer also believed, that through his death, Nolan was made the perfect scapegoat because 'dead men tell no tales'.[20] This was a view confirmed by other officers in letters home.[21] Lawrence Godkin, the 'Special Correspondent' for the *Daily News* also believed Nolan was being made the scapegoat; so too did his editor: 'Dead men cannot defend themselves; and this fact seems to have suggested the idea of casting the blame on a dead and voiceless man ...'[22]

The *Daily News* was convinced Nolan was innocent and the guilty parties were those who tried to cast blame upon him; furthermore the real culprit, they argued, was Lucan because 'the order conveyed by Captain Nolan was in writing' and he had misconstrued the order 'advance' for 'attack'. Furthermore, Lucan failed to use his discretion over the important word in the order 'try'.[23] The 'Special Correspondent' of *The Morning Chronicle* went further, calling the charge 'wilful murder'. It too was sure of Nolan's innocence, and that Lucan should have sent a request for further clarification to Raglan. Furthermore, *The Morning Chronicle* suggested that 'the noble earl was influenced by the petulance or eager spirit of the aide-de-camp' into making the charge, suggesting that Lucan's judgement was suspect.[24] The outspokenly Radical *Reynolds's Newspaper* laid the blame on Raglan for his poorly-worded, ambiguous orders 'which render them incomprehensible'.[25] *The Manchester Times* vociferously agreed.[26] Lieutenant John Image (21st Foot), writing on 27 October, thought that Nolan had given Lucan the 'wrong order': '"That he was to charge and retake the batteries" instead of "That Lord Cardigan was to use his discretion, and charge if necessary."'[27] A similar view was taken by the editor of the *London Standard* that the verbal order sent to Lucan ordered him immediately 'to storm the Russian guns with the Light Cavalry, *if* the manoeuvre was practicable' and that Nolan had, in the heat of the moment, mistakenly omitted 'if ... practicable'. The 'Special Correspondent' for the *London Standard* out in the Crimea, however, admitted that the details could not be verified but that his version of events were 'implicitly believed here'.[28] The same 'paper later changed its argument and suggested both Nolan and Lucan were to blame: Nolan for misconstruing the order and Lucan for not only obeying the order given to him by Nolan without question, and for letting his opinion of Nolan interfere with his judgement.[29] The 'Special Correspondent' of *The Morning Post*, after interviewing survivors and observers, suggested that the Light Brigade had been ordered to '... meet the advance of the enemy up an assent of considerable steepness, upon the top of which were redoubts deserted by the enemy were erected'. In other words, the Light Brigade had been sent to recover or prevent the guns being taken away from the redoubts on the causeway heights, rather than attack the Russian guns at the end of the north valley.[30] The 'Malta Correspondent' of *The Morning Chronicle* also shared this interpretation after interviewing survivors and eyewitnesses.[31] Lord George Paget, with the benefit of hindsight, thought that the original intent of the order had been for the Light Brigade to mount the Causeway Heights and recapture the guns. Owing to the difficulty of the ground to be crossed, however, sending cavalry against earthworks would 'have been attended with great difficulty', especially without infantry support.[32] Lawrence Godkin of the *Daily News* admitted that it would be easy to lay the blame – as many did – for the loss of the Light Brigade on the Turks (for supposedly not defending the redoubts) or on Nolan because he was dead. Godkin found it impossible to believe the assertions that the Turks or Nolan were to blame and instead suggested that Lucan or Cardigan were to blame for 'acting upon an impossible order'.[33] Neither Lucan nor Cardigan could agree as to the precise order given: Lucan asserted the order he gave his brother-in-law was 'to advance *steadily*' whilst Cardigan claimed it was 'you will *attack*'. Both, however, were certain Nolan was to blame.[34] The *Daily News* further suggested that the vitriol directed towards Nolan had been 'got up' by the surviving senior officers, and, in particular *The Times* and its 'Special Correspondent', W.H. Russell.[35]

Général Canrobert, the French C-in-C described the briefing of Nolan in great detail:

> Lord Raglan was anxious: he first sent an aide-de-camp, Commandant Witherall [*sic*, Wetherall], of his staff, to Lord Lucan, then after he called General Airey and spoke with him. We saw the latter taking his sabretache, using it as an improvised desk, to write a note in crayon. With the note written, the two Generals exchanged some further words, and Lord Raglan, calling Captain Nolan, of the 15th Hussars, aide de camp of General Airey, entrusted him with the paper to carry to Lord Lucan.[36]

Général, later *Maréchal* and future President of France, Patrice de MacMahon, who was present on the Sapoune Heights with Canrobert, described the events thus:

> [Lord Raglan] immediately despatched one of his orderly officers to General Cardigan. 'You will order him,' he said, 'to charge the Russians.' The orderly officer galloped off without saying a word. He took half an hour to get to General Cardigan, and, once he had gained that point, he saw the plain which had been previously concealed from his sight, and perceived behind the Russian cavalry, two divisions, of whose presence Lord Raglan had not been aware when he gave the order ...[37]

Canrobert further states that the batteries at the end of the north valley and on the Fedioukine Heights were visible from the heights but *not* from the valley floor, which made Raglan's orders and the subsequent action of the Light Brigade all the more confusing. Canrobert believed that if the Light Brigade had 'instead of going at the bottom of the funnel, [and] attack[ed] ... the other point of the horse shoe ... [they] would have succeeded'.[38]

According to MacMahon, Nolan transmitted the orders to Cardigan 'taking no account of the events which had altered the situation'. This was because 'He [Nolan] was not on good terms with Lord Raglan, who would not have forgiven his taking any initiative upon himself.' The blame, therefore lay with Raglan and the 'system' of the British army for not allowing his subordinates to use their own discretion or initiative.[39]

The French viewpoint

From his position on the Sapoune Heights, *Général* Canrobert and his staff had the same 'grandstand view' of the battlefield. Indeed, Canrobert described his position as

[like] on a racecourse ... and the staff found themselves installed on a crest, like spectators who would attend a spectacle especially given for them in their boxes or their chairs.[40]

Canrobert and other French officers considered the redoubts on the Causeway Heights to be insufficiently defended and 'built much too far away from any support' and therefore 'easily captured'.[41] Colonel Félix de Wimpffen (commanding officer of the *Tirailleurs Algerièn*), rather like Canrobert, though that the Battle of Balaklava should not have been fought at all if the British defences on the causeway heights had not been so feeble and unsupported – something which the Russians had discovered and used to their advantage.[42]

MacMahon described the battlefield as being triangular in shape, formed by the Chersonese Plateau, the Causeway Heights and 'Canrobert's Hill'.[43] Canrobert described the battlefield as being horseshoe-shaped, and that the Light Brigade was meant to attack one end of the horseshoe and the French *Chasseurs d'Afrique* and light troops (*Zouaves* and *Chasseurs à Pied*) the other.[44]

The Charge

Whatever occurred between Nolan and Lucan, Lucan ordered Cardigan to charge and attempt to capture the Russian guns, which may or may not have been out of sight at the end of the valley. An officer of the *Chasseurs d'Afrique* recorded that:

Lord Cardigan, in command of the Light Brigade, to whom the order was transmitted, observed that the battery against which he was to charge was flanked by two others, with a cross-fire on the ground to be traversed; that the distance was enormous; that the infantry would join its fire to that of the artillery, and that the Russian cavalry would be able to act in its turn.[45]

MacMahon records a similar conversation, adding that Cardigan thought, 'Lord Raglan must be mad!'[46] W.H. Russell of *The Times* records that at 11.10 a.m. precisely 'the Light Cavalry Brigade advanced'. The Light Brigade was formed in two lines:

	Left	Centre	Right
First line	11th Hussars	17th Lancers	13th Light Dragoons
Second line		4th Light Dragoons	8th Hussars[47]

The two lines were 200 metres apart, but Paget suggests the 11th Hussars gradually moved forward to the first line, whilst the 8th fell back to the interval between the 1st and 2nd lines and that he manoeuvred his 4th Light Dragoons into line with them.[48]

Up on the heights, the French could not understand what was happening; *Générals* Canrobert and Bosquet had expected the Light Brigade to make a ninety-degree turn to their right and mount the causeway heights:

'What are they doing?' Général Bosquet, turning to Mr. Layard, shouted to him, in front of everyone 'It is superb, but it is not war – It is madness!' 'Where are they going?' we repeated; and we remained amazed at this admirable and useless heroism.[49]

Général de Martimprey watched as, to everyone's surprise:

> ... the English cavalry moved forward, this movement not only exposed them to the frontal fire from the enemy's artillery, but also from a Russian battery placed under the protection of five Battalions, on the Hills of the Tchernaia, and which fired on the left flank.[50]

Capitaine Paul de Molènes of the *Spahis* thought the unfolding scene was 'like something from Shakespeare', somehow chivalric but he could not understand the sense in sending cavalry to charge the 'masses of bayonets and redoubts mounted with cannons'.[51] Another French officer saw how:

> The cavalry found itself exposed to a very violent cross-fire from the redoubts, which destroyed entire squadrons. The commander of the column launched without hesitation his men at the first redoubt. At the same instant, around ten o'clock, the French and English reinforcements appeared, which had been due soon, which will soon destroy, as you have seen, the resistance of the Russians. The redoubt and its guns fell immediately into our hands. But we did not pursue the enemy, who retired to the shelter of their camp established in the second plain, protected by their strong entrenchments.[52]

Yet another French observer described the Light Brigade as galloping into a trap:

> 600 English horsemen charged before [a] formed Russian infantry square, it opened suddenly and unmasked a strong battery that vomitted on them a rain of shot; the English then performed prodigies of valour, but when they managed to reform, approximately four hundred of them were missing.[53]

'Fortunately' for the Light Brigade, the 'French rescue arrived on time, and the enemy, after receiving several brilliant charges of two regiments of *Chasseurs d'Afrique*, was pushed into the ravines where the allies' artillery inflicted on him significant losses.'[54] A similar version of events was reported by a French officer writing to the *Constitutionnel* (6 November 1854):

> on the 25 October the Russians appeared on the heights in face of the redoubts of the Allies. Whether the Turks, according to their custom, were not on their guard, or were not in sufficient numbers to defend themselves is not known: but it is certain they abandoned their redoubts, after spiking their cannon, threw themselves in complete disorder into the plain ... The Division of Light Cavalry, under command of the Lord Cardigan, arrived first, and immediately charged the Russians, who [had] descended in good order into the plain in pursuit of the Turks. In spite of their courage, the three regiments which composed the Brigade in vain endeavoured to check the march of the enemy. The Dragoon Guards went to their aid, and were at first more fortunate; their ranks were broken by the artillery of the redoubts, of which the Russians had turned the cannon, after unspiking them, against the Allies. In the meantime the British infantry arrived in line. It held firm under the fire of the Russian infantry, and under that of the redoubts, and thus gave time for the Division of General Bosquet, the farthest from the scene of action, to come up, and form.

Russian Deployment

General Liprandi stated that in order to reinforce his right flank:

... Major-General Jabrokritsky with a detachment of the infantry regiment of Vladimir (three battalions) and that of Souzdal[,] ten guns of the battery of position No. 1, four guns of the light battery No. 2 of the 16th brigade of artillery, two companies of the battalion of riflemen No. 6, two squadrons of the regiment of hussars of the Grand Duke of Saxe-Weimar, and two detachments [*sotnias*] of the regiment No. 60 of Cossacks (of Popoff) advanced upon the heights to the left of our cavalry, and occupied them. Our cavalry hardly had time to form in order of battle beyond the right flank of our infantry, when, from the other side of the mountain, where the redoubt No. 4 was raised, the English cavalry appeared, more than 2,000 strong.[55]

Prince Menshikoff in his report, however, stated that it was 'Don Heavy Battery Number Three' which was charged in front by the Light Brigade in which 'several gunners were cut down'.[56] This is also confirmed by General Rhyzov,[57] whereas the artillery officer Stefan Kozhukhov thought it was two horse artillery batteries, one of which as 'Light Battery Number Seven', which were charged.[58] The cavalry officer, Lieutenant Koribut-Kubitovich also described the Russian deployment in detail:

Lieutenant General Liprandi guessed that the enemy intended to make an advance and saw that it was necessary to make some changes in his troop deployments and reinforce his right flank. Infantry occupied the heights as before. The right flank was deployed in stepped-back echelons and formed almost a right angle with our position's front. It consisted of the Odessa Jäger Regiment with eight guns [No. 1 battery, 16th Artillery brigade]. We too were moved from the left flank to the right and deployed between Redoubts No. 2 and No. 3. The hussar brigade and Ural Regiment were in the valley separating the Kadykioi heights from the Fedyukhin Hills, where General Zhabokritskii was located.[59]

He remembered the remainder of the force being formed as follows:

The hussars and Ural men were formed as follows: the Ural cossacks stood in front near elevated ground; to their right was a Don battery with a division of the Weimar [Hussar] Regiment on each flank for protection, in attack column; behind the Weimar men were the Leuchtenbergers with an extended front.[60]

One Russian officer was amazed how the Light Brigade 'attacked our Hussars and Cossacks' in spite of

... the fire of grape from the guns of light battery No. 7 of the 12th Artillery brigade, and battery No. 1 of the 16th Artillery brigade [silenced by the *Chasseurs d'Afrique*], and regardless of the fire of the Odessa Chasseurs. The English cavalry fought hand to hand with our Hussars and Cossacks, threw themselves on Don battery No. 3 and cut down the artillerymen.[61]

General Liprandi vividly described the Charge and repulse of the Light Brigade in his report:

The enemy made a most obstinate charge, and, notwithstanding the well-directed fire of grape from six guns of the light battery No. 7, and that of the men armed with carbines of the regiment of chasseurs of Odessa, and a company of the 4th battalion of riflemen at the right wing, as well as the fire of a part of the artillery of the detachment of Major-general Jabrokritsky, he rushed upon our cavalry; but at this moment three squadrons of the combined regiment of lancers attacked him in flank. This unexpected charge, executed with precision and vigour, was attended with brilliant success. The whole of the enemy's cavalry in disorder precipitated itself in retreat, pursued by our lancers and by the fire from our batteries. In this attack the enemy had more than 400 men killed and sixty wounded, who were picked up on the field of battle, and we made twenty-two prisoners, one of whom was a superior officer.[62]

Charge of the *Chasseurs d'Afrique*
Like their British allies, the French had similarly been on duty since before dawn; *Capitaine* Charles-Antoine Thoumas (*1e Batterie, 17e Artillerie* (*Montée*)) recorded that he and his men 'watched the charming spectacle' of first, the 'thin red streak' and then the Charge of the Heavy Brigade unfold before them as if they 'were at the hippodrome'.[63] Thoumas managed to grab a much-needed 'frugal dinner' (he had been in the saddle four hours), which he had stored in the caisson of number one gun before *Commandant* Durand de Villiers, *Officier d'Ordonnance* (Orderly Officer) to *Général* Canrobert, galloped up:

> 'From where do you come from?' our commander asked him – 'To bring [the] order to the *Chasseurs d'Afrique* [to come] down in [the] plain to support the English cavalry' – 'Without artillery?' 'He did not say anything to me.' 'Say then, on my part, the general-in-chief he must send a horse battery with the brigade of *Chasseurs*.' 'It is up to you to, mount your horses, [and] march.'[64]

Abandoning their coffee, Thoumas' battery mounted their horses, and trotted into the plain, and, after receiving an order from Canrobert 'the battery marched to battle in a perfect order, without the slightest delay'.[65] Canrobert thought that Thoumas

> ... commanded one of the most beautiful batteries one could see: superb and quivering horses, gunners, all experienced men ... At the call of the Aide de Camp ... the battery descended from the heights into the plain like a whirlwind.[66]

Seeing the Light Brigade charging the Russian guns in the north valley, Canrobert ordered *Général* Morris with his two regiments of *Chasseurs d'Afrique* (*1e* and *4e*) to charge the Russian guns and infantry on the Fedioukine Heights. Each regiment of *Chasseurs d'Afrique* consisted of some eight squadrons (*escadrons*); four remained in Africa and four were sent to the Crimea. Each squadron was commanded by eight officers and mustered eleven sub-officers, sixteen corporals and 140 privates. Total establishment of the four squadrons was around 700 sabres, giving 1,400 sabres in total for both regiments – more than twice the strength of the Light Brigade!

Two squadrons (approximately 350 sabres) from the *4e* commanded by *Major* Abdelal and *Captaine* Dancla deployed in skirmish order (*en Tirailleur*), 'the small horses galloped and leapt over the stones and undergrowth, crossing all the obstacles'. The remaining six squadrons (approximately 1,000 sabres) were deployed '*en bataille*', ready to charge.[67] Émile Hubaine, the Private Secretary to

H.I.M. Prince Napoléon, who was present with the French staff, in a letter of 27 October suggests that the attack of the *Chasseurs* was not initiated by Canrobert, but by Lord Raglan. The execution and success of the charge, however, was due to *Générals* Morris and d'Allonville.[68] The French official historian of the war, César Louis de Bazancourt, however, believed that the charge of the *Chasseurs* was done entirely on the initiative of *Général* Morris because of the imminent 'disaster' that was unfolding before him.[69] One officer of the 4th Light Dragoons and the Rev. W.S. Shipley (quoting Russel's despatches from the Crimea) thought the *Chasseurs* charged to 'alleviate the retreat' of the Light Brigade,[70] whilst W.H. Russell described it as an 'independent action' which was begun simultaneously with the Charge of the Light Brigade.[71] *Colonel, le Vicomte* de Noë (*1e Chasseurs d'Afrique*) wrote:

We left at the full trot, in column of *pelotons*; our two regiments of *Chasseurs d'Afrique*, because the *4e Régiment* had joined us, we went into battle. As soon as the movement was completed, a shell burst over the Eagle of the *1e Régiment*; but it did not hurt anyone.[72]

'Without hesitation' *Général* Morris launched the *4e Chasseurs* against the Russians: 'Two *escadrons* rushed bravely, sabring [the] two lines of Russian skirmishers' but broke off their attack when they came upon well-formed Russian squares.[73] Canrobert watched as:

... [they] reached the height of the battery, make a turn-round [*demi-tour*] and fell upon the Russian gunners from the rear. *Capitaine* Dancla, at the head, was knocked stiff and dead; but in flash his horsemen, without stopping, entered the battery, whose gunners, sabred and hustled, however managed to throw themselves on their guns, to bring the horses and to couple them up, and to make them slip away at the gallop, followed by the infantry.[74]

Bazancourt further adds that as soon as the Russian artillery was 'hastily limbered up and withdrawn' *Major* Abdelal 'threw himself in pursuit with his intrepid *Chasseurs*' only to be met with a 'thick line of sharpshooters [*Tirailleurs*]' which opened a 'terrible fire'. *Capitaine* Dancla was 'carried away by his courage' and 'threw himself upon the serried ranks of enemy bayonets and fell mortally wounded'. The *Chasseurs* who followed him 'rushed forward with heroic valour; nothing could stop them, and they made a bloody path in the Russian squares ... it was a hand-to-hand struggle'. *Général* Morris called off the engagement, however, 'seeing a regiment of Don Cossacks rushing to the rescue of the broken squares'. The *4e Chasseurs* rallied and formed line, behind the *1e Chasseurs*, one *escadron* of which was deployed as skirmishers.[75] The *4e Régiment* reformed on the left, the *1e* on the right with Thoumas' battery in the centre, 300 metres in front 'ready to engage the enemy should they charge'. Behind the *Chasseurs* was a battalion of French infantry. In their successful attack, the *Chasseurs* lost two officers and thirteen other ranks and sixteen horses killed, seven men and twelve horses wounded.[76] *Général* d'Allonville was distraught at such heavy casualties:

'All in one squadron!' [he] exclaimed in a tone that expressed surprise, *Général* Morris, and the other (they could not feel) [put on] a game face, [which] seems to answer 'What do you want me to do?'[77]

One Russian account of the charge of the *Chasseurs* suggests three, rather than four squadrons attacked the left wing of 'battery No. 1 of the 16th Artillery brigade', 'dashed through the cordon of rifles ... and began to cut down the men who manned the battery'. The Wladimir infantry regiment 'hastened to the relief of the battery' forcing the *Chasseurs* to retire.[78]

Capitaine Thoumas and his men watched as the shattered wreck of the Light Brigade passed them:

> From a knoll we saw the drama that went on in the plain. Just down [below us], we saw to a group of 15 to 20 English lancers [wearing] pearl-grey pants [with a] white band, bloody, messy, in disorder. That is, we are told, what remains of a regiment, the 17th Lancers. Then there is the 11th Hussars regiment, royal-blue dolman, with golden-yellow braids, amaranth coloured pants, with half-boot, wearing an elegant talpack, they are hardly more numerous and equally maltreated as the lancers.[79]

Later, in the evening, *Générals* Morris and Forton (commander of the Heavy Cavalry) caused 'much amusement' because before the battle they had rolled their handerchiefs [*mouchoirs*] and used them to tie their sabres to their wrist, and they had not untied them and *Général* d'Allonville recounted the charge to anyone who would listen.[80] As a reward for their services in the Crimea, the *4e Chasseurs d'Afrique* found themselves transformed into the *Chasseurs à Cheval de la Garde Impériale*.[81]

Letter from Private **William Pearson** (number 1353), 4th Light Dragoons, to his parents.[82]

Camp, near Sebastopol,
My Dear Parents,-   Oct. 26.

I take the pleasure (having stolen a few moments) to write these few lines to inform you that I am, God be thanks for it, enjoying good health, after having been engaged in a hard fought battle with the Russians on the 25th of October. I am, however, sorry to say that a great many of my poor comrades met with their death-wounds, but in an heroic manner. The Light Dragoon regiments got a dreadful cutting up, among which were my regiment (the 4th Light Dragoons), the 17th Lancers, the 8th Hussars, the 13th Light Dragoons and the 11th Hussars. Of the five regiments just mentioned we can scarcely muster what would complete one regiment. My regiment (the 4th Light Dragoons) came from England 300 strong and now we have not more than 100 left from deaths, from sickness, and killed in battle. However, what are left of us are all very thankful that we have been so fortunate, after the great hardships we have undergone since we left Old England. Oh! how thankful I am!

Dear parents, I am sorry I have not much time now, as we expect every moment to go and attack the enemy, who are in sight of us. We gave them a great slaughtering yesterday, and at day-break this morning our big guns are at work slaughtering at Sebastopol, which has been the case for the last 12 days. A great many of the Russian artillery soldiers, together with many of the townspeople, have been killed, and the town set on fire.

Dear mother, do not alarm yourself about me; I have a good opinion I shall see you again. I shall never forget the 25th of October – shells, bullets, cannon-balls [*sic*], and swords kept flying around us. I escaped them all, except a slight scar on my nose from the bursting of a shell, and a slight touch on the left shoulders from a cannon-ball, after it had killed one of our horses; but, God be thanked, it did not disable me. The Russians fight hard and well, but we will make them yield yet. Dear Mother, every time I think of my poor comrades it makes my blood run cold, to think how we had to gallop over the poor wounded fellows lying on the field of battle, with anxious looks for assistance – what a sickening scene! In one part of the battle I lost my horse, owing to the one in front of me being shot dead, and my poor horse fell over it, and I was unhorsed; but, fortunately for me, I saw another that some poor fellow of the 8th Hussars had been killed from; I mounted it in a moment and was in the rank again. On our return from the charge I got my own horse again; he had galloped to the camp, and, dear parents, I was glad when I saw him there, as if I had got half the world given to me!

Dear mother, after the battle of the Alma I wrote to [censored]; I hope she got the letter. Give my kindest love to her, as also to Mr. Grazebank and poor Agnes, grand-father &c. I have not time to say more, as things look rather queer, and as if we will soon be engaged again with the enemy. I hope to hear from you soon, and when I return to Old England, if God spares me, I will tell you all. Corrie, from Pooley Bridge, and Bob Mitchell, of Penrith Town-head are both well. I often think of you, and I am sure you daily pray for my safe return. Tell – to write to me. Will write again, but it is hard work to get stamps and paper. When I wrote to [censored], after the battle of the Alma, we had only lost two men: but in this battle we have lost the better half. But I keep in good heart. We have hitherto thrashed the Russians, and we shall do so again.

Letter from Cornet **Denzil Thomas Chamberlain**, 13th Light Dragoons, to his father.[83]

Balaklava,
Oct. 27

My Dear Father, -

I write a few lines to give you an account of the battle of Balaklava, which was fought on the 25th, between about 30,000 Russians and the whole available force in the valley of Balaklava, being certainly not more than 10,000, of which 5,000 were Turks, and those of little use. Our force included staff, artillery, marines, and, indeed, every man who could be of any use. There appeared to be some slight mistake with respect to the orders, but . . . we (cavalry) were formed upon parade on Wednesday morning, at five o'clock, and remained so until seven, about which time the guns on the hills round the valley began to play upon the enemy. These guns number about eight, and are played by twos at intervals upon the hills, commanding the north and east of the valley; they are ship guns, are entrenched, and are entrusted to the Turks. As soon as the firing commenced on the hills, the artillery and cavalry who had not turn in went to protect them, and the Turks in the valley and one regiment of Highlanders prepared for business and formed in line, protecting the roads to Balaklava. The 13th had to protect a battery of horse artillery, and formed up behind the hill on which it was placed; but we were in a tolerably safe position, only now and then catching a round shot and some splinters from shells, which wounded a few horses, but did not injure a man. After the firing had continued some time, the Russians advanced a little, being in great force, and the unfortunate Turks 'cut and run' with all speed, when the enemy was at least 600 yards off, and did not even spike the guns – which, however, I believe, was fortunately done by our own artillery. Consequently, the enemy obtained possession of the heights, but it did not do them much good, as the valley is so broad that nothing is within of shot from them. The artillery and cavalry then retired slowly back to their camp, when they formed up behind it. The Russians sent two strong forces of cavalry down towards the camp. The former was met by the regiment of Highlanders, the enemy at first fancying they were Turks; but they were soon undeceived, as they were met by an incessant and galling fire from the brave Scots, who did not take the trouble to form square, but remained merely in line, the Russians retiring in double quick time. The second force, sent against the camp, were met by the Scots Greys, backed up by the Royals and Enniskillens, who, after a short but rather desperate encounter, forced them to retire. After this we formed up in line- that is, the light cavalry and the "heavies" – behind on the hills. The enemy had possession of the low part of the valley (the valley beyond the hills), a very narrow long one, where they formed up their cavalry immediately behind 13 large guns, and within range of two of the four hills they had possession of. Now, began the slaughter of the day – as I can call it nothing else. Lord Lucan, who said he had Lord Raglan's authority for so doing, ordered us to charge the enemy, about a mile distant from us, so at it we went in earnest, trotting the first half and galloping the last part of the distance. Though the heavy brigade was formed up behind us, they had no orders to support us, so did not move. The sketch I send you will show the crossed fire to which we were exposed – round shot, grape, shell and bullets. The 13th and 17th were in front, the 8th and 11th behind, and then the 4th. At the outside, I should think there are not more than two-thirds of the light division of cavalry left. The 17th have about half left. The 13th as follows:- In the morning we turn out 9 officers and 110 men, or within five of that number; at about three o'clock in the afternoon, after the charge was over, we could only find nine *mounted* men out of the 120. At last the horses began to drop in, some without riders, others with, but most of them were brought back by Turks and camp-followers. To-day we reckon our loss thus:- 3 officers, 24 men, and 84 horses missing; and 3 officers, 26 men, and 5 or 6 horses wounded.

This is the loss in the 13th. In the morning we had nine officers with the regiment, viz.:-

Captain Oldham – killed, horse missing.
Captain Goad – badly wounded and missing, horse killed.
Captain Jenyns – wounded slightly, horse killed.
Captain Tremayne – escaped unhurt, horse killed.
Lieutenant Smith – wounded slightly, horse safe.
Lieutenant Jervis – escaped unhurt, horse killed.
Cornet Montgomery – missing, reported dead, horse missing.
Cornet Goad – wounded slightly, horse killed.
Cornet Chamberlayne – escaped unhurt, horse killed.

Our Colonel was unwell, and not with us, as also our volunteer, McNeill. Capt. Oldham is known for certain to have been killed, and Capt. Goad and Cornet Montgomery we have too much reason to fear so. Capt. Jenyns and Cornet Goad are hurt only by severe falls from their horses when they were shot, and Smith was wounded by a lance in the breast, but so slightly as not to incapacitate him from duty. Cornet Goad is the only one unfit for duty. I received a lance thrust in the stomach from the right, which fortunately just missed me, but broke my cap-pouch and ripped up my revolver case. I also received a sword cut on the arm, but it fell very lightly, as I shot the Russian dragoon through the head when his arm was raised. My poor charger Pimento was shot through two places in the flank with Minié balls, and one through the body with grape on our retiring. He was only just able to carry me out of the range of the enemy's batteries when he fell to rise no more. The enemy's cavalry was in immense force. I had very many hairbreadth escapes (thanks be to a merciful Providence). Returning was the worst part of the business. I was nearly the last out of about 35 that stared together to return, but I only saw nine when we got out of range. Men and horses fell about like nine-pins; it was an awful sight. I could have killed three or four more Russians with my revolver, but as they were a little detached from the main body I thought it would look too much like murder. Lord Cardigan fought most gallantly – like a true Briton. We drove the enemy's cavalry a considerable distance beyond the guns, but were eventually surrounded, and only escape (those who did) by reason of the cowardice of the Russians; in fact, the Light Brigade was almost cut to pieces, and were not backed up or supported by a single regiment. We were about 600 men, and their cavalry must have been about 2,000. We, however, frightened then a little, for although they have still possession of the heights they have not yet advanced an inch. They always kill the wounded men they find after an engagement (cowardly brutes!) Having no more time, believe me, your affectionate son.

Letter from Sergeant **William Garland** (number 954), 17th Lancers, to his brother, Rev. R. Garland, Curate of St Paul's, Warrington.[84]

My Dear Brother, -

Camp, Balaklava, Sebastopol
October 27.

Thank God, I am spared to write, for I can assure you that I had little hope when at the charge on the 25th, in which a large number of the Light Brigade of Cavalry was lost, killed, wounded, or disabled, that I should come out alive. And I may safely say that there were not twenty men of the 17th Lancers that did not receive some injury, or lost their horses, had them wounded, or some part of their appointments carried away by shell or shot; and there were very few that went from one end to the tother [*sic*] that got off so safe as myself. I only had my lance broken close to my knee, the broken part of it striking against the saddle flap, the grape shot passing through, and rubbing against the horse's rib bones, and he is now unfit for work.

Our Colonel having been sent onboard ship after the battle of Alma, Major Willet had command until the 22d ult., when he had a sudden attack of Cholera, brought on by being exposed the whole night before while on out-laying picquet [*sic*] duty with the remainder of the cavalry, and he died after about twelve hours' sickness. After this, Captain Morris came off Lord Raglan's staff and took command of the regiment, but his command lasted only a short time, for he got severely wounded on the head, and but little hopes were entertained of his re-covery [*sic*]. However, I hear he is better this morning.

Captain White, the next senior, got a severe wound through the flesh of his leg, and had his horse shot. Captain Winter is missing; he may have been slightly wounded by grape, but not severely, for I saw him half a mile past the enemy's guns, all right; but his horse came into camp without him, very much cut up, and he is still missing. Captain Welsh has lost his leg below the knee, and is doing well. Lieutenant Thompson was shot dead. Lieutenant Sir William Gordon has several lance and sabre wounds, but fought and kept his saddle out of the charge, and rode down to the hospital. The only officers that charged and came back all right, were Captain Morgan, Cornet Wombwell, and Colonel [*sic*, Cornet] Cleveland; the remainder were sick, or not in the charge, except Lieutenant and Adjutant Chadwick, whose horse was shot in several places, and he was afterwards taken prisoner. Of all the non-commissioned officers, we only lost Sergeant Talbot – shot dead – and three Corporals – Hall, Paget, and Wrigley. About forty men dead and missing, and about thirty wounded.

I have only had half-an-hours notice of post, which is now up; therefore I must conclude by telling you that we advanced with the 4th Light Dragoons, 8th Hussars, 11th Hussars and 13th Light Dragoons, to chase about twelve guns and eight squadrons of cavalry. We had not got more than half a mile, when some more guns which we had not seen, opened, and we found ourselves under the fire of about thirty – all 9-pound guns and 24-pound howitzers, with double lines of cavalry, the whole of which we put to the route.

Letter from Captain **William Morgan**,[85] 17th Lancers, to his father.[86]

Balaklava,
My dear Father – Oct. 27, 1854.
As usual, I am hard pressed to save the post, as, being always in momentary expectation of being turned out, it is just as much as we have time to do to get our horses fed and watered, and eat our rapid meals. I am at present commanding officer of the 17th Lancers, which gallant little regiment now consists of fifty men and horses fit for duty, and three officers.

I fear that before you receive this letter you will have heard some bad news of the cavalry light brigade. However, not to keep you in suspense, I will begin by saying that I am safe and well in my own person, having come out from that gallant, brilliant (but, as all add, useless) charge under a tremendous fire of all arms from front and flanks, and a perfect forest of swords and lances, untouched, with only a sabre cut on poor old Sir Briggs (my charger) head just over the right eye.

On the 25th, about half-past five a.m., when about to file in from our usual morning parade, we heard the report and saw the smoke of a gun from a Turkish redoubt, and soon perceived the Russians advancing, supported by heavy artillery, in number believed to be about 20,000 infantry and 3,000 cavalry.

At the first sight of them the Turks 'cut and run', forsaking their guns, and the Russians quickly brought their horse-artillery upon the heights. We retired out of range. Down came huge masses of cavalry upon us. The Greys and Enniskillens charged, and broke through them. The 4th and 5th Dragoon

Guards struck in; the Russians turned and fled right and left, and retreating over the hill, took up a tremendously strong position in the valley.

We waited about two hours for some infantry to come to our support, when an order arrived (as we must believe, by mistake) for the Light Brigade to charge the enemy's position. On we went – astonished, but unshaken in nerve – over half a mile of rough ground, losing dozens of men and horses at every stride, to attack horse artillery in our front, supported by three times our numbers of cavalry, heavy batteries on our right and left flanks, backed by infantry, riflemen &c. We took the guns, cut up the gunners, routed the cavalry, and amid a storm of shot, found ourselves very soon surrounded on all sides by the enemy, through whom all that remained of us cut our way back to our position. We went into action 140 strong. I numbered the regiment off 34, when we returned. The other regiments suffered nearly as much.

Letter from Private **Robert T. Chambers** (number 1252),[87] 11th Hussars, to his mother in Leeds.[88]

Camp, near the Heights of Sebastopol
My Dear Mother, -   Oct. 30, 1854.
Your affectionate letter, dated Aug. 26th, arrived here on Friday last, the receipt of which relieved me of a world of anxiety, and which I hasten to reply to, agreeable to your wish, in doing which I must on the present occasion be very brief as the enemy is encamped within sight of us. We sailed from Baltchik Bay, off Varna, on the 5th of September last, with our Allies, under a strong convoy, and anchored some 15 miles above Sebastopol; without the slightest resistance from the enemy we dis-embarked [*sic*] the whole of the Allied army, the place being so well adapted for such an operation. Our landing, including every department, was performed *within a week*, and without delay we proceeded en route for the intended point of Attack. The second night of our bivouac we received the compliments of the renowned Cossacks in the shape of a sharp volley of musket shots whizzing past our ears; luckily on that occasion no injury was done to us; of course, we were out for the expected encounter in a few minutes, but all them had mysteriously vanished over the hills. The following morning we proceeded on our march in battle array, and upon the summit of the first range of hills, which intersect the country between the place of our landing and our present position, we descried our adversary; we reconnoitred their position and supposed them to consist of about 15,000 comprising infantry, artillery, and cavalry, to oppose which force we had only the Light Cavalry brigade and one troop of Horse Artillery, the rest not being up with us. However, a skirmish between us (being the first exchange of shots in the present campaign) commenced about four p.m., 19th September. Having got rather too close to them for the safety of our small force, they brought their 36-pounders to bear upon us; having got our range admirably, they played upon us some time (we being formed in line, facing them) before our troop of artillery could bring their guns into action; they, however, quickly silenced the foe, and the first shot overturning one of their guns, they considered this sufficient for the day and withdrew themselves over the next range of hills. The damage we sustained on this occasion was one man's leg shot off and two or three horses wounded; the rest of the brigade (except the 13th Light Dragoons, who were on our left) escaped scot free.

The next morning early we continued our march, and came up with them in a most formidable position at a place called Alma, situate on a river of the same name. This place, we were afterwards told, they intended for the grave-yard of the Allied powers, but in that, through the Almighty's assistance, we deceived them. The particulars of the battle I must defer to a more convenient period; it was, however, with much regret I have to say the slaughter was terrific, and the sight that met our eyes after the foe were dislodged from their position in three hours, which they calculated on retaining six weeks, was truly appalling. The defeat was so astounding to them as to cause them to retreat into Sebastopol without halting. We remained on the scene of the action until the dead were buried and the wounded conveyed on board ship. Our course lay close to the beach all the way. This done, we followed the enemy till we arrived in sight of the splendid fortress of Sebastopol, where we assumed a defensive position – waiting most anxiously for the commencement of the siege; but an undertaking of so gigantic a nature as that in which we are now engaged required immense preparations before we could begin the deadly struggle, which, however, commenced on the 14th inst.,[89] and continues with unabated fury at the present moment, Sunday, 12 mid-day.

They have a large army in the rear, who advanced on our batteries at six o'clock on the morning of the 25th; we were in our saddles at the time, and ready for them. They succeeded, however, in taking three batteries manned by the Turkish infantry, and came down the hills towards the Highlanders, whom they speedily found were made of different metal, as they kept their position and opened a fire on their cavalry, which caused them to return faster than they came. They were then charged by our Heavy Cavalry, who drove them to their former position. We continued the engagement with little loss up to about midday, when the Order came down from Lord Raglan for the Light Cavalry to charge the enemy. They at this time occupied a position which threatened the entire destruction of any attacking force, they having possession of a large plain with hills on each side on which were placed their batteries of artillery and columns of infantry. We, however, were ordered, though *perfect madness*, to advance, and accordingly off we started in column or regiments at a gallop, and as soon as we neared the plain their terrific fire of artillery and musketry from the hills on each side opened on us, and a troop of guns ranged in front of us as we advanced. The plain was about two miles in length and two hundred yards wide, so you can form some idea how we were knocked over, and having no support from our own army of either infantry, cavalry or artillery, we charged immense masses of Russian cavalry and artillery, and on our return up the plain to our main body, their cavalry had re-formed across the plain to intercept our passage, which, however we broke through, when their batteries and infantry from the hills opened on us, horses and men falling every stride, and by the time we regained our former position the Light Cavalry regiments averaged about 40 each remaining, being when we entered the action about 150 in number, each regiment. This ended the fight for the day, there being great slaughter on both sides. Thank God I, up to the present date, have received no injury.

We have scare a night without a brush with them, they always retreating with much loss. There is no certainty on the issue of the siege, they having such inexhaustible resources in point of guns, ammunition, &c., &c., in fact everything supposed to stand a siege of three years; so you can form some idea of the job we have on hand, and of course expected by the "sages" at home to accomplish the job in "no time." However, here we are and likely to be for some time. The weather has set in bitter cold and raw, and the two armies facing each other like two bull-dogs ready to overwhelm its adversary the first chance. May the Almighty, in His omnipotent understanding, terminate the cause in favour of the righteous. I must now finish, to write again, if Providence shall so ordain, at a future day. I rejoice to hear you are all in pretty good health, and hope you may continue so. I am tolerably robust myself, for which blessing I endeavour to render thanks to my Divine Parent, whose will, not mine, be done. Please to express my warmest respects to C.F. and J.W., and tell them for the present they must make allowances for my not writing, and with love to all cousins, brothers, sisters, and kind regards to any inquirers.

Letter from an anonymous Officer of the 17th Lancers.[90]

We were ordered to charge some Russian batteries and cavalry, and the Light Brigade went down – the 17th [Lancers] and 13th [Light Dragoons] leading in Line; the 11th [Hussars] were ordered to hang back a little as support, the 4th [Light Dragoons] and 8th [Hussars] followers, in a sort of third line. We all knew the thing was desperate before we started, and it was even worse than we thought. In our front, about a mile and a half off, were several lines of Russian cavalry and nine guns – to get at which we had to pass along a wide valley, with the ground a little falling, and in itself favourable enough for a charge of cavalry; but the sloping hills on each side gave the enemy an opportunity (which they used) of placing guns on both our flanks as we advanced; and not only guns, but infantry with Minié rifles.

However there was no hesitation, down our fellows went at a gallop – through a fire in front and on both flanks, which emptied our saddles and knocked over our horses by scores. I do not think that one man flinched in the whole Brigade – though every one allows that so hot a fire was hardly ever seen. We went right on, cut down the gunners at their guns (the Russians worked the guns till we were within ten yards of them) – went on still, broke a line of cavalry in rear of the guns, and drove it back on the third line. But here our bolt was shot: the Russians formed four deep and our thin and broken ranks and blown horses could not attempt to break through them, particularly as the Russian cavalry had got round our flanks, and were prepared to charge our rear (with fresh men). We broke back through them, however, and then had to run the gauntlet through the cross fire of artillery and Minié rifles back to our own lines, with their cavalry hanging on our flank. The Heavy Brigade, which had made a good charge of its own in the morning, covered our coming out of action, and lost some men from the artillery.

There is no concealing the thing – the Light Brigade was greatly damaged, and for nothing! For though we killed the gunners and the horses of nine 12-pounders, we could not bring them away. Nolan (who brought the order) is dead. The first shall that burst hit him in the breast. He gave a loud cry, his horse turned, trotted back (with him still in the saddle) between the first and second squadrons of the 13th, and carried him so for some way, when he fell dead. He was hit in the heart.

In the two leading regiments, including Lord Cardigan (who led in person) and his staff, we had 19 officers. Only three came out of the action untouched, both man and horse; all the others were killed, wounded, prisoners, or had their horses hurt. The 17th had no field officers, but five captains. They came out of action commanded by the Junior Captain, I believe. [Captain William] Morris is severely wounded; [Captain John] Winter is supposed killed; [Captain Augustus] Webb is shot through the thigh; [Captain Robert] White through the leg; [Lieutenant John] Thompson is supposed to be killed. One of Lord Cardigan's Aides-de-Camp is wounded – Maxse; the other, Lockwood, is missing, and supposed killed. We have lost about 335 horses (exclusive of officers' horses), our of little more than 600 which we (The Brigade) had in the field; besides that a great number are wounded with gun-shot wounds, and about 25 have already been destroyed, and more will.

It was a bitter moment after we broke through the line of cavalry in rear of their guns, when I looked round and saw there was no support beyond our own brigade, which, leading in the smoke, had diverged, and scarcely filled the ground. We went on, however, and hoped that their own men flying would break the enemy's line and drive them into the river [Tchernaya]. When I saw them form four deep instead, I knew it was "all up," and called out to the men to Rally. At this moment a solitary squadron of the 8th came up in good order. This saved the remnant of us; for we rallied to them, and they, wheeling about, charged a line which the Russians had formed in our rear. You never saw men behave so well as our men did. As we could not hold our ground, all our dead and badly wounded were left behind, and know not who are dead or are prisoners. All this makes me miserable, even to write; but it is the naked truth. Our loss in men is not so great as that in horses; for men whose horses were shot in the advance got back on foot. I hear from a man who dined with Lord Raglan today, that they do us justice at Head Quarters, and say that our attack was an unheard of feat of arms, and that Lord Raglan says that the moral effect has been wonderful. The Russians prisoners taken at Sebastopol say the Russians were petrified at the audacity of the attack and the energy that could after such a fire break through their lines. These prisoners were taken in a very successful affair by Sir De Lacy Evans. Do the old fellow justice. He is a first rate division leader.

Letter from an anonymous Trumpeter of the 8th Hussars.[91]

I write this to you in haste to inform you that I have escaped unhurt up to the 25th of October. Oh, what a sight it was to see our cavalry charging at their cavalry, and coming into contact with each other; men were falling on both sides. It was worse for us, for our light cavalry had to charge their cavalry between two batteries, and they were firing on us for two miles and a half. As we were coming back, our regiment and the 17th Lancers were attacked by another lot of Russian cavalry, so we had to make the best of our way through them. Their artillery and infantry were firing on us all the time. Our regiment lost 38 men and two officers killed; seventeen men and two officers wounded. Capt. Lockwood is missing, we suppose him to be killed.[92] It was an awful sight to see our men falling on every side of me, but, thank God, I was spared. I had my horse shot under me, but I was no sooner down than I mounted a Russian's horse. I had not, however, the pleasure of riding it more than half an hour when one of the Russian lancers ran his lance through the horse's body. Then I was left without any, so I had to run for my life, which I did for three miles until I came to the French cavalry, where I remained until our regiment came back. You may guess I had a very narrow escape.

Letter from Private '**C.R.**' (Charles Randall [number 1062]?), 17th Lancers, to his mother.[93]

Balaklava,
My dear Mother, -   Nov. 1
I now take the opportunity of writing these few lines to you, hoping they will find you quite well, as I am happy to say it leaves me at present. I have a little news to tell you in this letter, although it is not very good. I left the Hospital at Scutari on the 20th of October, and joined the regiment on the 24th. When I got there they told me the Major had died a week ago of the cholera. The day after I joined the regiment we had an engagement with the Russians, which lasted for a few hours, and then the Light Brigade charged down a valley, between the fire of the Russians. Captain Nolan, of the 15th Hussars, led us, and he got shot himself, and nearly the whole Light Brigade was cut up. We had two officers killed, four wounded, and one taken prisoner; 22 men killed, 69 wounded, and seven taken prisoners. In fact, the whole regiment is nearly cut up, for when we came out of the field we could only mount 42 men. But, thank God, I came out safe myself. Joe I[censored] sends his best respects to all, and he is quite well. The whole of the Light are cut up the same as our own. They are still at Sebastopol, and they expect to take it in a few days. When that is taken there is a great talk of our coming home this winter; in fact, I think they will be obliged to send us home, for we are not much use now.

Letter from '**G.C.**' to Right Hon. Francis Henry FitzHardinge Berkeley, MP for Bristol.[94]

General Hospital, Scutari, Constantinople,
Honourable Sir, -   3rd November, 1854.
My last letter was just after the battle of the Alma. Well, we had a dreadful battle last week at Balaklava, about four miles from Sebastopol. I must first tell you how we were as regards our position. All the cavalry (in comparison to the cavalry of the Russians, and their hordes of Cossacks, a mere handful of men) were in the rear of the army besieging Sebastopol, and we had to act as their rear-guard, and to keep thirty thousand men (so reported) in check, and, those men continually threatening a forward movement. Many were the harassing days and nights we had. Every day they were trying to surprise our outlying pickets, and on the 25th October the whole of them advanced at about six o'clock in the morning; luckily we were quite ready for them; every horse saddled, every man at the head of his horse, ready to mount. Unfortunately, we were supported by no infantry but the 93rd Highlanders and about 2000 of those cowardly Turks, who had certain redoubts to mind, and who fired upon the Russians as they advanced. On they came however, and an immense

mass they were, not less I think than four thousand cavalry and artillery. Our cavalry, all told, heavy and light, could not have been more than about 1700 men, inclusive of artillery; perhaps 1800 men. This immense mass of the enemy came over a hill, taking the redoubts and driving the "bono Turcos" before them like chaff. They divided into two bodies, one went towards the Highlanders and Turks, who had pretended to reform on the Highlanders' flank, and the other came towards us, the cavalry. No doubt they thought to ride over us all at once. The body who approached the Highlanders and Turks, terrified the "Bonos" into immediate flight, and I daresay thought Highlanders would soon follow; but Donald was not to be got rid of so easily. Well did Old Scotland do its duty. They drew up in two lines, at which our old soldiers were astonished, expecting a regular Waterloo square. Not so, they tried their hands first at a long-shot, with decided, if not conclusive effect; but they gave the Moscows their dose complete at within a hundred yards; and when they bolted pelted them till out of reach of the Minié. The tumbling about of men and horses was very pleasant to our feelings, and the Russians, thinking they might meet with more grief, troubled the Highlanders no more. The body that advanced on the cavalry met with a very cordial reception. So confident were they of riding down our cavalry, that they stopped galloping, called a halt, and advanced in a steady walk. No sooner had they done this than the Scots Greys and Enniskillens had orders to charge them. They went on like a whirlwind through the Russians, with their swords at the "Engage," in two lines, our fellows cheering when within five yards of them, and broke through their regular cavalry, four deep – regulars, you will be pleased to understand, not rubbishing Cossacks. Such splendid cutting and thrusting never was seen; our heavy-Dragoon's swords are longer and straighter than the Russians, and about ten inches from the point they have a double edge; the Russian sword is a complete curve, and is not of the slightest use in giving point, so that all they could do was to cut at our fellows' helmets, which they did pretty heavily, but only dented them; their horses, little cats of things, could not stand the jumping forwards of our powerful animals, with a pair of spurs driven into their sides; in short, both horse and horse-men are no match for ours. Well, our fellows charged and re-charged, the Royals made in, and the end was a complete victory to our arms, the enemy being full four to one, and they rode off and took shelter with their guns, having had a precious mauling, and leaving many a stout horseman stark and stiff. The general opinion is that it would have been all over with them had it not been for some unfortunate mistake in orders delivered by Capt. Nolan, of the staff. The orders upon which Lord Lucan acted were, to send the Light Cavalry to take the guns from the Russian army – those pieces which "Bono Turco" had deserted – and to do this we were forthwith despatched. Lord Raglan never could have intended it [the Charge of the Light Brigade], but it is a mess made up between Capt. Nolan, Lord Cardigan and Lord Lucan; so think the branch of service to which I belong. Who is to blame God knows, and perhaps I ought to say no more, therefore sir, if I have gone too far, pray excuse me. Never I believe, unless at Chillianwallah, was such carnage. We had to charge on a battery of thirteen guns of the Russians, and our own guns (but they were said to have been spiked) all blazing away; as we approached, they fired grape and canister, and we had to undergo a flanking fire of musquetry to boot. Well, sir, here my narrative ends, my old mare was smashed by a cannon round shot, and went down heavily on me, beating the breath and sense out of me; on recovering my recollection and trying to extricate myself, a Cossack put his lance into my shoulder – those vermin are always prowling about and act independently; I staggered away to the rear, having taken a shot at this same Cossack fired with my carbine, while he was plundering a dead man, and got in by the time our poor fellows had returned and reformed behind the heavy cavalry – and a sad sight they were – I had just managed this when I was taken faint and carried to a hospital tent. I am now at Scutari, my wound is doing well, and I hope to join soon. I must say that the hospital fare is a complete luxury, as is a bed, to a man who has lived on salt pork and biscuits for two months, and slept on the bare earth.

Letter from Sergeant **John George Baker** (number 888),[95] 4th Light Dragoons, to his parents.[96]

Dear Father and Mother,-

Camp in Front of Sebastopol,
Nov. 7th, 1854.

Through the Mercy of God, and that alone, I am permitted to address you once more. I am happy to say I am still in the enjoyment of good health, and I trust this will find you all the same. I do not wish to say a word to make you uncomfortable or over anxious about me; but as I am on Guard, and have half an hour to spare, I wish to give you a few particulars. It is very pleasant to sit in a parlour in England, with a long pipe and a glass of grog, or a pint or half-and-half, and to talk of events that occur around us. I know, by the 'papers, there are many in England who think Sebastopol ought to have been taken long ere this, and may think that by this time it really is taken, but such is not the case. We have now laid by this town since the 27th of September; we commenced firing into it on the 17th of October, and are still firing while I am writing; and I firmly believe they may continue until next April, and then they will not give in. The fortifications are immensely strong. The men-of-war ships cannot assist us in the least, and it appears impossible to take it in any other way than at the point of the bayonet, which will cost an immense sacrifice of life; but I think an attempt will be made to storm it in a few days.

I must now tell you that I have narrowly escaped being taken prisoner twice – the first time I escaped by about five minutes, and the last time I escape through having a good horse and galloping through the enemy. The papers have ere this given you an account of the engagement of the Light Brigade under the Earl of Cardigan. I was with him on that ever-memorable day, and I shall not forget it, even to the last day of my life. We advanced on a level, between two hills, both well lined with artillery, and on one three battalions of infantry, and in our front artillery were planted also in very great numbers. We galloped through all this firing, which was almost as thick as hail, and the shot from the guns were as large as ordinary Dutch cheeses; and shells were bursting all around us. We reached the guns at the end, and cut down the gunners and drivers, and took possession of the guns; and then, to our mortification, we saw that the enemy had a large quantity of cavalry formed up ready to receive us. The consequence was, we were obliged to leave the guns, and to go three abreast back again through the same fire. And to make the affair still worse, during the time that we were cutting off the artillerymen, a party of cavalry, (about 1,000) came from behind a hill, and formed up, so that we had to cut out way through them on our retreat. We lost, killed, wounded, and missing, about sixty men. Our regiment is now only a skeleton. We have lost a great many also by disease.

You have seen in the paper the account of the skirmish[,] which took place two days afterwards; the cavalry was not engaged on that occasion. You have likewise seen an account of the battle that took place on Sunday, the 5th of November, which was more severe than at Alma; the ground would not allow the cavalry to act, but still, we were under fire; and had two men killed or wounded, and several horses killed.

We are now expecting that Sebastopol will be stormed every day, but do not know what day it will take place. In consequence of the lateness of the season, we do not expect to return to England before spring, but we cannot tell anything positively before the town is taken.

I was not able to finish this letter in time, and must wait for the next mail; I cannot get stamps for love or money, and my letters will be all unpaid. Although within a mile of cousin Robert, I have not seen him for some weeks: but as his regiment had not been engaged, I hope he is will. Since writing the above, our Colonel has left us and returned to England. I am also informed that Lord Raglan has declined storming the town; therefore I expect we shall have to lay here for months.

Since writing the above I have been appointed Serjeant, from the 20th of October; direct to me as such, for the future.

God only knows what will become of us: the weather is wet, windy and miserable already; but I hope it will please God to preserve us though all, and bring us safely back to Old England.

When war's proclaim'd, and danger's nigh,
God and the soldier, is the people's cry;
When was is o'er, and all things righted,
God's forgotten, and the soldier slighted.

Of course you will have seen by the 'papers, that we have a large army in rear of us. I shall now conclude with my kind love, to each an all, and that we may all meet again in this world, and dwell together at God's Right Hand for evermore in eternity, is the earnest prayer of your affectionate son.

Letter from an anonymous Sergeant in the 13th Light Dragoons to his brother in Stockport.[97]

Near Sebastopol,
Dearest Brother, -   7th November 1854.

I can say but a few words. When I last wrote to you, we were on the point of embarking for the Crimea. Unfortunately, I met with a severe accident, I fell down the main hatchway, and to thank God I was not killed. I went to the General Hospital at Scutari, consequently was out of Alma, but joined the Regiment as soon as possible, being able to participate in the next Honours. Joined at Balaklava where we passed some weeks in the most arduous and harassing duties, both of outposts and picquets, and surrounded by Cossacks, and we were obliged to be continually on the alert. At last we engaged them and I suppose, ere this, you have the account.

On the 25th of October the enemy advanced, and stormed our advanced positions on some hills, which were well fortified, and unfortunately occupied by the Turks, but the rascals fled before the Russians came within 150 yards of the forts; our artillery came up, and the Russians recovered the guns, where we were exposed to shot and shell for upwards of two hours, but the positions were lost, we slowly retired a short distance. The Russians advanced direct on to us, on the ground of our camp. Our heavy dragoons were ordered to charge them and they fled, although their numbers were sufficient to overwhelm our hand-ful of cavalry. At this time, the Light Brigade formed up on the left, on some ground which commanded a long valley about two miles long, at the end of which the enemy retired. By some misunderstanding, we were ordered to advance and charge the guns, which they had formed up full in our front at the extreme end, and here took place a scene which is unparalleled in history. We had scarcely advanced a few yards, before they opened on us with grape, shot and shell. It was a perfect level, the ground only enough for the 17th and 13th to advance, the rest of the brigade following. To our astonishment, they had erected batteries on each side of the hills, which commanded the whole valley; consequently, a dreadful cross-fire opened on us from both sides and in front, but it was too late to do anything but advance, which we did in a style truly wonderful, every man feeling certainly that we must be annihilated. Still we continued on, reached the very guns, charged them, took them; but, there being no support, we were obliged to retire, almost being cut up. Out of our regiment, we assembled only ten men mounted, and one or two officers. Our Colonel has gone home sick,[98] and major gone home,[99] we were commanded by the senior Captain.[100] Two captains were killed,[101] and one lieutenant.[102] Poor Weston[103] was killed, and two sergeant-majors taken prisoners.[104] The others were either killed, taken prisoners, or dismounted. Of the remainder we retired, and here the firing was hotter than ever, for the infantry aimed at us as we passed them. I escaped – thank God! – without a scratch; but my poor horse got shot through the head and in the hind quarters, and a lance was through my shoe bag. It was a most unwise and mad act. One thing, there is no blame attached to the Earl of Cardigan, for he *was ordered* to do it, and he did it most noble. We charged up to the very mouth of the guns, and since then the 17th and ourselves have scarcely been able to make one squadron between us. The 4th Light Dragoons are nearly as bad. The Earl is very cut up contemplating it, and points it out to the officers as the effect of charging batteries. The daring of the thing astounded and frightened the enemy. The shattered remnants of the Light Brigade moved up here (near Sebastopol) shortly afterwards, and have remained pretty quiet with the exception of the continual bombardment sounding in our ears from morning till night, until the next fighting of 5th of November, when the Russians appeared in force, and we had then a most glorious and awful day. They estimated the loss of the Russians from 13,000 to 16,000; our loss is very great. The Duke of Cambridge had his horses shot under him; General Sir G. Brown was wounded, General Lord Cathcart was killed, and many colonels and other officers are killed or dangerously wounded. The battled last more then seven hours, and the Grenadier Guards were cut to pieces. We brigaded, for the first time, with the French cavalry; but were not engaged this day, though exposed to shot and shell. We lost some horses, and a fine young fellow – an officer of the 17th Lancers – was killed. A shell burst in the midst of us and he was the only one hurt, and he survived but a few hours afterwards. We only lost a few men.

You will, I know, excuse this rambling scrawl, as I have been disturbed fifty times whilst writing it; but I am sure it will be welcome. Many many thanks for the newspapers – they are a source of great amusement and much gratification. I pray to God that I may be spared to see you some day; but He alone knows what will become of us if they keep us here much longer, as the weather is getting very cold. We are all in a [illegible] as to the fall of Sebastopol, and there is a great deal of dissatisfaction experienced at this procrastination; but I suppose our chiefs know well what they are about?

Letter from Trumpeter **Robert Nichol** (number 1027),[105] 8th Hussars, to his father James Nichol of Pitt Street, Newcastle.[106]

Balaklava,
Dec. 11, 1854.

Dear Father, -

We started for the Crimea on the 1st of September, in the "Himalaya", and were sixteen days on the water looking for a landing place. We landed all safe, and that day we went fifteen miles out and came back at night. We stopped on the beach for two days, and then marched for Sebastopol. On the first evening, the 19th, we met the enemy, and had a bit of a set-to. The next day, the 20th, we marched for Alma, and at this time we had no provisions for two days, except a bit of biscuit and a drop of rum. We went on about six miles, when we came to the heights of Alma. We met the enemy and took the hills in three hours and twenty minutes. We stopped there two days. The army then marched again, but my troop had to stop behind to see the wounded aboard of ship. Then we marched off at night and came within sight of some lights, which we thought were the enemy, so we stopped all night by ourselves, but the next day we went on again and joined our regiment. We went on pretty quiet to Balaklava, while they commenced work at Sebastopol. We remained quiet until the 25th October, when we had to charge some guns; we had to go through a triangular fire, and there was infantry on the right – that was how there were so many lost. When we got to the guns the Russian Lancers were charging us in the rear. We came Left About Wheel, and charged then, and very soon mowed our way through them. I came out safe, but a ball had gone through the end of my cloak. Tell L. that I saw [censored] sabred with a lance when we were retiring. The enemy remained quiet until the 5th of November, when they made another bolt, but they were forced to retire with great loss. They have not made another attack. We have been two months battering Sebastopol. I do not know what to say about it. Please God I live to return, I will be able to tell you a great many things. We had no tents for one month. I will not say any more about the war. We have nothing with us except what we have on our backs. We are in tents yet, and it is quite cold. Send me a newspaper as often as you can. By the time you get this letter I hope we shall be in Sebastopol. We are lying alongside of the 13th Light Dragoons, and have only sixty horses left of the regiment. Send me some stamps in your next letter and some paper, as they are not easy to get here.

Letter from Trumpet Major **William Gray** (number 392),[107] 8th Hussars, to a friend in Nottingham.[108]

In front of Sebastopol,
November 12th, 1854.

My Dear Friend, -

I received your kind letter dated October 18th a few days after the most bloody battle that ever was fought by the English army, which took place on Sunday the 5th of November. We had not idea of being engaged that morning, and consequently, we lost a great number of our poor men; I should say 400 killed and 1,000 wounded. The Russians brought a great force into the field, I should say 52,000, and out of that the number they lost 16,000 altogether in killed and wounded. Our cavalry lost a few men: we lost no men and only one horse, but I am sorry to say we fought a most dreadful battle on the 25th of October, in which we lost most of our light cavalry, as I told you in my last; we got under the most terrible fire that ever was known in the memory of any man for cavalry to be under. I shall just tell you the miraculous manner in which by the goodness of God my life was spared. On going down in the charge I was wounded in my right shoulder, but thank God, not dangerously; as soon as we got down about a mile in the valley, we had to meet a regiment of Polish Lancers, about 2,000 in number, we broke our way through them manfully, and left many of them dead alongside our poor fellows that had been killed by their cannon. On my coming back [from the guns] I received two balls, one on my thigh, but I am happy to say it did not take much effect, for in the pocket of my overalls I had my pipe which was broken in a hundred pieces, and the ball left there in my pocket; I gave it to one of our surgeons by request. Another ball was entered in my horse shoe case, I had a ball entered there, took part of my sword belts away from my sword, and only left part of my sword remaining, and thank God I am spared so far.

We had another engagement this morning but not with the cavalry much; our artillery walked into them nicely with great slaughter on their (the Russians') side, but none on ours, thank God. We have no been 26 days firing on Sebastopol, and can make no impression whatever. I do not know what we shall do in this state; here we are up to our knees in mud and water, and the weather most bitter cold. We brought no kitt [*sic*, kit] with us, and here we are just as we stand, nothing more to put on. No! if you only saw the state we are in you would pity us, but I shall say no more about it. I hope you have received my letters since the battle of the Alma, I have written two since then, and by your letters you have not received either of them. I am afraid we shall remain her all winter and if that is the case, we shall be lost with the cold and wet. You must excuse this letter, for I have only two hours for this and church parade. Pray give my love to the young ladies, and tell them I have been in three engagements, and God has spared my life so far. Give my love to your wife, and kiss the dear children for me.

Letter from Private **Samuel Walker** (number 688),[109] 8th Hussars, of Leeds, to his brother John Walker in Leeds.[110]

Scutari, Constantinople,
Nov. 18, 1854.

Mr dear Brother, -

I now take this favourable opportunity of writing these few lines to you, hoping to find you in good health, as thank God, they leave me at present, nearly recovered from a wound I received on each leg, which I got in an engagement at Balaklava with a lot of Cossacks. Dear Brother, I am very sorry to inform you that our regiment got wonderfully cut up. Out of 360 men, we have 100 remaining; and I am sorry to say that our brother Light Cavalry shared the same fate. We have been fighting night and day ever since we have landed in the Crimea. Dear Brother, we had a very sharp engagement on that memorable day, the 5th November, which I am sure will never be forgot for there were about 45,000 of the enemy came down from Silistria by forced marches, and they just reached Sebastopol before daylight that morning. They were made drunk as lords, and they fought with great courage whilst the liquor was in them, but as the drink died away, they died away likewise. It was calculated at the camp next day that the number of Russians killed, wounded, and taking prisoners, amounted to 3,000 or 4,000, with 90 officers included. Dear Brother, you will be surprised when I tell you that I had three horses shot from under me, and yet escaped with so slight a wound myself, which I am happy to say nearly recovered. We have now a reinforcement of Circasians (*sic*, Circassians), and we live in hopes of the war soon being brought to a close. Now, Dear Brother, for they are more devils than soldiers in the field, Jack; for there is no army in the world can that can stand before them; not even batteries or cannon can stop them; but I am sorry to say that the enemy being ten or more to one of us in the field, is the reason we lose so many gallant men. Dear Brother, you would think it a curious sight to go over a battle field the next day after a fight, and witness the scene of 5,000 or 6,000 dead and dying. Our regiment (8th Hussars) lost nearly all their horses; and the chief of them are now mounted on Russian horses, which we took from the Russian Cavalry. They are a very good breed of horse, something of the Arab Breed, and lighter than *ours*; we have taken some hundreds from them.

And now, dear Brother, I think I had said enough about the horrors of war, to make you think how comfortable you are to have your comfortable bed to lie in every night, whilst your brother has not stretched his weary limbs in a bed this last eight months; nor does there appear any likelihood of doing so at present. Dear Brother, this is a wild, barren country; not the slightest sign of cultivation, except in the odd valley or so. The fort of Sebastopol is the strongest fort in the world; it mounts 1,400 guns, and it is garrisoned by 70,000 men; and they have an army in the rear of us that we have to keep attacking, of 45,000 men, or we could have taken the fort long ago. So now, Dear Brother, my time is short, and I must conclude by wishing you a Merry Christmas; but I expect mine will be a Good Friday, what the Jew call a fast day. But never mind, there's a good time coming and give my kindest love to sister Mary and brother Ben and to all.

Letter from Private **William Henry Pennington** (number 1631),[111] 11th Hussars, to his father.[112]

General Hospital, Scutari,
Dec. 7th.

I received a letter this morning, in which I was surprised to hear that no letter from me had reached you, as I wrote a month since to my father, describing the Light Cavalry charge on the 25th October, so far as it concerned myself. I also received one in which you said that Mr. Angell, the postmaster at

Constantinople, had written to inform you that I was wounded. I am sorry to say that I have not had one of the newspapers which you say that you have almost daily sent to me. Though four months' pay is due me, I cannot get a penny – in fact, I should be glad to buy a loaf of bread, as hospital fare does not suit my appetite. My wound was from a musket ball through the calf of the right leg, but it is so far healed that I being to walk upon it for an hour or so in the day. I enjoy excellent health, as, thank God I have done since we left Turkey, though cholera and war have made sad devastation in our ranks. It was a made, though gallant charge made by our Light Cavalry at Balaklava. The newspapers will let you see our position at the time. The word was given to 'Charge Guns to the Front.' We advanced at a gallop to these guns, amid a fearful fire from the front, with 'ditto' on the right and left flanks, of grape, shell, and canister, and infantry also pouring in a tremendous fire. The effect was that horses and men fell thick and fast; but even this did not check our onward rush. All the Russian artillerymen were sabred, and for an instant, we were masters of the guns, but, having no support, could not keep them. In this condition we were charged in flank and rear by numerous regiments of Russian infantry and cavalry, and but for the desperation with which our fellow cut their way, there would not have been a single man return from that fatal charge. As for myself, I never reached the guns in front, as a grapeshot went through my 'busby,' about two inches above my head, knocking it on one side, another through the calf of my leg, and next through my horse's head (a fine black mare.) Well, here I was at the mercy of their Lancers, whom I saw lancing our dismounted men. The demons give no quarter when you are down. At this moment the 8th Hussars came by with a horse without its rider. This I mounted, and formed in rear of the 8th as if it were my own regiment, and dashed on, but, worse again, we were obliged to wheel 'Right About,' and to pass through a strong body of the enemy's cavalry which had gathered in our rear, cutting off our retreat.

Of course, with our handful it was life or death; so we rushed at them to break through them; but as soon as we got through one body there was another to engage. At any rate, with five or six of our fellows at my rear, I galloped on, parrying with the determination of one who would not lose his life, breaking the lances of the cowards who attacked us in the proportion of three or four to one, occasionally catching one a slap with the sword across his teeth, and giving another the point in his arm or breast. They still pressed on me till I got sight of our Heavies, when, thanks be to God, they stopped pursuing me, and I got clear without a scratch from their lances. Oh! The sabre before the lance! I found that I could not dismount from the wound in my right leg, and so was lifted off, and then how I caressed the noble horse that had brought me safely out! I will not disgrace you as a soldier, take my word.

Letter from Private **Thomas Dudley** (number 1134), 17th Lancers, to his parents.[113]

Scutari General Hospital,
Dec. 18, 1854.

My Dear Father and Mother, -

I hope this will find you and all my dear sisters well, as I am happy so say I am fast recovering, and hope soon to be as well as ever. In my last I only just told you I was alive, and my whereabouts. I have more leisure now, and am better able to write you a little more in detail. First, a little about that fatal 25th October charge. When we received the *order*, not a man could seem to believe it. However, on we went, and during that ride what each man felt no one can tell. I cannot tell you my own thoughts. Not a word or a whisper. On – on we went! Oh! If you could have seen the faces of that doomed 800 men at that moment; every man's features fixed, his teeth clenched, and as rigid as death, still it was on – on! At about 300 yards I got my hit, but it did not floor me. Clash! And oh God! what a scene! I will not attempt to tell you, as I know it is not to your taste, what we did; but we were Englishmen, and that is enough. I believe I was as strong as six men – at least I felt so; for I know I had chopped two Russian lances in two as if they had been reeds. Well, I got out of the melée, but, in returning, my poor horse was shot down, and me under him. Poor beast! I believe he struggled to release me. You will hardly think I took time to give the noble brute a last look, but I did though; he was a fine creature. Well I got to my legs, and was fortunate enough to catch an officer's charger, got up as well as I could, and so got to camp, and next day got packed off to this place, and many times have I thought it a very lucky hit for me in two respects: first, if it had been an inch further to my neck, it would have been all up with me; next it sent me here to be laid up in lavender – at least, compared with what the poor fellows are undergoing at camp; *but I dare say it is not all true that is said about that, any more than it is about this place.* By the bye, I stuck the paper you sent in the fire. The lies in it were shameful. Never was a place worse libelled. I don't believe there is a man here but would feel as I do about it. Why, here we have all the comforts we can desire; at least, well expect. A poor fellow can't utter a groan, or hardly a sigh, but some kind soul is at his pillow. If Miss Nightingale had been dropped by Heaven, she could scarcely have done more good. Talk of the men not being grateful! Many a noble fellow here would marry his nurse out of sheer gratitude, if he could do her the honour thereby, to say nothing about the thoughts of mothers and sisters: Yes, this will set a man thinking about his own fireside comforts and those that are far away. Of course, after a large and fresh arrival of sick and wounded here is some con-fusion – how should it be otherwise? But the next day all is set in order. The medical staff is, as far as I can judge, excellent; and I can say something about it, having been here nearly two months. I have written some scores of letters home for other poor fellows, and they all express themselves as I do. I know I am in no hurry to go back, but I suppose I shall soon. I believe I might get sent home if I wished, but they would say that looks like cowardice, so that won't do; but, however, I will make the most of it while I stop here. We hope to get a bit of old English fare at Christmas – a bit of plum pudding &c. I shall think of home and you all while eating it; so wishing you all a Merry Christmas and happy New Year, and better times, I leave you for the present.

Letter from an anonymous Troop Sergeant-Major of the 8th Hussars, to his father.[114]

Near Balaklava,
Dec. 22.
Dear Father, -
I have no doubt that you feel anxious to hear of my welfare in this truly dread-ful country, but I must not dwell on all we have suffered, or are likely to suffer before this fearful struggle is at an end.

With regard to myself, I am as comfortable as I can well be in the camp, as I fortunately have good clothes, but many of our poor fellows have hardly a shoe to their feet or clothes to their backs, and yet are obliged to do the most arduous duty, although so diminished in numbers; in fact the three troops in camp would hardly make one of the strength we came out.

The Troop which composes Lord Raglan's escort has not suffered much, as it was not at the horrible engagement at Balaklava, nor on the heights of Inkermann, where we lost so many horses through starvation and inclemency of the weather We are all better off now, as we are close to the town, and can get supplies for ourselves, but it is galling to think that we lost more horses, and men through the above means than we should probably from the most severe fire of the Enemy.

You received my former letter, describing the dreadful 25th. By the by, no better description can be given than that of "The Times" reporter, and I am glad to see our brave and gallant Colonel (Shewell) has been promoted through it. He richly deserves it; and but for his coolness and bravery there would have been an end to the Light Brigade. Well indeed our noble men followed his example. No men could work better, and their line in advance through the Russian artillery, as well as through their cavalry, could not be surpassed on Hounslow-Heath.

After we had sabred and passed their artillery at the end battery the word was given, "The Russian cavalry are in our rear; make ready to Charge!" Some officers gave the order "Retired by Threes from the Right." Our brave Colonel shouted immediately, "Steady, my brave men!" in a cool but determined voice, followed by "Right About, Wheel." We were at this time at a full gallop; and this movement brought the officers and front rank facing the Russian cavalry; and, when we were well in line, the brave fellow said, "Follow me – Charge!" He led us on, and how he escaped is a miracle, for he was the first who came up to that tremendous mass of horsemen. We followed close, and went through them like the wind, making clear way for the others to follow, after which our handful of men broke, and each as best he could, cut his way to the original ground. I shall never forget that day as long as I live. Only a handful of that devoted band of soldiers returned. We prize our gallant Colonel the more, because for several days previous he had been laid up in his tent, and even on the morning of the engagement was too unwell to attend parade; but, no sooner did he hear the cannons roar than he called his servant to inquire what was the cause, and, on being told, immediately ordered his horse to be saddled, but was obliged to be helped to mount it. He was no sooner seated than he clapped spurs to his noble beast and came up at a gallop to take command of us; and, as I said before, we indeed did he perform his part.

We are still in tents, and, I fear, are likely to be so; were they to send sheds, as there is a talk of doing, we could hardly spare men to put them up, although doubtless they would contribute much to our comfort, the weather being exceedingly wet and cold.

I have no time to write more at present. Give my love to all.

PS. We only lost two horses at the battle of Inkermann; the ground would not allow us to work. The played on us with their tremendous artillery.

Letter from Private **Thomas Williams** (number 1479)[115] 11th Hussars, to his father, a hatter in Colchester.[116]

Dear Father and Mother, -
Camp near Sebastopol,
Jan. 7, 1855.

I trust you will forgive me for keeping so long silent, but if you knew how we have been harassed about since we landed, I am sure I should obtain your forgiveness. I thank the Lord most fervently for His merciful goodness towards me, in giving me health and strength, and carrying me through the many difficulties I have had, with my poor comrades, to encounter.

I have been with the Regiment in all the skirmishes we have had, except Inkerman. I was then at the wounded horse depot at Balaklava, with three of our wounded horses. We lost one poor fellow there of my troop, and a Sergeant got his arm blown off; it was a well-aimed ball from the enemy's artillery. It first took the top of a horse's head clean off, took the rider's arm off, went through his rear-rank man, and put the next man's shoulder out of joint. That's all our casualties in our regiment on the 5th, which, I think, was more than sufficient after the cutting-up we got at Balaklava. I cannot help telling you a little about that affair, although, of course, you have heard more flowery accounts than I can give of it. At that time we had to turn out every morning before daylight, and soon after daylight we would turn in and go about our daily business. On this fatal morning we were just about to turn in when we heard a report from the Turkish batteries. We looked round and saw flash after flash. Of course if caused a bit of a stir in our ranks; we were mounted in quick sticks, and advanced. The shot and shell soon began to make themselves heard. Several passed through the rank, but did no harm. Presently we saw Master Turk retiring; then shells came quicker; and at last we retired behind a hill, out of sight of the enemy. We stopped here perhaps a quarter or half an hour, and it was while we were stationed here that the Heavies made their bold and daring charge, and drove the Russians back over the hills. Then we got the order to advance. I could see what would be the result of it, and so could all of us; but of course, as we had got the order, it was our duty to obey. I do not wish to boast too much; but I can safely say that there was not a man in the Light Brigade that day but what did his duty to his Queen and Country. It was a fearful sight to see men and horses falling on all sides. Thank God, I and my poor horse got through it without a scar, although I had two or three very narrow escapes. My sword scabbard had two or three very severe knocks; in fact a ball caught it about the centre, and cut it very nearly in two. How my leg escaped seems to me to be a miracle; but, thanks be to a kind Providence, I did escape, and hope, by God's assistance, once more to return to the bosom of my beloved family. If I should fall, you must console yourselves by the thought that I died in a Just and Honourable cause. But I do not despair; thank God I am in good spirits, as well as health.

There has been a great fall of snow here, and it is rather unpleasant to find it comes through the tent, and is wetting our blankets nicely. It has been freezing this last day or two. I woke up this morning and felt rather cold about the mouth; I put my hand up to it and found what little moustaches and whiskers I have frozen – rather a pleasant sensation! What think you? I am very sorry to say that poor Bill [his brother] has been very unwell. We left him at Varna when we started for the Crimea, and the silly fellow kept trying to join us, although he was not fit for it. He got his wish, and came to Balaklava a few days after our charge; but he was too weak to join his regiment, so he was sent back to Scutari, where he will be much more comfortable. He is all right, except weakness. I feel very thankful for the kind inquiries after my welfare by so many of my worthy townsmen; and pray remember me to all inquiring friends.

Letter from Captain **J.D. Shakespear**, Royal Horse Artillery, to the Editor of *The Times*.[117]

Hardwick-court, Glocester [*sic*],
March 31

Sir, -

Having been repeatedly asked to lay before the public what I know relative to the attack made by the Light Cavalry at Balaklava, and what was done, or not done, by the Horse Artillery, I have been induced to make the following statements:

It is well known that on Major Maude falling seriously wounded early in the day I, who had been with him in four previous actions and affairs, succeeded to the command of his Troop. Passing over all previous occurrences of that day, I had brought my guns up at a gallop on the left flank of the Heavy Brigade, while re-forming after their charge. The Light Cavalry, having passed along my rear, were on my left flank. It must now be remembered that the whole cavalry brigade were in the plain on the Balaklava side of the heights on which were the redoubts. My troop would be about 600 yards from the crest of these heights. Considering all immediate action over, if not, indeed, the whole thing for the day, I rode over to the heights to reconnoitre. I there met Lieutenant-Colonel McMahon, the Quarter-Master General of Cavalry. We were alone, and with our telescopes were examining the Russian Artillery in the bush on the opposite heights across the second plain. The distance would be about 1,500 yards. I had counted 10 guns; there were other guns further on to the left of these. There was cavalry, infantry, and artillery in the plain, nearly a mile away. I knew the Russians held Nos. 1, 2, and 3 redoubts, which, it must be remembered, faced the bush I have before mentioned. Captain Charteris rode up to us: he was accompanied, I think, by Captain Methuen, of the screw-ship 'Columbo'. The former said, "You will see something now; the Light Cavalry are going to attack down the plain." I exclaimed: "You will all be destroyed. I will go and bring up the troop and try and give assistance." I galloped back; I could not see Lord Lucan; but Major-General Scarlett being close at hand, I said, "Will you allow me to go to the support of the Light Cavalry?" His answer was, "Certainly." I moved off at a smart trot seeing the rear regiments of the Light Cavalry just slip out of sight over the heights. My horses were tired and reduced in numbers, several having been killed in the early part of the day; so I soon came to a walk. The Scots Greys had moved before me, and had halted in line just at the foot of the Heights. I passed through squadron at intervals. At this time, Major Walker, Lord Lucan's Aide-de-Camp, rode up to me, and, in a conversation I had with him afterwards, he said, "with an order for me to advance." I perfectly remember his being with me, but have *no* recollection of this order. He had brought me directions to do otherwise than I was doing, I should probably have paid more attention. Major Walker, in speaking to me on the subject afterwards said, "My life was probably saved by being sent back for you." I passed on over the heights with the troop; a heavy fire was immediately opened on me, happily without effect, from the artillery in the bush on the opposite heights; to this I could not reply, the range being too great for my light guns. I at once "Wheeled to the Right" and endeavoured to pass along the Balaklava side of the heights immediately below their crest, screened from the enemy's fire, and so come over, if possible, on the rear of our Light Cavalry but a cut down into the Woronzoff Road, past which I could not get my guns, prevented me. I wheeled about and followed the Heavy Cavalry, which had now come up, down into the plain in support of the Light Cavalry.

The fire at this time from the Russian front and flanks was tremendous. I halted for a moment in the rear of the Heavy Cavalry, but, not being able to make my guns of any use, seeing the disaster and knowing from previous observation that descending further into the plain was taking the troop to certain destruction and giving the guns intrusted to my care into the hands of the enemy, I retired at a walk to the crest of the heights on my own responsibility, fearing a second Chillianwalla, and was almost immediately followed by the Heavy Cavalry, who were indeed, close on to my guns when I reached the crest.

CHAPTER 6

Winter in the Crimea:
1 November 1854–1 March 1855

Aftermath of Balaklava: hospitals and prisoners

The wounded of the cavalry brigades received initial treatment in the temporary hospital set up in the Orthodox Church at Kadikoi; the more serious cases were transported down to Balaklava. The most seriously wounded were put onboard the transport *Australia* on 26 October, which conveyed them to the General Hospital at Scutari, a four-day voyage away across the Black Sea. Amongst their number was Lieutenant-Colonel John Yorke (1st Royals) who had had his ankle smashed.[1] Often described as 'horrific' with 'no beds, no bandages and no nurses' by the rabble-rousing press eager to make sales, this was perhaps not the case. Surgeon Scott (57th Foot) thought the Barrack Hospital was as 'comfortable as can be expected'. The wounded were all in 'wooden cots' and 'well supplied with good rations and warm dress'. The high rate of mortality was not due to the incompetence of the hospital staff but because the sick were 'already dead'; 'mere skeletons' from exposure and starvation brought on in the 'Crimea, that land of death': victims of the failed commissariat.[2] Another surgeon explained some of the difficulties encountered:

> ... you may easily imagine some of these experienced in accommodating 6,000 or 7,000 persons in a country where bedsteads, chairs, tables, fire-places, chimneys, knives and forks, are not known, and where all these things have to be made for us, or sent out from England.[3]

Those men who were taken prisoner were collected at the Russian HQ before being sent away from the immediate combat-zone to Simpheropol, arriving 10 November 1854. Those men who had been wounded were treated by the Russian surgeons. The food they received was not of the highest quality: 'There as not a sparkle of fat on top to lead the mind to suppose that there had been meet cooked in it [the soup]' and there was 'no flour to thicken ... but there were large lumps of cabbage and ... black bread floating [in it]'.[4] From Simpheropol the prisoners were marched to Melitopol (on the coast of the Black Sea) and then into Russia, as far as Voronesh where they spent a miserable winter.[5]

Letters from Lieutenant-Colonel **John Yorke** (1st Royal Dragoons) to his sister.

Arabia Transport,[6] Balaklava Harbour
Oct 27th

My dear Ethel, -
More bad luck, but do not make yourself very uneasy. I have been badly wounded in the late disastrous affair – a grape or canister shot caught me on the left shin bone, and smashed my leg badly, but I continued to ride down home, about 4 miles with my leg swinging about, I suffered considerable pain but did not faint, and the Doctors say I am unusually well. This is the 3rd day

since the accident, and I have continued to [illegible] a little sleep, and feel very confident my leg can be spared, but it must be shorter. I am going on board the Hospital Ship bound for Scutaria [*sic*], as I feared the voyage would do one last injury, & Captain Foust of the Arabia expressed the great esteam [*sic*] & every kindness, and if we move to Katcha River, it will be equally comfortable for me.

The Poor Light Cavalry Brigade is cut to pieces. It was madness advancing against a raking fire from the Right, Front & Left. The shells flew in every direction and it is most fortunate matters are not worse for me. 3 other Officers wounded slightly in the Royals. Cheer up my dear Ethel our losses might have been much worse ...

Arabia, Balaclava[7]

My Dear Ethel, -   Nov. 1st 1854
This is a very formidable affair and it is most difficult for even the Doctors to decide at this early stage as to my case, but Doctor Gorringe[8] of the Regt. who I have on board to attend to me, assures me he never saw a contused wound do better, indeed he is surprised at each dressing to observe its continual healing appearance, more particularly after my loss of rest for the pain of one fixed position puts sleep out of the question.

I have been to develop all sorts of contrivances of my own, and was actually carried from my sofa at the stern window to a birth which I had first prepared with [a] canvas *bottom in the centre* to afford me some relief from the pain which I suffered in the loins. The ball has never been found but it is evident it is of the Minié variety and not grape as the damage it has done to the bone led us to suppose, there is only one aperture in the overalls and it is hard to guess what has become of it may have fallen out in my long ride after the misfortune[,] but Guthries book[9] states that it does not always follow that it must be within.

The ship will eventually take sick to Scutari. It is difficult to write more at present. May God Bless you all and much love my dear Ethel.

Nov. 2nd 7 p.m.
The Doctor considered my leg better than ever this morning and I have had some refreshing sleep during the day.

Letter from an anonymous sergeant in the 5th Dragoon Guards to his parents in Manchester.[10]

Scutari,
November 2nd

Since I wrote to you last, I have undergone many hardships in this country; I not having anything of a pleasant nature to send you, I thought it useless to write. From the time we entered the country to the present we have been in the midst of pestilence and death, and to finish up we had a dreadful battle on the heights of Alma, on the 20th September, in which I got off safe; but I had not come off so easy on the 25th of October, when we had a battle with Cossacks and infantry, in which I had to fight hard for my life. The Russian cavalry came thick upon us, eight thousand in number, which caused us to do something else than play with them. At one time I was surrounded with about ten Cossacks, and with the assistance of my long sword (which is the only thing you can depend upon with those Cossacks), I got clear of them, with two wounds in my head and one in my right hand, all sabre cuts; and what is more remarkable, I have eleven cuts in my helmet. My helmet has been shown all over the hospital and barracks. Just fancy ten fellows cutting at you on all sides! The morning after the battle wounded were removed from the Crimea to the General Hospital; and I am glad to say my wounds are doing very well, and that I am in pretty good health. In Turkey I found my wife of great service, and I am glad that I did not leave her behind, as she has been employed in cooking and washing for the officers all the time we have been out. With her earnings she has made me very comfortable.

Letter from Private **Edward Edmonds** (number 1008), 4th Light Dragoons, to his wife in Littlehampton.[11]

I left the Regimental hospital, under the walls of Sebastopol, or rather the tent appropriated for the sick, on the 28th last month [November], and went on board ship at Balaklava, were her left on the 4th December, and arrived here on the 13th. We had on board 250 – I was going to say men – but I do not know what to call them, unless I call them the wrecks of good men – but our number was sadly reduced on our arrival at Scutaria [*sic*, Scutari]. Oh! What a tale might be told – it would defy my poor, simple, abilities to give the least idea of such a scene. Scarcely a morning came but two or three bodies were sewn up in a blanket and carried on shore while we were in harbour, or thrown overboard at sea. I must now tell you something of our reception at Scutaria Hospital. On our arrival we were put into a clean, warm room, stripped of our – I mean worldly – rags; our poor bodies were washed of their filth; we were put into clean beds, with plenty of clean good clothing, and supplied with arrow-root and wine by the charitable Miss Nightingale and her Christian band. No one could sufficiently describe the kindness and attention of that lady to the unfortunate. Every man can get a flannel shirt, a pair of drawers and socks from her, by requisition signed by the Surgeon of the war, and there is no stint of anything on her part to make the sick and weak comfortable. Oh! what a pattern she is to the ladies in England. I fear you will think this is a strange letter; but I have been called away very often, for as I am convalescent, it is my duty to render assistance to the helpless which I have received from others. What would I not give to see you and my dear boy now. Oh! what a change in two years: but I have another longing – it is for the blessing of health that I may return to my duty, for after the Alma and Inkermann, with all the hardships I have endured, I should not like to lose the honour of being present at the fall of Sebastopol.

Letter from '**P.H.J.**', 11th Hussars to his brother in Leeds.[12]

Military Hospital, Balaklava,
My Dear Brother, -   Nov. 28th 1854.
It is against inclination to heighten your anxiety concerning me, but upon receiving your letter bearing the Leeds post-mark of 1st November, I considered it a duty I owe myself, as well as to you, to let you know t hat ever since I landed in the Crimea I have suffered almost daily more or less from intermittent fever, accompanied by diarrhoea, which reduced me to almost a shadow before I gave up my duty. At length the severest snow, hail, and rain

storm that ever I witnessed visited us on the 14th instant, blowing two days, without covering of any sort, and up to our knees in mud. This became too much for me; and as I was sinking under it, Colonel Douglas ordered the doctor to make arrangements for me to be sent down to Balaklava on board the ship 'Trent' on the 16th, where I remained trying to make myself comfortable; but failing this, I got myself removed on the 24th to the General Military Hospital at Balaklava, where I have met with every kind treatment from the surgeon in charge, and am, thank Divine Goodness, again on my pins, recovering strength. This change in my situation has compelled me to purchase new under clothing and comforts which have been withheld [*sic*] from us all by the awful shipwreck which took place in the Bay a fortnight ago: the 'Prince' steamer having gone down with all our boots, flannels and blankets. As I have proceeded thus far the Doctor sends in the orderly to me with a 'Weekly Dispatch' our dear brother Jack has sent me, dated the 5th of November. It cannot, however, contain any account of the two dreadful engagements which have taken place at Balaklava and Inkermann, the accounts of which will be better detailed in the newspapers than I can give you. Suffice it to say, that I am, by an over-ruling Providence, spared from the effects of the sudden and terrible attack made upon our *then* weak position by the Russians. On the 25th [October] the wretched Turks, to whom we had entrusted the batteries protecting our position, gave way before the enemy, and let them through upon us before we had time to get all saddled. I was in a most critical dilemma, the Cossacks passing close by me, spearing and shooting the poor Turks, upon whom they seemed to direct their vengeance, whilst our cavalry go into position to repel the attack, which they did in masterly style but unfortunately followed the villains too far into their masked entrenchments, and the Light Cavalry were consequently nearly cut to pieces with grape and canister shot, and I narrowly escaped the Cossacks. In this terrible affair our regiment lost nearly one-half of the effective force, so that we are but a wreck of what we were six months ago. We have within the last ten days received reinforcements of about 25,000 men, and it is said Lord Raglan very shortly intends striking the blow. Yet it must not be supposed that when Sebastopol falls the war will be ended, although the Russian power will be completely prostrated by it. The weather here is miserably wet and dull, and will continue so until the middle of December, when the air becomes frosty and winter sets in. I find I cannot write much more, but will communicate with you when I am restored to duty, which is likely to be so far deferred as the new year, the Doctor thinks. The new Staff Corps which has just got to work at Balaklava are attacked with cholera, and two have died in the hospital here to-day [*sic*]. Our men are perfectly bare-footed, their toes out of their boots, and the mud gushing out at every step they take. Every thing is exceedingly dear here, and I thank God my pay is so good as to afford me a chance of getting commodities even at the dearest rates.

December 3rd.
The French torment the Russians sadly with their batteries almost every night, and get them to turn out a few thousand men from the fort to attack them, when they permit them to advance very close, and then charge them down the hill with a murderous fire, leaving numbers killed. We have succeeded in cutting off the communication, by one of the roads between the Fortress and

Osten Sacken's, and Liprandi's army in the rear; eventually all intercourse will be stopped, and the French are advancing their mines close up to the Russian works, so that there is a probability of the place eventually surrendering without our having to storm it at all.

Lord Raglan acts on the maxim, "Give them rope," which no doubt will succeed best. We are just stealing to the completion of a new battery, which will bear upon their shipping in the harbour, which sometimes annoys us by throwing over the heights shells into our camps; the siege guns are gradually being platformed in the Battery, and in a few more days it will open fire upon the shipping with red-hot stuff. As regards the Fortress itself, the Commander-in-Chief simply prevents the Russians from advancing any batteries nearer to us, whilst we are gradually gaining ground for future operations whenever he thinks proper to direct active measures to be taken against it. The army of 50,000 men in our rear has to be narrowly watched and eventually attacked, so as soon as the weather hardens; but since the battle of Inkermann, we have got out positions ten times more strongly entrenched and protected, sufficient to defy 100,000 men.

Letter from Private **Robert Martin** (number 1337),[13] 11th Hussars, to his family in Liverpool.[14]

My dear Wife and Mother, -

General Hospital, Scutari,
Dec. 9th, 1854

I am sorry to inform you I am severely wounded in the right arm, which I have no doubt you have long since seen in the papers. I am now looking over the paper and see my own name. I am doing very well, and expect to leave here for England about the end of the month, so you may expect to see me the beginning of the New Year. I have every attention paid to me here; I have as much wine as I can drink; also plenty of all kinds of things that I fancy. The doctors are very kind, and pay every attention to our wants and comforts. We have about 1500 here, and 170 officers. The weather here is beautiful, though this is the 9th of December, the sun out like a May day in England. Good old England. I shall be glad when I am there. My brother is quite well, and writes in love to you all. – I am your affectionate son and husband.

P.S. – You must excuse this short note, as a sick man cannot write a long letter.

P.P.S. – It is no use my keeping it any longer a secret from you; but I must tell you that I have lost my right arm about six inches below the shoulder. My arm is getting on very well indeed now, and I expect to be up in a day or two. I place my trust in the Almighty, and hope to see you both in a month or two. I shall have to go to Chatham first to get discharged and pension settled. Remember me to all inquiring friends.

Letter from Corporal **James Hall** (number 1051),[15] 17th Lancers, to his father, Staff Sergeant Thomas Hall of the Leicestershire Yeomanry.[16]

Dear Father,-

Near Balaklava.
October the 29th, 1854.

I am just about to send you a few lines to let you know that I am alive, for I have no doubt buy you will hear of the disaster which befell the Light Brigade of

Cavalry on the 25th; on which occasion I received a ball in my leg below the knee, which broke, but I have got it set again all right, and am getting on as well as can be expected for the time. I am a prisoner of war in the Russian camp, and am going to be sent to Simpheropol in the morning: There are about fifty prisoners here altogether (some very badly wounded) belonging to our Brigade. I cannot tell you the particulars at this time, but will embrace the first opportunity of writing again, and tell you more particulars about it, for I have only a short time to write as our letters are wanted to be sent away in a few minutes, so I thought I would prevent you from thinking that I might have been killed on the field, as the Regiment does not know what has become of me. The Russians have been very kind to us; in fact, I am scarcely able to return sufficient thanks to them. I only hope that they will be recompensed by the English army showing the same to those who have the misfortune to become prisoners of war.

Give my kind love to all at home ...

Letter from Private **Henry William Parker** (number 1484),[17] 11th Hussars, a Prisoner of War in Russia to his father, Mr George Parker, tailor, of Love Lane, Windsor.[18]

Simpheropol,
Dear Parents, -   Nov. 5. 1854.
I have no doubt you will be surprised when you read this to hear where I am, but let a few words suffice. I and a great many more were taken prisoners by the Russians on the 25th of last month in the skirmish at Balaklava. Dear Parents, I must thank the Almighty I was taken prisoner as I was, without being wounded in the slightest. I was only hurt a little in the fall from my horse, when it was shot from under me; but that wore off in a few days, and now, I am happy to say, I am in as good health as ever I was in my life. I must say, that since we have been in the hands of the Russians they have behaved like gentlemen to us in every respect; and we have been treated equally as well as if we had been with our own countrymen. They have even allowed us this very great indulgence of writing home. There is no telling how long we shall remain prisoners; perhaps until the war is ended, and perhaps not; it is quite uncertain, but sooner or later. I hope I shall keep in as good health as I am at present. Last Christmas-Day [*sic*] I was at home at dinner with you, but I doubt very much whether I shall be at home with you this Christmas-day. Dear Mother, you had better not write till you hear from me again, which will be the first opportunity. Remember me to all inquiring friends. I will now conclude with my love to all, and believe me your ever affectionate son.

Letter from Private **Thomas Perry** (number 597),[19] 8th Hussars, to his mother in Reading.[20]

Simpheropol,
My Dear Mother and Sisters,-   Dec. 22.
I have taken this the first opportunity of writing to you, to inform you that I am a prisoner of war in Russia, at a place named Simpheropol. I am in hospital here. I suppose you have seen by the English newspapers there was a battle fought on the 25th of October, at Balaclava, near Sevastopol, and the Light Brigade of Cavalry, that my regiment was in, charged the Russian lines, and we

were very much cut up by the enemy's cannon. I have since heard that about 160 were killed, and about the same number wounded, but I cannot tell you much about them, as I myself was shot through both thighs, and through the right shoulder, at the top part of the arm, two sword cuts in the head, and two lance wounds, one in the hand and one in the thigh; so I leave you to think I was in a bad state. I was taken up almost dead by the Russians; but after I got a doctor's attendance I began to do well. I am still in hospital, but I am happy to say I am enjoying as good health as I can expect. The Russians are very kind to us, as well as we can understand them; and I make myself as happy as I can, waiting for the time to come that I may see you all again, as I hope it will be the will of Almighty God to spare me, and send me safe back to you again in a few months. We have in attendance at the hospital some ladies who are very kind to us; they are what we call in England Sisters of Mercy or Charity.

Letter from Lieutenant **John Chadwick**, 17th Lancers, to his brother, James Chadwick.[21]

Karkoff,

My dear James, -   April 2, 1855.
I have deferred from day to day and from week to week writing to you, in the hope of having some definite news to give you as to what is likely to be done with me and the other officers, prisoners. All we know, however, is, that we are to be sent to Riazan, about 100 Versts from Moscow, where I suppose we shall remain until we are exchanged, which I sincerely hope will be this summer. We left Simpheropol on the 20th of January, and arrived here on the 15th of last month, so that you may imagine that we suffered some little inconvenience during that long march at such a time of the year; the distance was something like 700 versts (a verst is two-thirds of an English mile). We have a little more than that distance yet to traverse, but the Governor-General here has very kindly allowed me to remain a little to recruit ourselves and until the weather gets a little better for travelling: besides which we have been given to understand that the present Emperor has given an order that we are to travel alone with post horses and not in the same manner as we came here day by day with English, French, and Turkish soldiers, prisoners and Russian convicts on their way to Siberia. It would be quite useless for me to attempt to describe to you what we suffered on our journey here. I could not do it. Suffice it to tell you that I was impious enough to wish often that I had not met the same fate as my poor mare did at Balaklava.

I am in company with Captain Frampton, 50th Regiment;[22] Lieutenant Duff, 23rd;[23] Lieutenant Clowes, 8th Hussars; and a Mr Carrew, who was master of the 'Culldoen' transport which was wrecked on the 14th November; he, poor fellow, a few days before we reached here became idiotic and is now in hospital; he is nearly well now but weak. Of twelve men of the 17th Lancers who were taken prisoners on the same day that I was [25 October 1854], 5 only are living. Corporal Hall[24] and Private Jenner[25] are at Simpheropol, for former having had his leg taken off, and the latter his arm. Private Wightman[26] left sick at Alexandrioski on the way here, and Private Marshall[27] is here. Private McAllister[28] had gone on for his destination. The seven dead are Privates Harrison,[29] Ellis,[30] Young,[31] Kirk,[32] Edge,[33] Brown,[34] and Sharp;[35] the two latter started quite well from Simpheropol, but died on the journey. I wish you would write to Taylor, the Riding Master at the Depot, in order that he may cause their friends to be written to.

...

I know nothing, of course, about the state of affairs with the regiments at home, but hope you will give me in your next letter all the news you can, bearing in mind that your letter will be read, and not read me if it contains anything objectionable.

The Battle of Inkerman

During the evening of 27 October 1854, 'About 11 ½ pm ... we were alarmed by one of our pickets galloping in saying that there was a large body advancing in the plain.' The whole of the cavalry brigade turned out and guns and musketry was heard 'in the direction of Balaklava'.[36] This, in fact, was a false alarm. About 100 Russian horses had got loose and galloped across the plain toward the British camp near Kadikoi. The sound of approaching horses had naturally alerted the pickets, who instead of firing at the horses attempted to round up as many as possible. Amongst the Russian horses was the mount of Trumpeter Lovelock (4th Light Dragoons), which had been captured at the Battle of Balaklava, and it was suggested that it was this horse that had led the stampede toward the British camp. The Light and Heavy Brigade were therefore remounted courtesy of the Russians.[37]

On 28 October Lord Raglan ordered the cavalry to move their camp to the Inkerman Heights. The heights were exposed to the cold winds which blew across the Crimean Peninsula and offered little shelter from the elements or firewood for cooking fires. Lieutenant-Colonel Hodge 'banked up my tent inside and out to try and make it warmer and drier' with mixed success.[38] Two days later he wanted to move the camp of the 4th Dragoon Guards to a more sheltered spot, 'a sheltered valley close to water, and a little wood in it' about half a mile to the rear, but 'that obstinate mule Lord Lucan will not do it'.[39]

Under the cover of a dense fog at dawn on 5 November 1854 around 60,000 Russian troops attacked the British position on the Inkerman Heights and simultaneously a further 40,000 sallied from Sebastopol to attack the French siege works. The Light Brigade were ordered to mount and 'stand ready' just behind the front line in case they were needed under the command of Lord George Paget. Lieutenant-Colonel Hodge relates how 'we turned out without any breakfast and remained sitting on our horses until after 12½ o'clock'. He had just returned to the lines when Lord Lucan ordered him to take 'a squadron of the 4th, one of the Greys and the Royal Dragoons to the front in support of the Horse Artillery', arriving just 'as the business was over'.[40] Lord Paget with the Light Brigade had been ordered to 'Support the *Chasseurs d'Afrique* ... and went to the front to the support ... of General Bosquet.' The Brigade 'went on till we got into a heavy fire, when after some time they [*Chasseurs d'Afrique*] returned, and we also.'[41] Troop Sergeant-Major Smith (11th Hussars) recounted:

> The Enemy must have known where we were, for they dropped their cannon-balls just over the brow of the hill so that they passed through us about breast high. One struck a horse's head, knocking it to pieces, then took off Sergeant Breese's arm. It then struck Private White full in the chest, passing through

him. Another cannonball struck a man's leg just above the knee, taking it clean off, passing through his horse.[42]

By about 1 p.m. the Russian attack had faltered and by 3 p.m. all was quiet. The Heavy Brigade returned to camp about 5 p.m. but whilst at the front, Lieutenant-Colonel Hodge and Major Forrest's horses were stolen by a soldier from the 41st (Royal Welch Regiment) which meant that they had to 'trudge on foot to the camp of the Light Dragoons' where they were able to borrow some ponies to ride home on. The Provost Sergeant was informed about the theft, and around 2 a.m. on the 6 November the missing horses were returned but minus Hodge's pistol and water canteens. After dinner on 6 November Hodge rode over to the 41st 'and there I found the man who had carried off our horses, and from him I recovered the greater part of my things'.[43]

The outcome of the battle, however, meant that the 'siege, or rather assault, is to be given up for the year, until reinforcements come' and 'the occupations of the army are to be for the present confined to intrenching [sic] themselves'. Many officers, including Lord Paget, received leave to return home, but for the surviving men of the Cavalry Division a miserable four months on the Inkerman heights awaited them.[44]

Letter from Corporal **Thomas Morley** (number 1004), 17th Lancers, to his father.[45]

Near Sebastopol,
Dear Father, -   December 1.
I wrote my last letter to you about the end of October, after the Battle of Balaklava.[46] On the 2nd November we moved further towards Sebastopol, where we are at present. We are not more than a mile from the guns which are playing upon Sebastopol. We were sent here in order to have a little rest, but on the 5th of November we had a general engagement again. It began before day-break [sic]. The Russians lost about 16,000 men; the English did not lose as many hundreds. I do not know the loss on the side of the French, but it is not great. In our regiment we had one officer and one private killed; and one private had his arm shot off. The officer was just in front of me when he was shot. I dismounted in order to take him out of danger, as he was not then dead, but he died the next day. As we were carrying him, I and a private had our dress caps shot off our heads by the bursting of a shell. We laid him in a place sheltered from the cannon balls and shells. Our horses followed the regiment, which retired out of the way of the fire. We did not at first know where the shot came from, but we soon learnt that it came from the Russian ships. I had to run after the regiment for more than a mile. I would run about twenty yards, and then, as I saw the balls coming, I would fall down. I was glad when I got to my regiment. It is not very pleasant for a Light Dragoon to be off his horse in such a fire. Sebastopol is not yet taken, but I hope it will be taken soon. The weather is very cold; and with the rain we have had, the mud is up to our knees. It frequently happens that for two days we cannot light a fire to cook our food. One day it blew so hard that all our tents were thrown down. The rain also fell heavily, and we got wet to the skin. In addition to this we could not get anything to eat or drink. We shall have to move from here before long, as the horses are dying at the rate of four or five every night. We are returned as unfit

for service, and I think we shall be in quarters somewhere before long. The report is now that we are going to Scutari, in the vicinity of Constantinople, in a few days. If we do get into barracks, I will write the first opportunity. We may return, and get recruited afresh. At present we are neither useful nor ornamental. You never saw such a dirty set of fellows in your life. We do not wash our faces above once a month. We do not even get clean water to drink. I have seen water running down the channels in the streets clearer than that which we have to drink. If I can but get through this, I shall regard myself as a lucky man. The best thing we get is rum. We get a quartern a-day[*sic*] – that is, half of half a pint; and we get one half in the morning and the other half in the evening. George Harpham, of Wilford, is quite well. You must excuse my short letter, as I have not time to say more. I have plenty of news, but it would take me a month to write it. I must reserve it until I return, should I ever do so. I always think I shall. I am tired of hearing the guns go off at Sebastopol. I never thought we should have been so long here. Sebastopol is a very strong place, and we have a Russian army in the rear of us.

Letter from Sergeant **William Garland** (number 954), 17th Lancers, to his brother Rev. R. Garland.[47]

Camp, Balaklava,
My Dear –,   Dec. 20.
When I wrote my last I think we were lying near Balaklava. Soon after, the Light Brigade was removed to within a mile of Inkermann-Hill, and about 2 to 3 miles from Sebastopol. On the 5th of November, being a very foggy morning, we heard some firing in the direction of Balaklava, and remained in the saddle for about half-an-hour; we then dismounted, fled to the lines, and remained bridled and saddled, and ready to turn out at a moment's notice, when all at one we heard a very sharp file firing from the same direction. Soon after, a quantity of wounded were carried past to the different hospitals to get their wounds dressed, and it was then that we first heard what was going on – that the Russians had made a feint upon Balaklava and a real attack upon Inkermann, and had on the latter place concentrated all their force, and with the aid of their shipping, which did their work admirably, were throwing shot and shell of heavy weight right over the hill into the centre of the 4th Division. Their infantry advanced in heavy columns, right to the top of the hill, upon which was a strong entrenchment and wall – in endeavouring to scale[,] which hundreds fell at the point of the bayonet. At the flank of this wall we had some guns of a field battery – I cannot tell how many – but about and before them the Russians (the English having been carried away) were lying in masses next morning. The guns were taken and retaken several times, and it was at one of these takings that we were ordered to the front to support about 500 or 600 Chasseurs [*d'Afrique*], and when we got under fire in good range were halted and ordered to sit at ease. At this particular time a nice 8-inch shell would come near each of your heads, or perhaps over or against yourself or horse, with the intervals filled up with a few round shot from 9 to 24lbs. We remained thus about twenty minutes, when they thought fit to retire about a mile. The 17th Lancers lost a very fine young officer named Cleaveland [*sic*, Cleveland], one man killed and another lost an arm; several horses suffered. Sergeant-Major Duncan had a horse shot dead again. Several lances were shot away, and

all the other regiments lost more or less; I cannot say how many. However we could not get another "go in," and so were obliged to be content for a time. I went up next morning to see what had been done, and the ground was literally covered with dead men, wounded Russians and horses, principally artillery. There were burying parties out, and strong picquets some miles in advance of this, counting the dead, collecting the wounded, and so on. The reports I daresay you have already read in the 'papers. Sergeant-Major Fennell[48] died of cholera about Nov. 15; he was gazetted quartermaster, but had not the pleasure of seeing his name in print then.

Our horses have suffered very much on account of the late severe weather, and the want of forage while so far away from Balaklava. We could not get it up on account of the bad roads and loss of baggage animals. In five days the horses got 4lbs. of oats, and not forage or anything else; at the same time it was bitterly cold and wet. Certainly they did not do much work, because they could not. After this they brought us down to Balaklava, where they got as much or more than they could eat. A few could not rally, but most of them are now picking up very much, and they have also a set of clothing for the winter. The men have all had a good thick woollen Guernsey and one of socks served out, and are to have one pair of woollen drawers each, and I believe some high serviceable winter boots – all at the expense of the government.

The cavalry is principally engaged in finding outlying pickets and conveying rations up to the infantry in front, which latter they are obliged to do on account of the non-arrival of baggage animals. They (the Infantry) have been lately constructing some new batteries, mounting very heavy guns, and it is said have pushed their trenches within 100 yards of Sebastopol. But things in general are going on so quietly, and with so little noise, except from the reports of cannon, and they cause so little excitement in camp, that no one knows anything, and it would be impossible to say when the siege is likely to be over. There is one thing I forgot to mention, and that is that all vegetables received by the army will be free of cost; it is rather an uncertain issue, but when it does come it is very acceptable.

We are to be augmented to two troops, viz., 150 men and 120 horses. It is not known whether the men and horses will come out ready formed in England, or whether the men and horses will come out to be formed here, and this is a question that puts the whole of us in fidgets. I duly received the news-papers and letters addressed to me.

PS. We are to commence cutting out stabling on the side of a hill, which will be covered over with boards. The ground is marked out, but we have not got men to do it – nor can we have them until we can get struck off some of our present duties.

Letter from Troop Sergeant Major **Richard Lawrence Sturtevant** (number 868), Scots Greys, to the editor of the *Nottinghamshire Guardian*.[49]

> Heavy Cavalry Camp, near Sebastopol,
> 8th Nov., 1854.

On the 4th we had a very heavy day of rain, and early on the 5th morning the Russians came out of Sebastopol, and attacked the right of our lines. By the official details you will see the particulars. I am not able to give them, for the cavalry were not engaged, although a few officers and men were killed by some shells. The battle has been more severed than at Alma, and thousands have lost their lives. The Russians suffered most and fought well. They took one of our batteries, I hear, twice, which was re-taken by us. The fog and damp air with rain rendered the morning of the 5th so dark that the enemy made for our lines and were actually in our camp, even in some of the tents, before our men could get to arms. When they did, not above one piece in four or five would go off, and our men had to do much work with the bayonet. The Guards have been fearfully cut up, as also other regiments. We have buried all our dead, but the Russians are lying on the field. Such a sight to see, hewn down like walls, that horses turn from the place, the riders not being able to make them go over the dead bodies. The carnage has been awful, but a complete victory has been gained, and the Russians have been driven back. It is said that most of the enemy was a reinforcement from Odessa. The prisoners taken yesterday passed our camp – about 300 in number, some of them shockingly mutilated. It is said that the cause of their fighting so stoutly, was in consequence of their being nearly drunk. On many of the wounded were found spirits in their canteens – otherwise to look at them you would fancy they were paupers from some Workhouse. Sebastopol is still being bombarded night and day. The Greys, both men and horses, are doing well, and standing the climate better than was expected. It is certain we shall not leave this until Sebastopol falls. And I hear the mud huts are to be built for the army to remain all winter in, and that warm horse clothing has been sent for the cavalry.

The Great Storm; 'Generals December, January, and February'

Lieutenant-Colonel Hodge records how the weather began to turn after Inkerman and that men and horses were beginning to rapidly deteriorate. On 9 November, at 9.30 a.m., Lord Lucan 'had us all [Commanding Officers] to his tent' where he 'found fault ... with the dirty state of the men ... He ordered use all to get our men's kits for them, and also pipe-clay and oil.' Hodge thought it was 'no fault of the men' that they did not have their kit with them because the valises had been ordered to remain onboard ship, which meant that the men of the Cavalry Division had not had a change of clothes for five weeks. Furthermore, there was a lack of water so they were unable to either wash themselves or their clothing and 'continually under orders to mount at a moment's notice' so had no time in which to do so even if they did have the means.[50]

Hodge records in his journal:

10 November. The lines are a foot deep in mud and slush. The saddles are all lying in the middle of it ...

13 November. The state of our camp is beyond anything beastly. The mud is a foot deep all round the horses. The rain beats into our tents. How man or horse can stand it this work much longer I know not.[51]

At dawn on 14 November 1854 the Allied camps were wrecked by a hurricane. One Captain of the Royal North British Fusiliers wrote:

It commenced suddenly, at 6 o'clock in the morning and last 'til 12 o'clock. The wind blowing from the south directly on this bold and rugged shore. We had 16 vessels outside the harbour, some of the finest transports and steamers in our service, amongst them the 'Prince', quite a new vessel, she broke in half right in the centre, and sunk at once with 150 souls on board and a valuable cargo. The effect of this disaster is most serious to our proceedings, and it has thrown gloom over us all. Every vessel had stores and warm clothing for our poor but brave soldiers, so you may imagine how it will throw us all back. When the storm had moderated, I climbed to the top of a cliff, and from thence beheld one of the most awful sights ever witnessed by man (a sketch of witch I enclose). I counted 14 wrecks. Such a sea! The waves nearly equalled the height of the mountain on which I stood. You may guess the effect of this on the encampment. In a moment every tent was blown away: some were carried into the air like parachutes, those who indulged in sleep without their clothes were left in a state of nudity ... The Colonel was carried inside his tent, down the side of the mountain; he was much injured, and was immediately taken to the hospital.[52]

Lieutenant-Colonel Hodge's tent blew away at about 9 a.m., the pole having 'smashed into two pieces' and 'everything that could be blown away was blown away'. Sadly, nothing could be done for the horses, who 'got nothing [to eat] all day'. The horse lines were 'knee deep in mud and slush'.[53] Hodge thought the situation after the storm 'most critical': his men were short of supplies and completely without winter clothing. On 18 November Hodge reported that the 'Commissariat have nothing up here' for the cavalry and whilst the French were 'neatly hutted in' the British horses were 'in the open air'.[54]

Every day forage arrived at Balaklava for the cavalry and artillery, and due to the complete lack of any means of transporting it, those horses from the Heavy Brigade deemed fit enough were selected to make the fourteen-mile return journey down to the port to bring the forage up to the heights. One Guards officer blamed the death of the transport animals on them being kept in the open on the uplands rather than in stables in Balaklava so that they did not have to carry both their own forage and stores for the army up from the port. Furthermore the hired-in Turkish mule-teams were considered 'useless, filthy vagabonds', who did not care for their animals and had to be 'flogged out of their tents to feed their animals'.[55]

Conspicuous by their absence from the forage issued to British horses were oats, the main source of energy in equine food. This meant that they were eating barley straw and hay – which are used to bulk out food, to make horses feel 'full'. Straw and hay are of very low nutritional value and ironically uses more calories to eat and digest than it produces. Even this low-quality forage was only issued irregularly. By contrast, the hardier French horses were thought to survive on less rations but, crucially, their rations did have oats.[56] Thus, whilst British horses did have food to eat, the energy they gained was expended on eating and digesting their forage rather than being able to pull wagons. Therefore it is no surprise that they fell ill or were too weak to work, leading to the collapse of the British supply system. Furthermore, newspaper reports suggesting British horses were 'eating off their own tails' due to starvation is erroneous: the chewing of tails, mains and ears is not due to a horse being hungry, but either due to scabies (sarcoptic mange) or 'sweat-itch' an irritation and inflammation of the skin caused by fly bites, both of which indicate a very poor standard of equine management.[57]

On 1 December 1854 Hodge reported that he had 130 horses fit for duty and 100 men; four days later he described the cavalry as 'quite *hors de combat*. They are utterly done for.'[58] The Heavy Cavalry moved camp on 6 December to 'a snug valley near Balaklava' because they could 'no longer feed the horses where we were': the horses were so weak they could not 'struggle up the hill' from Balaklava with the sacks of forage. The horses were 'always out' and stood 'knee deep in mud' with on average twelve horses per night dying from exposure or starvation. Hodge believed that the cavalry had been 'sacrificed and neglected' and left to die.[59]

The daily routine of a cavalry trooper during the winter of 1854–5 was as hard as it was monotonous, and was described by the Earl of Lucan thus:

> He has to clean his own horse, appointments, arms and clothing; he has to clean the horses and the horse appointments of the sick, and all men on dismounted duties, such as camp guards, hospital orderlies, cooks ... &c.; to attend three stable hours; to water the horses twice daily ...; has to scrape and shovel away and remove to a distance all the dung, mud, &c. from the picket lines ... In bad weather he is constantly repitching tents and changing the ground for the picket lines. He has to go upon divisional, brigade, regimental and troop fatigues; to clean out the camp, draw provisions, fetch water and wood for the cooks ...; to bury dead horses ... and to attend funerals. To do this, besides the stable hours, in the short days, he cannot be said to have more than three hours.[60]

The French took a more practical approach to their equine management. Two, later all four regiments, of *Chasseurs d'Afrique* served in the Crimea, bringing with them their hardy little Barb horses. The *1e* and *4e Hussards* arrived without horses and were remounted using local animals, which avoided a lengthy acclimatisation process and meant that they were used to the rigours of the Crimean weather. However, the heavy cavalry (*6e* and *9e Cuirassiers*; *6e* and *7e Dragons*) brought their horses with them from France. During the winter of 1854–5 the French reduced their cavalry to a skeleton force – rightly concluding that cavalry was of little use in a siege and a severe winter would be the death of many horses, especially the European animals – and packed off the cavalry to spend the winter near Adrianople.

The final death-knell for the British cavalry came on 12 December 1854 when Lord Raglan ordered that in addition to their usual cavalry duties, the exhausted men and horses were to be seconded to the Commissariat. Lieutenant-Colonel Hodge wrote:

> we [the cavalry] are to give 500 horses a day to carry the provisions of the infantry to the front ... We are to be carriers to the Commissariat department, and then, when all our men's things are destroyed, saddlrey gone, and horses killed, they will tell us that we have neglected our regiments. It is too dreadful to think about.[61]

Letter from Lieutenant **Robert Scott Hunter**, Scots Greys, to his sister.[62]

My dearest Holly,

Lines before Sebastopol
Friday 17th November 1854

I have been expecting letters for two days now but the steamer has never come in & there is great fear that she has been lost in the hurricane we have wrestled with on the 13th. We turned out that morning as usual before day break in a storm of wind & rain, so violent that the parade had to be dismissed & just as we got off our horses such a blast suddenly burst on us as if by a cannon shot. The rain sleet & snow at the same time blowing so that we were obliged to lie down on our things wet as they were to prevent both them and ourselves from being blown away, for no mortal man could stand before it. My troop was startled by the falling tents &c. & at night 25 were still missing but we have recovered nearly all of them now. The worst of it was that we could get nothing to eat till near evening when the storm moderated & we got some ration mutton cooked (half) on green wood. For some days previous we had a great deal of rain, but the storm quite polished us off & we got all our things wet & uncomfortable. Our in spite of all this continues & the very next day I was on outlying picquet & had brought it on a black hill side all night, when I was nearly frozen. I stood on my feet from 12 at night to nearly ½ past 4 when I was so done and weak I could hardly stand & my right side was quite paralyzed. Ever since I have been all over acute rheumatism & yesterday & the night before had a good deal of fever, but today I am *all right* with the exception of a very sore throat and pains in my left arm & shoulder. This is truly miserable work I can tell you & now we have real hardships to contend with. A lot of our ships have been [illegible] anchor & wrecked, amongst them some of our men of war & a lot of transports, including all our horse forage for 27 days, an awful loss & one ship with all the men's warm winter clothing *which they need much nor poor fellows*. *30 men* died of *cold* in the trenches the night of the storm, & every night night now our horses share the same fate, 2 or 3 per regiment. We cannot take this place now this year & so shall have to be here all winter. Im afraid it will be the last to many amongst us. I suppose you will have heard of the Battle of Inkerman by this time, fought on *Sunday* the 5th November. We gave them a tremendous drubbing. The Russian loss cannot be under 10,000. Ours about 2,000, but a very large proportion of *officers*. We were not engaged as the Enemy could not get their cavalry up & there was no place for us to act as the battle was fought in a little valley with hills on both sides & covered with brush-wood. We have all along been expecting them to attack Balaklava but we have got the heights commanding the gorge so long defended by artillery & earth intrenchments that I suspect they mistrust their ability to take it. I hope you got my last letter safe & have written about the 'Gazette'. News-papers are a scarce commodity here, & we are only getting accounts of the Battle of Alma *now*. We knew the day we landed but when or how is this war to finish? I can't see my way out of it at all.

... I have a view of Sebastopol from my tent door now. We shuffled camp again the day before yesterday & now have a fine sea view & the prettiest glimpse of the town *between* two downs. I can't see the batteries but only the smoke of each gun, but our view comprises some public buildings & private houses, & looks joley [*sic*, jolly] & like home. In S[ebastopol] is very English looking & there are such swell houses in it. Our Quarter Master[63] is just starting for Scutari to bring up necessaries for our Brigade. So I shall get some warm things soon now. Our Encampment is on the open steppe in view of the town, very high & therefore cold in proportion. I never felt it colder than this in England & this is only the beginning of winter, & the transition from heat to cold has been so sudden, only 3 weeks also we were walking in our shirts sleeves and could not keep ourselves cool & now it is vice-versa but I daresay we feel it more from just coming from Constantinople ...

Letters from Troop Sergeant-Major **Richard Lawrence Sturtevant** (number 868), Scots Greys, to the editor of the *Nottinghamshire Guardian*.[64]

Camp before Sebastopol,
Nov. 23d, 1854.

... On the 20th the rain fell in torrents, running through the tents, and such a mess of things by such inclement weather it is impossible to describe, at least amongst the cavalry. The Greys have lost altogether since leaving England 40 horses, and many of those are very little fit for work. The other cavalry regiments have lost more in proportion; and the weather now indicates much wet. We are of course under canvas. The Turks likewise, but they have nearly finished their winter quarters. Holes are dug some four feet deep, some 10 or 12 feet wide, and about 20 long. Two firm supports are in the centre at either end, about four feet above the ground; a pole traverses these on the top, and then supports for the roof of sticks are place from the ground to the above. Mud is then used, and fine stuff it is; in my experience I never saw such stuff to make bricks or tiles with as on this position in the Crimea. However, we have heard that contracts were entered into at Constantinople for the supply of wooden huts and stables for the cavalry, but the contractor has failed in his contract so far as regards time. We shall all be glad to get them, for the weather, although not so cold (if we could get at a fire after being some time out in it), but under canvas, without that accompaniment, it is cold and raw, the ground damp, and when we have now pitched the tent some eight days the ground inside is as damp and moist as outside. This, therefore, cannot be healthy, and we are looking forward to some more substantial covering.

Sebastopol is still being bombarded with all vigour, and holds out well. Sorties are often made, in which the Russians lose many. Our men being entrenched, the loss is trifling to them. It is expected an attack will be made on the army in the rear in a day or so, to drive them away. The French are very anxious for it, and have been watching their movements with much interest; and as Balaklava serves us well, taking a great part of our army to watch it, I think it is not improbable that they will drive them away, when perhaps we can erect batteries on the north side of Sebastopol, and indeed completely surround it, which I have no doubt would have been done long before but for the large force it would take, owing to the extent of the ground.

Of course official despatches will give you lists of killed, and indeed all casualties. I trust that you will take pleasure in occasionally hearing from me, as I am aware of the great interest the inhabitants of Nottingham take in the welfare of their countrymen. I may here state that from the Camp to Balaklava the road has become very heavy, on account of the many stores being brought up, and troop horses are sent down and sack of corn is put on each, as the mule carts can only now bring half of what they did formerly. Yesterday we had no hay for the horses; it is through the Commissariat not providing a store at camp when they had the fine weather for brining it up. Of course that will be looked to by superior authorities. The health of the men is not bad, but on account of such very inclement weather cases will occur as the human frame is tried to the utmost.

23rd, Morning: I wrote the above late last night. Just as I finished your letter the rain came in torrents, with tremendous gusts of wind. The rain penetrated the tents like a sieve, and thankful am I that it did not come down like on the 14th, when so much of the shipping was damaged. As I write, 7½ a.m., the firing on Sebastopol is still proceeding. The weather this morning is fine; but if you are a sportsman you can recognise the state of the ground after a very heavy rain all night. I have now to go to post, six miles, and an ugly road, so good bye ...

Before Sebastopol,
24th November, 1854.[65]

Since I wrote to you last the troops have suffered much from the wet weather. On the 25th the rain fell like torrents, and penetrated inside the tents like a sieve; this lasted the whole day. The ground consequence is extremely soft; where the cavalry are it is from six to eight inches deep of soft mud. The horses are dying fast. They have had but little hay for five or six days, and only the usual quantity of corn. The commissariat department have a difficulty in getting the provisions up, as the roads are so heavy. On the 26th morning all were agreeably surprised by a glorious sun bursting through the fog. Everything was taken out of the tents, and laid to catch its feeblest rays. Thank God it continued fine all day, and you could see in man and beast the effects of that blessed luminary. The army in our rears continues peaceful, and no demonstrations have yet been made by them or us. The bombardment of Sebastopol has been heavier than formerly, and I am sorry I cannot furnish you with a detail of the artillery batteries. Some French Cavalry and Infantry landed this day, and we have disembarked at Balaklava the new police (mounted), I think called "Guides."[66] They all looked very smart in their scarlet body frocks, trimmed with lace, and a kind of fireman's helmet. I thought they would not look so smart after a few duckings from Crimean showers, and lying upon the ground with only one blanket and coat to cover them I see it is the intention of Government to send out an extra suit of clothing to the cavalry (not before it was needed). I learn that the sick at present here and at Scutari amounts to nearly 9,000; this is enormous, but it must be borne in mind that this includes all the wounded. It is rumoured that about the 1st of December every preparation will be completed, viz., erecting fresh batteries, &c., and that a heavy bombardment will be kept up for several hours when it is expect the place will be stormed. I ought to have before remarked that although the weather has been very unfavourable, we have little sickness with it, and the spirits of the men are as good as ever.

On the 27th the weather was good, wind changed, and every appearance of cold weather setting in. The 9th Foot landed at Balaklava this day in excellent condition.

Evening of 2nd December, 1854.

Since I wore last the weather has continued severe and is much felt by us all. The siege of Sebastopol continues with unabated vigour, and I hear that probably in a few hours we shall have a battery erected of 24 guns, which will command the entire fleet in the harbour. Should this be the case you no doubt will soon learn that the place is ours. Great execution was done last night on a party of Russians who sallied out. Report goes that upwards of a thousand of the enemy were killed, while the loss on our side was comparatively small.

Letter from Corporal **Thomas Morley** (number 1004), 17th Lancers, to his father.[67]

Balaklava,
Dear Father,-   7th Dec. 1854.

I received your kind and welcome letter yesterday. The little bag of camphor and the pens arrive quite safe, but I have not yet received the newspaper. I think you should put stamps upon the newspapers when you send them, so that I might receive them sooner. I have already received several, but t they are very old. I sent you a letter five days ago, but there were no stamps upon it, and I had nothing to seal it with, excepting a bit of biscuit[,] which I chewed. I heard to-day [sic], that the Russians had been attacking us again in the same place as on the 5th of November. If they did attack us here there have got "bell tinker," as there are now a thousand English and French soldiers at that place, where there was only a hundred before. Many thousands have joined us since the 5th of November. I think we have done all the fighting we have to do; we have not got ten horses in the regiment worth 2d., and I think they will all die in another week or two. One or two die every night and sometimes more. They will be obliged to take us somewhere before long, unless they are going to make foot soldiers of us. We have only got 40 or 46 horses in the regiment now, and when we came out we had 300. When we shifted camp two days ago we had to walk and lead the horses, and then you could trace the road all the way back from where we had left by dead horses upon the ground. We are a curious looking lot now. We had not boots to our feet nor a shirt to our back until to-day [sic] when they provided us with good thick knitted worsted shirts and drawers which fit close to the skin, and boots and shoes. You said in your last letter there were stables coming. It will not take many stables for the light cavalry. I am the oldest corporal doing duty in the regiment now, and as there are vacancies for two sergeants, I think before many days have elapsed I shall be promoted to a full sergeant. Young Neepe and Joseph Slack are doing well.

Letter from an anonymous non-commissioned officer of the Inniskilling Dragoons, to relatives in Leeds.[68]

Camp Before Sebastopol,
My dear Harriet, -   7th Dec., 1854.

My letter in reply to yours of October must not have reached you, or I should have heard from you again before this. I have received three letters and two papers from you since I have been in this country – two written in September and one in October – the last of which has not been answered.

Mr dear H. do not blame me for not writing more frequently, as I assure you we have many hardships and privations to endure in this country. I will just give you an idea of it. We are encamped about four miles from Balaklava, and the road to that place is cut up in a frightful manner that the bullocks and dromedaries are not able to pull the arabas[69] through it, consequently we are obliged to go to that place for our forage and provisions, and the horses are actually up to their bellies. The weather is getting very severe. We have had not but rain for the last fortnight. The horses are standing to their knees in mud – of course the men have to share it with them. Many days we get we through, and in wet clothes we have to lie – (I cannot say sleep) – at night. We furnish strong outlying picquets and patrols; and allow me to inform you that it's no joke to remain on top of those hills, having nothing but our cloaks for twenty-four hours; and besides, we have to go daily to Balaklava; each man takes a led horse, which he loads with hay, oats, or biscuit, as the case may be. We get nothing but salt pork and biscuit, and two allowances of grog daily. When there is a very wet day (which is too often the case) the men cannot stand out to cook, consequently they are obliged to go without food for that day. Our horses are dying very fast. I have seen them lay [*sic*, lie] down near their men, or on the road, and die. We have not one-half left. If we remain here all winter we shall no have no horses, and I fear very few men.

No doubt you will have heard of our being engaged at Balaklava, on the 25th of October, and on the 5th of November – two hard days. On the latter, the rain fell in torrents, and the bullets like hailstones. We had two men killed and two wounded the first day [25th October]. One serjeant has died since of his wounds – he had his leg shattered by a splinter of a shell – I was near him at the time. Thank God I escaped without a scrape, although I was in the midst of them. I certainly lost my horse in the first charge, but I soon succeeded in catching a splendid black Russian charger, fully accoutred, which I have ridden ever since. We have a number of their horses.

The enemy's army consists of 32,000 men, and are encamped within sight of us, their videttes and ours are daily posted on the neighbouring hills, within shot of each other. I don't know what their intentions are respecting Sebastopol. They keep on continual cannonade from that place; so much so that we cannot sleep at nights for them. We are in sight of the town.

And now, my dear H., do not be displeased with me for not writing oftener, as you see I have scarcely a moment to spare. Paper is very hard to be go; postage stamps are not procurable at any money, those who have them will not part with them, and they are not sold in the village. Anything that is sold here is unreasonably dear, and of an inferior quality. If God spares me to return, I shall be able to tell you some amusing tales about the campaign. I often heard of the battle field [*sic*], I have now had an opportunity of seeing it, and I never want to do so again. You could see nothing but heaps of dead and wounded men, and field covered with dead and wounded horses. We daily and nightly expect another attack, but are prepared for them.

Give my love to father, mother, Edwin, and Fred. I hope they are good boys.

Letter from an anonymous private of the 1st Royal Dragoons, to his brother in Liverpool.[70]

The Camp on the Heights
before Sebastopol,
Dec. 11, 1854.

My Dear Brother,-

The Lord has spared me once more to write a few lines to put your mind at ease for a time about me. I am sorry to say that I am not near so comfortable as when I wrote last; the winter is showing itself more and more every day. The fatigues and hardships are double what they used to be. I could stand it all with a good will if I only knew that I should, after all was over, return safe to Old England. Seeing so many dead and dying about every day gives no encouragement at all. It is next thing to a wonder that any us are alive, when we have been wet for so many days together, lying on the field, which is flooded, and the best place in our tents and have had to shovel out the mud; as long as two days unable to light a fire to cook any meat. No change of clothing; I have been nearly two months without a shirt. It is not joke and yet I can scarcely help laughing when I mention it. I never laughed so much in my life as when we had every tent blown down, to see the figures that were inside them – many undressed and exposed to the storm. I would not see it again though, for any more, the poor sick shared the same fate. There are some quite merry when nothing but death stares them in the face – it was so at Balaclava [*sic*]; that was the hardest fighting we had, but I have seen a greater slaughter. It is awful to see our poor horses – the Light Brigade is completely unfit for service, and that makes the duty heavier for us; they cannot muster enough for one outlying picket. I have seen our horses eat the ropes they were tied to there, and also a part of their saddles, then commence at our tents. We would try to stop them at that, and then they have actually eaten one another's manes and tails off; they are dying by the dozen every night, and often when we take them to the water place we leave two or three behind. The road between Balaclava [*sic*] and Sebastopol is covered with carcasses of mules and horses; the men are not much better – they are half of them sick. I could tell you much more, but it would only disgust you. Call on Mr. Whitington and inquire if he received my letter, dated the same as this; he will expect you. Give my love to all old friends; tell them that I am alive and well. Write as often as you can – I like to hear from home. Sebastopol is still standing, but fall it must. I suppose you often look at the 'Illustrated [London] News'. I have seen some very good plates – could not be better; they cannot picture it any worse than it really was, and yet it was not so bad as the continual harassing and fatigue that we have had to undergo. We have forgotten what it is to be comfortable; it might turn out better yet – I hope it will. I hope I will find you in Liverpool if I return, and we will try to make up for [illegible]. If I can get any Russian or Turkish coins I shall send you some just for curiosity. I am not certain whether I can get any stamps for this. Tell me in your next what you have to pay when previously stamped. I can send you no news about the war, as you can see it much sooner in the papers. Some of the Russians that are behind us have retreated a short way so we cannot see them now.

18th December
My dear Brother, I received your most kind and affectionate note when in our outlying picket. It did me more good than anything I had had for many days. As you said, the new you sent was too good, I am afraid, to be true. I am happy to tell you that I am more comfortable these last few days than I have been since I arrived in Turkey. I hope to God you will succeed in your undertaking. I will write a note to Mr. J[censored], as I and Corporal Taylor[71] opened his note, and found it for one of the same name, but not a Corporal, and he opened it by mistake. He is dead; he died from wounds received at Balaclava. I shall write again within a week, and enclose a note for aunt T[censored] and one for aunt H [censored], and for Harriet and Mary. Give my love to them all. If you write before me, enclose paper and envelopes. Accept my kindest love, from your ever faithful brother, [censored], 1st Royal Dragoons, Army in the East.

You see that the other part of my note was written some days since. I should have finished it, but I was ordered for an out-lying picket, and whilst I was on the hill I received your most kind and welcome letter. I was quite well at the time. I could not answer it at the time. You must excuse this scrawl, and the paper; it is very scarce, and rather a rum place to write on. We have had fine weather for a few days; but just as I am writing the rain is coming down in torrents, just as usual – about the worst thing we have. If I have time I shall enclose a note in this for Mr. James J [censored]; if not, you can inform him of the untimely death his old friend met with. It is dark now; so I must leave off, and finish another day. I almost forgot to thank you for the paper you were so kind to send me. I suppose you often look at the paper. You may depend upon hearing from some of my comrades should anything happen to me. I dare say you think a person must feel a very curious sensation come over him when going in to battle. I know I did; but not that we have been a few times before the enemy the men are quite wild to have a charge at them. I am sorry to sat that there was a little bad management at Balaclava, or we should have taken all prisoners, excepting a few stragglers might have got away, for we them down the valley. It was not in the first place that the Light Brigade lost so many, and it was all musketry and balls that killed them. Sword cuts are nothing; they can only dash away when they have about six to one. I have seen as many sword wounds as six on each arm, besides other parts of the body. My hands are so cold, and the wind blowing, I cannot write. I see by the papers that there are a great many false reports. We have for a long time never seen any of the Russians except on the heights, about a mile or a mile and a half from our outpost; there is one party much bolder than the other, but they are very mean, for they like to take advantage of a small party. At the engagement on the 5th of November all the prisoners were quite tipsy; each had a bottle of spirits, which they call arrack. We call it a drink, or something of such kind. As to the strength of Sebastopol, it is one of the most wonderful places in the world; to think of so many of us, and not able to get into it. They are erecting a new battery of 21 guns, which they expect to be ready about next Sunday, but this rain, I am afraid, will put it further off. The roads are in an awful state; you cannot see where the old original one was, for there is about two or three feet of mud each side for a mile in length, and in some places about a mile wide. The road between Balaclava and Sebastopol is covered with dead horses, mules and oxen. I have actually counted four within ten yards of each other. They never bury any of them: there is an awful stench as you go along. I have been patrolling along the road all times at night in charge of a small party of four or six. It is a very dangerous duty, especially with the cowardly set we have to deal with. As we go along the road we trust to our ears and the horses. Perhaps we stumble across a carcase or into a ditch, or the horses shy at some poor dying horse in the road. I dare say you saw an account of some of the enemy's horses cutting from their lines and disturbing the whole of the British army in the night. The horses came galloping up the hard road, then slap into our camp. I really thought they were down on us then, to hear the officers shouting "Turn out!" the out-lying picket coming in out of breath, with foam from head to foot. Lord Raglan has often said in our hearing that he can walk into Sebastopol any time, but he wants reinforcements, and to do it with as little loss of life as possible. When you write again, send me a little paper and envelopes and stamps, as we cannot get them for any money and when we come across them the paper is 7s. a quire, and envelopes at no price. I wish you a happy new year and a merry Christmas. I shall not fail to drink to your good health on New Year's Day; and on that night week after, should this reach you in time, do the same. God bless you.

Letter from Corporal **John Selkrig** (number 807), Scots Greys, to friends in Camarthan.[72]

Cavalry Camp, near Sebastopol,
Dec. 12.

My ever dear Friends, -

I send you this as a token of my remembrance, to show you that I am not unmindful of last December in Camarthen. I am happy to inform you that I am quite well and hearty, and have escaped as yet without a scar, though, as you will see by the papers, the Greys have done their share since coming to the Crimea. I need not give you any particulars, as you will have got all the news, and my time will not permit it; but I will give you a summary. We landed in the Crimea from Kulalie, near Constantinople, on the 24th of September, and marched on the same day a few miles, and joined the army. On Monday, the 25th, we were out reconnoitring, and came on the rear-guard of the Russian army. We had no fighting, for they fled at once, and we followed them, and took a good many prisoners, and a great part of their baggage and ammunition. A part of them fled into the brushwood on the road side, and the troop I belong to was dismounted with their carbines to scour the brushwood. I never had such a job in my life. I was with the officer, and we went too far, and lost our way in the wood, and were nearly an hour and a half beating through – no joke, with a long sword dangling after you, spurs, the [shoulder] scales on our coats, and big Grenadier caps, all which were very cumbersome for "Riflemen." However, we got safe to our horses again, very tired. The next day we got into the valley of Balaklava. I never saw a more beautiful spot in my life; it is (or rather, was) covered with vineyards, and we encamped in the centre. I could pull beautiful ripe grapes from any spot I chanced to be. There were also plenty of almost every kind of fruit for the pulling. We had a good deal of shifting and turning out to receive the Russians, but nothing particular occurred until the 25th of October, when we had to go to the front of Balaklava, which, by-the-bye, is a most beautiful harbour, and I believe that the name signifies the same. I had my horse shot under me in the very first, and had only time to take off my carbine, and lost all my kit. I got hold of an old horse belonging to the 1st Royals, the rider of which had been killed. It was nearly knocked up, and I had a sore job to keep it on its legs during the great charge. I went through the enemy's ranks as far as my comrades, and did my duty. I will not say I killed great numbers, but, like a good many more who said they did a great deal, I frightened some. I then exchanged horses with a doctor of the 1st, who had mounted one of ours, and went down the valley after the Light Brigade to assist then, but we could do no good, and only exposed ourselves to three different fires of the enemy. We may be in engagements for years, and never see such a destructive fire again; but our regiment escaped most providentially. During the whole day we only had two killed on the field, but we had about 50 wounded, some very slightly, but the greater part rather severely. I think we have had eight or ten dead since of their wounds. We have had no other engagements since. We were on the field at Inkerman, but not required.

We have knocked about since – duty very hard and very bad weather, and always in expectation of something to do.

I will now let you know the fate of some of your old friends in the "Greys." Sergeant Kneath was very severely wounded, but is now nearly fit for duty again. Peter Morrison, who was at the "Angel," was also very severely wounded, and, I have heard, has died at Scutari, the sick depot; Findlater [*sic*, Findlatter] is now in hospital, very bad with fever and ague. Sergeant-Major Graves [*sic*, Grieves] is now Regimental Sergeant-Major, but took very badly with fever, and was sent to Scutari, and I have not heard how he is since. G. Ewing died of Cholera, and W. Connell got wounded with a ball in the shoulder, and sent to Scutari, but it now getting better. Sergeant Taylor was taken badly when we came to the Crimea, and has never been seen since. Sergeant McGregor is knocking about, as childish as possible. Andrew Gray got very severely kicked on the head when we were at Kulalie, and was thought by the Doctor to be of no more use for the service, as his brain was impaired; but he has since come to use again, and is doing very well, though his eyes show that there is something wrong. All the rest of the different parties that were in Camarthen, as far as I mind, are all well, Peter is quite well now, but was bad for some time with the Diarhoea. As for myself, I was for a few days troubled with a bowel complaint, but, on all, I never was in better health in my life.

Our rations are very good. We have one pound of biscuit, one pound of salt-meat (with now and again a dinner of fresh meat), coffee morning and evening when we can get it ready, but the weather has been so coarse, and fuel so scarce, that often we are left to forage for ourselves. We get also rice daily, and two glasses of rum, one in the morning and another in the evening. We depend on the grog in very coarse weather more than anything else, and it certainly does us good. I wish I had a teetotaller for a comrade, but I am afraid he would not be one long. I am worst off for clothing, as I lost all my kit, and am nearly naked; but we are getting out winter clothing piecemeal, and I am improving. I want boots very bad, and so do nearly all of our men, as the very wet weather (after the scorching dry season) spoiled our boots altogether; but we hear there is a good supply on the road, which will be a great blessing. We can also get some luxuries to buy in Balaklava when we can get money – tea, 4s. per lb.; sugar, 1s.; cheese, 2s.; butter, 1s. 8d.; onions, 4d.; porter, 1s/6d. per bottle; pepper, a tablespoonful for 3d. each, & c.

The weather when we first came to the Crimea, was very warm, and we bivouacked at night round our fires, as we had no tents. The nights were very cold, with very heavy dews, so it was very disagreeable. We got our tents when we were about a month here – just in time, as after that the weather got very cold and wet. Our horses have been in very bad condition, as they are exposed to all weathers, and generally up to the knees in mud. We have lost a great many. We have four or five in a morning, after a very coarse night. This week past, the weather has undergone a complete change. Again, this week, we can scarcely lay [*sic*, lie] in the tents for heat, and the sun is as strong as in the month of June at home, and both horses and men are recruiting; but I am afraid it will not last long.

Sebastopol is not yet taken, but we are in daily expectation of something particular. Our enemy is an army of Russians in rear trying to get into Sebastopol, or to get possession of Balaklava. We expect to hear some news on Friday, when a new 30-gun battery is to open on the sipping in the harbour. The Russians sallied out of Sebastopol last night, and attacked the fort, but after a skirmish of four hours, were repulsed. We have a picket of 40 men watching the enemy's movements. We have a vidette on the top of a hill, and they have one on another knoll of the same hill, watching one another like cats. It is a very disagreeable job that same picket. We have to stand to at our horses' heads, with their bridles in their mouths, for twenty-four hours, whether it is rain or shine. I was out twice, when it rained and blew the whole time. We were wet to the skin, and dare not move. I must cut short, as the post leaves immediately, but I trust this will find you all well, and that you may all enjoy yourselves during the holidays is the earnest wish of yours every sincerely.

Letter from an anonymous 1st Royal Dragoon to relatives in Liverpool.[73]

My Dear Friend, -

Camp before Sebastopol,
December 14, 1854.

At last I have found time to scribble a few lines. I might have written several times while in Turkey, but then I had nothing worth notice. We are now continually on the move dodging the enemy; even now while I am writing they are giving an order to be in readiness to turn out at a moment's notice. I think that it has nearly come to a point with Sebastopol. The Cossacks have returned in rear of us, and burnt all the huts we had built. I cannot describe what an awful thing a winter's campaign is in the Crimea. The cavalry are nearly unfit for service; as for the Light Brigade, they are completely done up – they cannot even find one outlying picket; so it all falls upon us, and I can assure you it is no trifle, for I have many times remained out in the rain for 24 hours. That would be nothing at home in England, but here, when we get into camp, there is no fire, nothing warm, and we are obliged to keep our things on till they get dry. Frost is nothing; we can warm ourselves then, but the rain and wind make an awful mess among us. I have seen everything down, impossible to put them up again, having the sick without any shelter, and many without clothing, exposed to the storm. After one of these storms I have seen nearly all the horses loose from the bridles, eating their saddles and everything they come across; and, more than that, you can inquire if it not true they have eaten one another's manes and tails completely out. Everything is marked by them, even one's clothing; it is more than we can do to keep them out of the tents in any regiment. There are three or four dead horses every morning. Half the men are sick. The scurvy is raging amongst them. None of us look like the same persons. I never think of changing my linen; and as for a wash, it is never thought of. Water is scarce. I have offered a shilling for a drink and could not get it for 50. Excuse this scribble, as I am on guard, and writing on my knees. I am nearly dropping with fatigue. Rest is one of the principal things I want. It is ten times worse than on the battle field [*sic*]. I am quite tired of if. I wish I was once again in the hammock you were so kind as to give me, and on my way home; but I am thankful that I am as I am – that the Lord has spared me so many times.

Balaklava was the hardest fighting had, but I have seen more slaughter than that. My hands have had blood on for three weeks together. I tore up shirts to bind up wounds, and have gone two months without one. I could say much more if I had time, but it would only disgust you. I don't know when I shall be able to post this, and I am afraid I cannot get a stamp. We cannot buy anything. Money is no object. I hope this will find you and all the family in good health. We are nearer Balaklava than we have been yet. If I am spared until after the downfall of Sebastopol I shall write again. It is a strong place, but down it must come, and we are all ready to give a hand, for we are very anxious to get under a roof again. I have not been in a house since that night in Liverpool, excepting to pull it down to get wood to make a fire.

Letter from an anonymous Subaltern in the 5th Dragoon Guards.[74]

Camp near Balaklava,
Dec. 17th-

We are now in a nice warm valley close to Balaklava, and can get our forage without much trouble. We are to hut ourselves – just like everything they do, beginning to hut us when nearly all the horses are dead; and it will be more than a month before the huts can be finished. They make us do Commissariat Duty. We send 120 horses every day for biscuits for the infantry. There are the French, with a good Commissariat, plenty of hay and corn for their horses, and rations for their men. We have to bring our own hay and corn, and biscuits for the infantry. Then we have no means of carrying our sick, the carts and waggons are too heavy, and are to be seen fast in the mud with 10 horses attached to them, and are obliged to be left there. The French are now bringing the sick down for us; they brought about 1,800 poor men the other day, who would otherwise have been left in the hospital tents to die, and men ad horses are beginning to look a little better, but we have again had rain and snow for 24 hours. I am trying to get warm things from Constantinople; they will be very acceptable as I am in rags. My clothes are rotten and as black as your hat. I am sorry to say my poor horse (Thirsk) is dead. After carrying me safely at the Battle of Balaclava, he died from the fever, which so many have done, and the veterinary surgeon has no medicines for the horses. I must finish this letter sooner than I intended, as I am just ordered up to the front with biscuits – six hours' work – and the post will be gone before I return.

Letter from an anonymous NCO of the Scots Greys.[75]

Camp, Hadikor [*sic*. Kadikoi],
22nd December, 1854.

... On account of the great sickness prevalent in all ranks, it leaves double and more work for those remaining. We have in the Greys at this present moment, nearly 70 men sick and wounded, at Scutari. Amongst those, one is Regimental Sergeant Major, and two Troop Sergeant Majors. I have now to do the duty of the first, my own office duty, and also that of a Troop Sergeant Major. This leaves little time on my hands. It would be useless to write an account of the war, popular as it is; but I can assure you, that never in the annals of British History, has England had such a handful of difficulty, trying as she is to destroy the stronghold of Southern Russian (so callen by Nic[holas], may the Devil take him) in the shape of one of the strongest fortifications the known world has in it, and with an immense army in our rear. The troops decimated by sickness, those who are killed the very elements at war against an European constitution, – these, taken altogether, will satisfy you that my conjecture is correct. To shew you how even our horses stand it, I have only to tell you that we came out after leaving Nottingham with 249, and we have now in the lines 181 – 68 of which are sick, leaving only 113 fit for work. These are fully employed the greater part of the day in carrying biscuit to the different divisions of the Infantry, and in fetching from Balaklava *their own fodder*. This became indispensable, as the baggage, animals and carts of the commissariat could not get along the roads, which are so heavy on account of the continued heavy rains. I must however say that the spirits of the Greys are indomitable, and we all look forward with deep anxiety, but deeper certainty, for the downfall of Sebastopol. A new battery is erect and now nearly fit for the great work of destruction. I believe it comprises some 30 guns, and is in such a situation that it commands the whole of the ships in the harbour. It is intended to shell the place night and day from this battery, besides pouring in red-hot shot night and day for the purpose of doing all possible preliminary damage previous to the storming. I am afraid we shall spend a poor Christmas, but we must do the best we can. We are getting salt meat now, which had continued for some time, though we expect some fresh for the festivities.

A parralel [*sic*] was taken by the Russians on the morning of the 20th, and all the picquets made prisoners. The 50th Regiment on duty. One of the officers taken was a nephew of Bt. Major Clarke, of the Greys.

Letter from Lieutenant **Robert Scott Hunter**, Scots Greys, to his sister.[76]

> Balaklava
> December 26th 1854

... Get me a copy of the Army List & put it in along with the other things. I expect I shall be senior Lieutenant very soon now, so please the Lord I shall get my troop sometime next year if I am spared. There are a great many reports of *peace* going about here. God knows they may be true, for any lot of soldiers so thoroughly sick of 'war Alarms' as this army I hope it will never be my bad luck to see again. Have you seen that we are where our /54 medal issued immediately?? You see, or will see, by the number of clasps issue that we are not considered worthy of a clasp for "Balaklava". Well, it can't be helped! We fought hard & well, & have at any rate the satisfaction of thinking that we did our duty, & a clasp more or less would hurt, but still, we would have been proud what had it. I am all *right now & getting rapidly strong*, & content to return (DV) to the regiment tomorrow. The last two days have been lovely clear frosty weather with a warm sun. The hills are just white & that's all but in the plains & on the steppe the ground was too wet for the little snow we had to lie. Today looks duller but the glass is high & we hope the fine weather has set in for some little time. The Russians we hear have hutted themselves, they have left the redoubts & gone to the side of the hill opposite, where they are intrenching themselves, & now only one solitary Cossack vidette, with his absurdly long lance is to be seen. The siege as it is was & has been, going on slowly. The French have about 130 pieces in battery ready to open when *we* are ready, & we are getting enormous quantities of ammunition on shore. Nothing of course is known of when the assault is to be, but I *should not think* much will be done for the next three weeks yet. The 71st arrived here, at least part of them, last week & the 18th are expected in today. They are outside the harbour now, this will make up a very strong reinforcement, we have received during *the last month*. I think with many others, that they ought to strike while the iron is hot, & go in at it, before the new fresh regiments are decimated by disease, which must be the case. Most of *our* regiments are only about 200 or 250 strong, & they came out 800 & 1100. I saw a poor fellow an officer of the 90th carried on board the Medway yesterday dying of dysentery. He has not been in this country for *three weeks* yet. This is a fearful climate & the exposure to wet & hold & hot, which cannot be avoided is nothing more than certain *death*! Proved daily by the deaths in the trenches, & the hundreds of sick sent down to Scutari every day. I hear Miss Nightingale has done good already there, but everyone says that her staff of young Lady nurses have not been judiciously selected, & that when once the enthusiasms of the thing wears off they will sicken of their work, wounds are things which new Doctors dislike to dress on account of the horrible Effusions, the wounded wards are dreadful in spite of the ventilation, & I cannot think that young ladies of 25 & 30 will or can stick out – you rather want some more *matronly* nurses, who tho' not quite so enthusiastic would understand it much better. They *will not* however look at the officers as they are considered *able* to pay for attendance & *therefore* confine their good offices strictly to the men ...

I had a much more jolly Xmas than I suspected. Dined on board the Medway & had Roast Beef (worthy of capitals) & mince pies, there was a *plum pudding but it was a failure*. You never saw anything like the fellows from camp scraping for dinner on that date. All the stewards of the ships lately arrived made a fortune & one told me that he had cleared about £150 *in half an hour for poultry alone*. They are a set of robbers and want flogging. As long as they can screw out money they wont cease asking those ridiculous prices ...

Letter from Sergeant **Edward C. Davies** (number 1175) 1st Royal Dragoons to his brother in Preston.[77]

	Camp, Before Sebastopol,
Mr Dear Brother, -	Dec. 28, 1854.

Thank God that I am able once more to address you in a few lines; you must excuse this scrawl, as it is very cold. I am happy to say that I am in good health, and doing very fair. I feel in very good spirits ever since your last note. I wrote one since then which I hope you have received. Although the winter is severer than it has been, yet we do not feel it any more, because we have had a good stock of warm clothing, and expect more yet. It is a great pity to see the poor horses die as they do. We are digging holes in the ground, and going to cover them over to make stables of them. We carry biscuits for the infantry up to Sebastopol, and carry their sick down to Balaklava every day, and it is very hard work I can assure you. I can find more time now to write than since we landed on the Crimea. Poor Fitzmorris,[78] he that was with us at Preston, has lost the use of one side completely.

You would have been quite surprised to see us preparing for Christmas-Day. The first thing we did was to dig holes in the ground and build cooking houses, so as to defy the wet weather, which we managed very well. We got some plum puddings and hams boiled, but the price was really extortionate. I shall make mention of the market prices by-and-by. The French came down from the hills with fine French brandy at 5s. a bottle, which we made very free with. We enjoyed ourselves very much, and had several French friends with us. They are very good company, and first-rate singers. The day was very wet, and, of course, out here every day is the same. But at night, if you stood anywhere near the cavalry camp you could hear singing going on in every tent. It was something like a country-fair at night. I only hope I shall never see a worse Christmas; it was all "Success to the canvass we're under." I am sorry I had not this note written last night when the post left.

Now for the prices – flour, 1s. to 1s. 6d., raisins 1s., butter 2s. 6d, to 3s., and cheese 2s 6d, per lb. Bread we can only get about once a month, and there is such a run for it then, it is above 1s. per 1lb. Sugar is 1s. per lb., and their pounds are Turkish – about eleven English ounces to the pound. Everything is the same; and we cannot get these things when we like neither; we mest [*sic*, must] wait for a chance to go on duty to Balaclava. When we could not buy anything we did not know what to do with our money, but now we know very well.

. . .

There was a request sent to each regiment from Lord Raglan that no officers or non-commissioned officers would get their letters published in England; but it did not matter about private soldiers. Keep up your spirits; you can say that a brother of yours has worn a medal in the great Russian war. I only hope I shall live to get over it. The Queen's speech and thanks to the army and navy was read to us yesterday, and all the men heard it with great pleasure.

Letter from Private **Thomas Sawbridge** (number 1507),[79] 11th Hussars, to his mother in Costock, Nottinghamshire.[80]

My Dear Mother, -

Balaklava,
January 2nd, 1855.

I dare say you have been in a sad way after hearing what the 'papers have stated, but you may depend upon it that I am quite safe and well – thank the Lord for his kindness to me. I have been in every engagement, and came out without a scratch. But I must tell you that I had a very narrow escape on the 25th of October. I had my horse shot under me, and I had to run for my life. The shot and shell were flying like hail in all directions. After running about a mile over the dead and dying I fell down on my face, I was so fagged out; but I got up and reached my regiment after a hard struggle.

We are in a dreadful state here. We are laying on the wet ground under thin canvas, and if we move we are up to our knees in wet and mud. We have had very little frost yet, but continually wet cold weather, and no signs of any change. Everything is very dear here. We have to pay through the nose for everything that we get. Cheese is 4s a lb., and there are only twelve ounces to the pound; butter is 2s. and sugar 1s. per pound; tea about 10s.; and everything in like manner.

There is no chance of coming home yet, for they keep on firing at Sebastopol day and night. They seem to make no progress, but they say they intend to set the town on fire, if they do not come to terms. The Commander-in-Chief sent word to the people that they were to leave the town as soon as possible before he set fire to it.

Now, my dear Mother, I must conclude, with my kind love to all, and my best respects to my kind friend and pastor Mr. [censored] and all his family, and I remained your dutiful and affectionate son.

Letter from a 'Young Officer in the Heavy Cavalry.'[81]

Jan. 3 – This has been a dreadful day, nothing but snow, and I have been on duty. It is pitiable to see the unfortunate horses and Turks – the latter are dying in hundreds at Balaklava, and the former suffer awfully; one died with me between this and Balaklava (two miles' distance), and one in another troop going to the front, and two troopers died last night. I do hope they will send out more officers, for we are tremendously worked.

Jan. 4, – The winter seems to have set in real Russian fashion. All yesterday, last night, and to-day it has been snowing continually. The wooden houses and the winter clothing, of which we have heard so much, have not yet arrived; and, as for our horses, every cavalry officer is disgusted with the way the cavalry is treated. We have to fetch all the forage for our horses, which the Commissariat ought to bring up. We have to take up rations for the infantry – also the business of the Commissariat, we have to bring the sick and wounded from the front, and, of course, conveyances for them. Then the officers are not allowed a farther [*sic*] if their horses die from the inclemency of the weather, or from the hard work which subaltern officers' horses have to do. Then, there is the clothing sent out for the horses; but if an officer applied for any, the Quartermaster-General says, "Oh no, officers are not entitled to any." Now, look at the French. Most of their horses are hutted, their forage is brought up for them, and their sick are taken away in vehicles for the purpose, and the consequence is, their cavalry is fit to be called cavalry and to do its work as such, while ours are only dying animals. Oh! how all wish that some one would write and represent all this. Then, of the things that are sent to us by friends at home, not half, not a quarter ever reach their destination. I have heard that there is a box for me on board the "Cosmopolitan," but that it is under so many other packages that I cannot get at it. All being to complain, and very properly, at the mismanagement of everything.

Letter from Trumpet-Major **William Gray**, 8th Hussars.[82]

Balaklava,
My Dear –,   January 4th, 1855.
I am sorry I was not able to write a few lines to you last post, as I had only just time to give my brother Henry a turn. The weather has been very bad this last three weeks. Rain! Rain! Everyday, and now it has turned to snow up to our very knees. This moment the snow is coming down in torrents. I never saw snow so think in all my life. I am sure we can never stand this. If we remain in this state much longer we shall all be lost with the cold. We have not any warm clothing as yet, and are completely lost for want of boots. Unless we get some clothing of some kind, we are done men. Our poor horses are dying very fast. It would surprise you to see the number of dead horses that are lying about the place done up with hard work. The roads are quite impassable. There is not a night passes in our light brigade without three or four horses being taken out

of the lines dead, and if this weather continues another week we shall not have one left. The French have had another turn with the Russians. I was going up with letters to Lord Raglan's in the morning, very early – I should say about seven o'clock – and I saw the whole of them parading ready to advance on the Russians. The attack was on the army in our rear. They completely routed them, took six field pieces, and turned the pieces on the forts which the Russians took from the Turks. They also took eight head of cattle and plenty of poultry. The firing is still very brisk on Sebastopol, and the French have taken another battery from the Russians. I believe, however, they have plenty to do to keep it. Two attempts have been made to retake it, and the Russian shipping does them much harm. The Russians have made two sorties two nights running, but were repulsed each time.[83] They wish to take advantage of the weather. They seem to think we cannot stand the cold, and I think they are about right. I am sure something will be done shortly. While I am writing these few lines we have lost five horses from the Light Brigade. They went up to the trenches with provisions and the road is quite impassable.

Really it would make your very heart sink to see this place. The number of dead horses is awful. What do you think the Russians did in Sebastopol last night? They even rung the joy bells on account of the bad weather; that is a fact.[84] I am afraid before morning we shall not get out of our tents for snow. My hands are very cold, so you must excuse my writing more. I hope yourself and family are quite well. Give my kind love to all. I shall write home this post, and also to my brother. What will our poor men do in the trenches, 10 hours at a watch? *God help them!*

Letter from Corporal **Norman Stevenson** (number 1050), Scots Greys, to Mr Samuel Lee, landlord of the Shakespeare Inn, Mansfield Road, Nottingham.[85]

Heavy Cavalry Brigade
Before Sebastopol,
8th Jan., 1855.

Mr Dear Sir, -

I dare say you will be thinking I have almost forgotten you and my promise as well. However, suffice it to say, I have not half forgotten you or any of my old Nottingham friends. I have been waiting for the fall of Sebastopol before writing; but, after waiting all this time, I cannot speak definitely anything about its approaching downfall. All I can say is that the siege operation are going on with as much vigour as ever. I sincerely trust that these few lines will find Mrs Lee and family and the large circle of your friends enjoying good health, as I am also happy to state they leave me. Since I left Nottingham there have been many things transpired which my little space does not allow me to mention. I have no doubt you have anxiously watched the actions of the regiment since their leaving England, and I sincerely trust that the Scots Greys in their encounters with the enemy – of which I have no doubt you have full particulars – have not in any way betrayed the confidence the Nottingham people reposed in them. I think myself every man did his best to keep up our good name.

The weather here of late has been very unpleasant – heavy rains, cold winds, and for the last few days a heavy fall of snow combined with a very severe frost. You may guess, therefore, it is not very pleasant to be lying out with a frail bit of canvass [*sic*] for covering, and men are every day undergoing unparalleled hardships. However, I hope it will soon be all over.

The Greys are greatly thinned since they left England. A great many men have died through disease brought on by cold, and a great number have been killed and wounded at Balaklava. Many are laying sick at Scutari, and our horses are dying very fast, the average being nearly two every night. But after this month I trust what is left of us will soon recruit again. At present, however, everything looks cold, dismal, and uncheering [*sic*]. Notwithstanding this disheartening state of affairs, I do think every soldier does his duty without murmuring. He knows that his countrymen are doing everything for his welfare, and that the Peace of Europe depends on his exertions.

The Russians are reinforced in great strength here, and it is very probable we shall soon be meeting them again. However, I think one man of ours is equal to at least three Russians of the Cavalry, and if they meet our diminished number again we will, I dare say, prescribe something at the end of the sword which will put them past their oilcake in the evening.

I am sorry to inform you that Trumpeter Mitchell[86] died here of Cholera, and Heywood[87] got wounded in the hand, and he is going home to England. When did you hear of the Depot in Newbridge? Let me know is Lee is still in the regiment; also all the news you can give me. Corporal Dawson desires to be remembered to you as one or your old Orchestra; also remember me to all your friends. If ever I meet a dog that comes from Nottingham I shall take it in and give it a feed out of respect for the old town. I shall conclude this time with the hope that you will kindly overlook all the defects of this half-written scribble.

Letter from 'J. M^cL.', Scots Greys, to his father in Glasgow.[88]

Balaklava,
Jan. 10., 1855.

Dear Father, -

I received your letter this morning, and was very glad to hear from you, but I am sure you will be thinking, from the long silence caused on my part, that something serious has happened to me, but, thank God, I am well as yet; but I am sure you will excuse me when you get this letter. In the first place, since I came here I have not had an opportunity of writing, as there is no getting of paper, pens or ink; and, in the second place, there is very little time, for there are so few of our men fit for their duty, it comes the hard on us who are strong. Dear Father, if you would see us rise out of our tents in the mornings here with nothing but our cloak and blanket to cover us, and the ground that we are lying on frozen below us, you would excuse my writing. If you believe me, this morning when I got up, my boots were so frozen that it took me about an hour before I could put them on; however, I will be able to write to you oftener now, as we are near the village of Baliklava [*sic*], and I believe there are a few things sold there, so I will try and write you oftener now.

Dear Father, I dare say you will have heard of the Battle of Balaklava. It was an awful day; the large cannon balls were flying among us for above four hours like hail, and comrades falling on every side. If you only saw it – it was a fearful scene – I never thought I should have seen the like. But, when we came to be engaged hand to hand, and sword to sword, we let them see what we were made of. As, I suppose, you will have seen in the newspapers before this time, they are still blazing away at Sebastopol with very little effect.

We are lying at present between two high hills, and our horses are tied in lines, but I am sorry to say there are very few of them left, as they are dying three and four every morning with cold, so they will not last long as this rate. There are a great many of our men badly too, and a great many of them have died since we came out here, besides those who were wounded in the field; but, God be thanked, I am still in good health. The snow is about four feet deep and hard frozen, but I believe there is some clothing coming out to keep us warm, and I wish it were to come.

There is no use of giving you any further particulars about this place, as you can see in the newspapers better than I can inform you. There is one thing, they are not going to be so easily beat as we thought when we came out. We can see the Russian sentries about four miles from us, watching us, and we often get a shot at them, but they always run away when we come near them. I will conclude now for want of time and daylight, for there are neither coal nor candle here.

Letter from Private **R. Jennings**, Scots Greys, to his parents in Nottingham.[89]

Dear Father and Mother,-

Camp,
January 15th, 1855.

I write these few lines to you, and hope they will find you and my brother and sisters all in good health as they leave me at present, thank God. We are still in the same place, looking at our friends, the Russians, at whom we now and then take a random shot. The weather is now very cold. The ground is covered a yard deep with snow, but, thank God Old England – the Land of Paradise – has not forgotten us. We have each had delivered to us a very good pilot cloth coat, good flannels, and drawers, and these, with the sheepskin cloak, that serves either for a cloak or a bed, given to us by the Sultan, renders us pretty comfortable. The only articles that we are in want of are boots and fur caps. These, I suppose, will arrive in due course from England. Everything is very dear at this place. We have to pay 1s. 6d. a lb for bread; 2s. 6d. a lb. for butter and cheese; 1s. 6d. a lb. for sugar; and 1s. 6d. a pint for ale. By the bye, I may say the Ale here is not so good as that at home. You can tell the good people of Nottingham that there are more people here than Scots Greys who can drink Nottingham Ale. I really believe the Nottingham people think there is not another regiment to be compared with the Scots Greys for charging. I can only say the old 5th Regiment charged the Russians as well and with as much effect as the Greys, and did not retire quite as soon. But we do not hear a word about that regiment. I have not time to write more. Give my best respects to all inquiring friends, and accept the same yourselves from your affectionate son.

Letter from Corporal **Henry William Stancliffe**, 4th Light Dragoons, to his cousin, Mr James Sheard, in Huddersfield.[90]

Mr Dear Cousin,-

Balaklava, Crimea,
January 17th, 1855.

Your very kind and welcome letter only reached me about three or four days ago. This I attribute to its coming via Southampton instead of France; had it left have come this latter way you might have had my reply long 'ere this. I am exceedingly sorry that I should have occasioned the slightest anxiety to my poor mother, but I cannot get a letter from them. I have written several times, and am totally at a loss to know the reason I receive no reply. I am much afraid my letters have never been received, Until very recently there has been great difficulties in obtaining stamps, paper, &c., and I have found that all letters not properly stamped, that is to say, unless they have three upon them, and sent via France, are sent per sailing vessel or any other merchantman bound for home, and thereby are much delayed and frequently lost. Your letter was 46 days instead of about 14 before I received it.

I am, thank God, in most excellent health, and have enjoyed it ever since I have been in the country. I have been in three engagements, and several skirmishes with the Enemy. I was at the battles of Alma, Balaclava, and Inkerman without a scratch. Our brigade lost few men in action except at Balaklava, and there in one short half hour we lost more than one-half; the five regiments comprise the brigade, but all this you have seen in the newspapers. Every person will long remember the charge of the Light Brigade. Our horses are nearly all dead; we have few left, and what we have are almost useless; in fact the Light Brigade is a complete wreck, – we are of no service whatever, and what they intend to do with the few that are left I do not know. I think it will be impossible to make us up here. Report says we are to be relieved by the Light Cavalry now at home. I hope, if please God, such may be the case. The miseries of a camp at this season of the year are intolerable; the ground is covered with snow to the depth of two or three feet, and is likely to be for some time, a very cold wind blowing from the north, and freezing hard. I never experienced anything so cold before. We have been served out with good warm clothing, thank to the people of England, or I do not know how we should have got ours. There is nothing on earth can afford me so much pleasure here as to hear from any of my friends, and I always feel great pleasure in replying when I have an opportunity to do so. I have not heard from my wife for some time. Now I am afraid my letters have not reached her; I wrote to her and mother also about Christmas. I should be very glad if you will please say now whether mother has received my last letter, if not you will relieve her of a world of anxiety by acquainting her of my existence, and how I am. I am corporal, and doing very well, – promotion is rapid, and whether I come home or not, 'ere long I shall be full sergeant, – if I am lucky. I hope you will not fail to give my kind love to all relations and friends, and hope God willing, 'ere long, to be in my native Land. Please to favour me with all the news you can, and I shall feel for ever [*sic*, forever] obligated. I am indeed very anxious to hear from my mother and wife, and whether they have received my last letters. I am exceedingly obliged for the stamps you sent me. I hope you have had a merrier Christmas than I, and I wish you all a happy new year. I have fallen much short of spice cake and cheese this year. With sentiments of the greatest respect.

PS Address for me, 4th Hussars [*sic*, Light Dragoons], Crimea, *via* Marseilles. You will please excuse my not having given you a description of the various actions &c. I am afraid the news will be old, and the scenes of a battle are horrible beyond description. It is truly painful to dwell upon the subject.

Letter from Corporal **George Senior**, 13th Light Dragoons, to his brother in Huddersfield.[91]

Balaclava,
Dear Brother,-   1st Feb., 1855.
I have no news of any interest to communicate; we have had no Almas or Inerkmans since I last wrote you, but have experienced one of the three "generals" which, I understand, the Emperor of Russia calculated a good deal upon – January, February, and March. The former has now, thank God, done his worst, with not much effect, although the former part of his career was any-thing but comfortable, burying him in about two feet of snow and frost, which we sometimes experience in England in one of our severe winters; and when we calculate the difference between stone walls and canvass [*sic*], in the shape of shelter, it will be (*minus* canvass) very much; and so we have felt it. I would have given anything to have been under a roof of slate during the night; the frost penetrates through the tent and freezes everything in it; our boots we are obliged to hold to the fire to thaw before we can put them on; the clothes which cover us are frozen or wet with the damp arising from the ground; but still, with few exceptions, our brigade has not suffered in health very much; still we have a great deal to contend with, but, thank God, the latter part of January we have had fine open weather – warm during the day and frosty nights – the snow having gradually disappeared; and we have now, to all appearance, not much to fear from the Emperor's second "general," for the weather is more than we could wish for, and I trust sincerely, that it may continue so. It is rumoured that the Emperor's sons are again at Sebastopol; an officer of the Russians having given himself up to us the day before yesterday says they are again about to attack us at Balaklava, and, if unsuccessful, are going to burn down Sebastopol and the shipping, and leave the Crimea. Whatever truth there may be in the report we are, at all events, under orders to be ready to turn out, for we are expecting an attack this very night; and previous to your receiving this letter you may have heard of a battle lost or won; for should they again attack us at Balaclava it will be, I feel certain a final attempt on their part, and no doubt a very determined one. We are, I may say, almost impregnably forti-fied, and, before they take the place will lose as much almost as they will gain should they succeed. However, I feel indeed our brigade very easy, knowing we have four Highland regiments, sailors, batteries, and marines, besides a French battery on an eminence which overlooks the plain, in which direction the enemy will have to come previous to t heir entering the road leading into Balaclava, and the latter battery commands that road; and again, before they reach the road our shipping, with their heavy guns, will have full play, and the road leading into the town being very narrow, lying between two high hills, will rake them very much before they could get possession of it.

With regards to the privations and hardships which we have had to endure, and which according to your letter has been represented as very severe, I can only say (speaking of our brigade) that we are not very badly off under present circumstances. That we have some hardships to contend with must be expected, but not of that severity which might be represented in the 'papers. We are certainly better off than when camped near to Inkerman, having no boots or winter covering, but thanks to the benevolence of or feeling countrymen, whom I have inwardly thanked hundreds of times – and I feel certain that there is not a soldier in the Crimea who has not expressed himself grateful for the many unexpected presents sent out to this country, and everything so good and serviceable that we can now defy the cold. Every solider cannot but feel the many compliments paid to their bravery, which so many deserve and which all share in, and which I feel certain is a great encouragement to further acts of daring which may yet be wanted. The Infantry divisions suffer much more than us, as night after night, they are in the trenches, which we are not, and being so many of them I dare say all have not yet been furnished with all their winter coverings, and the difficulty of transport from Balaclava to their encampment is the principal drawback to their getting many things which are now laying at that place, but every day fresh clothing for them is going up, but I question whether all will get what they are entitled to before the winter is over, wing to the latter reason. I must say this that hundreds of sick come down almost every day from their encampment near Sebastopol, – that must prove their hardships must be great, when the cavalry have almost as few cases of sickness as it at home, and look as well, or even better, than when in Old England. It you were only to see me dressed up on a very cold day (commencing with the feet), with a good pair of "Benevolence" stockings (which we call those given by the country), and another pair over them of Turkish make – being of a coarse material, cut out and stitched together in many fanciful shapes, and figured with black braiding, giving them quite an Eastern appearance – coming up to the knee, – with a splendid pair of Northampton-made boots, which I had served out to me two days ago, coming up to almost the same height as the stockings. Together these are almost impregnable to cold, but not to the wet soaking through them, but which we must put up with; on my upper person I have a most fanciful shaped lamb-skin jacket or coat (for it certainly has something in the shape of lapelles [*sic*, lapels] upon it) with the woolley [*sic*, woolly] side in, and the outside figured with flowers in many colours running up the back, makes one look like a "Bono Johnny;" when without my pea coat, which covers all when on, and which is the most useful article we have, and quite supersedes our cloaks, which we never use except to cover us during the night; and to crown all, on my head I have a sheep-skin cap, wool both in and outside, something in the shape of a sweep's, made to come well over the ears, and if pressed on the top makes a regular Russian head-dress, which the peasants wear, but a first-rate article when on guard or picquet duty during these frosty nights.

I have no news regarding the siege operations; it is going on much as usual – sometimes hearing reports that Sebastopol is going to be stormed at such and such a day, while we await its coming with the greatest anxiety, and then are doomed to disappointment, the long-looked-for day has not yet come. We have latterly been expecting an attack from the Russians at Balaclava; but these last three or four days the weather having broken, from fine frosty open weather to rain, sleet, and snow, at intervals, with high winds, makes camp life most uncomfortable, and consequently we have not much fear of an attack from the enemy, the ground being too heavy for working their heavy field pieces. I shall be glad when the campaign is over; but should it continue I am ready to go with my regiment, and, thank God, in most excellent health, never better; and if God in His goodness will continue to bless me with that blessing, which is the first in this world – health – I have no fear but I shall return to Old England, let the campaign be over so long.

Letter from Lieutenant **Robert Hunter**, Scots Greys, to his sister.[92]

Balaklava
February 5th 1855.

... I am writing from my hut, which I got into a couple of days ago. It is better than a tent if that's anything about the most of it. It is built of wood, & there is a fireplace in it, but owing to some misconstruction it smokes obnoxiously that with the wind in some quantity I can't make use It, so am obliged to do without a fire. However the I'm pretty well accustomed to that now & don't mind cold & wet – much. I have grown quite stout in spite of hard living, & carry more flesh now than I did when you saw me last. I am I think better in health bearing that confounded rheumatism the terrible consequence of always having wet feet & damp clothes, which of course are not to be avoided out here. One ought to be pretty hard after this but I suspect we shall suffer the effects of it all, if [illegible] we are spared to return home. The navvys have arrived & the Railway is begun, but whether it will soon be finished is a matter time will shew. I think not before we don't want it much. We are all utterly disgusted with this business & I for one am not ashamed to say that I wish I was well out of it. I don't know of cause whether it is *the fault* of ministers or generals. I think *both* but it is & has been all along a botched business & the sooner its over the better. I hope to goodness Nicholas is [illegible] his signing of points, &c., but of course there is no depending on him & Im only afraid that the *fifth one* includes the dismantling of Sebastopol, & reduction of the Black Sea fleet which I don't think there is a ghost of a chance of his acceding to, unless we are by that time in possession of both town & fleet.

... My horses are pretty well & under cover, but only one of them has ever done me his work the other my second charger went in the near fore on the march & now is laid up with sore back.

Letter from Troop Sergeant Major **Matthew Brown** (number 517), Scots Greys, to his cousin in Glasgow.[93]

Camp, Off Sebastopol,
My Dear Cousin, -   11th Feb., 1855.

I received your welcome letter, and was glad to see by it you were all well, as this at present leaves me, thank God; and as for my spirits, they are up to concert-pitch.

I suppose you will think as I am on the sport I can give you a detail of what is going on here at present; but I can assure you I know little about it, except when I pick up an old paper a month old. Yet, I am happy to inform you that Sebastopol *will fall*, and soon, if not before you receive this. We are nearly read, and some of these fine mornings the Russian will get a start that will surprise the world. We are all eager for the fray, and the day will be ours. I see by the papers a great many accounts of what we are suffering in the way of hardships. Although great, if I have my health, and be able to return to my family with honour to my "Queen and country," it will repay me for all I have gone through. The rations are very good and plenty at present, but they were rather scanty a month ago.

The "Greys" have suffered a good deal: and if you saw us at present you would stare. We have only 40 horses fit for duty, out of 200 – about 90 died since 25th October; but still the same spirit remains in us as at Balaklava, and although nearly dismounted, we can fight on foot if required.

I am sorry to say that we have lost a great many men – no less than 17 died last month at the hospital at Scutari. We are nearly 100 men short. We suffered a deal at Balaklava; there was scarcely a man that did not receive a wound, and a great many have died through them. My wound is well, and I am able to handle the claymore once more.

I should have said more, but as I am writing this on the ground, it being rather awkward, I will say more in my next. If you would send me a paper it will be a great treat. If you will put two stamps on it I will repay you for it.

CHAPTER 7

Remounts and Reinforcements: March–June 1855

Rebuilding the Cavalry

In the Spring of 1855 the British army was faced with the prospect of having to rapidly rebuild its mounted arm before the campaigning season opened. Lord George Paget wrote in his diary on 23 February 1855 that the entire cavalry division numbered 400 horses, and in March confided that the Light Brigade had forty-four horses of which 'about 12 are serviceable. Scarlett ... has told Raglan that he had better send home the Light Brigade.'[1]

Even before the worst of the winter weather hit, Lord Hardinge, the Commander-in-Chief at Horse Guards, wrote to General Richard Airey (Quartermaster General in the Crimea) informing him that to relieve the man-power crisis (letters home presenting the Siege of Sebastopol in a far from positive light had a major negative impact on voluntary enlistment) the minimum height requirements for enlistment into the cavalry had been dropped by one inch (from the regulation 5ft 5½in) and the bounty increased from £4 to £6 – it was later to rise to £10. Cavalry regiments were also to be augmented from six troops (i.e. three squadrons) to eight troops of seventy-five men, six troops for war service and two to act as the home depot.[2] This augmentation would increase the cavalry force in the Crimea by an extra 1,500 sabres.[3] Hardinge was also able to report that he had managed to procure 2,000 five-year-old horses as remounts and only wished he was 'able to get recruits in larger numbers' as 'finding the 2,000 [to ride them] will be another affair ...'.[4] The *Daily News*, however, reported that nearly 200 re-mount horses 'from the northern and eastern counties had passed through the Metropolis' *en route* to the Cavalry Depot at Maidstone to be 'trained for cavalry service.' The horses were mostly browns and bays and 'three-quarter bred ... average price of each £28'.[5] *The Morning Post* on 11 December 1854 reported that the Maidstone Depot had received 120 horses for the 13th Light Dragoons during the last week and that officers from the 10th Hussars and 12th Lancers had arrived to inspect the remounts.[6] During the first week of January 1855, the Maidstone Depot was home to detachments from 1st and 2nd Life Guards, the Royal Horse Guards, 3rd Light Dragoons, 7th and 15th Hussars, and the 6th Dragoon Guards undergoing basic cavalry training, and in theory, not meant to be sent to their regiments until June. In order to provide space for the much-needed re-mounts for the Crimea, however, they were to be dispatched as soon as possible. At the same time, the Depot was ordered to procure 240 horses with which to entirely remount the 13th Light Dragoons, but only had eighty with which to do so![7]

By the New Year of 1855 Hardinge was beginning to despair in finding men and horses for the cavalry:

> In order to complete the Cavalry in the Crimea to 10 Regts. of 4372 ... we shall have to take almost every available Dragoon in England. Horses ... we are buying seasoned horses at £40 each ...[8]

Those regiments selected to be sent to the Crimea as reinforcements in December 1854 included for the Light Brigade the 10th Hussars and 12th Lancers, and for the Heavy Brigade the 1st (King's) Dragoon Guards and 6th Dragoon Guards (Carabiniers).[9] Both the 15th Hussars and 16th Lancers, only recently returned from India, had received orders to embark for the Crimea and were to be increased in strength from 600 sabres to 800.[10] The 10th Hussars and 16th Lancers, however, had retuned from India as mere 'skeletons' – the 16th Lancers, for example, returned 300 strong whilst the 10th Hussars could 'scarcely muster 600'.[11] Regimental agents were sent to the major Horse Fairs, but due to the inflation in the price of horses caused by the war meant that many regiments were unable to acquire remounts; the Government allowed up to £40 for a heavy cavalry horse, £30–£35 in the light cavalry, but horses were selling for twice the amount. The Scots Greys 'made a few purchases' at the Limerick Horse fair in November 1854 as did the 7th Dragoon Guards but the 8th Hussars, 16th Lancers and the 4th and 5th Dragoon Guards were unable to buy remounts.[12] The same was true at the Lee Gap horse fair near Leeds and also at Doncaster.[13] At the Chesterfield Horse Fair in February 1855 'good' horses fetched as much as £45 and many dealers were 'quite astonished' at the price horses sold for and 'the brisk demand'. Also present at the Chesterfield Fair were French cavalry agents looking to purchase remounts for their artillery.[14] The regulations concerning the age of the horses, so long as they were 'of sufficient height', were also relaxed to as young as three years in order to increase the number of animals theoretically available to the army.[15] Horse Guards also placed adverts in the newspapers inviting 'gentlemen', 'sportsmen' and also cab-owners and hauliers to 'volunteer' their horses for the cavalry.[16] In order to make good the deficiency in trained cavalry, various schemes were proposed, including using the Yeomanry cavalry as a trained cavalry reserve or the formation of volunteer cavalry units, such as that forming in Manchester, trained and equipped as Mounted Riflemen.[17] An 'ex-Dragoon' wrote to *The Morning Post* suggesting that the enlistment bounty for the cavalry should be increased to £10 and that the suggestion by Horse Guards that a raw recruit into the cavalry could become an efficient soldier in the six weeks that they envisaged was ludicrous; what was needed was an 'entirely different plan' for recruiting and training for the cavalry.[18]

By 8 January 1855 Hardinge was able to report that 500 enlisted men and 1,000 trained cavalry horses were ready to be dispatched to Constantinople and a second batch were being prepared for embarkation a month later.[19] Indeed, Hardinge gleefully informed Airey that there were 1,500 cavalry recruits at their depots

> ready to join in April and trained by 9 Regts. at home, 400–1,000 volunteers from Regts. at home ... We have 1,000 very fine horses 5 to 8 years old and rather more than 1,400 at the Hd. Qrs .... We can double this no. and train them, before the middle of April so I can feel certain of sending Lord Raglan 4,000 good horses before the end of April.[20]

In order to increase the cavalry establishment in the Crimea the Horse Guards proposed to 'take 140 old soldiers from each of the 19 Regts. at home' to form nine squadrons for immediate active service. Each of the 140 'old soldiers' was to take 'a seasoned horse' with him.[21] The 3rd and 7th Dragoon Guards, for example, each transferred forty-two horses as remounts for service in the Crimea.[22] The 4th Dragoon Guards received '42 seasoned horses' from the 2nd Dragoon Guards (Queen's Bays) whilst the 5th Dragoon Guards received a similar number from the 3rd Dragoon Guards. The 16th Lancers sent fifty horses to the 17th Lancers.[23] Not only horses, but men too were transferred from home regiments to those being sent to the Crimea; the 1st Dragoon Guards (barracked in Edinburgh) sent men to the Scots Greys; the 2nd Dragoon Guards supplied men for the 4th Dragoon Guards; 3rd Dragoon Guards men for the 5th Dragoon Guards and the 7th Dragoon Guards for the Inniskillings.[24]

Hardinge also took the unprecedented step of establishing a Forward Remount Depot at Constantinople – rather as the French had – ready to accept the remount horses where they would be acclimatised for one month before being sent on to the Crimea. The lack of acclimatisation of the horses had been one of the major causes of death. The Remount Depot was to be capable of stabling 1,000 horses and the 'invalids or men from the Cav. Divn. to take care of them'.[25]

However, things did not go according to plan. Whilst in March 1855 there were 1,000 horses and 500 recruits 'ready' at the home depots, they were unable to be drafted due to 'want of shipping'.[26] The *Daily News* reported that 'unremitting exertions' were being made to reorganize the cavalry, stating that 1,600 horses were being trained for cavalry service at Newbridge Barracks and a further 340 were at Dublin Cavalry Barracks ready to be sent to the Crimea. In Manchester, the Hulme Cavalry Barracks had been considerably enlarged to hold a further 112 horses and men.[27]

By the end of March it was discovered that the 'Cavalry can only send 550 men and 1,100 horses' in the first embarkation to the Crimea. It was hoped the second embarkation would include '1 squadron … [from] each of the 9 regts. at Home, if Old Soldiers, & 1170 picked horses'. The third embarkation was to consist of:

> … 1,350 Recruits of the 10 Regts. amongst which the remainder of the Old Soldiers at Balaclava will be intermixed – so that the 10 Regts. will then hopefully have 1,300 Seasoned men and 1,500 Recruits with horses from 5 to 8 yrs. Old, and the 10th Hussars complete.[28]

The issue of remounts and augmenting the cavalry was even raised in the House of Commons; Sir Frederick Peel MP (Under-Secretary of State for War) stating that

> … each regiment of cavalry in this country should raise for active service about 120 men and 300 horses. The cavalry force in the Crimea had been increased by bringing from India two cavalry regiments …[29]

In addition, '550 men and double that number of horses' were reported to be on their way to the Crimea.[30] Horse Guards estimated that by the end of April Lord Raglan would have under his command 3,000 sabres – considerably less that the number they had promised in 1854 – and 600 'reserve' horses at Constantinople.[31]

Letter from Farrier **W.H. Elam** (number 1202), 17th Lancers, to his father Mr Elam, a Veterinary Surgeon, in Huddersfield.[32]

Balaclava,
My Dear Father, Mother, Brother, and Sisters, -   March 6, 1855.
I was glad to receive a letter from you this afternoon. You may think it strange that I have not wrote to you before this time, but I have a great deal to tell you now, for it is nearly twelve months since I embarked onboard of ship to go to foreign lands. I have seen Gibraltar, Malta, and Constantinople, and several other places in Turkey since then, but now I am in the Crimea, about five or six miles from Sebastopol. I can now hear the cannons roaring from the above-mentioned place while I am lying on my bed writing this letter to you. You all think Sebastopol might have been taken before this time, but if you saw it you would think it impossible to be took from them at all, for there is no end of batteries all round the exterior of it, and very heavy metal they carry. The English and French have been erecting batteries in front of Sebastopol for sometime past, and that is no easy work, for the Russians will sometimes knock them down with shot and shell as fast as they can put them up; but of late we have taken a fresh plan, that is, the English erect batteries during the night, and at the same time the French keep up the firing at another point to attract their attention from the English while they are doing their work, and by this means they complete their ends without any interruption. The batteries belonging to the English and French are almost completed, so God help the Russians and Sebastopol when the English and French open fire on them, which will not be very long now, and I may say that it will fall to the ground by the time you receive this.

Letter from an anonymous private from Stockport in the 10th Hussars, to 'a friend in Manchester'.[33]

Balaclava,
May 2nd 1855.
... We were three months on the march from India, crossing the desert from Suez in three days, embarking at Alexandria and landing in the Crimea last month, amongst the thick of it, being present on the right rear of the besieging army before Sebasotopol. The report of guns of all calibres is incessant. Our business at present is to keep in check a body of Cossacks who continually keep us on the alert. They come down from the hills about Inkerman, when we have to meet them, and as yet have managed to drive them back, with the assistance of some Horse Artillery, who present samples of their bomb shells, &c., which they (the Cossacks) return, and then gallop off: believe me it is a peculiar sight. Prisoners are brought in every day. Thousands of troops, as far as you can see, in whatever direction you may be sent. The worst of it, to us "Indians" is the cold weather, which is extreme. We certainly are well supplied with warm clothing, as well as body linen, all but free of exposure; but the rations are rather scanty and precarious, as well as expensive. Bread alone is 1s. 3d. per loaf; butter, such as it is, 2s. per lb. &c. There is nothing but desolation and cannon shot. I am now writing after bedtime, small as the allowance of that is, the regiment being 18 out of the 24 [hours] either under arms or on duty of some kind of another. There are twelve of us, without any distinction, put up in

a small tent, not so large as one half of a third-class railway carriage on the Stockport line! You would smile to see me in large brown leather jackboots, very rough leather-lined pilot coat, sharpened sword, and thirty rounds of ball ammunition. Under all circumstances horses are nearly always saddled; unbridled to feed, and then on with it again; gather a few sticks, knock up a fire, boil or roast what you can get hold of, despatch same as quick as possible, and then look out for the squalls. Sebastopol has been on fire on the south side this morning, and there is some fresh movement on the tapis, some of our cavalry having marched to some quarter, where at present we know not. Troops, both French and English, are daily going to the front, and wounded to the rear.

Letter from Private **William Clark** (number 874), 12th Royal Lancers, to his parents in Stockport.[34]

My Dear Mother and Father,-

Camp Karana, Crimea,
12th Sept. 1855.

Having a few spare moments I have taken this opportunity of sending you a few lines. Since I wrote to you last I have been nearly all over the world. The Regiment marched from Bungalore on the 25th January, and we had a very pleasant march to a place called Shangalore, distant about 200 miles. We arrived at that place and remained there two days, and then embarked on board a steamer called the 'Pottinger', and had a very pleasant voyage out to Suez; we had very good rations and plenty of grog. We landed at Suez safe and sound, without the slightest accident; we stopped there three days, to give the horses a little rest previous to their march across the Sandy Desert. It would astonish any person to land here and have them march that we have had; we had to cross the Red Sea that you hear spoken of. There is many a Gentleman in England would give a great sum of money if he had the opportunity of seeing the sights across the Desert – for instance, the Pyramids of Egypt; we kept *them* in sight three days' march, and I think they are the most wonderful things I have ever seen. We arrived in Cairo, the principal city in Egypt, and the Pasha lent us a very fine barracks. We remained there about a fortnight, and had a chance of going about the place. The Egyptians are a very strong race of people, but very dirty in their persons and manners. You recollect, Egypt was visited with a plague of flies, I think that they have never cleared out, for I never saw so many in all my life. If you leave food or drink for a minute, you will not be able to see it for flies. We marched away from Cairo, and arrived at Alexandria, which is a very large, splendid place; the inhabitants are principally French, Italian, and English; we remained there two days, and then embarked on board the celebrated 'Himalaya', and had a pleasant trip to Balaklava. Previous to making for that place, we steamed round to Kamiesch Bay, and reported our arrival to the admiral of the fleet, and received orders where to land. The Captain of our vessel took us in front of Sebastopol, so that we had a good view of the harbour and city, and all our army and navy. I think it was one of the strongest places in the world: of course you know that we have taken it, and that it is in our possession. We landed at Balaclava on the 9th May, in good spirits and health. We have been out several times. We were at the storming of the 18th June, and at the engagement on the banks of the Tchernaya. We repulsed the enemy, and killed a great many of them. We are up every morning at two o'clock, saddled, and standing to our horses, ready to mount if required; although we often go up to the Russian lines to entice them out, but they will not come. In your letter you mention that you have heard of the deaths of poor brothers James and John, for which I am exceedingly sorry, and hope they are better off, for I can assure you that this is not a very pleasant place to remain at, and I hope before long to make a move toward Old England, to enjoy a quart of good old English beer, at a reasonable price, for which we pay one shilling and sixpence a quart, and everything else in proportion ... Trusting this finds you in good health and spirits, as it leaves me at present; accepting my kind love and respects to all my brothers and sisters.

Spring Amusements

For those officers, men and horses who had survived the winter, Spring 1855 was a chance to 'let off steam' and enjoy themselves, especially the officers, with race meetings and picnics. Lord George Paget relates how he had little else to do other than 'rides out' as far as the French camp and 'rambles' in the surrounding countryside during March.[35] Mrs Duberly recorded in her journal:

> Saturday, 24th [March]- Can this be a journal of a campaign? I think I must change its name to a new edition of the Racing Calendar. The French races today were very amusing. The course was crowded, the sun shone, and French officers were riding at the full gallop everywhere, and making their horses go through all the tricks of the *manège*.[36]

There were further race meetings on the following day (Sunday 25 March) and then during the week from 26–31 March. The Light Division held its own races on 7 April.[37] Yet another officer reported:

> Cricket is now the grand sport of the day. Nearly every day a match of some sort comes off on a good piece of ground behind the third and fourth divisions. One day is the cavalry against the infantry, and on the other the Guards against another division. To-day [*sic*, today] it was Harrow against Eton, and, although there was some little difficulty in getting together eleven of the former, the Harrovians gained a complete victory.[38]

Letter from Private **Edward Kirkwood** (number 1160), 5th Dragoon Guards, to his family in Belfast.[39]

Camp, Kadikoi,
March 8, 1855.

Dear Mother and sister, -

You wish to know if we have been so badly off as the papers reported us to be. We were not quite in so bad a condition, for we had plenty of clothes, though they were not suited for the stormy weather. However, we got warmer clothing before the winter was much advanced. The Sultan gave each of us a fur coat and a pair of Turkish boots, and we had from England, each of us, a blue pilot coat, a long pair of boots which covered the knees, two Guernsey shirts, and two pairs of flannel drawers. I myself happened upon a very good kit, for, after the battle of Bala Klava [*sic*], a great many grey Russian horses which broke away from the Russians came into our camp, and I caught one of them, which had a fine kit, and a pair of pistols, belonging to a Russian officer. The valise contained three fine linen shirts, three pairs of drawers, three pairs of socks, a beautiful pocket-handkerchief, and a nice cap with a big silk tassel. I was not long, I can tell you, getting into a Russian shirt and drawers. As to our having gone without trousers and shoes, there was nothing of the kind. The Light Brigade were rather worse off then we were, for they were more put about, and suffered more severely at the battle of Bala Klava than we did.

You want to know what sort of meat we get. Well, it is mostly either salt beef or pork, but about one in each week we get fresh meat. We have to cook in the open air. Sometimes we get a few fresh potatoes, and occasionally some pre-served ones, with cabbage and pease-soup. After the day I received your letter, we had a great hunt after some bullocks which broke loose from Sebastopol, and were running on the hills near our camp. Our commander, Mr Thompson,[40] a fine officer from your neighbourhood, and who has a brother living at Muckamore, shot one, and we brought it to camp. You were just right in your conjecture about what I felt when I lost my horse in the battle. I was not thinking where or how I should get another, but whether I should live to ride one, I had to make my way through a multitude of straggling horsemen, who were galloping about among the dying and dead Russians lying on the ground. These Russians are stout, hardy-looking men, but not hardy enough to stand the British steel, for they soon retired from it; yet, as for as numbers went, they might have eaten us, such a mere handful were we compared with them. This place is getting better every day. They are making a fine railway from Bala Klava to Sebas Topal [*sic*], which will bring up everything the soldiers require. When we came here first, the country was lovely with beautiful vineyards, the grapes bending down the branches to the ground. Now these vineyards have become so many grave yards. The weather has again become very fine, and the season is like May at home, every-thing springing up around us. Give my love to all old Friends.

Letter from Private **James Cooper** (number 941),[41] 1st Royal Dragoons, to his family in Spring Vale, Birmingham.

                                                    Camp near Balaklava,
My dear Brother, Mother, and Sister, -   March 14, 1855.
With pleasure I embrace the opportunity of answering your letter of the 18th of February. We[42] were both glad to see by it you were all well: hoping in God this may you all still the same. I am happy to say we are both in good health. For my part, I never enjoyed better health at home than I do in this country, which is one of the greatest blessings we have here. We have lost some-thing like sixty poor fellows out of our regiment (1st Royals), and about the same number sick. We have very fine weather now; I doubt very much if you have such weather in England as we have here. I suppose you have heard of the good news of the Russian Nicholas being dead. It may be the means of bringing the war to a close a little sooner. I must acknowledge we have had hard fighting here most fearful to relate. I can clearly say we have been for a fortnight together and never had a dry thread to our backs, with scarcely a bit of shoe to our feet, and the mud half way up to our knees; but, thank God, the worst of the time is over now. We have good boots and good clothes, which will keep out a good storm.

We were all turned out this morning (14th March) expecting an attack to be made on us by the Russians. They showed a very good front, supposed to be about 30,000 of them, to attack Balaclava, but they were not game to try their luck; if they had they would have met with a very warm reception from out batteries which we have erected. If peace is made, you will have a chance of knowing before we shall here. I have not received the parcel of pens, ink, and papers, &c., yet. I hope I shall have no need to use them in this country, for we all think we shall shortly see dear old England again. We have got wooden houses to live in now during the fine weather. We ought to have had these good things a long time ago, and that would have been the means of saving the lives of many thousands of our poor comrades; they have lessened our army greatly. But with all our losses we can still wollop the Russians, for all their superior numbers. I hope we shall soon hear from you all again. Brother Henry joins with me in love to you all. Please not forget us to all friends. I am glad to tell you we are very happy now, for we are truly like being in Heaven to what we were. It makes us more comfortable, having under gone the hardships we have, and then come to have a change. I think God for His kindness to us. It is amusing to see the railroad from Balaklava to Sebastopol. It is about half done now. Sebastopol still stands, but I should think before long you will hear of it being ours. I don't care how soon. I now conclude with all my love to all. I am just going to retire to bed, so good bye and God bless you.

Letter from Private **Benjamin Driver**, 4th Dragoon Guards, to Mr Frank Butler 'furniture dealer, Barnsley'.[43]

Sebastopol,

Dear Frank, -   March 18, 1854 [*sic*, 1855]
You must excuse me for not writing to you before but the reason of my not doing so was because it was waiting to send you the result when I did write, but things remains in the same state as before with bits of skirmishes now and then, but no general field fight. The devils are afraid to meet the British in the field. The army has suffered very much this winter. It has been wet nearly every day, and we have had nothing to put on except one blanket and our cloaks, and to lie on the cold ground at nights, but, thank God, I have got over all; but I may tell you I have seen many a fine fellow die. The warm clothing the country sent out to the army was too late, as winter was nearly all over. The fine weather is now coming on, and the Russians are showing themselves again, but I can tell you that our men are only waiting to have a chance to be at them. I have got a medal and the five pounds awarded to me for bravery in the field at Balaklava, on the 25th of October, but we are not to get them until the regiment comes home. Our pickets are taking prisoners every day, and sorties are made on us every night by the Russians, but they always come off the worst; and their cavalry have been afraid of ours ever since Balaklava; but I can tell you that I should like to be on my road home once more, but I am afraid that it will be some time first. I wish all the regiments would come out and march up the country, but I am afraid a great many of the young men who are coming out will die off very fast, for the country here is very unhealthy, but the Old Hands are getting used to the country. The French are fine soldiers, but the Turks are not worth anything. It is very hard to be on salt meat for so long, and the men look very unhealthy from bad feeding, but they are in fine spirits and get a drop of brandy. No one can stop John Bull.

Letters from Lieutenant **Robert Scott Hunter**, Scots Greys, to his sister.

March 26th 1855[44]

... There has been some pretty hard fighting in the trenches lately in which, I'm sorry to say the French have not behaved as was supposed of them for nearly every sortie lately. Mr Johnny Frenchman has *bolted* fairly & now the Russians are getting up in pluck, & lick them nearly every night. I am perfectly *certain* now that the place is impregnable, & on account of the large armies the Enemy have at the other side of the Tchernaya, & between the Belbec & Alma we cant get round with our present force. If the war lasts I suspect there will be a battle for the Crimea which we will all three of our present victories quite into the shade, as it will be fought between the reinforced armies of the Allies and the Concentrated Russian forces. It will end but by our side on the other going to the wall with a vengeance. However if it does happen Im sure we'll lick them. They cant stand before us on the open tho' they certainly can thrash us behind trenches. I send you a lot of violets from the field of Inkerman, they grew where many a brave fellow fell, and their roots have been moistened with something more valuable than water. I daresay they will be a rather interesting relic of the battle. It is curious to see these little sweet blue flowers growing up by the side of broken fragments of shell, pieces of pouches & belts – stained with blood – & heaps round shot, & rifle bullets without number but the ground is covered & *quite blue* in some places with them, & they scent the whole of the place. This is a very hot day. We were called up at 3½ this morning expecting an attack but it never came off & I have been so long out of bed (for it was such a lovely morning, I had not the heart to go to bed again) it is now 11½ by our time, that Im getting quite sleepy.

... There is a good deal of fun going about in the Camp. Today there are races at the 4th Dragoons. Tomorrow running in sacks &c. & Wednesday is our 3rd Cavalry Division Spring Meeting. The two French ones have gone off well & there has been some good riding. The Officers of the Chasseurs d'Afrique had a good steeplechase on Saturday & I believe some of them are good riders. Their horses are mostly Barbs, but a few have English horses.

Camp,
April 6th 1855[45]

... nothing has been begun yet, tho we have an immense number of guns up & ammunition in proportion & I don't think field operations are thought of as we are completely hemmed in by the Enemy in rear who have fortified every road, height and valley around our present positions. I hope however the either peace will come or an order to go in at everything we can lay hands on, & I'll bet any odds that fearful as the odds are against our comparatively small force, we'll give an account of the Russians that will make them sing "Je Bleu" the wrong [illegible]. There is a great deal of amusement going on about the camp. Capital races &c. two or three times a week. There to be capital races tomorrow at the 4th Division Camp. I get the M I G pretty regularly, & for the number of the 17th March today[.] [T]he ham is excellent, it was a little mouldy outside so I had it paired and walk but it was uncommonly good at breakfast. The mince pies inwardly are splendid, but the crust is so tough that no dental teeth could chew, or rather digest it. So we got the inside (the best bit) and look at the outside. Bannocks capital but we get them fresh baked now. Mr Peter Primrose a Scotch baker has set up a shop in Balaklava & I get a loaf of white bread & bannocks when I want them. Every day. You may see I appreciate the paper & am writing on the book. The Cheese, Oh! What a charming cheese it is! Im going in at *he* at dinner today. All the other things are equally good but about *four months* behindhand. I am very well & jolly. I am going to write to AKH to send me a new forage cap so you can send the pipe in it. If can cover by post if you put lots of stamps on it.

Letter from Regimental Sergeant-Major **John Grieve** VC (number 774),[46] Scots Greys, to Mr E.G. Pickering of the Long Row, Nottingham.[47]

Heavy Cavalry Camp,
Sir,   2d April, 1855.
I beg to acknowledge the arrival of the following barrels of Ale, from the inhabitants of Notting and neighbourhood, viz.-

One from Mr Dickinson 'The Butchers' Arms; one from the landlord of the 'Lord Nelson'; one from Mr Hickling, 'Rose and Crown'; one from Mr. G. Spencer, of Nottingham; one from Mr. J. Birkin, Farmer, of West Bridgeford; one from Mr. J. Pilkington, Artichokes, Nottingham; one from Mr. J. Eyre, 'Albion', Southwell Road, Nottingham; one from the landlord of the 'Wellington', Eastwood.

They have all been issued to the Troops, who have desired me to thank the presentees of it, through the medium of the "Nottinghamshire Guardian", and to say that it will ever be a source of pride and gratification to hear of the welfare and happiness of all who have so liberally come forward to testify their appreciation of us as defenders of the *true faith*, fighting for right against might and tyranny. Much more might I say of such generosity did time allow me, but let me assure you that our thanks are heartfelt.

There is still more ale in the stores at Balaklava, but which are so blocked up that we are at present unable to obtain it, but expect to do so shortly, when I shall also acknowledge that. I now beg to conclude, and hope before many posts to have the pleasure of announcing to you the fall of the Tyrant's Stronghold, as vast exertions are being made for that purpose.

Letters from Corporal **Thomas Morley** (number 1004), 17th Lancers, to the Editor, *Nottinghamshire Guardian.*

Camp Near Balaklava,
April 16, 1855.[48]
In my last I said that our Siege fire had opened. They are still at it hard and fast. Firing, I am afraid is not of the least avail. It does not make the least impression on the place. They give us back shot for shot. Such terrific firing was never heard in this world. There have been a great many lives lost since the opening of the siege; at the Sailor's Battery in particular. I went down to Balaklava the other evening, and saw a great many wounded men of the artillery being taken off the railway trucks. All the wounded were brought down on the railway, which is a very good thing for them in place of the ambulance waggons, which are enough to shake your insides out. I was glad to notice that every attention was paid to the poor fellows whilst being taken on board ship. Everything in fact is carried out much better than formerly. I am not able to state the

number killed since the opening of the siege; but I believe that the sailors lost in one battery one hundred in the course of four days. I think that in the other batteries there are however, more wounded than killed.

The sortie made by the Russians last night (the 15th) was more like a battle than a sortie. It lasted for a long time. The sortie was made on our counter and left. I am told there were neither many of ours nor of the French, but that there were a great many of the Russians killed. I believe that we took a grand battery from the Russians and that the French sprung a mine under the Round Tower and blew it up; but I am sure that Sebastopol never will fall from the firing on it. They must storm the place, otherwise we shall never have the town. It was expected that the shipping would aid in the attack on Saturday last. But as yet they have done nothing.

Omar Pasha's army has arrived here. They are fine looking men. I believe they are going to take possession of the same redoubts which the Turks lost at Balaclava. I don't think the Russians could take them from these fine men. I went to witness this morning the landing of the whole of the 10th Hussars from India. So fine a lot of horses I never saw in my life. They must be six hundred sabres. The 12th Lancers will be here in a fortnight. I am still in hopes we shall have peace. Within these five minutes they have left off firing; for what purpose I cannot say. It is quite a treat not to have the guns roaring in your ears. It is now past ten o'clock p.m. and there is only one person in the tent with me.

April 20th.
We have certainly failed in this siege in taking Sebastopol. This is the second time we have made the attempt and failed. The bombardment has stopped for these two days; but I believe we intend trying once more. They are getting up twice as much shot and shell as they had before, and if this does not do, we shall have to raise the siege and take the field, and best the army in our rear. It is rumoured that Lord Raglan and Canrobert have had some words about the affair. Lord Raglan is willing to storm the town – but General Canrobert is not; he says the place must be invested. Every one is very much down in the mouth about the matter. In fact our men expected to storm the town two days after the opening of the siege; the men were actually told off for it: and there was a *reconnaissance* made on the morning of Thursday the 18th. They assembled in Balaklava plain betwixt four and five in the morning. I think that there must have been altogether 20,000 French, English and Turks, led by Omar Pasha. Of our cavalry, there were two strong squadrons of the 10th Hussars, and a strong troop of the Greys, together with a troop of the 4th Dragoon Guards. As for our Light Brigade – God help us! We could not muster 20 horses! So they took none of us. The 10th Hussars don't know what to make of this work yet. They went five or six miles into the country and returned with only one Cossack. The Russian army has left our rear and gone into Sebastopol. In the sortie made last night, the 10th, there occurred, I am sorry to say, a little loss of life on our side. We have lost one brave officer, the Colonel of the 77th Regiment, and two other officers besides; but I believe there are only four or five of the men killed, although there were forty wounded. By this sortie we have taken what we call the Gravel pits, which were considered good places by the Russians, and these pits certainly annoy our men very much. The Russians

came thither in great force – the French having undertaken to carry these pits before but failed. The Russian position annoyed our 8-gun battery exceedingly; and we therefore carried these pits with the point of the bayonet. To-night all is as quiet as if we were not at war. Everyone has given the matter up for a bad job. I am afraid this war may last for some time. If Sebastopol should fall, I think, however, we should have peace. But I am sure we never shall subdue the town by firing on it. We shall have to starve them out of it. You must not believe all that appears in the papers. What I say you will find to be correct. The railway has got as far as Lord Raglan's – a distance I should say of five miles. I believe they are going to branch it off by divisions, so that each division of the army may have every requisite brought directly to it. I really do not know what we should have done without the railway. Then men are now enjoying the best of health and spirits. It is now past one o'clock a.m. I must close for the night – there is an odd shot going now and then.

21st April, 1855.
There was a sortie last night which lasted for sometime. The firing was terrific.

Balaklava, Friday Evening,
May 25, 1855.[49]

I have this day received your very kind letter. I think I told you in my last that there was a move upon the board. I am glad to inform you that the move had been made. But I must first mention what took place on Tuesday night last, the 22nd. There was a sortie made by the French, and they have taken three batteries – the Flagstaff Battery is one – the names of the other two I cannot tell you. I am sorry to say that the French met with tremendous loss of life – it is supposed to have amounted to twelve hundred on that night alone. On the next night the Russians came to see whether they could not take these batteries back again. But they did not and could not succeed. They (the Russians) came back again last night (Thursday), the 24th, but I have not heard the result of last night's works. I am told, however, that the Russians are lying in thousands about the batteries – dead.

Our Field Army has left this at last. They number I am told 80,000 men. They left this morning, and were crossing the heights of Balaklava at six o'clock. The Russians were taken completely by surprise; so much so that our men came in for a good hot breakfast in a small village not far from Balaklava. An engagement then took place and we completely routed them and drove them from their entrenchments. I do not think that there was much loss on our side. No doubt before this reaches you – you will have heard tell of many engagements. I am inclined to think that Sebastopol will soon be in our hand. It was reported that the final bombardment would take place on the Queen's Birthday [24 May]. Such has not been the case.

I have just been looking at the heights of Balaklava. Only last night there were nothing to be seen save a solitary Cossack on No. 3 Redoubt. Now the heights are arrayed all over with tents facing the valley where we light cavalry were slaughtered. On the Queen's Birthday there was a review of all our cavalry. I was not mounted myself; but I am told it was a superb sight. A strong reinforcement left this on Thursday last, for Kertch; it took nearly two days to effect their embarcation [*sic*], including English, French, and Sardinians. I think it was 50,000 that went. I hope they will get a safe landing. But it is rather strange that no other cavalry went with this expedition except the 8th Hussars – of whom there are 50 men and four officers mounted on good horses under the command of Col. De Salis. There were only a few men and horses left behind. There has been a good deal of amusement going on in each camp. We have had races, jumping in sacks, foot racing for prizes, &c. The Guards had some very good sports.

It is now 10 o'clock [p.m.]. Firing very slack. Our shipping, however, are doing good execution to-night. There is no firing from the batteries – it is all from the shipping.

Balaklava,
Monday night, June 4 [1855].

I really don't know what to give you in the shape of news. Of course the news I should give you I know you have it as soon as we have it ourselves. You never can get, however, the true statement of anything that is done unless you happen to be present yourself. The [Kertch] expedition is still absent. They have done very well in taking those provisions and stores. There were provisions for an army for six months, and a great quantity of ammunition. We have heard here that in one of the vessels taken there was a great deal of money. I did expect that the army encamped near the Black River [i.e. Tchernaya] would have made an advance before this to get on to the north-road. The army at Kertch I think are waiting for them to get in sight. I was out riding one day last week and went as far as the Black River and watered my horse. I was very glad to get back again. I was not aware that I was within range of the enemies' batteries, however, until just a few yards before I got to the river bang! went a 32-pounder and lodged a ball only three yards over my head. I saw a splendid horse belonging to one of the French officers killed a few yards from me. The French cavalry are obliged to water their horses there, as there is no other place nearer them. The Russians are very strong in position – having batteries two miles in length. When we do make the advance movement, it will be *a second Alma*. The batteries are all arranged along a very high cliff. I never saw hills so steep in my life. On my way back I had a look at the valley where we Light Brigade was mowed down by the Russian guns. I could hardly keep from dropping a tear when I came into the valley. A number of the poor fellows are not half buried – only just a little earth thrown over them. Some of our men went and dug larger holes for them. I saw two large pits. I suppose the remainder of the poor fellows are in them. A great number of the horses are not under ground. There was a sortie made last night. We have taken two more batteries, one with 31 guns in it – the other with mortars. I am sorry to inform you that cholera is very prevalent in some parts of the camp. The Guards loses a number every day. There were four of the 10th Hussars died this morning. I am glad to say that it has not made its appearance in our Light Brigade.

CHAPTER 8

Mopping Up:
September–December 1855

The Allied cavalry were at their busiest during the summer offensives of 1855 – particularly the French cavalry. French, British and Sardinian cavalry were all present at the Battle of Traktir (16 August) but were not engaged. Nor were they engaged during the final assault and capture of Sebastopol on 8–9 September 1855. French, British and Turkish cavalry played a very active role around Kertch and Eupatoria mopping up the Russians and attempting to blockade the Russians in the north side of Sebastopol. It is no exaggeration to suggest that the British cavalry saw more action in the three months following the fall of Sebastopol than during the preceding year.

The 10th Hussars at Kertch

The 10th Hussars formed part of the British garrison at Yenikale. On 21 September the *Chasseurs d'Afrique* and British Hussars were engaged with the Cossacks outside Kertch. The French troops were under the command of *Colonel* D'Osmont, and he had received information that Cossacks were 'collecting and driving away all the arabas from the neighbourhood'. In order to prevent this he ordered the *Chasseurs* and 10th Hussars on a sortie against the Cossacks and reconnoitre the villages surrounding Kertch. Two troops of the 10th Hussars, commanded by Captains the Hon. E. Fitzclarence and Clarke were attached to an equal number of *Chasseurs* and French Dragoons. The *Chasseurs d'Afrique* departed before the British Hussars; the troop under Captain Fitzclarence rendezvousing with the French at the village of Koss Serai-Min. Fitzclarence then sent an order to Clarke to 'join him that night' but 'the order was unfortunately not delivered until the following morning.' Whilst marching to the village, Captain Clarke's troop, numbering only thirty-four men

> fell in with a body of about fifty Cossacks, which he immediately charged and pursued, but as they were soon re-inforced [*sic*] by upwards of 300 [Cossacks], but he was forced to retire upon the village, with the loss of his sergeant-major, farrier, and thirteen men.[1]

Captain Fitzclarence and the French, having seen 'a large body of the enemy', 'skirmished with them at some distance, and moved in the direction of Serai Min' where they found the remains of Captain Clarke's troop. However 'at about the distance of half-a-mile from the village they were attacked by a large body of Cossacks, who were, however, beaten back by repeated charges'.[2] One French officer wrote:

> ... at Kilai, about eight leagues from Kertch. A handful of English Hussars and French *Chasseurs d'Afrique*, who had made a rather venturesome dash into the interior, fell in with the enemy's cavalry. The Russian General sent against

them eight squadrons of Cossacks and Dragoons, who completely surrounded our 200 horsemen. The Hussars and French *Chasseurs* replied with the point of their swords to the invitation of surrender addressed to them in French by an officer of Dragoons, and after prodigies of valour, succeeded in opening a passage for themselves and returning to Kertch. In that hand-to-hand engagement our *Chasseurs* lost eight men, who were so closely pressed that they could not make use of their arms ... The English Hussars lost 17 men ...[3]

The loss of the 10th Hussars were two privates killed, one wounded, one sergeant-major, one farrier, thirteen privates and fifteen horses taken prisoner.

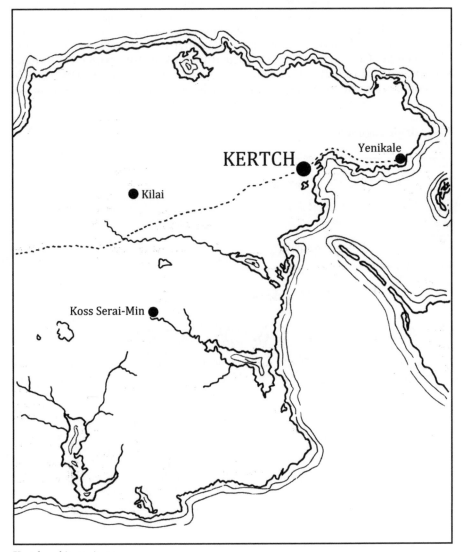

Kertch and its environs.

Eupatoria
Following the fall of the south side of Sebastopol to the Allies on 8 September 1855, attention shifted to pinning-down remaining Russian forces and cutting-off the north side of Sebastopol. This was done using a method developed in Algeria by the French called *Razzias* – using highly mobile, self-contained 'flying columns' to seek out the enemy and to destroy his means of communication and supply. To this end, *Général* d'Allonville was ordered to immediately take a strong French force into the field at Eupatoria to cut-off the Russian supplies entering the Crimean Peninsular via Perekop. D'Allonville was appointed '*Général en Chef*' of the expedition and under his command was a strong Turkish force under Ahmed Pasha. *Sous-Lieutenant* Charles Silbert de Cornillon (*6e Dragons*) *Offiçier d'Ordonnance* to *Général de Brigade* Ferdinand Esterhazy, Inspector General of Cavalry in the Crimea, noted on 7 September that the cavalry was being concentrated in the Tchernaya valley and being prepared immediate service.[4] On 17 September Charles announced his departure for Eupatoria with some trepidation, not knowing whether they were to over-winter in the town, which he hoped was not the case due to the 'arid steppes. We have few resources, and then we will be distant from everyone and everything.' He also thought the position of *Général* Esterhazy was 'bizarre' being a General of Brigade but in reality only commanding a single regiment.[5]

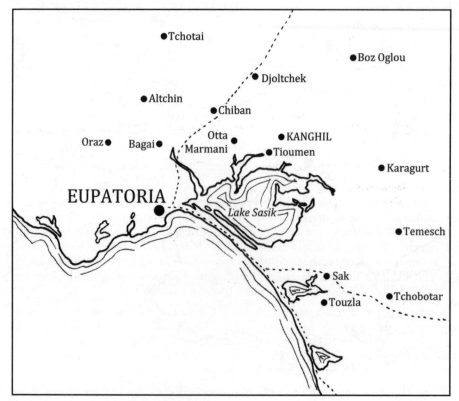

Eupatoria and its environs, showing Kanghil.

The French force consisted of:

1e Brigade – Général de Brigade d'Esterhazy
   4e Hussards (4 squadrons) *Colonel* de la Mortière

2e Brigade – Général de Brigade du Champéron
   6e Dragons (4 squadrons) *Colonel* Ressayre
   7e Dragons (4 squadrons) *Colonel* Duhesme.

1 battery, *Artillerie Montée* (*Capitaine Armand*)

The *1e Hussards* had been earmarked to form part of the *1e Brigade* but they were retained in Sebastopol on staff duties. The expeditionary force left Kamiesch on the evening of 18 September, landing at Eupatoria unopposed two days later.[6] *Sergent* Mismer (*6e Dragons*) noted that the hospitality afford by the British on the two 'giant steamers' in which the French had embarked, was great and impressive, even laying-on a special table at dinner for the Sub-Officers; during dessert the ships' Petty Officers and Engineers came to sit with the French and drank beer and sang songs with them. The landing was effected in the evening, and Mismer, much to his alarm found himself 'on a foreign beach, in the dark'.[7] *Sous-Lieutenant* de Cornillon thought that voyage from Kamiesch to Eupatoria was 'charming. The sea calm, like oil, as we say in Marseilles, the sky pure, and your Don Carlos in his black humour.'[8] *Général* Esterhazy and his *Ordonnance* found themselves installed in a mansion – 'a bedroom and a *grand salon* for the Général, a dining room, one room for the Aide-de-Camp, one for me, a kitchen, a wood-shed, a cellar, an attic, stables, a courtyard etc ...'.[9]

The Turkish garrison at Eupatoria – which had been blockaded by the Russians since 17 February – consisted of 15,000 men and 30 guns and were found to be suffering greatly from lack of water, typhus and scurvy.[10] D'Allonvile wrote:

The town of Eupatoria, with the fortified camp which protects the town, with a development of parapets for around 8 kilometres, and we observe Cossacks at a distance of 1 or 2 kilometres from our works; I decided to exclude those inconvenient observers and study the land on which I was operating ...[11]

Sous-Lieutenant de Cornillon had mixed feelings about the Turkish army:

It is clean, disciplined, more presentable. The infantry is poorly clothed, but not bad at the manouevres; the cavalry, consisting of lancers, has a bright spirit; artillery is what is the best. The general officers commanding these troops speak good French, and have an air of intelligence ... With this troops is an irregular cavalry, a bizarre assemblage of Turks, of Tatars, the bandits of all countries ... some armed with long lances, others with muskets ornamented with brilliant fittings, carrying curved, gilded sabres, pistols tucked into the belt, mounted on small ponies but strong and robust.[12]

In consequence of the constant raids by Cossacks, D'Allonville sent a strong reconnaissance towards Sasik and Touzla. He directed 'several squadrons and battalions toward Oraz and I went the same day towards Sak with four battalions, ten squadrons and six field pieces'. The forces left under the cover of darkness and at 4 a.m. near Lake Sasik d'Allonville found:

The Russians surprised in their cantonments; the Cossacks retreated over the ground, the signal rockets broke out on all sides, when suddenly arose a thick fog which does not [let us] see twenty paces ahead, and that forces us to completely stop our movement. It was not until 8 o'clock that this mist dissappears, and we were permitted to continue our march towards Sak.[13]

Several squadrons of Russian Uhlans appeared to the left of the village, accompanied by 'three or four' Russian field guns. At the approach of two Egyptian battalions, who were supported by the French cavalry, the Russians retreated into the village which they 'evacuated with great precipitation'. The French returned to camp around 6 p.m.[14]

Information from Tatar spies and from Russian deserters suggested two Russian forces, one composed of infantry, dragoons and Cossacks protecting the Simpheropol Road (about 80km distant), and the second of Grenadiers, Cossacks and Uhlans covering the route to Perekop (around 180km distant). D'Allonville therefore sent out a second strong reconnaissance to locate the Russians, and, if possible, bring them to battle.[15] Mismer recorded that on 25 September a strong Franco-Turkish force was despatched toward Perekop: the *Bachi-Bazouks* (aka *Spahis d'Orient*) formed the advance guard; the *Dragons* the 'first line' and the Turks the reserve. The French discovered at sunrise that they had been shadowed by Russian cavalry:

As the horizon lightened we saw before us, cannons and a dozen [Russian] squadrons formed in battle; this cavalry has always maintained the same distance, stopping when we stopped when we moved backwards. Sometimes our artillery sent him a few rounds. When the projectile was fired we could clearly see the disorder in the [Russian] ranks. The Russians made an about-turn and moved out of range. At the time we stopped to feed the horses, the *Bachi-Bazouks* offered a spectacle, a fantasy. Individual riders advanced at the gallop up to the face of the enemy, discharged their weapons, and galloped back straight away the way they came. The Russians, disdaining this bravado, did not reply.[16]

In order to break the monotony of the march, some of the dragoons took to hunting the numerous 'hares who scampered through the legs of our horses'. Finding themselves low on fuel and water, and that the Russians were constantly retreating before them, refusing to give battle, the column returned to Eupatoria, the men having been in the saddle for fourteen hours.[17]

The Battle of Kanghil, 29 September 1855

A large reconnaissance was sent on before dawn on 29 September, consisting of three columns; the right-hand column of Egyptian infantry and artillery directed towards Sasik; the left-hand column of Turks and the central, Franco-Turkish, column under d'Allonville consisting of twelve squadrons (*4e Hussards, 6e* and *7e Dragons*), one battery of artillery and four Egyptian battalions. The *Bachi-Bazouks* formed the head of column to scout ahead.

A French cavalry regiment consisted of six squadrons; four of which were 'war' squadrons with the remainder forming the depot. Each squadron was commanded by a *Chef d'Escadron* (Squadron Leader) or senior *Capitaine* and consisted of eight officers, eleven sub-officers, sixteen corporals, thirty-two privates first class and 108 privates second class for *Hussards* and ninety-eight for regiments of *Dragons*. Each squadron also had two trumpeters, a master farrier, shoeing smith and a saddle maker. In total, therefore the *4e Hussards* mustered around 700 men at full strength whilst the *6e* and *7e Dragons* around 660. The total French cavalry force – excluding the *Bachi-Bazouks* – was around 2,000 sabres.

The column left Eupatoria at 3 a.m., and after passing the Joseck defile:

> the division formed in order of battle, driving before it the Russian positions. Contact is made by *Bachi-Bazouks* with Cossacks foragers. These are multiplying, a platoon of the regiment [*4e Hussards*], commanded by Lieutenant Garcin, is sent to support, then a division of the 4th Squadron was launched to clear the area [of] swarms of Cossacks.[18]

Général d'Allonville records that at daybreak the *Bachi-Bazouks* began skirmishing with Cossacks and one *peloton* of the *4e Hussards* was sent forward to support them on their right. *Général* d'Allonville wrote:

> I perceived, on the Chiban Heights, eight squadrons of Uhlans descending on the right, on the Djoltchak, and eight others debouching at Tioumen and obviously seeking to cut off our retreat, driving us to the edge of the lake. The First squadron of the *Hussards*, the Head of Column, received the order to go to their right to maintain the offensive. On the left, the second division of the fourth squadron is made ready to charge ... through the mist which attended the horizon, I perceived the Russian cavalry searching for a manoeuvre against our right flank.[19]

According to Prince Gortchakoff's report, the Russian force was commanded by Lieutenant-General Korff (who was taken prisoner) and consisted of the 'Regiment of Lancers of Her Majesty the Grand Duchess Catherine Mikhailova', the 'Regiment of Lancers of Archduke Leopold' and 'Light Horse Battery No. 19'. A Russian Lancer Regiment had eight squadrons, each 170 men strong (1,360 in total). The combined strength of both regiments would have been around 2,700 – significantly more than the French cavalry force.

The Russians had been taken somewhat by surprise by the French: Gortchakoff had ordered Korff to retire to the villages of Karagout and Boz Oglou if a superior force presented itself. Major-General Terpelevsky, commanding the 'Lancers of Archduke Leopold' fell back on Boz Oglou, but Lieutenant-General Korff commanding the 'Lancers of Grand Duchess Catherine' and 'Light Horse Battery No. 19' lost contact with the enemy before arriving at Karagout and therefore decided to march in support of Major-General Terpelevsky and halted at Kanghil. He ordered his men to dismount and rest and for the guns to be unlimbered. Gortchakoff noted that he 'did not dispose his advance posts in convenient order, and at the requisite distance from his position.' The result was, therefore that the French surprised him.[20]

Général Coste de Champéron had also spotted the Russian movement and he ordered his men to prepare for action. At 10 a.m. the column had covered four leagues when they were ordered to rest, 'in full view of the enemy'. Here they adjusted the saddles and harness and rested the horses. This halt was also to allow the supporting Turkish infantry to catch up with the French cavalry.[21] An hour later they halted again in order to water the horses, but due to a lack of water they were given a feed instead. *Sergent* Mismer remembered that during this halt, the *4e Hussards* suddenly remounted and advanced at the trot towards the Russians, perpendicular to the right flank of the *Dragons*, towards the village of Kanghil. The first three squadrons of the *6e Dragons* were soon given orders to follow the *Hussards*, 'the enemy multiplying at each moment on different points'. The fourth squadron – of which *Sergent* Mismer was a member – was ordered to protect the accompanying artillery battery.[22]

The French cavalry advanced in columns, diagonally across the Russian front, *4e Hussards* leading; half an hour later the leading elements of the *Hussards* were in full view of the Russians. D'Allonville disposed his troops with six squadrons formed in line of battle, the left flank covered by two squadrons near the village; to the rear eight field guns and reserve squadrons.[23] *Général* Esterhazy wrote that:

> At midday, or thereabouts, after a night march and a rapid movement onto the line of retreat of the enemy, we came to the small village of Kanghill. The *4e Hussards*, which composed my brigade marched at the right of the column, and the brigade of *Dragons* on the left. I received the order to charge immediately.[24]

From his position with the artillery, *Sergent* Mismer watched as:

> All at once the *Hussards* were a thousand metres ahead of us, disappearing behind a fold in the terrain, and we heard two cannon shots. So we went at the gallop. Our first three squadrons disappeared in their turn. Soon we arrived at a sudden dip in the Steppe, marking a new difference in the level of the three steps. The scene is uncovered and we saw a brigade of Russian Lancers at the gallop, chased by our *Dragons*. In the foreground, the *Hussards*, who had charged head-on, were reforming their ranks.[25]

This flank movement is confirmed by Gortchakoff's report: 'a great part of the enemy's cavalry, numbering from two to three thousand men, making a rapid movement to the right, appeared on the right flank and the rear of Lieutenant-General de Korff'.[26] *Général* Pélissier's despatch noted that:

> The *Général* D'Allonville, with the support of Muchir [Ahmed Pasha] by two regiments of Turkish cavalry and six Egyptian battalions diverged on the tip of lake to surround the enemy. The promptness of the movement allowed the *4e Hussards*, conducted in the first line by the *Général* Walsin-Esterhazy, to approach the enemy with the armes blanche, while the *Général* Champeron with the *6e* and *7e Dragons* in the second and third line overpowered the Russians Hulans [*sic*, Uhlans] and forced them to a precipitous retreat during which they were harassed for more than two leagues.[27]

Général Esterhazy placed himself at the head of the *4e Hussards*, in the centre of the regiment; to his right was *Colonel* Simon La Mortière and to his left his ADC, *Capitaine d'État Major* Pujade and his *Offiçier d'Ordonnance*, *Sous-Lieutenant* Silbert de Cornillon, seconded from the *6e Dragons*. The first two squadrons were commanded by *Chef d'Escadron* Tilliard; the remaining squadrons by *Capitaine* d'Anglars. Esterhazy drew his sword, and with a shout of '*En Avant! Vive l'Empereur!*' launched the charge against the Russians. As the *Hussards* raced towards the Russian lancers, at about 400 metres, they opened their ranks to unmask a battery of horse artillery, which fired case-shot into the oncoming French, causing 'great disorder in our ranks'. *Capitaine* Lenormand at the head of the 1st Squadron, changed the direction of its charge and 'launched it with terrible élan on the cannons, they were also tackled with the same energy [by] the *Capitaine* Galibert with the 2nd Squadron, while the other two (the *Captiaines* d'Anglars and Charmeux) charged the enemy line as they tumbled [into them]'.[28] *Sergent* Bourseul of the 2nd Squadron captured one of the Russian guns and during the melee received 'five sword cuts to the head, five lance wounds in the posterior region of the trunk, two lance thrusts in his right arm, two lance wounds in his right hip, a lance thrust in his left knee, a lance wound to the neck, and finally a lance wound in the epigastric region'.[29]

Général Esterhazy described what happened:

> The charge is launched; our *Hussards* approached the enemy with an admirable cheerfulness. Sibert [de Cornillon] my Aide-de-Camp and I penetrated the first rank of the enemy, but we only had four squadrons, the enemy had eight, many irregular Cossacks and a battery of six guns. We captured the artillery, but the [enemy] squadrons came on our flanks and rear.

Twenty-one-year-old *Sous-Lieutenant* Silbert de Cornillon found himself encircled and cut off from his comrades. He would have presented an easy target – wearing the uniform of the *6e Dragons* amongst the braided dolmans of the *4e Hussards*. His horse was killed under him and he received no fewer than eighteen sabre or lance wounds from which he later died. He was posthumously awarded the *Legion d'Honneur*.[30] *Capitaine* Pujade was severely wounded – *Sergent* Mismer saw him 'covered with blood' – and one poor *Hussard* 'crawling on all-fours, head [cut] open, crying out for water'. The *Hussards* captured three guns and drove off the gunners, but the Russians, sensing their numerical superiority, counter-attacked with two squadrons (approximately 340 sabres) of Lancers into the flank of the *Hussards*. *Général* Esterhazy, seeing the movement of the Lancers, ordered *Chef d'Escadron* Tilliard to rally and reform, and prepare to receive the Lancers. The Russians attacked the 3rd and 4th Squadrons of the *Hussards*, and were received with a volley of musketry from their carbines.

Galloping to their rescue came *Général* Coste de Champeron at the head of the *6e Dragons* who attacked the left of the Russian line: 'the enemy squadrons, on all their points, hesitated, and again abandoned the ground … and disappeared in all directions.' *Sergent* Mismer graphically describes the arrival of his squadron and the *Bachi-Bazouk* marauders looting the wounded Russians:

> We passed at a gallop, men and panting horses. Here is a Russian cannon brought by overjoyed *dragons*. And other vehicles besides: caissons, and a forge, thirty vehicles in total. In fact, a complete battery. Prisoners arrive escorted one by one and in groups. On the right, a *Bachi-Bazouk*, dismounted, the reins of his horse through his arm, trying to pull boots off a Russian crying for help with all his might. 'Get this scum to go away', said my *Capitaine*. The order was fortunate. I had a grudge against the *Bachi-Bazouks* since one of them killed, before my eyes, a wounded Cossack on the road from Balaklava to Baidar. I diverted my horse, but with a leap, the other is in the saddle and ran away at full speed. I suspected that I would have to turn back. He came in and fired a few shots at the Russian's feet, in punishment for crying out. This time, I broke him. He reached when he rolled left in the dust. I shot him with my pistol without stoping my horse and doing a half jump, I joined my squadron. When I regained my rank the artillery had stopped. Our horses were covered with

foam, heads sank between his front legs and lungs sounded like the bellows of a forge.

Off into the steppe, scattered *dragons* fired gunshots into the crowd of Russians who had halted. At the other end of the horizon [the] *7e Dragons*, recognizable [from the] reflection of his [*sic*, their] helmet, arrived raising a cloud of dust. In view of these reinforcements, the Russians rapidly withdrew. Our halt was prolonged to give [the] artillery horses time to catch our breath and to join the regiment.[31]

The Russians were pursued by the *Dragons*, but due to their horses being exhausted and the undulating nature of the ground, pockmarked with undulations and rivulets, they found it difficult going which gave the Russian Lancers time to regroup:

We then learned that the Russians, having realized the small number of horsemen in pursuit, had done an about-face to take the offensive, pushing heroically but their horses refused service … At the apporach of the *dragons*, the enemy turned away with their tails between their legs.[32]

Général Champeron sounded the rally and one company of the *6e Dragons* fanned out as skirmishers (*en Tirailleur*) to cover this movement. The victorious French returned to camp at around 7 p.m., having taken 170 prisoners (of which two were senior officers), six field pieces, twelve artillery caissons, one field forge and 250 horses. The French losses were fourteen dead and twenty-two wounded from the *4e Hussards* and one officer and four men wounded in the *6e Dragons*.[33]

British Reinforcements

On 8 October d'Allonville sent out another reconnaissance in force towards Perekop, where they encountered 'several squadrons of cavalry and several *sotnias* of Cossacks, who refused to engage. The *Bachi-Bazouks* … burned the abandoned villages.' On 14 October the Expeditionary Force was reinforced by an Infantry division commanded by *Général* de Failly and a British cavalry brigade under Lord Paget.[34] The British cavalry consisted of the 6th Dragoon Guards (Carabiniers), 4th Light Dragoons, 12th Lancers and 13th Light Dragoons as well as C Troop Royal Horse Artillery and a detachment of the Land Transport Corps. The British were operating under French orders.

The first Anglo-French reconnaissance was led by d'Allonville was led by him on Monday 22 October – it had taken several weeks for the British to organize themselves, Paget declaring his Brigade ready for the field on 20 October. The reconnaissance in strength was formed into two columns; the first under Muchir Ahmed Pasha consisted of mostly Turkish troops but accompanied by French artillery; the second under d'Allonville consisted of four Turkish battalions, two French infantry battalions and a battalion of *Chasseurs à Pied*, half the *Bachi-Bazouks*, twelve Turkish squadrons, twelve French squadrons, all the British cavalry and six guns. Brigade Orders stated that reveille in the British camp was to be sounded at 5 a.m.; everything was to be ready to move by 6.15 a.m. and the column would move out at 7.15 a.m. The men were to take with them one day's barley for the horses, firewood and cooked rations for one day. The first column was directed to Sak whilst the second proceeded to Karagurt.

On the first day, Lord Paget reported 'we marched at daybreak and arrived at Karagurt (eighteen miles) about 4pm, where we bivouacked for the night, and which village, before leaving, we destroyed'. They had only march a further three miles, however, before they came across 'about twenty squadrons of Russian cavalry, who retired before us after some shots from the French horse artillery, which told with some effect'.[35] The following day (23 October) the column proceeded to Temesch where again they made contact with a large Russian force: 'a body of Russian cavalry, considerably superior in numbers to that we had seen the evening before, a strong force of guns, and, I believe, some battalions of infantry. This body also retired before us.' At the village of Tuzla, d'Allonville took position on 'some rising ground' and 'offered battle'. C Troop RHA under Captain Thomas 'firing several shots with precision, which were answered by the enemy without any effect'. After two hours the Russians retreated; after joining-up with the column under Muchi Ahmed Pasha, the joint force marched to Sak 'where we bivouacked, destroying the town and considerable Russian cantonments'. On the 24 October the two columns returned to Eupatoria.[36]

Another reconnaissance was sent out three days later, via Sasik Guilore where they found a Russian force in a similar location to that identified during the previous reconnaissance. D'allonville was once again determined to bring the Russians to battle. Lord Paget wrote in his report:

> General d'Allonville ... opened fire with much effect, which continued for nearly an hour, and which was warmly responded to by the enemy. Captain Thomas's Troop of horse artillery was supported by the 12th Lancers; the Carabineers, 4th and 13th Light Dragoons were in second line in Reserve. The loss to the Allies on this occasion was nineteen killed and wounded, one English artilleryman having been slightly wounded, two horses killed and three wounded.[37]

The following day the cavalry and horse artillery proceeded towards Temesch 'in endeavour to turn the right of the enemy' but the Russians would not be drawn into battle, so they returned to their bivouac at Sak. Because of a 'total want of water' in and around Sak the Allies had to retire to Eupatoria; lack of food and water would become a major limiting factor to the Allies' operations.[38]

A much more successful 'flying column' was sent out on 2 November: a column commanded by General Ali Pasha consisting of the *Bachi-Bazouks*, two regiments of Turkish cavalry, two squadrons from the *4e Hussards* and two squadrons from the 12th Lancers (commanded by Lieutenant-Colonel W. Tottenham) departed Eupatoria at 4.30 a.m. towards Tchotai. Lieutenant-Colonel Tottenham reported that:

> At daylight we march through Altchin to Tchotai, a village about fifteen miles from this – the Turkish cavalry in advance, supported by English and French squadrons. We arrived at Tchotai about 11.30 A.M., and captured a Russian commissariat officer, a Cossack, about forty Arabs, and 3000 head of horses, camels, oxen and sheep. Three Russian carriages were brought in, and a considerable number of inhabitants of the village. We started our return at 1.30P.M. and set fire to the village, and destroyed thirty large ricks of hay. We arrived in camp about 8.30 P.M.[39]

British cavalry were also involved in a *Razzia* on 16 November. One squadron each of the 6th Dragoon Guards, 4th and 13th Light Dragoons, two squadrons of 12th Lancers and C Troop RHA assembled with French infantry commanded by *Général* Failly. Major Brown (4th Light Dragoons) commanded the three squadrons of Dragoons whilst Captain Oakes (12th Lancers) was to command the two squadrons of Lancers, the whole Brigade under the command of Lieutenant-Colonel Tottenham (12th Lancers). They force-marched towards Oraz, returning via the villages of Bagai, Chidan and Ortamamai the same day. Lieutenant-Colonel Tottenham reported that the column 'destroyed or carried away all the firewood in those villages and that the column saw only a picket of sixty Cossacks at Ortamamai, who retired as soon as the allies appeared'.[40]

With the winter fast approaching, the French set-to establishing winter quarters at Eupatoria, whilst Lord Paget organized winter quarters for the cavalry at Scutari. The embarkation of the British cavalry began in late November and by 7 December Paget was able to report that would be completed by noon the following day.[41]

Despite the fall of Sebastopol, and the sorties around Eupatoria and Kertch, the War was still not over, and grumbled on until 30 March 1856 when peace was signed in Paris.

Notes

Introduction: Letters Home

1. M. Hudson & J. Stanier, *War and the Media* (Stroud: Sutton Publishing, 1999), Chapter 1.
2. Ibid., pp. 19–20.
3. H. Barker, *Newspapers, Politics and English Society, 1695–1855* (London: Longman, 2000), p. 222; O. Anderson, *A Liberal State at War: English Politics and Economy during the Crimean War* (New York: Macmillan, 1967), Chapter 2.
4. H. Streets, *Martial Races: The Military, Race and Masculinity in British Imperial Culture* (Manchester: Manchester University Press, 2004), pp. 23–4; O. Figes, *Crimea: The Last Crusade* (London: Allen Lane, 2010), pp. 467–9; D. Russell, '"We carved our way to Glory" the British soldier in music-hall song and sketch' in J.M. McKenzie, ed., *Popular Imperialism and the Military 1850–1950* (Manchester: University of Manchester Press, 1992), pp. 59–60.
5. S. Hazareesingh, *The Saint-Napoleon. Celebrations of Sovereignty in Nineteenth-Century France* (Harvard: Harvard University Press, 2004), pp. 35 and 74.
6. Hazareesingh, *Saint-Napoleon*, pp. 80–5; http://www.stehelene.org accessed 02-12-2011 @ 17.33.
7. Barker, *Newspapers, Politics and English Society*, p. 222; Anderson, *A Liberal State at War*, Chapter 2.
8. Ibid.
9. L. Brown, *Victorian News and Newspapers* (Oxford: Oxford University Press, 1985), pp. 27 and 32–45; L. Brake & M. Demoor, eds, *Dictionary of Nineteenth Century journalism in Britain and Ireland* (London: The Academic Press, 2006), pp. 354 and 571–2.
10. Hudson & Stanier, *War and the Media*, pp. 12–14; I. Stewart & S.L. Carruthers, *War, Culture and the Media* (Trowbridge: Flicks Books, 1996), pp. 148–51.
11. J. Sweetman, *Raglan, from the Peninsula to the Crimea* (Barnsley: Pen & Sword, 2010), pp. 270–80.
12. Ibid., p. 292.
13. E.M. Spiers 'Military correspondence in the late nineteenth-century press', *Archives*, vol. 32 no. 116 (2007), pp. 28–31.
14. J. Tosh, *The Pursuit of History* (Harlow: Pearson Education, 2010), fifth edition, pp. 319–22; P. Fussell, *The Great War and Modern Memory* (Oxford: Oxford University Press, 2000), second edition, Chapters 4 and 9.
15. Fussell, *The Great War*, p. 311; A. Green and K. Troup, *The Houses of History* (Manchester: University Press, 1999), p. 231.

Chapter 1   Going to War: 1 May–1 September 1854

1. Marquess of Anglesey, *A History of the British Cavalry* (London: Cooper, 1973), vol. 1, pp. 82–93.
2. Ibid., p. 164.
3. Ibid., pp. 174–5; 'National Defence', *Daily News* (24 January 1852).
4. Marquess of Anglesey, *Little Hodge: his letters and diaries of the Crimean War 1854–1856* (London: Leo Copper, 1971), pp. 2–3.
5. Ibid.
6. 'The British Cavalry in the Peninsula', *The United Service Journal and Naval and Military Magazine for 1832*, part 3 (1832), p. 37.
7. Captain T. Robbins, *The Cavalry Catechism* (London: Longman, Green, Longman, Roberts & Green, 1858), pp. IX–X. Robbins first published in 1841 for internal use in the 5th Dragoon Guards but felt compelled to publish nationally after the Crimean War to help educate cavalry officers.
8. Lieutenant-General Sir W. Napier, *Life and Opinions of General Sir Charles Napier* (London: John Murray, 1857), vol. 2, pp. 244–50.
9. C. Woodham-Smith, *The Reason Why* (London: Constable, 1953), pp. 21–5 and Chapters 4 and 5.
10. A. Clayton, *The British Officer: Leading the Army from 1660 to the Present* (London: Longman, 2007), pp. 107–8; Woodham-Smith, *The Reason Why*, pp. 139–40.
11. 'The Earl of Cardigan and the 11th Hussars', *The Times* (17 September 1840); 'The Earl of Cardigan and Captain Tucket', *The Times* (21 September 1840); 'Court-Martial of Captain

R A Reynolds', *The Times* (26 September 1840); 'To the Editor of the Times', *The Times* (26 September 1840); 'Editorial', *The Times* (30 October 1840). See also Woodham-Smith, *The Reason Why*, Chapters 4 and 5.

12. Cartoon 'The Plunger in Turkey', *Punch Magazine*, vol. 27 (1854), p. 126.
13. C.J.H. Dickens, 'The Modern Officer's Progress', *Household Words*, vol. 1 (1850), pp. 304–7, 317–20, 353–56.
14. Anglesey, *Little Hodge*, p. 5.
15. *Wakefield Journal & Examiner* (31 March 1854).
16. 'Drogheda May Fair – Friday 12 May', *The Belfast News-Letter* (15 May 1854).
17. *Leeds Mercury* (7 April 1854).
18. T. Brighton, *Hell Riders* (London: Penguin Books, 2005), p. 13.
19. 'A Gallant Hussar', *Wakefield Journal & Examiner* (29 December 1854); see also 'A Balaklava Hussar', *Daily News* (26 December 1854).
20. Brighton, *Hell Riders*, p. 13.
21. 'Preparations for War', *The Manchester Examiner & Times* (18 March 1854).
22. 'Preparations for War', *The Morning Chronicle* (13 March 1854).
23. Flintshire Record Office (FRO), Acc. D/E/1545/2, Ethedlred Yorke, Mss. Lieutenant-Colonel John Yorke to Etheldred Yorke, 12 May 1854.
24. FRO, Acc. D/E/1542/302, Erddig Moluments, Mss. note from Lieutenant-Colonel John Yorke, ND.
25. FRO, Acc. D/E/1542, Erddig Moluments, Mss. , Lieutenant Colonel John Yorke to Simon Yorke, 12 May 1854; FRO, Acc. D/E/ 1545/2, Etheldred Yorke, Mss., Lieutenant Colonel John Yorke to Etheldred Yorke, 12 May 1854.
26. 'Preparations for War', *The Preston Guardian* (1 April 1854).
27. L.G. Crider & G. Fisher, eds., *Recollections of One of the Light Brigade* (Crimean War Research Society, 2009), p. 7.
28. G.L. Smith, *A Victorian RSM* (Winchester: Royal Hussars' Museum, 1987), p. 79.
29. Crider & Fisher, *Recollections*, p. 7.
30. 'The Right Way and the Wrong Way of Shipping Horses', *Daily News* (13 April 1854).
31. J.W.H. Greaves, 'A horseman at war', *Gwent Local History: the Journal of Gwent Local History Council*, no. 68 (Spring 1998), pp. 46–8.
32. Ibid., p. 49.
33. 'Naval and Military News', *The Morning Chronicle* (11 May 1854).
34. Anglesey, *Little Hodge*, pp. 9–11.
35. 'Narrow Escape of the Harkaway Transport', *Nottinghamshire Guardian* (25 May 1854), p. 8.
36. 'Reported burning of the Europa Transport Ship and Loss of Life', *Daily News* (16 June 1854).
37. 'The Scots Greys', *Nottinghamshire Guardian* (6 July 1854).
38. 'Departure of the Scots Greys from Manchester', *Manchester Examiner & Times* (26 July 1854).
39. Lincolnshire Archives (LA), Acc 1-Dixon 22/12/3/1, Lieutenant Robert Hunter, Mss., Hunter to Helen Carnegy Hunter (sister), 27 July 1854.
40. 'Arrival of the Scots Greys at Malta', *Nottinghamshire Guardian* (24 August 1854).
41. Robert Scott Hunter was born in Brechin, Angus in 1831: he purchased a Cornetcy in the Scots Greys 17 June 1851; Lieutenant 17 February 1854; Captain 13 September 1855. Transferred to the 6th Dragoon Guards 1860 and retired in 1863. He married Clara Maria Middleton in 1861 and according to the 1881 census was living in Alyth, Perthshire.
42. Lincolnshire Archives (LA), Acc 1-Dixon 22/12/3/1, Lieutenant Robert Hunter, Mss., Hunter to Helen Carnegy Hunter (sister), 27 July 1854.
43. The *Himalaya* was owned by the Peninsular & Orient Steam Navigation Company (P&O). She was built by C.J. Mare & Co. of Leanmouth, London: laid down in 1852, and launched 24 May 1853 and subsequently purchased by the Royal Navy as a troopship in July 1854 for £130,000 – the cost to build and fit her out. She was retired as a troop ship in 1894 and became a Royal Navy coal hulk in 1895. She was sunk on 12 June 1940 by German dive-bombers. She displaced 4,690 tons, was 340ft (100m) long with a beam of 46ft (14m).
44. HMS *Duke of Wellington* was a 131-gun First Rate man-of-war launched in 1852. She had originally been designed (1849) as a sailing ship, but before her launched was converted to screw-propulsion. She was cut in half, lengthened 30ft and steam engines installed. She was 240ft (73m) long.
45. Probably Captain William Miller, the Adjutant. He was well known in the regiment for his stentorian voice. He joined the Scots Greys in 1827 as a Private; gazetted to Cornet and Adjutant 7 July 1846; promoted to Lieutenant 20 June 1850 and Captain 30 September 1854. He became

Adjutant at the Cavalry Depot in Maidstone, Kent in 1856 and retired on full pay in September 1862 and was made Honorary Major December 1862.
46. Probably Sergeant John Hill (number 976). The letter is initialled 'J- H- Sergeant 1st Royals Dragoons' and the only sergeant with those initials is John Hill. He had his horse shot from under him during the Charge of the Heavy Brigade.
47. 'A letter from the camp', *Reynolds's Newspaper* (27 August 1854).
48. 'Arrival of the Scots Greys at Malta', *Nottinghamshire Guardian* (24 August 1854).
49. "Cheer boys, Cheer" by Henry Russell (1812–1900) was perhaps the most popular song of the Crimean War (and later sung by both sides during the American Civil War) and was written in 1841. Russell's most famous song is 'A Life on the Ocean Wave' written in 1851.
50. 'Tullochgorum' and 'Flowers of Edinburgh' are both ancient Scottish Reels.
51. 'Arrival of the Scots Greys in the Bosphorus', *Nottinghamshire Guardian* (31 August 1854), p. 4.
52. Probably Captain Samuel Toosey Williams (1823–54); he rode in the Charge of the Heavy Brigade (25 October 1854) where he was wounded and he died in the hospital at Pera, 23 November 1854 from 'low fever, the result of exposure, privation, and excessive fatigue'. His funeral oration described him as a brilliant horseman and 'A more honourable and brave officer never existed'. (*Nottinghamshire Guardian*, 21 December 1854).
53. Lieutenant-Colonel Henry Darby Griffith (1810–87), son of Major-General Matthew Darby Griffith. He was Colonel of the 5th Lancers 1872–87. Gazetted Cornet 25 November 1828; Lieutenant 25 November 1831; Captain 1 August 1834; Major 6 November 1846; Lieutenant-Colonel 24 August 1852; Colonel 28 November 1854. He was promoted to Major-General in 1856.
54. 'Letters from the Seat of War', *Daily News* (31 May 1854).
55. 'Letter from Varna', *Wakefield Journal & Examiner* (4 August 1854).
56. Anglesey, *Little Hodge*, p.16.
57. 'Pictures of the War', *Lloyd's Weekly Newspaper* (2 July 1854).
58. S.T. Peters, *Epidemic! Cholera. Curse of the Nineteenth Century* (New York: Benchmark Books, 2005), Chapter 1.
59. Anglesey, *Little Hodge*, pp. 21–2.
60. 'Progress of the Cholera in the Eastern Fleet and Armies', *The Times* (2 September 1854).
61. 'The Fifth Dragoon Guards. To the editor of The Morning Chronicle', *The Morning Chronicle* (15 November 1854).
62. 'Naval and Military', *Daily News* (9 November 1854); 'Naval & Military Intelligence', *The Morning Post* (9 November 1854).
63. H. Franks, *Leaves from a Soldier's Notebook* (Colchester: C.W. Poole & Sons Ltd., 1979), p. 57.
64. 'Souvenirs de la Guerre de Crimée. Lettres du Commissaire de Marine Garreau', *Carnet de la Sabretache*, vol. 21 (1912), p. 78.
65. 'The War. From our Special Correspondent', *The Times* (12 July 1854), p. 9.
66. Earl of Cardigan, *Eight Months on Active Service* (London: Clowes & Sons, 1855), pp. 12–13*ff*.
67. Anglesey, *A History*, p. 37.
68. C. Kelly, ed., *Mrs Duberly's War. Journal and Letters from the Crimea* (Oxford: Oxford University Press, 2008), p. 40.
69. NAM Acc. 1958-04-32, Major W.C. Forrest, Mss. Forrest to mother, 18 July 1854.
70. Ibid., Forrest to Mother 27 August 1854 and 12 October 1854.
71. Portal, cited by Brighton, *Hell Riders*, p. 17.
72. C.S. Paget, ed., *The Light Cavalry Brigade in the Crimea. Extracts from the letters and journal of the late General Lord G. Paget* (London: John Murray, 1881), pp. 216–17.
73. Ibid., pp. 217–18.
74. Kelly, *Mrs Duberly's War*, pp. 33–4.
75. Corporal Thomas Morley (1831–1906), author of *The Cause of the Charge of the Light Brigade* (Nottingham: 1899). Enlisted in the 17th Lancers in Nottingham in 1849; fought at Balaklava where he and TSM Dennis and Pvt. O'Hara rescued Cornet Cleveland. Purchased his discharge 1857; in June 1862 he joined the 12th Pennsylvania Volunteer Cavalry and was commissioned as a Lieutenant; taken prisoner at Bull Run. Promoted to Captain February 1865 and signed his commission April 1865. Returned to Britain but returned to America in 1884 and subsequently took US Citizenship. Returned (again) to Britain 1893 and died in Nottingham in 1906.
76. 'Letter from a Nottingham Soldier at the Seat of War', *Nottinghamshire Guardian* (13 July 1854), p. 5.
77. 'Letter from a Lockwood Man in the Eastern Army', *Huddersfield Chronicle* (22 July 1854), p. 5.

78. The infamous 'Sore-back' reconnaissance led by the Earl of Cardigan, which departed 24 June 1854 from Varna. Cardigan took with him 200 men from the 8th Hussars and 13th Light Dragoons and some Turkish cavalry. They covered 300 miles in 17 days; nearly 100 horses out of the 280 present died or were unfit for further work.
79. 'Letter from a Soldier in the East', *Nottinghamshire Guardian* (10 August 1854), p. 8.
80. FRO Acc. D/E/1545/10, Etheldred Yorke, Mss., Lieutenant-Colonel John Yorke to Etheldred Yorke, 7 August 1854.
81. Probably Lieutenant John Glas Sandeman (1836–1922): gazetted to the 1st Royals as Cornet 10 June 1853. During the Charge of the Heavy Brigade, his horse Toby was killed under him. He had Toby's body shipped to England to be buried at Hayling Island where the Sandeman's resided.
82. FRO Acc. D/E/1545/11, Etheldred Yorke, Mss., Lieutenant-Colonel John Yorke to Etheldred Yorke, 12 August 1854.
83. LA Acc. 1-Dixon 22/12/3/2, Hunter Mss., Hunter to Sister 22 August 1854.
84. Major-General Prince George, Duke of Cambridge (1819–1904) was the cousin of Queen Victoria and commanded the Brigade of Guards in the early months of the Crimean War. He was created 'General Commanding-in-Chief of the British Army' in 1856, promoted to Field Marshal in 1862 and 'Commander-in-Chief of the Forces' in 1887, serving as Commander-in-Chief for some thirty-nine years!
85. Probably Major Simon Philip Townsend Royal Artillery: he was killed at the Battle of Inkerman (5 November 1854) and is buried in the British cemetery on Cathcart's Hill.
86. 'Piastra' from the Italian meaning 'a thin plate'; the main Turkish currency available in 1, 5, 10 and 20 Piastra coins. A Piastra was worth about 2d.
87. Richard Lawrence Sturtevant was born in Bethnal Green in 1825; he married Mary Ann Sadler in 1844 and joined the army the following year. His wife died childless in April 1852 and eight months later he married Elizabeth Buncle, in Worcester (she would die in Edinburgh in June 1867). He was discharged from the army in 1867 and held five good conduct badges. He was a Mason and member of the Burdett-Cutts Lodge (No. 1278). He died 25 October 1900 at Buxted, Sussex.
88. 'Another letter from the Scots Greys', *Nottinghamshire Guardian* (14 September 1854).
89. Probably Hospital-Sergeant William Todd.

Chapter 2   Invasion of the Crimea: 14 September–1 October 1854
1. Crider & Fisher, *Recollections*, pp. 27*ff.*
2. Ibid., p. 28.
3. Paget, *The Light Cavalry Brigade*, pp. 17–18.
4. A.J. Guy & A. Massie, eds., *Captain L.E. Nolan, 15th Hussars. Expedition to the Crimea* (London: National Army Museum, 2010) p. 47.
5. Ibid., pp. 47–48.
6. Ibid., p. 48.
7. Ibid., p. 49.
8. Paget, *The Light Cavalry Brigade*, p. 18.
9. Crider & Fisher, *Recollections*, pp. 29–30.
10. 'Une lettre écrite au *Moniteur de la Flotte*', *Le Moniteur de l'Armée* (11 Octobre 1854), p. 3.
11. Dr. Cabrol, *Le Maréchal de Saint-Arnaud en Crimée* (Paris; Tresse & Stock, 1895), p. 277.
12. The main body, usually cavalry, of an advanced guard.
13. M.O. Cullet, *Une Régiment de Ligne pendant la Guerre d'Orient: Notes et Souvenirs d'un officier d'Infanterie* (Lyon: Librairie Générale Catholique et Classique, 1894), pp. 70–1.
14. J.J.G. Cler, trans. Colonel G.B. McClellan, *Reminiscences of an Officer of the 2nd Regiment of Zouaves* (New York: D. Appleton & Co., 1860), p. 124.
15. Capitaine Minart, 'Lettres écrites pendant la Campagne de Crimée par les frères Charles, Alfred et Édouard Minart'. 2e Partie, *Carnet de la Sabretache*, vol. 9 (1910), pp. 418–19.
16. Cabrol, *Le Maréchal de Saint-Arnaud*, pp. 276–7.
17. 'Une lettre écrite au *Moniteur de la Flotte*', *Le Moniteur de l'Armée* (11 Octobre 1854), p. 3.
18. 'The Skirmish on the 19th.', *The Sheffield & Rotherham Independent* (14 October 1854), p. 11.
19. Ibid.
20. Guy &. Massie, *Nolan*, p. 52.
21. Smith, *A Victorian RSM*, pp. 99–100.
22. Guy & Massie, *Nolan*, p. 52.
23. Ibid.

24. Crider & Fisher, *Recollections*, pp. 33–35.
25. Captain W.P. Richards to aunt Robe, 30 September 1854 via http://www.victorianweb.org/history/crimea/richards/richardsov.html, accessed 23 April 2012.
26. 'The Battle of the Alma', *Leeds Mercury* (14 October 1854).
27. 'Letter from a Leeds Soldier', *Leeds Mercury* (16 December 1854).
28. 'The Battle of the Alma: Letter from a Leeds Soldier', *Leeds Mercury* (21 October 1854).
29. Sir E. Colebrooke, Bart., *Journal of Two Visits to the Crimea in 1854 and 1855* (London: T & W Boone, 1856), p. 17.
30. Cullet, *Une Regiment de Ligne*, pp. 70–1.
31. 'Une lettre écrite au *Moniteur de la Flotte*', *Le Moniteur de l'Armée* (11 Octobre 1854), p. 3.
32. Colebrooke, *Journal of Two Visits*, p. 17.
33. Ibid.
34. 'The Skirmish on the 19th', *The Sheffield & Rotherham Independent* (14 October 1854), p. 11.
35. Ibid.
36. Guy & Massie, *Nolan*, pp. 52–3.
37. French Staff Corps. A distinct 'branch of service' created by *Maréchal* de St Cyr in 1817 (*Corps d'État Major*). Not truly analogous with the British staff.
38. National Army Museum, London, Acc. 1973-11-170, Nigel Kingscote, Mss., Kingscote to Father, 5 June 1854. See also S.J. Calthorpe, *Letters from Headquarters: or, The realities of the War in the Crimea* (London: John Murray, 1856), vol. 1, pp. 38–9.
39. Culllet, *Une Regiment de Ligne*, pp. 70–1; Cabrol, *Le Maréchal de Saint-Arnaud* , p. 278.
40. Anon, *Campagnes de Crimee, D'Italie, D'Afrique, De Chine et de Syrie 1849–1862* (Paris: Librairie Plon, 1898), pp. 100–2. Letter 65: Jean-Pierre Vico to Marechal de Castellane, 21 Septembre 1854.
41. Minart, 'Charles, Alfred et Edouard Minart', pp. 418–19
42. Cabrol, *Le Maréchal de Saint-Arnaud*, p. 279.
43. 'The Army in the East', *The Bristol Mercury* (23 September 1854).
44. A reference to the popular comic song: 'Cheer up, Sam; Don't let your spirits go down. There's many a girl that I know well. Is waiting for you in the town.' Naturally, there were more bawdy soldier's versions.
45. According to W.H. Russell in *The Times* Longmore was 'seized with the illness' on Saturday 2 September at 8 p.m. and died at 11 a.m. the following morning (Sunday 3 September); 'He was an excellent officer, and Lord Cardigan spoke highly of his conduct . . .'. Fanny Duberly relates how his 'death rattle' could be heard by other officers on board the *Himalaya*.
46. John Chadwick (1817–69) was the Adjutant of the 17th Lancers: he was wounded and taken prisoner at the Battle of Balaklava after having his horse shot from under him. He had enlisted in the 17th Lancers in Manchester in July 1835. He was 5ft 10in tall and weighed 11 stones 4lbs. He had been promoted to Regimental Sergeant Major by 1851; gazetted Cornet 27 February 1852 and appointed Adjutant 12 March 1852. Promoted to Lieutenant 25 October 1852. Exchanged to the 15th Hussars on half pay 29 April 1856. He retired from the army in 1867 and died from cirrhosis on 25 March 1869 in Liverpool.
47. 'The Battle of the Alma', *The Manchester Courier* (21 October 1854), p. 7.
48. The famous line of defences ordered to be built by Wellington (designed by Sir Richard Fletcher) to defend Portugal – notably Lisbon – from French invasion 1809–10.
49. 'Letter from another Leeds soldier', *Leeds Mercury* (2 December 1854).
50. 'The War. The Cavalry in the Crimea', *The Standard* (23 October 1854), p. 1.
51. 'Letter from the Crimea', *Lancaster Gazette* (4 November 1854).
52. 'Letter from a Huddersfield Man in the Cavalry Brigade in the Crimea', *Huddersfield Chronicle* (28 October 1854).
53. 'A Private Soldier's Letter from the Alma', *Nottinghamshire Guardian* (2 November 1854), p. 5.
54. 'The Crimea', *The Bristol Mercury* (11 November 1854). The same letter also appeared as: 'Private letters from the Seat of War. Letters from Soldiers', *Daily News* (14 November 1854).
55. Anglesey, *Little Hodge*, p. 27.
56. Ibid.
57. *Leeds Mercury* (28 October 1854).
58. Guy & Massie, *Nolan*, p. 65.
59. Ibid., p. 67.
60. Ibid., pp. 68–9.
61. Ibid., p. 69.
62. Ibid.

63. Ibid.
64. 'The March on Balaklava', *Leeds Mercury* (14 October 1854).
65. Guy & Massie, *Nolan*, pp. 71–2.
66. FRO, Acc. D/E/1545/14, Etheldred Yorke Mss., Lieutenant-Colonel John Yorke to Etheldred Yorke, 3 September 1854.
67. FRO, Acc. D/E/1545/15, Etheldred Yorke Mss., Lieutenant-Colonel John Yorke to Etheldred Yorke, 16 September 1854.
68. Probably Lieutenant Richard Henry Currie; Cornet by purchase 16 April 1852; Lieutenant 15 July 1853; Captain 19 January 1855.
69. FRO, Acc. D/E/1545/16, Ehteldred Yorke, Mss., Lieutenant-Colonel John Yorke to Etheldred Yorke, 30 September 1854.
70. The military term for a Troop Horse, not the soldier who rode him.
71. Private George Hunt (number 754) was born in Clerkenwell, Middlesex. He was 'effective' from 1 October 1854 to 27 November 1854; he was sent ill to Scutari the following day, where he wrote his letter to his family. He was discharged 10 February 1859.
72. 'From Private Hunt, of the 1st Royal Dragoons', *Daily News* (2 January 1855).
73. 'Another letter from the Scots Greys', *Nottinghamshire Guardian* (26 October 1854).
74. LA Acc. 1-Dixon 22/12/3/3, Hunter Mss, Hunter to sister 30 September 1854.
75. Probably Captain John Arthur Freeman; Cornet by purchase 7 August 1846; Lieutenant 21 June 1850; Captain 11 November 1853. Died 27 September 1854 from cholera.
76. 'Private letters from the Seat of War: Specially Communicated', *Nottinghamshire Guardian* (18 November 1854).
77. Probably Trumpet-Major **William Forster** (number 581) whose letter home is reproduced below.
78. Lieutenant-Colonel **John Yorke**, Commanding Officer of the 1st Royals notes that his regiment lost 150 horses 'more than at Waterloo' in a storm at sea on 26 September 1854. The 1st Dragoons embarked at Varna with 255 horses and only had 182 effective on 1 October 1854.
79. The Light Brigade provided thirty-five remounts to the Heavy Brigade.
80. Probably Troop Sergeant-Major George Tripp (number 414); born in Alderby, Suffolk in 1811 he enlisted 21 September 1833 and was discharged on medical grounds after 25 years service in 1857. He was awarded the Distinguished Conduct Medal in February 1855, which granted him an annuity of £20 per year.
81. Probably Troop Sergeant-Major George Cruse; enlisted in the 1st Royals (11 July 1838). Promoted Corporal 30 June 1840; Sergeant 1 December 1842; Troop Sergeant-Major 1 April 1848; Regimental Sergeant-Major 4 November 1854. Promoted to Riding Master 16 March 1855 (without purchase). He retired in 1871 as an Honorary Captain and died 9 February 1878.

Chapter 3   Prelude to Balaklava: 1–24 October 1854

1. 'Correspondence from the Crimea', *Reynolds's Newspaper* (26 November 1854).
2. W. Douglas, *Soldiering in Sunshine and Storm* (Edinburgh: Adam & Charles Black, 1864), p. 181.
3. Ibid.
4. Lieutenant-Colonel St.V.W. Ricketts, *Standing Orders of the 2nd (Royal North British Dragoons)* (London: Parker, Furnival & Parker, 1852), pp. 22–3, 39–41, 55.
5. Guy & Massie, *Nolan*, pp. 77–9.
6. 'Journal des Operations de l'armée devant Sebastopol, du 1er au 22 Octobre', *Le Moniteur de l'Armee* (11 Novembre 1854), p. 2.
7. 'Skirmish at Balaclava', *The Daily News* (24 October 1854).
8. Guy & Massie, *Nolan*, pp. 77–9.
9. Guy & Massie, *Nolan*, p. 79.
10. Ibid.
11. 'Journal des Operations de l'armée devant Sebastopol, du 1er au 22 Octobre', *Le Moniteur de l'Armée* (11 Novembre 1854), p. 2.
12. 'Preparations against the attack: Letter from Balaclava, Oct. 16', *Supplement to the Illustrated London News* (11November 1854), p. 494.
13. Ibid.
14. 'Warning of the Russian Attack: Letter from Balaclava October 13', *Supplement to the Illustrated London News* (11 November 1854), p. 491.
15. 'Balaclava: Letter from an Officer, October 18', *Supplement to the Illustrated London News* (11 November 1854), p. 491.

16. 'Balaclava: Letter from an Officer of Royal Marines, Oct. 22', *Supplement to the Illustrated London News* (11 November 1854), p. 491.
17. Ibid.
18. G. Bapst, *Le Maréchal Canrobert. Tome Second: Napoléon III et sa cour, la Guerre de Crimée* (Paris: Plon-Nourrit et Cie., 1912), 7e Edition, pp. 306–7.
19. 'Balaclava: Letter from an Officer of Royal Marines, Oct. 22', *Supplement to the Illustrated London News* (11 November 1854), p. 491.
20. Bapst, *Canrobert*, p. 307.
21. Ibid., pp. 308–9.
22. 'The Siege of Sebastopol', *Supplement to the Illustrated London News* (11 November 1854), p. 496.
23. 'Balaclava: Letter from an Officer of Royal Marines, Oct. 22', *Supplement to the Illustrated London News* (11 November 1854), p. 491.
24. The assistant-surgeon of the 8th Hussars in the Crimea was Anthony Home.
25. 'The Crimea', *Daily News* (27 October 1854), p. 3; the same letter also appeared as 'Letter from the Crimea', *The Morning Chronicle* (31 October 1854), p. 6.
26. This caused considerable controversy: the Rev. H. Egan, Chaplain to the Light Division wrote to contradict the writer of this letter stating that Captain Crofton was *'buried as a Christian'* and his cousin, Captain J.G. Drewe of the 23rd (Royal Welch) Fusiliers wrote to *The Morning Post* refuting the claim as well. ('Capt. Crofton of the 77th', *The Morning Post* (14 December 1854), p. 4).
27. FRO, Acc. D/E/1545/17 Etheldred Yorke, Mss., Lieutenant Colonel John Yorke to Etheldred Yorke, October 1854.
28. William Scott (26 October 1849).
29. 'Private letters from the Camp', *Manchester Guardian* (12 November 1854), p. 11.
30. A Chibouk is a large, long-stemmed Turkish pipe for smoking tobacco. The bowl often has a decorative lid or cover. In other words, the flashing light striking of tinder boxes and lighting of pipes was mistaken for musketry.
31. FRO, Acc. D/E/1545/18 Etheldred Yorke, Mss., Lieutenant Colonel John Yorke to Etheldred Yorke, 22 October 1854.
32. Probably Lieutenant-Colonel Uick de Burgh, Lord Dunkellin (1827–67), Coldstream Guards.

Chapter 4   Charge of the Heavy Brigade: 25 October 1854

1. 'Journal of Operations before Sebastopol', *Wakefield Express* (18 November 1854), p. 2.
2. Lieutenant Koribut-Kubitovich, 'Recollections of the Balaklava Affair 13 October 1854', *Voennyi Sbornik*, no. 2 (1859), translated by Mark Conrad (1999) via http://marksrussianmilitaryhistory. info/Kubitovich.htm; 'Iz Krymskikh Vospominanii o Poslednei Voine', *Russkii Arkhiv*, vol. 7 (1869), pp. 381–4, translated by Mark Conrad, via http://marksrussianmilitaryhistory.info/ Kozhukhov.htm.
3. 'Correspondence from the Crimea', *Reynolds's Newspaper* (26 November 1854).
4. 'Letter from the Crimea', *Glasgow Herald* (24 November 1854).
5. 'Exploits of the Greys at Balaklava', *Nottinghamshire Guardian* (16 November 1854).
6. 'Letters from a Dragoon and a Sailor to Leicester Friends', *Leicester Chronicle* (23 December 1854); 'Letters from the Crimea', *Daily News* (28 November 1854).
7. Paget, *The Light Cavalry Brigade*, p. 164; Brighton, *Hell Riders*, p. 82.
8. Brighton, *Hell Riders*, p. 82.
9. Ibid. Smith, *A Victorian RSM*, p. 125.
10. Paget, *The Light Cavalry Brigade*, pp. 161–2.
11. Ibid., p. 162.
12. D.J. Austin, 'The Battle of Balaklava and the 4th Chasseurs d'Afrique', *The War Correspondent*, vol. 26, number 3 (October 2006), p. 32; P.E.A. du Casse, *Précis Historique des Opérations Militaire en Orient de mars 1854 à Septembre 1855* (Paris: E. Dentu, 1856), p. 161; 'Journal du Siège', *La Presse* (18 Novembre 1854).
13. Brighton, *Hell Riders*, p. 89.
14. Brighton, *Hell Riders*, p. 90.
15. 'France', *The Morning Post* (14 November 1854).
16. 'Correspondance Particulière', *La Presse* (17 Novembre 1854).
17. 'Affaires d'Orient', *Journal de Toulouse* (13 Novembre 1854), p. 1.
18. 'Correspondence from the Crimea', *Reynolds's Newspaper* (26 November 1854).
19. 'Correspondence. Letter from a Lancaster Soldier to the Editor of the Lancaster Gazette', *The Lancaster Gazette* (24 March 1855).

20. 'Letters from a Dumfrieshire Dragoon', *The Morning Post* (1 February 1855), p. 3.
21. Angelsey, *Little Hodge*, p. 47.
22. 'The Scots Greys at Balaklava', *The Morning Post* (23 November 1854).
23. Paget, *The Light Cavalry Brigade*, pp. 165–6.
24. 'Private Letters from the Seat of War: Specially Communicated', *Nottinghamshire Guardian* (23 November 1854).
25. A.W. Kinglake, *The Invasion of the Crimea: Its origins and an account of its progress down to the death of Lord Raglan* (London: WIlliam Blackwood & Sons, 1889), vol. 5, plate 1.
26. 'From a Colour-Serjeant of the 93rd Highlanders to his Friends in Glasgow', *Glasgow Herald* (19 February 1855).
27. Dr S. Summerfield, *pers. comm.*, email 16-11-2012.
28. Kinglake, *The Invasion of the Crimea*, Vol. 5, pp. 418–21.
29. 'The Siege of Sebastopol', *Colburn's United Service Magazine for 1854*, part III (1854), p. 486.
30. 'Report of Lieutenant General Liprandi, chief of the twelfth division of infantry, to Aide-de-camp General Prince Mentschikoff [Menshikov], dated October 26th [14th Old Style], [No. 3076]', *Russkii Invalid* (No. 237), translated by Mark Conrad (2002) via http://marksrussianmilitaryhistory. info/Liprandi.htm.
31. Ivan Ivanovich Ryzhov, 'On the Battle of Balaklava; Notes of Lieutenant General Iv. Iv. Ryzhov.', *Russkii Vestnik*, vol. 86 (April 1870), pp. 463–69, translated by Mark Conrad (1999) via http: //marksrussianmilitaryhistory.info/Ryzhov.htm.
32. V.I. Genishta and A.T. Borisevich, *Istoriya 3-go dragunskago Ingermanlandskago polka 1704–1904* (St. Petersburg, 1904–1906), Vol. 2, pp. 129–209, translated by Mark Conrad (1999) via http: //marksrussianmilitaryhistory.info/Inger-html.htm.
33. 'Letters from a Dragoon and a Sailor to Leicester Friends', *Leicester Chronicle* (23 December 1854): 'Extract from a letter of an officer in the heavy brigade', *Manchester Times* (25 November 1854).
34. 'Report of Lieutenant General Liprandi, chief of the twelfth division of infantry, to Aide-de-camp General Prince Mentschikoff [Menshikov], dated October 26th [14th Old Style], [No. 3076]', *Russkii Invalid* (No. 237), translated by Mark Conrad (2002) via http://marksrussianmilitaryhistory. info/Liprandi.htm.
35. Ivan Ivanovich Ryzhov, 'On the Battle of Balaklava; Notes of Lieutenant General Iv. Iv. Ryzhov'. *Russkii Vestnik*, vol. 86 (April 1870), pp. 463–9, translated by Mark Conrad (1999) via http: //marksrussianmilitaryhistory.info/Ryzhov.htm
36. Lieutenant Koribut-Kubitovich, 'Recollections of the Balaklava Affair 13 October 1854', *Voennyi Sbornik*, no. 2 (1859), translated by Mark Conrad (1999) via http://marksrussianmilitaryhistory. info/Kubitovich.htm
37. W.H. Russell, *General Todleben's History of the Defence of Sebastopol, 1854–1855. A Review* (New York: Van Norstrand, 1865), p. 121.
38. Ryzhov, 'On the Battle of Balaklava; Notes of Lieutenant General Iv. Iv. Ryzhov.'
39. V.I. Genishta and A.T. Borisevich, *Istoriya 3-go dragunskago Ingermanlandskago polka 1704–1904* (St. Petersburg, 1904–1906), Vol. 2, pp. 129–209, translated by Mark Conrad (1999) via http: //marksrussianmilitaryhistory.info/Inger-html.htm.
40. Ryzhov, 'On the Battle of Balaklava; Notes of Lieutenant General Iv. Iv. Ryzhov.'
41. Ibid.
42. V.I. Genishta and A.T. Borisevich, *Istoriya 3-go dragunskago Ingermanlandskago polka 1704–1904* (St. Petersburg, 1904–1906), Vol. 2, pp. 129–209, translated by Mark Conrad (1999) via http: //marksrussianmilitaryhistory.info/Inger-html.htm.
43. General Sir C.P. Beauchamp Walker, *Days of a Soldier's Life* (London: Chapman & Hall, 1891), pp. 134–5.
44. FRO, Acc. D/E/1330, Erddig Mss., Sir John York to Etheldred Yorke, 5 December 1854.
45. Austin, '4th Chasseurs d'Afrique', p. 33.
46. Ibid; P. de Molènes, *Commentaires d'un Soldat* (Paris: Librairie des Bibliophiles, 1886), pp. 110–11.
47. Austin, '4th Chasseurs d'Afrique', p. 33.
48. LA Acc. 1-Dixon 22/12/3/5, Hunter Mss., Hunter to sister 27 October 1854.
49. Walker, *Days of a Soldier's Life*, pp. 134–5.
50. FRO, Acc. D/E/1330, Erddig Mss., Sir John York to Etheldred Yorke, 5 December 1854.
51. NAM, Acc. 1958-04-32, Forrest, Mss., Forrest to Brother, 27 October 1854.
52. 'Extract from a letter of an officer in the heavy brigade', *Manchester Times* (25 November 1854).
53. 'Exploits of the Greys at Balaklava', *Nottinghamshire Guardian* (16 November 1854).

54. 'Letter of a Lancaster Soldier', *The Lancaster Gazette* (30 December 1854); 'Correspondence. Letters from Lancaster Soldiers', *The Lancaster Gazette* (13 January 1855); 'Correspondence. Letter from a Lancaster Soldier to the Editor of the Lancaster Gazette', *The Lancaster Gazette* (24 March 1855).
55. 'Letters from Lancaster Soldiers', *The Lancaster Gazette* (27 January 1855).
56. 'Correspondance. Letters from Lancaster Soldiers', *The Lancaster Gazette* (13 January 1855).
57. 'Correspondence from the Crimea', *Reynolds's Newspaper* (26 November 1854).
58. 'Private Letters from the Seat of War: Specially Communicated', *Nottinghamshire Guardian* (23 November 1854).
59. 'The Siege of Sebastopol', *Colburn's United Service Magazine for 1854*, part III (1854), pp. 486–8.
60. FRO, Acc. D/E/1330, Erddig Mss., Sir John York to Etheldred Yorke, 5 December 1854.
61. Angelsey, *Little Hodge*, p. 44.
62. 'Letter from a Dumfries Dragoon', *Glasgow Herald* (29 January 1855); 'Letters from a Dumfrieshire Dragoon', *The Morning Post* (1 February 1855).
63. 'The Battle of Balaklava', *The Manchester Times* (20 January 1855).
64. 'Letters from a Dragoon and a Sailor to Leicester Friends', *Leicester Chronicle* (23 December 1854).
65. 'Letters from a Dumfrieshire Dragoon', *The Morning Post* (1 February 1855), p. 3.
66. Walker, *Days of a Soldier's Life*, pp. 134–5.
67. LA, Acc. 1-Dixon 22/12/3/5, Hunter Mss., Hunter to sister 27 October 1854.
68. 'Extract from a letter of an officer in the heavy brigade', *Manchester Examiner & Times* (25 November 1854).
69. 'Letters from the Crimea', *The Morning Chronicle* (21 November 1854).
70. NAM, Acc. 1958-04-32, Forrest Mss., Forrest to Brother, 27 October 1854.
71. V.I. Genishta and A.T. Borisevich, *Istoriya 3-go dragunskago Ingermanlandskago polka 1704–1904* (St. Petersburg, 1904–1906), Vol. 2, pp. 129–209, translated by Mark Conrad (1999) via http://marksrussianmilitaryhistory.info/Inger-html.htm.
72. FRO, Acc. D/E/1330, Erddig Mss., Sir John York to Etheldred Yorke, 5 December 1854.
73. Angelsey, *Little Hodge*, p. 44.
74. 'Letter from a Dumfries Dragoon', *Glasgow Herald* (29 January 1855); 'Letters from a Dumfrieshire Dragoon', *The Morning Post* (1 February 1855); 'The Battle of Balaklava', *The Manchester Times* (20 January 1855).
75. 'Letter of a Lancaster Soldier', *The Lancaster Gazette* (30 December 1854).
76. FRO, Acc. D/E/1330, Erddig Mss., Lieutenant Colonel John York to Etheldred Yorke, 5 December 1854.
77. NAM, Acc. 1958-04-32, Forrest Mss, Forrest to Brother, 27 October 1854.
78. 'Mr Kinglake's Invasion of the Crimea: Letters to the Editor', *The Times* (19 August 1868).
79. 'Correspondence from the Crimea', *Reynolds's Newspaper* (26 November 1854). Extracts from this letter also appeared in *Lloyd's Weekly Newspaper* (26 November 1854); *John Bull* (18 November 1854); *Bradford Observer* (16 November 1854); *The Times* (16 January 1855).
80. Probably Lieutenant-General Lord Lucan.
81. There were two Trumpeter Staceys in the 1st Royals: George Andrew Stacey (number 1107) and William S. Stacey (number 885); the former was 'severely wounded' during the Charge and was sent to Scutari hospital 26 October 1854 – 31 December 1855. He was returned home in January 1855
82. Possibly Private James Richard Aslett (number 1268); aged only 19, he was 'severely wounded' and had his right humerus smashed by a roundshot, and he had his arm amputated at the shoulder joint and sent to Scutari hospital 26 October 1854 where 'the stump soon united without a bad symptom'. He returned home in May 1855 and was recommended for the Distinguished Conduct Medal.
83. Possibly Sergeant Maillard Noake (number 995) (1828–1914); he was wounded in the Charge and was sent to Scutari hospital on 26 October 1854 and sent home on 20 December 1854. He was recommended for the Distinguished Conduct Medal in January 1855.
84. 'The Battle of Balaklava', *Manchester Times* (22 November 1854).
85. LA, Acc. 1-Dixon 22/12/3/5, Hunter Mss., Hunter to sister 27 October 1854.
86. Daniel Moodie was commissioned as Cornet without purchase from Regiment Sergeant-Major 30 September 1854; promoted Lieutenant 7 February 1856. Resigned Adjutancty 1858; appointed Instructor of Music 10 April 1862. Transferred to 60th Rifles 31 March 1863 and retired on half pay 1865.
87. 'Exploits of the Greys at Balaklava', *Nottinghamshire Guardian* (16 November 1854).

88. Probably Brevet-Major George Calvert Clarke (1814–1900): Ensign 89th Foot 30 May 1834; Lieutenant 7 October 1836; Captain 20 September 1839. Transferred to Scots Greys as Captain 28 March 1845; Major 26 February 1858; Brevet Lieutenant-Colonel Scots Greys 12 December 1854. Went onto half-pay 1869; Major-General 1869; Lieutenant-General 1877. Colonel Scots Greys 1891.

89. Probably Cornet Lennox Prendergast (1830–?): Cornet 11 March 1853; Lieutenant 3 December 1854; Captain 13 June 1856; Major 3 February 1869. Half pay 1869; retired 1881.

90. Probably Private Henry Campbell: born in Louth, Ireland and enlisted in the Scots Greys April 1846. He was killed at the Battle of Balaklava.

91. Probably Private Thomas Traill: born in South Leith only served in the Greys for two years, enlisting on 7 January 1852 and dying from wounds received at Balaklava 26 October 1854.

92. The official casualty returns were two other ranks killed and fifty-four wounded, and four officers wounded.

93. Probably Private McAdam Galbraith: born in Dalamillington; he enlisted in the Scots Greys on 2 December 1845. He is listed as 'severely wounded' at Balaklava and was sent to the hospital at Scutari on 26 October 1854 where he died from his wounds.

94. Probably Sergeant Thomas Kneath: born in Bath and enlisted in the Scots Greys on 25 March 1846, listing his occupation as 'Yeoman'. He was severely wounded at Balaklava and sent to Scutari hospital 26 October 1854 and returned to Camp 29 December 1854. He died on 17 July 1855, probably from cholera.

95. Probably Corporal William Seggie; promoted to Corporal 31 December 1854 following the death of Corporal Francis Campbell who died on 29 December 1854 at Scutari from wounds received at Balaklava.

96. Probably Private Alexander Douglas Gardiner: born c.1826 in Norwich, son of Troop Sergeant-Major Alexander Gardiner of the Scots Greys, and enlisted in the same regiment aged 22 on 14 April 1848 in Athlone. He was 'severely wounded' at Balaklava and was dismissed from the army on 23 October 1855 in 'consequence of being disabled by amputation of the left thigh at its centre after cannon shot wound received at Balaklava'. His life was saved by Private Henry Ramage VC who 'dashed to his rescue and carried him to the rear', following Gardiner's leg being 'shattered by round shot'. The *Oswestry Advertiser* suggests that Gardiner was presented with a cork leg by Queen Victoria in March 1856. He died in 1879 aged 52.

97. There is a Private William Donaldson who was with the regiment and severely wounded at Balaklava but no A. Thomas Donaldson.

98. Possibly Private Andrew Scott Laing who appears on the Casualty Roll as 'A S Long'. He was 'severely wounded' at Balaklava and sent to Scutari hospital on 26 October 1854. He was recommended for Distinguished Conduct Medal in 1855.

99. There are two Edward Morris, both of whom were wounded at Balaklava: Edward Morris (number 740) was sent to Scutari hospital on 27 November 1854. The second is Edward Morris (number 1188 or 1088) who was at Scutari January–March 1855.

100. Probably Troop Sergeant-Major Matthew Brown, whose letters are printed here.

101. Probably Troop Sergeant-Major James Dearden: born 1823 in Edinburgh, he enlisted in the 11th Hussars 23 January 1841, aged 18. Promoted to Corporal December 1845 and transferred to the Scots Greys September 1848. Again promoted to Corporal December 1849; Sergeant November 1852 and Troop Sergeant-Major July 1854. He was 'wounded in the left thumb by Grape Shot received in action at Balaklava 25th October 1854'. He was in Scutari hospital from October 1854 to January 1855, when he was transferred to Abydos during February and March, returning to his unit in April. He was discharged from the army in 1865 and died sometime after 1881 – on the census of that year he was living with his wife Mary in Cheshire and was listed as being unemployed.

102. Probably Troop Sergeant-Major James Davidson: born in Roxburgh and enlisted on 9 August 1842. He was wounded in the Charge and sent to Scutari on 26 October 1854, returning to Camp on 10 November 1854,but was sent back to Scutari on 3 December 1854 where he died on 2 January 1855.

103. Probably Troop Sergeant-Major James Wilson: he was severely wounded in the Charge and sent to Scutari hospital on 26 October 1854, returning on 10 November 1854. He had in fact been under arrest on 25 October 'for a minor offence' but he apparently reported to the Adjutant, informing him 'I have broken my arrest, Sir, as I could not see my Regiment going in to action and remain quiet in camp.' He was wounded by a roundshot when the Greys manoeuvred in support of the Light Brigade later in the day.

104. Probably Troop Sergeant-Major David Gibson who was promoted to Cornet on 5 November 1854.
105. Probably Private Andrew Paul Clifford: born in Dumbarton, Kilpatrick, he had been with the regiment a little over a year, having enlisted on 7 January 1853 by the time of his death on 25 October 1854.
106. 'Extract from a letter of an officer in the heavy brigade', *Manchester Times* (25 November 1854).
107. Lieutenant-Colonel Darby Griffiths.
108. Probably Captain John Augustus Oldham, 13th Light Dragoons: gazetted Ensign by purchase 1 April 1842 in the 86th Foot; Lieutenant 23 June 1843. Transferred to 55th Foot 11 June 1847 at Lieutenant; Transferred to 13th Light Dragoons as Lieutenant 6 August 1847. Promoted to Captain 4 May 1849. He commanded the 13th Light Dragoons at Balaklava in absence of Lieutenant-Colonel Doherty, who was sick. Oldham was killed in the Charge: 'a shell which burst under his horse and knocked over two or three others. It blew the mare's hind legs off, and he jumped up himself, not hit, when next moment he threw up his hands and fell dead on his face.'
109. Probably Captain Augustus Frederick Cavendish Webb: born 1832 at Barnard Castle, Durham. Gazetted Cornet 17th Lancers December 1848; Lieutenant March 1850; Captain 1853. He died from wounds received during the Charge of the Light Brigade on 6 November 1854, and there is a memorial to him in St Mary's Church, Barnard Castle.
110. Probably Private Michael McNamara (number 743).
111. Probably Corporal James Taylor (number 1086).
112. Unknown? Not listed as being killed in the battle.
113. Two men with the surname Donnelly are listed in the 5th Dragoon Guards: Private Malachy Donnelly (number 1028) and Private Michael Donnelly (number 756). They were possibly brothers.
114. Possibly Captain William Inglis (1830–1900). Cornet 2 February 1849; Lieutenant 22 February 1850; Captain 3 March 1854; Brevet Major 12 December 1854. Retired 16 August 1859.
115. 'Letters from the Crimea', *Morning Chronicle* (21 November 1854).
116. Probably Corporal James Taylor (number 1086); born in Lancaster and enlisted in the 5th Dragoon Guards 15 August 1850 and was killed in the Charge (25 October 1854). His Lieutenant, Richard Temple Goodman wrote 'our Corporal was nearly cut to pieces, his left arm nearly severed in four places. I suppose there must have been a good many at him at once, as he was a strong and good swordsman.' (P. Warner, ed., *A Cavalryman in the Crimea* [Barnsley: Pen & Sword, 2009], p. 76).
117. Probably Private Bernard Callery (number 1115); born in Neath, and enlisted 30 July 1851, listing his occupation as 'Hawker' (i.e. door-to-door salesman). He was killed in the Charge.
118. Probably Cornet Hon. Grey Neville; he was severely wounded in the Charge and died from his wounds on 11 November 1854. Temple Goodman noted that 'Neville being a bad rider, and too weak to use his sword well, was soon dismounted and had it not been for one of our men who stood over him, Private Abbot, he would have been killed. He was wounded in the head and in three places in his back, and they fear that his liver is injured, in which case he cannot recover...' (Warner, *A Cavalryman in the Crimea*, pp. 76–7). A second account of Neville's death suggests 'He became separated from his troop and saw several Russian cavalrymen ride towards him. According to a friend 'he thought it was better to attempt to ride through them and rode with all his might against the centre of the party. The concussion knocked him off his horse and knocked his antagonist, horse and all, down, and, he thought, killed him. He was then on the ground and was wounded while moving away and, thinking they were gone, raised his head to look, but a Russian Dragoon dismounted and cut him with his sword over his head. His helmet saved his scalp but his right ear was cut in two. Some cavalry rode over him and he felt dreadfully hurt by the horses' hooves.' (M. Barthop, *Heroes of the Crimea: The Battles of Balaklava and Inkerman* [London: Blandford Press, 1991], p. 47).
119. Probably Captain Frederick Hay Swinfen; Cornet (by purchase) 5th Dragoon Guards 1849; Lieutenant 1850; Captain 1854. Listed as 'slightly wounded' in the Charge.
120. Probably Captain Alexander James Hardy Elliot; Cornet 9th Lancer 18 July 1848; Lieutenant 5th Dragoon Guards 14 June 1850; Captain 2 December 1854; Brevet Major 17 July 1855; Major 29 July 1856; Brevet Lieutenant Colonel 29 May 1863; Colonel 1 February 1871; Major General 1 July 1881. Colonel 6th Dragoon Guards 3 January 1892; Colonel 21st Lancers 18 February 1902. Died 1 July 1909, aged 83.

121. Probably Sergeant James Shegog (number 409); born 1811, County Monahan, Ireland. Enlisted 21 December 1834. He served for twenty-one years and was discharged in 1856. He died in Tasmania on 24 April 1896.

122. There are two Private Abbots in the 5th Dragoon Guards at Balaklava: Charles Abbot (number 1053) and John Abbot (number 1095), the latter receiving the Distinguished Conduct Medal (for his action at Balaklava?). 'Private Abbot, hearing his [Neville's] calls for help, dismounted and lifted him from the ground and made him stand for a moment. He tried to walk but was so weak he could not and wanted to lie down again. The soldier would not leave him and ended finally by dragging him by bodily strength to a place of safety.' (Barthop, *Heroes of the Crimea*, p. 47). Sergeant-Major Henry Franks (number 669) also recounts the death of Neville and the bravery of Abbott (Franks, *Leaves from a Soldiers Notebook* [Brightlingsea: Mitre Publications, 1979], p. 81).

123. Probably Private Michael McNamara (number 743). He is mentioned in the letter by Corporal Joseph Gough (number 1020), below.

124. Probably Regiment Sergeant-Major Erasmus Green (number 425); born in Kilebagen, County Westmeath in Ireland and enlisted at Kildare, Ireland, 22 August 1832. Upon enlistment he was 5ft 9in tall, with a 'fresh complexion, grey eyes, light brown hair'. Promoted Corporal 13 October 1836; Sergeant 29 October 480; Troop Sergeant-Major 15 September 1848; Regimental Sergeant-Major 5 November 1854. He was discharged in December 1856 as being 'medically unfit for further service'.

125. Probably Troop Sergeant-Major William Stewart; born 1814 in Perthshire and enlisted in the 5th Dragoon Guards 16 November 1837 in Glasgow aged 23. He was over 6ft tall. Promoted to Corporal September 1847; Sergeant June 1852; Troop Sergeant-Major September 1854. Troop Sergeant-Major Henry Franks recounts that TSM Stewart had three horses shot under him: 'The first one was by a rifle bullet. Stewart caught another horse belonging to the 4th Dragoon Guards, and he had hardly mounted him when a shell burst under him and blew him up. Stewart escaped without a scratch and managed to catch another loose horse which he rode for a while until a cannon ball broke one of the horse's legs ... He then procured another horse which made the fourth he had ridden that day.'

126. Probably Troop Sergeant Major James Russell (number 553); born 1819 and enlisted in the 5th Dragoon Guards 30 October 1837 in Glasgow aged 18. Troop Sergeant-Major Franks notes that Russell was riding to his right and Trumpeter Edward Baker on his left, when a shell exploded, throwing Russell over his horse's head, dismounting him, but luckily he was not injured (Franks, *Soldier's Notebook*, p. 76).

127. 'Correspondence from the Crimea', *Reynolds's Newspaper* (19 November 1854); the same letter also appeared as 'The Scots Greys at Balaklava', *The Nottinghamshire Guardian* (14 December 1854), p. 5.

128. Probably Lieutenant Lennox Prendergast; born 12 May 1830, son of Guy Lennox Prendergast MP for Lymington. Cornet by purchase 11 March 1853; Lieutenant 3 December 1854; Captain 13 June 1856; Major 3 February 1869. On Half-Pay 30 June 1859. Brevet Lieutenant-Colonel 1 October 1877. Retired 1 July 1881. He married in 1860 and had four children.

129. Probably Lieutenant Henry Edwardes Handley; Cornet by purchase 30 September 1853; Lieutenant 29 December 1854. He left the regiment in 1858. He is recorded as being 'severely wounded by a lance-thrust' during the Charge.

130. A reference to Dollond & Co. of London, founded in 1750 by John Dollond, makers of telescope and other optical instruments. They were awarded a First Class medal at the Great Exhibition (1851) for their optical instruments. They merged with Aitchinson & Co (established 1889) in 1927 to form Dollond & Aitchinson.

131. 'Battle of Balaclava – Cavalry Charge', *Huddersfield Chronicle* (25 November 1854), p. 3.

132. 'Black Water' is a translation of 'Tchernaya'.

133. Probably Captain William de Cardonnel Elmsall (1824 – ?); Cornet by purchase 1 July 1842; Lieutenant 13 October 1843; Captain 4 September 1849. Major in the 5th West York Militia 1858, resigned 1860. He was the son of Joseph Edward Greaves who had served in the 1st Royal Dragoons at Waterloo. He is listed as being 'severely wounded' in the Charge and was returned home in November 1854, sailing on the *Cambria* (*The Times*, 12 December 1854).

134. Probably Captain George Campbell; Cornet by purchase 25 February 1848; Lieutenant 4 September 1849; Captain 1 April 1853. He was shot through the shoulder during the Charge and was in hospital from 25 October 1854 to 18 November 1854. He had been sick 'on board ship' during the first week of October 1854. He retired on 10 February 1859.

135. Probably Lieutenant William Wrey Hartopp; Cornet by purchase 11 March 1853; Lieutenant 8 December 1854. He was 'severely wounded' in the leg during the Charge; he served with the Royal Horse Guards from August to November 1855. He died on 20 July 1870.
136. 'Letter from the Crimea', *Glasgow Herald* (24 November 1854).
137. 'Exploits of the Greys at Balaklava', *Nottinghamshire Guardian* (16 November 1854).
138. Probably Cornet Henry Edwardes Handley; gazetted Cornet, Scots Greys 30 September 1853; Lieutenant 29 December 1854 and resigned his commission in 1858.
139. 'Letters from the Seat of War', *Nottinghamshire Guardian* (23 November 1854), p. 8.
140. 'Private letters from the Crimea: An Enniskillen Dragoon in Battle', *Daily News* (24 November 1854).
141. 'Letters from the Crimea', *Daily News* (28 November 1854).
142. 'The Scots Greys at Balaklava', *The Morning Post* (23 November 1854).
143. 'The British Troops in the Crimea', *Berrow's Worcester Journall* (2 December 1854).
144. 'The Crimea', *The Bristol Mercury* (16 November 1854).
145. 'From one of the 1st Royal Dragoon Guards', *Daily News* (3 January 1855).
146. 'Letters from a Dragoon and a Sailor to Leicester Friends', *Leicester Chronicle* (23 December 1854).
147. Trumpeter, later Sergeant, Thomas Monks was the Brigade Trumpeter to General Scarlett, the commander of the Heavy Brigade at the Battle of Balaklava, and he sounded 'The Charge' of the Heavy Brigade. He was born in Lancaster and died in April 1902 in Shrewsbury.
148. 'Letter of a Lancaster Soldier', *The Lancaster Gazette* (30 December 1854), p. 5.
149. Lieutenant-Colonel Sir John Yorke (1813–28 March 1890); Ensign by purchase 21 December 1832; Lieutenant 5 December 1834; Captain 14 December 1841; Major 4 September 1849; Lieutenant-Colonel 4 February 1853. Colonel 23 March 1856. He was seriously wounded when the Heavy Brigade supported the Charge of the Light Brigade. Upon his return home, he was presented with a Sword of Honour and a purse of 120 guineas by the Town and District of Wrexham.
150. FRO, Acc. D/E/1330, Erddig Mss., Sir John York to Etheldred Yorke, 5 December 1854.
151. 'Squibbing' is a West-country slang term for fireworks or firecrackers; hence the expression 'a bit of a damp squib' i.e. a firework which did not go off.
152. 'The Scots Greys', *Glasgow Herald* (29 December 1854).
153. 'A letter from a Private in the 1st Royal Dragoons – A Native of Wrexham', *Wrexham and Denbigh Weekly Advertiser* (6 January 1855).
154. 'Letters from the Crimea', *The Morning Post* (26 January 1855), p. 3.
155. 'The Crimea – from a Corporal of Scots Greys', *The Hull Packet and East Riding Times* (19 January 1855).
156. 'Correspondence. Letters from Lancaster Soldiers', *The Lancaster Gazette* (13 January 1855).
157. This is a very common myth from the Crimean War, that the British horses were so hungry they ate each other's tails off: Horses, in fact, do not 'eat' tails and manes out of starvation. The chewing of another horses' mane, tail and ears is actually an indicator of Psoroptic Mange which is caused by mites in the thickly haired regions of the body, such as under the mane, the tail, between the hind legs and under the chin. It is highly contagious and is due to the animal's coat being in poor condition.
158. Private James Auchinloss is shown as being 'effective' from October to December 1854. He was 'slightly wounded' in the Charge of the Heavy Brigade and returned to England in spring 1855.
159. 'Letters from a Dumfrieshire Dragoon', *The Morning Post* (1 February 1855), p. 3.
160. Lieutenant-Colonel Edward Hodge (1810–94). According to his own diary, Hodge was ill from 23 September 1854, 'very unwell, with pain in my stomach, and dysentery'; he does not mention leaving HMS *Sans Pareil* on 17 October but felt 'so much better' on 21 October that he went ashore at Balaklava the following day. He was 'quite weak' on 23 October and slept 'very well' 24 October and resumed his place with his regiment on 26 October (Anglesey, *Little Hodge*, pp. 28–52.)
161. Probably Hospital Sergeant, Sergeant-Major Joseph Drake (number 199). Colonel Hodge said of him 'He is a thoroughly honest man, never drinks, and is most methodical and regular in his habits' (Anglesey, *Little Hodge*, p. 142).
162. Private Isaac Stephenson was born in Lancaster in 1827, enlisting in Manchester 27 July 1849 in the 4th Dragoon Guards. He was 'effective' from July to December 1854 and was ill at Scutari hospital from July to December 1855 and embarked for England in February 1856. He was promoted to Corporal December 1857 but purchased his discharge (at Aldershot) 11 March 1859.

163. 'Letters from Lancaster Soldiers', *The Lancaster Gazette* (27 January 1855), p. 8.
164. 'Correspondence. Letter from a Lancaster Soldier to the Editor of the Lancaster Gazette', *The Lancaster Gazette* (24 March 1855).

Chapter 5   Charge of the Light Brigade

1. Crider & Fisher, *Recollections*, pp. 55*ff.*
2. M.J. Trow, *Pocket Hercules. Captain Morris and the Charge of the Light Brigade* (Barnsley: Pen & Sword, 2006), pp. 91–2.
3. Woodham-Smith, *The Reason Why*, p. 232.
4. Ibid.
5. Anon, 'Sir Richard Airey in the Crimea', *The United Service Magazine for 1856*, part I (1856), p. 521.
6. Ibid.
7. 'The Charge of the British Cavalry at Balaklava. By One Who was There', *The United Service Magazine for 1856*, part I (1856), p. 551.
8. Ibid.
9. Paget, *The Light Cavalry Brigade*, pp. 169–70.
10. Anon, 'Sir Richard Airey', p. 521.
11. Ibid.
12. Ibid.
13. Ibid., pp. 521–2.
14. 'The Light Cavalry Charge at Balaklava', *The Morning Chronicle* (6 March 1855).
15. 'The Siege of Sebastopol. Camp Before Sebastopol Feb. 13', *The Times* (1 March 1855).
16. 'Notes from the Camp', *The Times* (2 March 1855).
17. 'Letters from the Crimea', *The Morning Chronicle* (18 January 1855); 'The Battle of Balaklava', *The Manchester Examiner & Times* (22 November 1854).
18. 'Imperial Parliament', *Daily News* (3 March 1855); 'Lord Lucan and Lord Raglan', *Daily News* (7 March 1855).
19. 'Letters from Balaklava', *Daily News* (15 November 1854).
20. Ibid.
21. 'Captain Nolan', *The Sheffield & Rotherham Independent* (25 November 1854).
22. 'The Cavalry at Balaklava', *Daily News* (14 November 1854).
23. Ibid.
24. 'The Battle on the 25th October', *The Morning Chronicle* (13 November 1854).
25. Lord Raglan's Promotion – Dangerous Favouritism at the Horse Guards', *Reynolds's Newspaper* (26 November 1854).
26. 'Captain Nolan', *The Manchester Examiner & Times* (17 November 1854).
27. 'Private letters from Sebastopol', *Daily News* (15 November 1854).
28. 'Extraordinary Gazette. The Battle of Balaklava', *The Standard* (13 November 1854).
29. 'Lord Lucan', *The Standard* (3 March 1855).
30. 'The Attack on Balaklava', *The Morning Post* (13 November 1854).
31. 'From our Malta Correspondent', *The Morning Chronicle* (17 November 1854).
32. Paget, *The Light Cavalry Brigade*, p. 205.
33. 'Letter from Balaklava', *Daily News* (18 November 1854).
34. Brighton, *Hell Riders*, p. 108.
35. 'Let Byegones be bygones', *Daily News* (25 November 1854).
36. Dr. D.J. Austin, 'The Battle of Balaklava and the 4th Chasseurs d'Afrique', *The War Correspondent*, vol. 26, no. 3 (October 2006), p. 34. See also G. Bapst, *Le Maréchal Canrobert. Tome Second: Napoléon III et sa cour, la Guerre de Crimée* (Paris: Plon-Nourrit et Cie., 1912), 7e Edition, pp. 319–20.
37. 'Marshal Macmahon on the Charge of Balaklava', *Freeman's Journal* (22 May 1888).
38. Austin, '4th Chasseurs d'Afrique', pp. 34–5. See also Bapst, *Canrobert*, p. 320*ff.*
39. 'Marshal Macmahon on the Charge of Balaklava', *Freeman's Journal* (22 May 1888).
40. Austin, '4th Chasseurs d'Afrique', p. 32. See also Bapst, *Canrobert*, p. 313.
41. Ibid; 'Correspondance Particulière', *La Moniteur de l'Armée* (21 Novembre 1854).
42. Anon, *Campagnes de Crimée, D'Italie, D'Afrique et de Syrie 1849–1862* (Paris: Librairie Plon, 1898), p. 131: Letter 79. Colonel de Wimpffen to Marechal de Castellane, 2 December 1854; M.O. Cullet, *Une Regiment de Ligne pendant la Guerre de Crimée* (Lyon: Librairie Generale Catholique et Classique), p. 103.
43. 'Marshal Macmahon on the Charge of Balaklava', *Freeman's Journal* (22 May 1888).

44. Austin, '4th Chasseurs d'Afrique', p. 35.
45. 'A Letter from the French Camp before Sebastopol', *The Morning Post* (15 November 1854).
46. 'Marshal Macmahon on the Charge at Balaklava', *Freeman's Journal* (22 May 1854).
47. Paget, *The Light Cavalry Brigade*, pp. 177–9.
48. Ibid., pp. 181–2.
49. Austin, '4th Chasseurs d'Afrique', p. 35.
50. 'Correspondance Particulière', *La Moniteur de l'Armée* (21 November 1854).
51. P. de Molènes, *Commentaires d'un Soldat* (Paris: Librairie des Bibliophiles, 1886), pp. 112–14.
52. 'Correpondance Particulière de La Presse', *La Presse* (17 Novembre 1854).
53. 'Affaires d'Orient', *Journal de Toulouse* (13 Novembre 1854), p. 1.
54. Ibid.
55. Ibid.
56. 'General-Adjutant Prince Menshikov's report on the offensive operation by Lieutenant-General Liprandi's force against the camp of the allies' who are covering the road from Sevastopol to Balaklava.' Via http://marksrussianmilitaryhistory.info/Liprandi.htm.
57. 'O srazhenii pod Balaklave; Zapiska General-Leitenanta Iv. Iv. Ryzhova', *Russkii Vestnik*, vol. 86 (April 1870), pp. 463–9.
58. 'Iz Krymskikh Vospominanii o Poslednei Voine', *Russkii Arkhiv*, vol. 7 (1869), pp. 381–4.
59. 'Vospominaniya o Balaklavskom dele 13-go Oktyabrya 1854 goda', *Voennyi Sbornik*, No. 2 (1859), via http://marksrussianmilitaryhistory.info/Kubitovich.htm.
60. Ibid.
61. 'Russian accounts of the Campaign in the Crimea. Drawn up by Anitschkof, Captain in the Russian Imperial Staff. The Battle of Balaclava, October 25, 1854', *The United Service Magazine for 1860*, part II (1860), p. 36.
62. 'Report of Lieutenant General Liprandi, chief of the twelfth division of infantry, to Aide-de-camp General Prince Mentschikoff [Menshikov], dated October 26th' via http://marksrussianmilitary history.info/Liprandi.htm.
63. C.-A. Thoumas, *Mes Souvenirs de Crimée* (Paris: La Librairie Illustrée, ND), pp. 131–2.
64. Ibid., p. 132.
65. Ibid.
66. Austin, '4th Chasseurs d'Afrique', p. 35.
67. Ibid.
68. 'On nous communique la lettre suivant, écrite par un personne attachée au siège', *La Presse* (13 Novembre 1854).
69. C.L. de Bazancourt, *L'Expedition de Crimée jusqu'a la Prise de Sebastopol* (Paris: Librairie D'Amyot, 1857), Special Edition for the Army, Vol. 2, pp. 31–2.
70. 'To the Editor of the Times', *The Times* (16 August 1864); 'The Battle of Balaklava: To the Editor of the Times', *The Times* (20 September 1864)
71. 'The Battle of Balaklava: To the Editor of the Times', *The Times* (23 September 1864).
72. Vicomte L.R.J. de Noë, *Souvenirs d'Afrique et d'Orient* (Paris: Michel Lévy, 1861), p. 232.
73. Ibid., p. 233.
74. Austin, '4th Chasseurs d'Afrique', p. 35.
75. Bazancourt, *L'Expedition*, p. 32.
76. Thoumas, *Souvenirs de Crimée*, p. 133; Bazancourt, *L'Expedition*, p. 33.
77. Thoumas, *Souvenirs de Crimée*, p. 133.
78. 'Russian account of the Campaign in the Crimea', p. 37.
79. Thoumas, *Souvenirs de Crimée*, p. 132.
80. Ibid., p. 133.
81. L. Delpérier, B. Malvaux and A. Joineau, *La Garde Impériale du Napoléon III* (Nantes: Éditions du Cannonier, 2000), p. 205.
82. 'From a Soldier of the 4th Light Dragoons', *The Times* (21 November 1854).
83. 'The Light Cavalry Charge at Balaklava', *York Herald* (16 November 1854).
84. 'The Light Cavalry Charge on the 25th of October', *John Bull* (18 November 1854), p. 734. It also appeared as 'The 17th Lancers at Balaklava', *The Lancaster Gazette* (25 November 1854) and in a slightly different form as 'Letter from Balaklava', *The Era* (26 November 1854).
85. Captain the Hon. William Godfrey Morgan (1831–1913), later 1st Viscount Tredegar was the son of Sir Charles Morgan of Tredegar Park. He purchased his commission as Cornet, 17th Lancers aged 19 in 1850; Lieutenant 1851; Captain 1854.
86. 'Letter from the Crimea', *Morning Chronicle* (16 November 1854); the same letter also appeared as 'The 17th Lancers at Balaklava', *Lancaster Gazette* (25 November 1854).

87. Chambers enlisted in the 11th Hussars in May 1846; promoted Corporal 1 January 1855 and Sergeant 25 May 1855.
88. 'The Battle of Balaklava', *The Morning Post* (27 November 1854).
89. He was mistaken: the formal Siege of Sebastopol commenced on 17 October.
90. 'Letter from an Officer of the Light Brigade', *Wakefield Journal & Examiner* (17 November 1854). Extracts from this letter also appeared as 'The Cavalry Charge at Balaklava', *The Bradford Observer* (16 November 1854). Given the publication date in the newspaper, this letter was probably written in October.
91. 'Good accounts of the Cavalry', *Daily News* (24 November 1854). Given the publication date of the letter, it was probably written during October 1854.
92. Probably Captain George Lockwood (1818–54). Gazetted as Ensign 75th Foot 11 July 1837; Lieutenant 28 August 1840. Transferred to 8th Hussars 17 May 1844 as Lieutenant; Captain 26 December 1851. There are two conflicting accounts as to the actions of Captain Lockwood at Balaklava: A.W. Kinglake suggests Lord Lucan had sent him to enquire as to the readiness and whereabouts of the Infantry and thus missed the 'Charge' but was killed during the retreat as he tried to find the Earl of Cardigan. Lieutenant Fitz Maxse, ADC to the Earl of Cardigan, however, asserts Lockwood was riding next to or near Lord Cardigan ('Captain Lockwood', *The Times* (28 July 1868).
93. 'Letters from the Crimea, from Various Sources', *The Morning Post* (21 November 1854).
94. 'Battle of Balaklava', *Bristol Mercury* (25 November 1854).
95. According to his obituary, John George Baker served in the 4th Light Dragoons for twenty-four years and 'went through the memorable charge uninjured'. He died in May 1893 'at an advanced age' in High Barnet ('One of the heroes of the Balaklava Charge', *The Standard* [13 May 1893], p. 5).
96. 'Soldier's Letter from the Crimea', *Leeds Mercury* (30 December 1854); also reproduced in the *Daily News* (2 January 1855).
97. 'Letter from the Light Brigade', *Stockport Advertiser* (1 December 1854), p. 4.
98. Probably Lieutenant-Colonel Charles Edmund Doherty who did not ride in the Charge due to being ill; Cornet 24 April 1835; Lieutenant 6 January 1837; Captain 4 September 1840; Major 23 June 1848; Lieutenant-Colonel 12 October 1852; Colonel 28 November 1855. He died 14 August 1866 in Brighton.
99. Probably Major William Gore who was invalided to Scutari Hospital.
100. Probably Captain John Augustus Oldham, who was killed in the Charge. He was succeeded by Captain Soame Gambier Jenyns (1826–73); Ensign 86th Foot 1 April 1842; Lieutenant 23 June 1843; transferred 13th Light Dragoons 6 August 1847; Captain 4 May 1849.
101. Probably Captains Thomas Howard Goad and John Augustus Oldham both of whom were killed in the charge.
102. Probably Cornet Hugh Montgomery who had only recently joined the 13th after leaving Cambridge, 17 January 1851.
103. Probably Troop Sergeant-Major John Weston (number 715). Recorded as being killed in the Charge.
104. Troop Sergeant-Majors John Linkon (number 762) and George Smith (number 1106) (1820–71) who are recorded as being taken prisoner, the latter being seriously wounded.
105. Robert Nichol was born 11 September 1834 in Coventry and enlisted in the 8th Hussars in October 1848; he was a labourer prior to enlistment. He was perhaps not the most reliable of soldiers: he was in jail in Exeter 25 January 1854 to 31 January 1854 and a prisoner in custody 12 to 14 July 1854. Finally he was court-martialled 24 August 1855 and sentenced to twenty-five lashes. Arrested 25 November 1855 and court-martialled for a second time 27 November 1855 and sentenced to fifty lashes and three months imprisonment. He was discharged the following year. He died in 1897 in Newcastle.
106. 'Letters from the Crimea', *Newcastle Courant* (5 January 1855).
107. Trumpet-Major Gray was born in Woolwich in March 1817 and enlisted in the 8th Hussars in April 1832 aged fifteen. He was made Trumpeter December 1836 and Trumpet-Major on 3 June 1851 and was discharged from the army ten years later. He died in December 1883 in Islington.
108. 'Private letters from the Seat of War: Specially Communicated. From Trumpet-Major Wm. Gray, 8th Hussars', *Nottinghamshire Guardian* (7 December 1854), p. 5.
109. Sam Walker enlisted in the 8th Hussars in 1840. He fought at Balaklava where he was wounded; he is listed as being in the General Hospital, Scutari November 1854; invalided home January 1855.
110. 'Letter from a Leeds soldier', *Leeds Mercury* (9 December 1854).

111. Pennington was born 26 January 1833 in Greenwich and enlisted in the 11th on 29 January 1854 at Portobello Barracks, Dublin. He was wounded in the Charge and invalided to Britain 30 June 1856 and was discharged 20 September 1856. He died 1 May 1923 in Stoke Newington, London. He wrote 'Last of the Six Hundred' in 1887 and presented a copy to Queen Victoria.
112. 'From a private in the 11th Hussars, who enlisted last spring', *Glasgow Herald* (29 December 1854); the same letter also appeared as 'A Gallant Hussar', *Leeds Mercury* (30 December 1854); the *Oldham Chronicle* (30 December 1854) and *The Times* (26 December 1854).
113. 'Letters from the Crimea', *The Morning Post* (1 February 1855), p. 5.
114. 'From a Troop Sergeant-Major of the 8th Hussars', *The Times* (16 January 1855). The same letter also appeared as 'The Charge of the Light Brigade', *The Lancaster Gazette* (20 January 1855), p. 8.
115. Thomas 'Old Taffy' Williams was born in Southwark and enlisted in the 11th in June 1850; his younger brother, William 'Young Taffy' Williams (number 1571), enlisted in the 11th two years later. Both were members of G Troop. He was discharged c.1856 and became Master of a Manchester Workhouse and thence Master of the Birkenhead Workhouse (Liverpool) from 1873. He died on 19 May 1887, aged 57, in Liverpool. According to *The Illustrated London News* (23 October 1875), p. 414, he wrote a 'most interesting pamphlet' entitled *Personal Reminiscences of the Crimean War*.
116. 'The Cavalry Charge at Balaklava', *The Morning Post* (1 February 1855), p. 1.
117. 'The Light Cavalry Charge at Balaklava', *The Times* (3 April 1855), p. 10.

Chapter 6   Winter in the Crimea: 1 November 1854–1 March 1855

1. Brighton, *Hell Riders*, p. 205.
2. NAM, Acc. 1993-07-39, Surgeon J.J. Scott, Mss., Journal, entry 26 January 1855, 28 January 1855, 1 February 1855 and 7 March 1855.
3. 'Extracts from the letter of a volunteer surgeon at Scutari', *Leeds Mercury* (24 February 1855).
4. D. Inglesant, ed., *The Prisoners of Voronesh* (London: Unwin Brothers, 1977), p. 17.
5. Ibid., passim.
6. FRO, Acc. D/E/1545/19, Etheldred Yorke, Mss., Lieutenant-Colonel John Yorke to Etheldred Yorke, 27 October 1854.
7. FRO, Acc. D/E/1545/20, Yorke Mss., Yorke to York, 1 November 1854.
8. Probably Dr. John Gorringe MD, Assistant Surgeon (8 June 1849).
9. A reference to Dr. George James Guthrie's 1814 book 'On Gunshot Wounds of the Extremities Requiring the Different Operations of Amputations, and their After Treatment'; the 6th Edition was published in 1855. Guthrie had served as surgeon through the Peninsular War.
10. 'Letter from one of the 5th Dragoon Guards', *Manchester Times* (22 November 1854).
11. 'Extracts of a letter dated Scutaria Hospital ...', *Hampshire Telegraph & Sussex Chronicle* (6 January 1855).
12. 'Extracts from a Letter received in Leeds from one of the 11th Hussars', *Leeds Mercury* (23 December 1854).
13. Robert Martin was born around 1828 in London and died in the Royal Infirmary, Liverpool, on 25 July 1900 and is buried in Bebington Cemetery. His reminiscences of the campaign were published by the *Birkenhead and Cheshire Advertiser* (28 October 1899).
14. 'Correspondence from the Crimea', *The Liverpool Mercury* (23 January 1855).
15. Corporal James Hall enlisted in the 17th Lancers in September 1850 and had been a servant prior to enlistment. Despite the 'very kind' treatment from the Russians, Hall died at Simpheropol probably during the amputation of his right leg.
16. 'The Cavalry Charge at Balaklava', *The Leicester Advertiser* (18 November 1854).
17. W.H. Parker was born in Windsor in July 1831 and he enlisted in the 11th Hussars on 27 August 1850, having been a domestic servant in London prior to enlistment. He was wounded and taken prisoner in the Charge and repatriated in autumn 1855. He transferred to the 1st Life Guards 1 March 1857; Corporal of Horse 8 January 1862; discharged 12 October 1864. As a POW Parker took part in theatricals put on by other prisoners; he was taught to 'tumble' and was described by one POW, George Newman of the 23rd (Royal Welch Fusiliers) as 'bright young fellow.' (Inglesant, *The Prisoners of Voronesh*, pp. 244–8.)
18. 'English Prisoners of War in the Crimea', *Sheffield & Rotherham Independent* (23 December 1854), p. 5.
19. Thomas Perry was born in Reading in 1822 and enlisted in the 8th Hussars in May 1838. He was wounded in both legs and taken prisoners by the Russians and exchanged 29 August 1855 at

Odessa; landed from HMS *Furious* 2 September 1855 and left Scutari Hospital October 1855. He died in London on 24 September 1884.

20. 'Letter from a Captured Hussar at Simpheropol', *Huddersfield Chronicle* (24 February 1855).
21. 'Letter from an Officer, a Prisoner in Russia', *The Nottinghamshire Guardian* (17 May 1855), p. 7.
22. Lieutenant Frampton was taken prisoner during the Russian sortie of 20 December 1854 after being wounded. Captain Clarke was also taken prisoner.
23. Probably Lieutenant James Duff who had been taken prisoner during the Battle of Inkerman (November 5 1854) along with twelve other men of his regiment, one of whom was Sergeant Newman who left an account of his captivity in Russia (D. Inglesant, ed., *The Prisoners of Voronesh. The Diary of Sergeant George Newman* [London: Unwin Brothers, 1977]).
24. Probably Corporal **James Hall** (number 1051), above.
25. Probably Private Alfred Jenner (number 1118). Enlisted in the 17th Lancers 3 May 1852, his previous occupation being a domestic servant. He was with the Riding Establishment at Maidstone Barracks in Kent from 1 January 1854 to 22 February 1854 prior to embarkation. He died in captivity.
26. Probably Private James William Wightman (number 1177) (c.1835–1907). He enlisted in 1852 and taken prisoner in the charge being repatriated in Autumn 1855. He fought in the Indian Mutiny and resigned in 1868. He published his memoirs of the campaign and captivity ('Balaclava and Russian Captivity', *Nineteenth Century Magazine* [May 1892]).
27. Probably Private Thomas Marshall (number 1010).
28. Probably Private James McAllister (number 997). Taken prisoner during the Charge and repatriated Autumn 1855. In the cells 5 December 1855 prior to Court Martial 8 December 1855.
29. Probably Private William Harrison (number 1131). Taken prisoner in the Charge although listed as being killed in the 'papers.
30. Probably Private Henry Ellis (number 1022) who was wounded in the Charge and taken prisoner.
31. Probably Private Henry M. Young (number 1078). Taken prisoner during the Charge and died from his wounds at Simpheropol in May 1855 aged 23 (*Illustrated London News* [9 June 1855]).
32. Probably Private William Kirk (number 842). He was taken prisoner in the charge after having had his horse shot under him. Private Wightman's account of his captivity mentions Kirk twice as something of a brawler and he suspected he had been poisoned.
33. Probably Private Robert Edge (number 696). A labourer prior to enlistment on 1 July 1848. He died at or on the way to Simpheropol.
34. Probably Private Thomas Brown (number714) – not to be confused with two other Private Browns (Peter, number 862 or John, number 455).
35. Probably Private Thomas Sharpe (number 940). Taken prisoner during the Charge, he died a POW in the hospital at Hartnoff, 27 February 1855 and was buried in the cemetery at the expense of the English expatriates living there.
36. Anglesey, *Little Hodge*, p. 52.
37. Brighton, *Hell Riders*, pp. 205–6.
38. Anglesey, *Little Hodge*, p. 52.
39. Ibid., pp. 53–4.
40. Anglesey, *Little Hodge*, p. 54.
41. Paget, *The Light Cavalry Brigade*, p. 81.
42. Smith, *A Victorian RSM*, p. 153.
43. Anglesey, *Little Hodge*, pp. 54–5.
44. Paget, *The Light Cavalry Brigade*, p. 83
45. 'From Corporal Morley, of the 17th Lancers', *Nottinghamshire Guardian* (21 December 1854).
46. The *Nottinghamshire Guardian* published a resumé of this letter on 16 November 1854, p. 6.
47. 'Letter from the Crimea', *Daily News* (17 January 1855); originally published in the *Warrington Guardian*.
48. Probably Regimental Sergeant-Major Charles James Fennell (number 699).
49. 'From the Scots Greys', *Nottinghamshire Guardian* (30 November 1854).
50. Anglesey, *Little Hodge*, p. 56.
51. Ibid.
52. 'Letter from the Crimea', *Wakefield Journal & Examiner* (15 December 1854).
53. Anglesey, *Little Hodge*, p. 57.
54. Anglesey, *Little Hodge*, p. 59.
55. West Yorkshire Archive Service (WYAS), Bradford, Acc. SpSt/10/4/1, J. Studholme-Brownrigg, Mss., Brownrigg to Major General Spencer Stanhope, 2 January 1855; NAM 1964-02-33, Lieutenant H. Clark, Mss., Clark to family 27 December 1855.

56. NAM, Acc. 1962-10-95, General J.B.B. Estcourt, Mss., Estcourt to General G.A. Wetherall, 13 December 1854 and Estcourt to Wetherall, 17 December 1854.
57. 'The starved horses in the Crimea', *Lloyd's Weekly Newspaper* (4 February 1855); 'Letters from the Crimea', *The Standard* (26 December 1854); 'State of the Army Before Sebastopol', *Liverpool Mercury* (16 March 1855); R.O. Parker, *Equine Science* (New York: Thomson Learning, 2003), 2nd edition pp. 392–9.
58. Anglesey, *Little Hodge*, p. 62.
59. Ibid., pp. 62–3.
60. *Report of the Board of General Officers* ... (London: HMSO, 1856), pp. 187ff.
61. Anglesey, *Little Hodge*, p. 64.
62. LA, Acc. 1-Dixon 22/12/3/7, Hunter Mss., Hunter to Sister, 17 November 1854.
63. Probably Quartermaster Thomas McBean: appointed Quartermaster, Scots Greys 16 August 1850, he served throughout the Crimean campaign with the Greys. He was later involved in a gunpowder explosion at the Barracks, Great Brook Street, Birmingham on Tuesday 8 March 1864.
64. 'Private letters from the Seat of War, Specially Communicated', *Nottinghamshire Guardian* (14 December 1854).
65. 'Private letters from the Seat of War: Specially Communicated', *Nottinghamshire Guardian* (21 December 1854).
66. Probably the 'Mounted Staff Corps' who wore red jackets with black lace and helmets. They were organised from London and Irish mounted police to act as orderlies and Provosts.
67. 'Private letter from the Seat of War: Specially Communicated. From Corporal Thomas Morley of the 17th Lancers', *Nottinghamshire Guardian* (28 December 1854), p. 8.
68. 'Letter from another Leeds Soldier', *Leeds Mercury* (30 December 1854).
69. A crude, four-wheeled cart used in Turkey: instead of the wheels rotating on the axle, the wheels were fixed to the axle and the whole assembly rotated in wooden bearings. They were not very efficient.
70. 'Letters from the Seat of War', *Liverpool Mercury* (23 January 1855).
71. Probably Corporal George Taylor (number 876); recorded as being 'severely wounded' in the Charge: a musket ball lodged in his abdomen and two passed through the upper part of his right arm. He was sent to Scutari hospital 26 October 1854 where he died 14 November 1854.
72. 'Letters from the Crimea', *The Morning Post* (10 January 1855). The same letter also appeared as 'Letters from the Crimea', *The Morning Chronicle* (11 January 1855).
73. 'Letters from the Crimea', *Liverpool Mercury* (2 January 1855).
74. 'War Items. Extracts from a letter of a subaltern in the 5th Dragoon Guards', *The Leicester Chronicle* (13 January 1855).
75. 'Private News from the Scots Greys at the Crimea', *Nottinghamshire Guardian* (11 January 1855).
76. LA, Acc. 1-Dixon 22/12/3/8, Hunter Mss., Hunter to Sister, 26 December 1854.
77. 'Christmas in the English Camp', *The Huddersfield Chronicle* (27 January 1854).
78. Probably Private Lewis Fitzmorris (number 985).
79. Thomas Sawbridge was born in Nottingham and enlisted in the 11th Hussars 17 June 1851, having previously been a shoe maker. He was taken to Scutari Hospital January 1855 where he died 28 January 1855.
80. 'Letter from Balaklava', *Nottinghamshire Guardian* (1 February 1855).
81. 'Extracts from a letter of a Young Officer in the Heavy Cavalry', *North Wales Chronicle* (3 February 1855); see also 'Extracts from a letter of a Young Officer in the heavy cavalry', *Sheffield & Rotherham Independent* (3 February 1855), p. 3.
82. 'Private Letter from the Seat of War: Specially Communicated', *Nottinghamshire Guardian* (25 January 1855), p. 8.
83. These two sorties by the Russians are confirmed by the French official historian, César Louis de Bazancourt (Bazanvourt, *L'Expédition de Crimée. 5e Édition* [Paris: Librairie d'Amyot, 1857], pp. 134–7); Additional colour is added by a French officer writing in the *Journal de Toulouse* (31 December 1854) who says the Russians attacked the French lines on 10 December (twice) and again on the 12 December where 'the enemy was warmly received and forced to retire in great disorder'.
84. This is not quite the case: the Orthodox Church celebrates Christmas on 7 January so the ringing of the 'joy bells' was probably associated with Christmas.
85. 'Private Letters from the Seat of War', *Nottinghamshire Guardian* (1 February 1855).
86. Probably Trumpeter David Mitchell (number 794).

87. Probably Trumpeter William Heywood (number 1038); born in 1834 he was aged 20 at Balaklava having enlisted in the Greys in 1851. Promoted to Trumpeter following the death of David Mitchell. He lost three fingers on his left hand at Balaklava and was in Scutari hospital 26 October 1854 to 11 January 1855 when he was sent home. He appeared before Queen Victoria in the Mess Room at Brompton Barracks 3 March 1855.
88. 'Letter from a Soldier in the Scots Greys to his friends in Glasgow', *Glasgow Herald* (5 February 1855).
89. 'Private letters from the Sea of War: Specially Communicated', *Nottinghamshire Guardian* (8 February 1855), p. 8.
90. 'Another letter from a Huddersfield Man in the Crimea', *Huddersfield Chronicle* (10 February 1855).
91. 'Letter from a Non-Commissioned Cavalry Officer from Lockwood', *Huddersfield Chronicle* (10 March 1855).
92. LA, Acc. 1-Dixon 22/12/3/9, Hunter Mss., Hunter to sister, 5 February 1855.
93. 'Letter from Troop-Major Brown, Scots Greys, to his Cousin in Glasgow', *Glasgow Herald* (12 March 1855).

Chapter 7 Remounts and Reinforcements: March–June 1855
1. Paget, *The Light Cavalry Brigade*, pp. 85–7.
2. Herefordshire Record Office (HRO), Acc. E47/G/IV/A, Richard Airey Mss., Lord Hardinge to Airey, 30 October 1854.
3. Ibid., Hardinge to Airey, 9 November 1854.
4. Ibid.
5. 'Naval and Military', *Daily News* (8 December 1854).
6. 'Maidstone Cavalry Depot', *The Morning Post* (11 December 1854).
7. 'Maidstone Cavalry Depot', *The Morning Post* (6 January 1855).
8. HRO, Acc. E47/G/IV/A, Hardinge to Airey 9 November 1854; Hardinge to Airey, 5 January 1855.
9. 'Reinforcements for the Crimea', *Lloyd's Weekly Newspaper* (17 December 1854).
10. 'Reinforcements and Supplies for the Crimea', *The Hampshire Telegraph* (3 February 1855).
11. 'Naval and Military Items', *Lloyd's Weekly Newspaper* (11 March 1855); 'Troops from India', *The Morning Chronicle* (12 March 1855).
12. 'Ireland. Price of Horses', *Daily News* (2 November 1854).
13. *Leeds Mercury* (4 November 1854).
14. 'The Chesterfield Cattle Fair', *Sheffield & Rotherham Independent* (3 February 1855).
15. 'Remounts for the Cavalry', *Daily News* (4 November 1854).
16. *Leeds Mercury* (3 February 1855).
17. 'The Yeomanry Cavalry', *Daily News* (23 December 1854); 'Rifle Corps', *Sheffield & Rotherham Independent* (23 December 1854).
18. 'Cavalry Recruits and Remounts', *The Morning Post* (3 February 1855).
19. HRO, Acc. E47/G/IV/A Hardinge to Airey, 8 January 1855.
20. Ibid., Hardinge to Airey, 9 February 1855.
21. Ibid.
22. 'Naval and Military', *The Morning Chronicle* (25 December 1854).
23. 'Naval and Military News', *The Morning Chronicle* (27 December 1854).
24. 'Naval & Military', *Daily News* (12 January 1855).
25. HRO, Hardinge to Airey, 9 February 1855.
26. Ibid., Hardinge to Airey, 5 March 1855.
27. 'Naval and Military Intelligence', *Daily News* (2 March 1855).
28. Hardinge to Airey, 5 March 1855; Hardinge to Airey, 30 March 1855.
29. *Hansard*, House of Commons, Deb 26 April 1855, vol. 137, cc1787–8.
30. Ibid.
31. Hardinge to Airey, 14 April 1855.
32. 'Letter from a Huddersfield Man', *Huddersfield Chronicle* (7 April 1855).
33. 'Private Letter from the Crimea', *Ashton Weekly Reporter* (2 June 1855), p. 2.
34. 'Letters from the Crimea', *Stockport Advertiser* (5 October 1855), p. 3.
35. Paget, *The Light Cavalry Brigade*, pp. 87–90.
36. Kelly, *Mrs Duberly's War*, p. 157.
37. Ibid., pp. 158–60.
38. 'Letters from the Crimea', *Wakefield Journal & Examiner* (7 September 1855).

39. 'Letter from the Crimea', *The Belfast News-Letter* (25 March 1855).
40. Probably Captain Richard Thompson; Cornet by purchase 25 February 1842; Lieutenant 17 November 1843; Captain 3 May 1848 and Major 22 December 1854. He retired on Half Pay 2 December 1859. He was sent out from the Depot to command the regiment in the absence of any other senior officers. Lieutenant Temple Godman described him as 'as great an ass as ever' and ' he is sure to make a mess of it [the command], pretending to know more than he does, and he will contradict himself often enough' (Warner, *A Cavalryman in the Crimea*. pp. 93 and 202).
41. James Cooper was born in Edgbaston (near Birmingham) and was a butcher prior to his enlistment on 20 October 1845. He completed 30 years' service and was discharged 23 May 1876 in York, having reached the rank of Sergeant.
42. Both James and his brother Henry (number 1174) served in the 1st Royals. Both survived the war.
43. 'Another Letter from Sebastopol', *Leeds Mercury* (7 April 1855).
44. LA, Acc. 1-Dixon 22/12/3/10, Hunter Mss, Hunter to sister 26 March 1855.
45. LA, Acc. 1-Dixon 22/12/3/11, Hunter Mss., Hunter to sister, 6 April 1855.
46. Regimental Sergeant-Major John Grieve (1822–73) was a Scot, born in Midlothian. He was awarded the Victoria Cross for his bravery during the Charge of the Heavy Brigade 'for saving the life of an Officer in the Heavy Cavalry Charge at Balaklava, who was surrounded by Russian Cavalry, by his gallant conduct of riding to his rescue and cutting off the head of one Russian, and disabling and dispersing the others'. He was promoted to Cornet without purchase 4 December 1857, appointed Adjutant 15 February 1859 and promoted Lieutenant 30 January 1863.
47. 'The Present of Ale to the Scots Greys', *Nottinghamshire Guardian* (19 April 1855), p. 5.
48. 'Private letter from the Seat of War: Specially Communicated', *Nottinghamshire Guardian* (10 May 1855), p. 8.
49. 'Private Letter from the Seat of War. Specially Communicated', *Nottinghamshire Guardian* (7 June 1855), p. 8.

Chapter 8   Mopping Up: September–December 1855

1. 'Cavalry Engagement with the Russians', *Reynolds's Newspaper* (14 October 1855).
2. Ibid.
3. 'The Late Cavalry Skirmish', *The North Wales Chronicle* (3 November 1855).
4. G. Bertin, 'Les 6e Dragons en Crimee', *Carnet de la Sabretache*, vol. 10 (1912), p. 617.
5. Ibid., pp. 622–3.
6. Bazancourt, *L'Expedition*, pp. 471–2.
7. C. Mismer, *Souvenirs d'un dragon de l'armee de Crimee: Avril 1854 – Juillet 1856* (Paris: Librarie Hachette et Cie., 1887), pp. 222–3.
8. Bertin, 'Le 6e Dragons', pp. 622–3.
9. Ibid., p. 625.
10. Bazancourt, *L'Expedition*, pp. 472–3.
11. Ibid., pp. 473–4ff.
12. Bertin, 'Le 6e Dragons', p. 625,
13. Bazancourt, *L'Expedition*, p. 475.
14. Ibid., pp. 475–7.
15. Ibid
16. Mismer, *Souvenirs*, pp. 227–8.
17. Ibid.
18. *Histoire du 4e Regiment des Hussards*, via http://military-photos.com/kanghil.htm, accessed 22-5-2013.
19. Bazancourt, *L'Expedition*, p. 478.
20. 'The Cavalry Action near Eupatoria: Prince Gortchakoff's Report', *Daily News* (18 October 1855).
21. *Histoire du 4e Regiment des hussards*, via http://military-photos.com/kanghil.htm
22. Mismer, *Souvenirs*, pp. 231–3; Bazancourt, *L'Expedition*, pp. 477–8.
23. Bazancourt, *L'Expedition*, p. 480,
24. Bertin, 'Le 6e Dragons', p. 630.
25. Mismer, *Souvenirs*, pp. 232–3.
26. 'The Cavalry Action at Eupatoria. Prince Gortchakoff's Report', *Daily News* (18 October 1855).
27. Bertin, 'Le 6e Dragons', p. 627.
28. Bazancourt, *L'Expedition*, p. 482; Léon Guérin, *Histoire de la dernier guerre de russie* (Paris: Dufour, Mulat et Boulanger, 1859), vol. 2 pp. 460–1.
29. *Registre Metricule du 3e Regiment des Hussards*, via http://military-photos.com/kanghil.htm.
30. Bertin, 'Le 6e Dragons', p. 625

31. Mismer, *Souvenirs*, p. 234.
32. Ibid., p. 235.
33. Bazancourt, *L'Expedition*, pp. 484–5; Guerin, *Histoire*, p. 461.
34. Bazancourt, *L'Expedition*, pp. 485–6.
35. Paget, *The Light Cavalry Brigade*, p 284.
36. Ibid.
37. Ibid., p. 298.
38. Ibid.
39. Ibid., p. 304.
40. Ibid., pp. 318, 323–5.
41. Ibid., pp. 335–7.

Index

Abdelal, *Major* (*1e Chasseurs d'Afrique*) 131–2
Airey, General Sir Richard (Quartermaster General) 30, 60, 64, 124–5, 127, 193
Allonville, *Genéral* Armand-Octave-Marie d' 132–3, 208–12, 214, 215
Alma, River 28, 29, 40–1, 147
Alma, Battle of 37, 39, 40–1, 43, 45, 58, 104, 136, 139, 145, 147
Arbuzov, Lieutenant 77–8, 80
Auchinloss, Private (4th Dragoon Guards) 75, 118

Baker, Sergeant John George (4th Light Dragoons) 144
Bingham, George, 3rd Earl of Lucan 13, 14, 31, 38, 44, 45, 47, 48, 49, 61, 62, 70, 73, 74, 111, 113, 123–5, 127–8, 135, 143, 155, 163, 169
Bosquet, *Genéral* Pierre 61, 86, 129, 163
British Army
  Artillery
    Royal Artillery 39, 72
    Royal Horse Artillery 6, 37, 38, 40, 44, 45, 46, 48, 57, 60, 67, 138, 145, 196, 214, 215–16
  Cavalry
    1st Life Guards 193
    2nd Life Guards 193
    Royal Horse Guards 193
    1st Dragoon Guards 194, 195
    2nd Dragoon Guards 195
    3rd Dragoon Guards 6, 195
    4th Dragoon Guards 5, 6, 7, 13, 14, 47, 51, 60, 66, 78–80, 90, 108, 111, 118, 120, 121, 137, 163, 194, 195, 200, 203
    5th Dragoon Guards 13, 16, 21, 22, 51, 67, 70, 72, 78–80, 89, 90, 92, 94, 101, 108–9, 111, 120, 121, 137, 157, 180, 187, 194, 195, 198
    6th Dragoon Guards 193–4, 214–15, 216
    7th Dragoon Guards 194, 195
    1st (Royal) Dragoons 5, 9, 20, 22, 47, 52, 53, 54, 57, 65, 70, 72, 79–80, 81, 83, 96, 97, 106, 110, 111, 112, 115, 125, 143, 156, 163, 174–5, 177, 179, 182, 199
    2nd (Royal North British) Dragoons (Scots Greys) 5, 8, 10, 23, 24, 37, 38, 39, 47, 48, 55, 56, 57, 59, 67, 72, 78–80, 81–2, 84–5, 86, 87–9, 90–1, 92, 93, 96–7, 98, 100, 102, 104, 107, 110, 111, 112, 114, 115,

116, 119–20, 120, 121, 134, 137, 143, 145, 163, 166, 167, 169, 171–2, 177–8, 180–1, 185–6, 187, 191–2, 194, 195, 201–2, 203
    6th (Inniskilling) Dragoons 13, 47, 50, 51, 70, 78, 80, 85, 87, 98, 99, 104, 105, 107, 108, 109, 111, 113, 114, 115, 116, 120, 121, 134, 137, 143, 173, 195
    3rd Light Dragoons 193
    4th Light Dragoons 6, 8, 27, 28, 44, 47, 72, 73, 85, 91, 96, 101, 124, 128, 133–4, 137, 140, 144, 146, 158, 187, 214–16
    13th Light Dragoons 7, 14, 16, 17, 18, 26, 28, 30, 32, 35, 36, 37, 40, 42, 44, 47, 85, 88, 96, 128, 133, 134–5, 137, 138, 140–1, 145, 146, 147, 189, 193, 214, 216
    7th Hussars 193
    8th Hussars 16, 17, 18, 32, 35, 37, 44, 45, 46, 47, 48, 49, 62, 85, 91, 124, 128, 133–4, 137, 140–1, 147, 148–9, 150, 151, 152–3, 161, 184, 204
    10th Hussars 194–5, 197, 204, 206, 207–8
    11th Hussars 6, 28, 36, 37, 43, 44, 47, 49, 73, 85, 91, 125, 128, 133–4, 137, 138, 140, 149, 153, 154, 158, 160, 161, 163, 183
    15th Hussars 193–4
    12th Lancers 193–4, 197, 203, 214–16
    16th Lancers 194, 195
    17th Lancers 6, 7, 15, 17, 18, 19, 32, 33, 35, 37, 44, 45, 46, 47, 48, 56, 60, 70, 75, 85, 88, 91, 95, 123, 128, 133–4, 136, 137, 140–1, 146–7, 150, 160, 162, 164, 165, 173, 195, 196, 202
  Infantry
    7th (Royal Fusiliers) 30, 35, 41
    19th (Green Howards) 35
    23rd (Royal Welch Fusiliers) 35, 39, 41, 64
    33rd (Duke of Wellington's) 39, 41, 46
    42nd Highlanders 96, 97
    49th Regiment 83
    55th (Westmoreland) 39, 41, 63
    68th (Durham Light Infantry) 24
    77th Regiment 64, 203
    79th (Cameron Highlanders) 20, 22
    88th (Connaught Rangers) 29, 39, 41
    92nd (Gordon Highlanders) 11
    93rd (Sutherland Highlanders) 60, 61, 67, 75, 76, 77, 90, 96, 97, 103, 104, 108, 113, 117, 121, 123, 142

95th (Derbyshire) 39
Brigade of Guards 35, 37, 39, 41, 64, 69, 81, 146, 167, 198, 205
Rifle Brigade 24, 26, 39, 45, 46, 82, 92, 101, 177
Royal Marines 62, 75, 92, 134
Brown, Sir George 29, 35, 37, 64, 146
Brown, Sergeant-Major Matthew (2nd Dragoons) 10, 87, 191
Brudenell, James Thomas, 7th Earl of Cardigan 5, 13, 14, 19, 28–9, 31, 33, 36, 38, 48, 67, 74, 93, 123, 127–9, 136, 141, 143, 144

Campbell, Captain (1st Dragoons) 52, 82, 84, 97, 107
Campbell, General Sir Colin 60, 62, 64, 68, 69, 74, 103
Canrobert, *Général* François Certain 28, 29, 31, 32, 61–2, 74, 76, 78, 127–8, 131, 209
Cathcart, Sir George 64, 146
Chadwick, Lieutenant John (17th Lancers) 35, 137, 162
Chamberlain, Cornet Denzil Thomas (13th Light Dragoons) 134, 135
Chambers, Private Robert (11th Hussars) 138
Champéron, *Général* Coste de 209, 211, 213–14
Charteris, Captain 74, 105, 135
Cholera 10, 13, 20–2, 33, 45, 49, 136, 142, 178, 186
Clark, Private William (12th Lancers) 197
Clarke, Brevet-Major (2nd Dragoons) 87, 91–2, 181
Cler, *Colonel* Jean Joseph Gustav (*2e Zouaves*) 29
Cleveland, Cornet (17th Lancers) 137, 165
Commissariat 22, 50, 156, 171–2, 184
Constantinople 11, 12, 15, 19, 23, 60, 150, 165, 170, 194–5, 196
Cooper, Private James (1st Royal Dragoons) 199
Cornillon, *Sous-Lieutenant* Silbert de (*6e Dragons*) 208–9
Cullet, *Capitaine* Marie Octave (*20e Légère*) 31–2

Dancla, *Capitaine* (*1e Chasseurs d'Afrique*) 131–2
Davies, Sergeant Edward (1st Royal Dragoons) 182
Devna 9, 17–19
Driver, Private Benjamin (4th Light Dragoons) 200
Duberly, Mrs Fanny 14, 198
Dublin 6, 7, 195
Dudley, Private Thomas (17th Lancers) 150

Edmonds, Private Edward (4th Light Dragoons) 158
Elam, Farrier W.H. (17th Lancers) 196
Elmsall, Captain (1st Dragoons) 82, 84, 97
Esterhazy, *Général* Ferdinand 208–9, 212, 213
Eupatoria 62, 208–9, 216
Evans, Sir George de Lacy 60, 141

Failly, *Général* Pierre Louis Charles de 215
Food, cost of 15, 19, 20, 24, 25, 68, 99, 116, 153, 159, 178, 180, 183, 187, 196
Forrest, Major (4th Dragoon Guards) 14, 75, 79, 80, 164
Forster, Trumpet-Major (1st Dragoons) 75, 96
French Army 63, 82, 86, 101–2, 117, 169, 173, 182–3, 184, 200
  Artillery 131, 181, 209
  Cavalry 58, 124, 146, 172, 205, 206
    Bachi Bazouks (*Spahis d'Orient*) 66, 210–13, 214, 215
    Chasseurs d'Afrique 97, 128, 129, 130, 131–3, 163, 165, 169, 201, 206–7
    6e Cuirassiers 169
    9e Cuirassiers 169
    6e Dragons 169, 208, 209–14
    7e Dragons 169, 209–12, 214
    1e Hussards 169
    4e Hussards 169, 209–14, 215
    Spahis 78, 129
  Infantry 173
    20e Légère 29
    1e Zouaves 29, 32
    Chasseurs à pied 128, 214

Garland, Sergeant William (17th Lancers) 136, 165
George, Duke of Cambridge, Prince 37, 64, 146
Gibraltar 9, 11, 196
Gibson, Sergeant David (2nd Dragoons) 112
Goad, Captain (13th Light Dragoons) 26, 88, 135–6
Godkin, Lawrence (*Daily News*) 12, 126–7
Gorchakov, Prince Alexander 211
Gough, Corporal Joseph (5th Dragoon Guards) 72, 75, 89
Grand Crimean Central Railway 122, 199
Gray, Trumpet-Major William (8th Hussars) 148, 185
Grieve, RSM John, VC (2nd Dragoons) 178, 202
Griffith, Lieutenant-Colonel Darby (2nd Dragoons) 12, 86–7, 91, 98

Hall, Corporal James (17th Lancers) 160
Handley, Cornet (2nd Dragoons) 91, 98

Hardinge, Henry, 1st Viscount Hardinge (Commander-in-Chief) 193–5
Hartopp, Lieutenant (1st Dragoons) 82, 84, 97
Himalaya, SS 7, 8, 10, 12, 32–3, 55, 91, 147, 197
Hill, Sergeant John (1st Royal Dragoons) 9
Hodge, Lieutenant-Colonel Edward Cooper (4th Dragoon Guards) 5, 7, 12, 13, 47, 79–80, 119, 163–4, 167–9
Horne, Gunner John (RHA) 38
Horses
  acquisition of 5, 6, 194–5
  feeding and care of 22, 29, 168–9
  loss of 14, 21, 47, 51–3, 65, 106, 109, 112, 135, 149, 152, 165–6, 168–9, 171, 173, 181, 184, 192, 199
  poor condition of 48, 154, 168–9, 173, 176, 177, 179, 181, 184, 192
  transportation of 12, 17, 26, 47, 48–9, 51, 53–4, 65
Hunt, Private George (1st Royal Dragoons) 53
Hunter, Lieutenant Robert Scott (2nd Dragoons) 8, 23, 56, 72, 79, 84, 169, 181, 191, 201–2

Inglis, Captain William (5th Dragoon Guards) 72, 75, 79, 90

Jakobritsky, Major-General 76, 130
Jennings, Private R. (2nd Dragoons) 187

Kadikoi 60, 114, 156, 198
Kamara 72, 80, 108
Kanghil (village) 211–12
Kanghil, Battle of 205, 206–7
Kerch 205, 206–7
Kirkwood, Private Edward (5th Dragoons) 198
Korff, Lieutenant-General 211
Koribut-Kubitovich, Lieutenant 130
Koulalie 23, 24, 194

Lawrenson, Lieutenant-Colonel John (17th Lancers) 7, 70
Leeds 2, 194
Liprandi, Lieutenant-General Pavel 76, 130, 160
Liverpool 6, 7, 12, 175
Luders, General Alexander von 47, 64

Mackenzie's Farm, skirmish at 38, 39, 43, 46–7, 48, 55–6, 102–3
MacMahon, *Général* Patrice de 127–8
Malta 9, 10, 11, 196
Manchester 1, 6, 10, 194, 197
Martimprey, *Général* Edouard, Comte de 129

Martin, Private Robert (11th Hussars) 160
Maude, Captain George Augustus (RHA) 6, 38, 40, 45–6, 57, 60, 61, 155
McGrigor, Sergeant-Major (2nd Dragoons) 97, 178
Menshikov, Prince Alexander 29, 130
Mismer, *Sergent* Charles (*6e Dragons*) 209, 211–14
Mitchell, Private Albert (13th Light Dragoons) 7, 26, 30
Molenes, *Capitaine* Paul de (*Spahis*) 78, 129
Monks, Trumpeter Thomas (6th Dragoons) 75, 79, 109, 116, 121, 173
Montgomery, Cornet (13th Light Dragoons) 88, 135
Moodie, Lieutenant Daniel (2nd Dragoons) 72, 86
Morgan, Captain William (17th Lancers) 7, 137
Morley, Corporal Thomas (17th Lancers) 2, 15, 17, 19, 165, 174, 202–5
Morris, *Général* Louis-Michel 131–2
Morris, Captain William (17th Lancers) 123, 136, 141

Nichol, Trumpeter Robert (8th Hussars) 147
Nightingale, Florence 159, 182
Nolan, Captain Louis Edward (15th Hussars) 6, 26, 27, 29, 30, 47, 48, 59, 60, 81–2, 84, 93, 105, 125–8, 140, 142–3
Norris, Sergeant-Major John (1st Royal Dragoons) 57
Nottingham 10, 11, 186, 187, 202

Oldham, Captain (13th Light Dragoons) 88, 135

Paget, Lord George (4th Light Dragoons) 14, 73, 75, 145, 164, 193, 198, 215, 216
Parker, Private Henry William (11th Hussars) 161
Pearson, Private William (4th Light Dragoons) 133
Pennington, Private William Henry (11th Hussars) 149
Perry, Private Thomas (8th Hussars) 151, 161
Prince, Private James (5th Dragoon Guards) 72, 101

Raglan, Lord 2, 13, 22, 40, 47, 49, 50, 63, 74, 81–2, 85, 86, 87, 104–5, 106, 123–7, 136, 141, 143, 160, 169, 195, 203–4
Randall, Private Charles (17th Lancers) 142
Rhyzov, General 76–7, 130

Russian Army
  Artillery 60, 75, 76, 81, 83, 84–5, 113, 115,
    129, 130, 137, 139, 140, 141, 147, 150,
    152, 211–12
  Cavalry 28, 32, 60, 77, 85, 86, 87, 89, 90, 91,
    108, 111, 112, 113, 114, 123, 135, 137,
    139, 140, 141, 146, 149, 150, 152, 157
  Lancers of Archduke Leopold 211
  Lancers of Grand Duchess Mikhailova
    211
  Leuchtenberg Hussars 74, 76–8, 130
  Orenberg Lancers 76
  Saxe-Weimar Hussars 74, 76–8, 130
  Siberia Lancers 76
  Cossacks 26, 27,28, 29, 30, 31, 35, 38, 45,
    47, 57, 58, 60, 63, 66, 67, 68, 74, 81,
    84–5, 91, 93, 94, 96, 98, 103, 106, 108,
    112, 114, 117, 120, 121–2, 142–4, 145,
    149, 157, 159, 179, 181, 196, 204, 206–7,
    209–13, 214, 215, 218
  Don Cossacks 130, 132
  Ural Cossacks 76–7, 130
  Infantry 62, 84, 96, 103, 129, 137, 139, 140,
    141, 150
  Odessa Jager 130–1
Russell, William Howard (*The Times*) 1, 3, 31,
  125, 127–8, 132

Saint-Arnaud, *Maréchal* Jacques Leroy de
  28–9, 32
Sawbridge, Private Thomas (11th Hussars)
  153, 183
Scutari 25, 36, 40, 41–2, 53–5, 102, 112, 142,
  145, 148, 149, 150–1, 155, 156, 157, 158,
  162, 165, 178, 182, 186, 216
Selkrig, Corporal John (2nd Dragoons) 114,
  177
Senior, Corporal George (13th Light
  Dragoons) 17, 40, 189
Shakespear, Captain J.D. (RHA) 155
Shaw, Sergeant James (13th Light Dragoons)
  36
Shewell, Lieutenant-Colonel Frederick George
  (8th Hussars) 14, 124, 152–3
Sickness and wounded 64, 66–7, 70, 89, 105,
  106–8, 148, 151, 154, 156–7, 158, 160,
  161–2, 163–4, 165, 167, 170, 172, 174–5,
  177, 178, 179, 180, 182, 186, 190, 200,
  202–3

Smith, Sergeant-Major George Loy
  (11th Hussars) 7, 30, 73, 163
Stancliffe, Corporal Henry William (4th Light
  Dragoons) 187
Stephenson, Private Isaac (4th Dragoon
  Guards) 79, 120, 121
Stevenson, Corporal Norman (2nd Dragoons)
  185
Sturtevant, Sergeant-Major R.L.
  (2nd Dragoons) 2, 24, 55, 79, 98, 166,
  171–2

Tents 26, 27, 38, 44, 63, 95–6, 98, 105, 109,
  169–0, 173, 175, 180, 185–6, 189, 191,
  196–7, 200
Terpelevsky, Major-General 211
Thoumas, *Capitaine* Charles-Antoine
  (*17e Artillerie*) 131, 133
Times, The 1, 3, 13, 126, 152
Todleben, General Alexander 76
Tottenham, Colonel William Heathcote
  (12th Lancers) 215–16
Turkish Army 74, 75, 81, 84–5, 86, 87–8, 90,
  91, 92, 93, 94, 95, 96, 97, 98, 103, 106,
  110, 113, 114, 117, 123, 125, 134, 137,
  142–3, 154, 159, 171, 200
  Cavalry 206, 214, 215
  Infantry 108, 112, 139, 210, 211, 214

Varna 13, 15–16, 17, 18, 23, 32, 33–5, 48, 112,
  138, 154
Vico, *Chef d'Escadron* Jean-Pierre 31–2

Walker, Captain C.P. Beauchamp
  (5th Dragoons Guards) 78, 79, 115–16
Walker, Private Samuel (8th Hussars) 148
Webb, Captain Augustus (17th Lancers) 88,
  141
White, Major (17th Lancers) 7, 70, 137
Williams, Private Thomas (11th Hussars) 154
Winter, Captain (17th Lancers) 137, 141
Wombwell, Cornet (17th Lancers) 60, 137

Yorke, Lieutenant-Colonel Sir John (1st Royal
  Dragoons) 6, 20, 21–3, 47, 48–53, 54,
  65, 70, 78–80, 82, 84, 97, 107, 110, 113,
  156–8